# The Law of the Future and the Future of Law: Volume II

Sam Muller, Stavros Zouridis, Morly Frishman and Laura Kistemaker (editors)

2012
Torkel Opsahl Academic EPublisher
The Hague

This and other books in the Law of the Future Series may be openly accessed and downloaded from www.fichl.org. This site uses Persistent URLs (PURL) for all publications it makes available. Printed copies may be ordered through online distributors such as www.amazon.co.uk. This book was first published on 31 October 2012.



**ISBN 978-82-93081-80-7**

# PUBLICATION SERIES PREFACE

This Series is the result of a rather unique endeavour of HiiL: to research the law of the future. Driven by research results that were coming from HiiL and from the small but growing engagements of others (Anne Marie Slaughter's *New World Order* stands out as an early pioneering work), we had a clear sense that the global legal environment was changing, and that legal and justice actors were both shaping those changes and were constantly working to adapt to them.

To understand law's futures, we started a process in which we asked 52 thought leaders in different legal areas to reflect on law in their field two decades away. Their think pieces became *The Law of the Future and the Future of Law*, volume one. One thing led to another, and with the tremendous support of our hugely innovative publisher, the *Law of the Future Series* was set up.

The Series is meant as a focal point for publications that reflect on the challenges connected with law's futures and what we can do to deal with them. It is perhaps a forum for a new discipline, legal futurology, although the Series is not meant for Jules Verne or George Lucas fantasies (however much we admire and enjoy them). It is a place for serious and thorough thinking about the future place in our lives of a commodity the future badly needs: good rule systems that support stability, prosperity and human dignity.

We welcome your ideas and submissions.

Sam Muller<br>
*Director, HiiL*

Stavros Zouridis<br>
*Professor of Public Administration, Tilburg University*

Larry Catá Backer<br>
*Professor of Law and International Affairs, Penn State University*

# LAW OF THE FUTURE AND THE FUTURE OF LAW

This is the second volume of *The Law of the Future and the Future of Law*, and a reflection of our continuing efforts to map trends in the global legal environment. In this volume, we focus on areas that received less attention in the 2011 volume. There is, for example, less on criminal law, and more on intellectual property and trade law. We start the volume with an introduction in which we set the stage. The volume ends with some concluding thoughts by Professor Jan Smits, who was amongst the earliest of law of the future thinkers. He reflects on common threads in the think pieces. We extend our appreciation to him for his willingness to take the time to do this.

Once again, it has been a very inspiring endeavour to work with outstanding thought leaders from very different fields. It was at times a tight process, which asked a lot from the authors. We thank them for their patience and commitment.

We would also like to thank our copy editing team, Wendy Bremang, Kaitlyn Jones, Sarah-Louise Todd, Lisa-Felicia Akorli, Tsvetelina Mihaylova, Lara Schaefer and Kate Elliot, led by the indefatigable and ever meticulous Alexander Orona. We thank Alf Butenschøn Skre and Morten Bergsmo from Torkel Opsahl Academic EPublisher, for their patience, and endurance with our inability to stick to deadlines. We are humbled by your continuing belief in us and treasure our cooperation. Lastly, a special word of thanks to Dessy Velikova, who managed the whole process with both softness and determination.

Sam Muller, Stavros Zouridis,
Morly Frishman and Laura Kistemaker

# TABLE OF CONTENTS

CHAPTER III
THE PERSPECTIVE OF TECHNOLOGY:
HOW IS TECHNOLOGY AFFECTING LAW?

CHAPTER IV
THE PERSPECTIVE OF STATES:
WHAT IS CHANGING OR NEEDS TO CHANGE?

# Introduction: The Law of the Future Continues

**Sam Muller**[*], **Stavros Zouridis**[**], **Morly Frishman**[***] **and Laura Kistemaker**[♦]

## 1. Why and How

In June of this year, the world convened in the Rio+20 Conference to tackle huge global environmental challenges, and the leaders of the G20 met in Los Cabos, Mexico to deal with the global economic crisis. What can these events tell us about the future? An obvious conclusion is that there continue to be global challenges for which global approaches are clearly needed. We also see different approaches to these challenges. Rio+20 was a conference under the auspices of the United Nations (UN), a formally structured international organisation. Los Cabos was host to the meeting of an informal leaders network; reviews of both conferences were generally of 'the glass is half empty' type. Not enough real progress, not enough real change. Looking deeper, however, the two events also reveal an 'iceberg' effect with most media reviews focussing on the top of the iceberg (the States and leaders that met). Underneath that top, however, a huge swathe of non-State Parties met, interacted, committed, and participated. This lower part of the iceberg is more difficult to see and understand, and is more chaotic. What does jump at you, however, is that there is a lot of organisation of interconnectedness around challenges happening in smaller, more local networks. Both events also show the interconnectedness of things: the conclusions of both conferences do not only relate to 'the environment' and 'the economy', but include many other areas and challenges, such as social exclusion, rule of law, equality, and so on. The events also reveal different uses of law: Rio+20 is largely

[*] **Sam Muller** is Director of the Hague Institute for the Internationalisation of Law (HiiL).

[**] **Stavros Zouridis** is affiliated with the Tilburg Law School as Professor of Public Administration.

[***] **Morly Frishman** is Justice Adviser at HiiL. Laura Kistemaker is Head of External Relations, at HiiL.

[♦] **Laura Kistemaker** is Head of External Relations at HiiL.

grounded in the language and mechanisms from the more formally organised UN system of organisations and treaties. The Los Cabos language and approach seems less formal and legalistic.

All this is the law of the future at our doorstep: using law as a tool to deal with societal challenges and to organise stability and prosperity. Law's future should mobilise at least as much scholarly attention as law's past and present. This conviction inspired us to develop a Law of the Future network that aims to provoke future research and debate on law and legal institutions. As we soon found out, however, researching and debating something that does not yet exist cannot be done with familiar methods. Mapping the highly uncertain future of law requires specific methodologies and strategies derived from the field of foresight studies. Because of the specific nature of law, these methodologies and strategies cannot be mechanically transplanted to the legal realm. Gradually, we have thus developed a research strategy for legal futurism. It builds on in-depth expert knowledge of lawyers and legal scholars; the trends and developments observed in different areas of law; the imagination of leading thinkers, researchers, and practitioners; and, most of all, critical reflection and debate. This volume is an expression of this strategy.

As said, the future of law does not exist yet and we assume that it is highly uncertain and complex. This should, however, not withhold us from systematically analysing and scrutinising it. In our view, ignoring or merely speculating is not an option. Ignoring the future opens the door to law becoming irrelevant, unstable, and dysfunctional because it cannot keep up with societal developments and is not constructed systematically enough. It also bereaves the world of fully using a tool, which if used well, can contribute tremendously to stability. But how to systematically analyse and scrutinise something as complex as law that is not even there?

A first step requires mapping of what *is* there: major trends observed in different areas of law. Together with the first edited volume of *The Law of the Future and the Future of Law* (published in 2011), this volume aims to provide a contribution to such a map. Both volumes comprise of think pieces, written by leading thinkers and doers in the field of law. In these think pieces, the authors address a set of questions based on their expertise on specific areas of law or legal issues. The questions we have posed to the authors are:

> What legal trends are we likely to see in your field in the coming two to three decades? How do these trends relate to

> the grand societal challenges that the world faces? In light of these trends, what do you see as the most significant challenges for the development of the law? And, which recommendations would you have in terms of (i) strategies/policies; (ii) research agendas; (iii) training/education for the lawyer of the future?

Thus, the authors were asked to reflect on *what they think will happen* in the coming decades. The think pieces are not meant to be elaborate academic papers, but short essays in which the authors can freely share their thoughts on the future. Therefore, the authors were asked to minimise the use of footnotes when making references. "Sources and Further Reading" sections included at the end of think pieces list sources provided by the authors and additional literature for further reading. We think this may strengthen the ability of the book to serve as a catalyst at this stage of development of this new field.

Mapping legal trends and challenges provides some clues on the future of law, but whether these trends will continue or reverse is highly uncertain. Rather than work on predictions (impossible), we work on preparedness. We therefore used the think pieces that we collected in *The Law of the Future and the Future of Law* volumes to build scenarios. What will happen if the trends stop or even reverse? What will be the impact on the future of law? A second edition of the *Law Scenarios to 2030* was published in June 2012 (http://www.hiil.org/publication/law-scenarios-to-2030).

But mapping legal trends and building scenarios once is not enough, because new trends may evolve. Any serious attempt to grasp the future of law should therefore continuously include new trends, new ideas, and new imagination. This understanding has led to this second volume on *The Law of the Future and the Future of Law*.

Again, the volume has been built upon three assumptions. First, it is impossible to predict the future – there is too much uncertainty and complexity for that. However, we can face the future better by mapping macrotrends and microsignals and preparing for plausible scenarios. Second, the future of law can only be understood by deploying a multi-disciplinary approach – law is not something that can be separated from life. Lawyers and legal scholars have written many think pieces in this volume but we have also included think pieces by scholars from adjacent academic disciplines. Third, law's future can only be understood if a variety of approaches, areas of law, and ideas are taken into account. As Surowiecki has convincingly argued, the wisdom of crowds is largely based on diversity, different ideas, observations and opinions.[1]

The final step of our research methodology consists of exchange and debate. What the thought and practice leaders have written here and what we have deduced from that in this introduction and in the *Law Scenarios to 2030* should be subject to constant discussion and exchange. Earlier this year, for example, we engaged justice leaders from Tunisia with the *Law Scenarios*, trying to work out what some of the trends that emerge mean for national strategies to reform the legal system. We also continue with the Law of the Future conferences, bringing people together around future challenges. The 2012 conference will focus on rule-making.

## 2. Previous Findings

The internationalisation of law and the rise of private legal regimes were the main legal trends observed in the first volume. The internationalisation of law, understood as both the rise of international law and growing interconnection between national legal systems as a result of international interdependencies (economic, social, political, technological, and so on), appeared to be a predominant trend in many different areas of law. National legal systems are also increasingly confronted with private rule regimes. These regimes sometimes pose either soft or hard rules and standards that compete with national legislation. If these regimes engage in settling disputes, they compete with national courts. As argued in the first volume, both internationalisation and the rise of private legal regimes are complex phenomena that can easily be misunderstood. We can also not be sure whether these trends will continue the next decades, as they have to date. Internationalisation and the rise of private legal regimes do appear to be the key design parameters of the law of the future, but these trends may as well reverse. Instead of extrapolating these trends, we have therefore used them as contingencies. With that, we developed four different scenarios that picture possible futures of the global legal environment.

---

[1] J. Surowiecki, *The Wisdom of Crowds. Why the Many Are Smarter than the Few and How Collective Wisdom Shapes Business, Economies, Societies, and Nations*, Doubleday, New York, 2004.

| | Mixed or private legal regime | Predominantly public legal regime |
|---|---|---|
| Continued internationalisation of law | Legal Internet | Global Constitution |
| Reversed internationalisation of law | Legal Tribes | Legal Borders |

If the expansion of international rules and institutions continues, and most of the heavy lifting is done by States and public actors, we may expect that the global legal environment will slowly develop as the European Union has been developing: into a robust legal order of its own that is highly integrated with national legal systems. We have referred to this scenario as Global Constitution. International rules and institutions can also further expand as part of a process of shifting emphasis from law created and enforced by State-connected institutions to private governance mechanisms and private legal regimes. If this happens, the Legal Internet scenario will evolve. The combination of a reverse process of internationalisation with simultaneous strengthening of law created and enforced by public authorities will result in the Legal Borders scenario. Finally, there is a theoretical possibility that the process of internationalisation will reverse as private legal and governance mechanisms grow. The global legal environment will then become dispersed, highly chaotic, and have diminishing importance. Because of the lack of State power, communities will depend on local and private legal and governance regimes. We have referred to this scenario as Legal Tribes. In each of these scenarios we have dealt with four questions: (1) what is the main ordering?; (2) who makes the rules?; (3) how are rules enforced?; and (4) how are conflicts resolved? It will come as no surprise that the answers to these questions are very different in each scenario.

We see aspects of these four scenarios and answers to these four questions in all think pieces contained in this volume.

## 3. Outline and Structure

Like the previous volume, we maintained a thematic structure, rather than, for example, a more traditional division in accordance with the field of doctrinal law. We believe such a thematic division offers a more interesting read, as it is better suited to help exploring issues 'out of the box', thereby promoting critical thinking about the inter-linkages of different areas of law with each other and with other realms such as politics, technology, and economics. Each ordering of the book is to a certain extent arbitrary, because most of the think pieces address several issues. Moreover, the trends and challenges signalled in the think pieces are connected. For example, globalisation is at least accommodated by revolutionary communication technologies. But new communication technologies also cause severe enforcement problems in some areas (for example, the enforcement of intellectual property law).

We have divided the think pieces into six sections, each with different perspectives. There is no claim that any of these perspectives are dealt with exhaustively. Rather, aspects are highlighted, connected with trends and challenges percieved by the author. Below, we discuss these sections, providing a short summary of the think pieces. After that, we will draw some general conclusions.

## 3.1. The Global Law Perspective: To What Extent are We Moving towards a Global Legal System?

Some authors emphasise the impact of processes of internationalisation and the consequences of these processes for law and the legal field. **William Twining**'s think piece is an excellent opener for this section, and the volume as a whole, as it nails to the door ten theses about ways in which a global perspective about law and its evolution challenges some widespread assumptions underlying Western traditions of academic law and legal discourse. Twining suggests that when thinking about the future of law from a global perspective, we need to try to break free of simplicities like depicting our world in terms of concentric circles neatly organised in a single hierarchy, or assuming that the centre of the universe is where one happens to be. His first thesis cautions against the temptation to generalise about law beyond our capacity, as, in fact, we (still) lack concepts, well-constructed hypotheses, and reliable data to make many evidence-based generalisations about law in the world as a whole. The second thesis is that a picture of law cannot sensibly be confined to the Westphalian duo of municipal State law and classical international law, as one must acknowledge the place of many forms of non-State law, such as religious law, customary law, transnational commercial law, new forms of regional and supranational ordering, and various forms of 'soft law' at different levels. The remaining eight theses relate to issues such as sub-global patterns of law, the diffusion of law, legal and belief pluralism, secularism, and ethnocentrism. On the whole, for Twining, a 'global perspective' on law must aspire to be the recognition of views from almost everywhere, rather than a view from nowhere. Accordingly, a global perspective can help us to recognise the diversity and complexity of systems of ordering human relations in the world and to realise that nobody is located uniquely at its centre.

In her think piece, **Elisa Morgera** illustrates much of the complexity of law and globalisation as described by Twining, with respect to the particular field of environmental law. Using international biodiversity law as a testing ground, Morgera argues that 'global environmental law' represents the future of law in the environmental arena. Global environmental law is a concept emerging from the promotion of environmental protection as a global public good through a plurality of legal mechanisms relying on a plurality of legal orders. It emphasises the functional role of States as protectors of the environment as a common interest of humanity and the considerable role of global institutions in international law-making and compliance monitoring. Global environmental law further underscores how international environmental law increasingly affects individuals and groups in society, and private operators, within and across national boundaries. It also points to the growing role of international private law in the environmental arena.

**Frank Vibert** offers a critical account regarding the role played by international institutions in multilevel governance. According to Vibert, it is widely acknowledged that international rule making is undemocratic, and there is also increasing awareness that these rule makers are far from infallible. As examples, he mentions the International Monetary Fund's (IMF) acknowledgement of its failure in the 2008 international financial crisis; the World Health Organisation (WHO), which has been criticized for its handling of avian and swine flu; and the International Panel on Climate Change (IPCC), which has been attacked for its handling of the evidence behind its analysis of the human contribution to global warming. Given these shortcomings of international organisations, Vibert's think piece focuses on the potential contribution of judicial review to combating both the democratic deficit and the problem of functional failures – real or alleged. Whereas at present, no coherent system exists for the judicial review of international bodies and most operate without the possibility of judicial challenge to their decisions, this think piece sketches alternative approaches to help constructing such a system of judicial review.

It should be mentioned that Vibert rejects what he describes as the conventional analysis, according to which the democratic deficit can best be diagnosed through theories of multi-level governance and/or principal/agent theory. The reason for rejection is that both theories involve normative bottom-up constructions (what should happen), while Vibert urges us to acknowledge the empirical reality that international rule making is top-down.

The top-down or bottom-up dilemma is also central to the think piece by **Colin Scott**, though in a different sense and context. Scott begins by stating that one of the central challenges of contemporary governance is the steering of organisational and individual behaviour. His main argument is that highly prescriptive approaches to regulation are frequently ineffective or even counterproductive. One reason for this is that we show considerable ingenuity in turning demands to change our behaviour to suit our own interests rather than meeting the public interest. Other reasons include the limited knowledge about the behaviours to be steered and limited capacity for monitoring and enforcement held by governments. He therefore suggests an alternative way to think about the problem of steering behaviour. The alternative is to reduce the emphasis on top-down control and instead seek to exploit the capacity of targeted individuals and organisations alike to regulate them, to monitor each other, and to learn how they may benefit from pursuing more public-oriented objectives. Corporate social responsibility initiatives provide only one example of such a process at play. His piece evaluates the potential as well as the known shortcomings of this meta-regulatory approach to governance, as a basis for developing regulation that is both more effective and more efficient. **Ellen Lawton's** think piece illustrates some of the arguments put forward by Colin Scott. In her think piece, she makes the case for learning from experiences gained within the health sector as a way to innovate the legal field. The legal field should use the knowledge and experience of the health sector to measure impact and quality, to use trend data, and to invest in interventions with a focus on prevention.

### 3.2. The Perspective of Connections: What Connections with Global Issues are Emerging?

According to some think piece authors, law is or will be confronted with some new and persistent challenges. Whether law will prove to be the solution is seriously questioned, but in order to become a solution for these challenges law has to meet some new requirements. **Hassane Cisse**, **Christina Biebesheimer** and **Richard Nash** discuss the connection between law or justice, and development. Many around the world, they explain, no longer view development equated solely with 'growth' at all costs as the optimal means for a country's path towards prosperity. Indeed, all these terms – development, growth and prosperity – have over the years become expanded to become broader and generally more inclusive. More and more indications seem to point towards a more vocal and powerful demand for more equitable and inclusive growth at the macro-, meso- and micro-levels. Development organisations, including the World Bank, will have to adapt to this new trend and be able to respond to it adequately if they are to provide the services that countries and people demand. A key element of this is likely to be more support for social justice interventions through a variety of stakeholders, which will have to inform a new global development pact more aligned with the needs and demands expressed by the people.

**Claudia Dumas** discusses the large and increasing number of legal initiatives to curb corruption and bribery and comes to the conclusion that the situation is actually worsening rather than improving. Dumas also explores the rise of soft law initiatives and takes the indications that corruption is not declining globally as a starting point to call for (i) an analysis of the assumed causal relationship between hard and soft law mandates and new understandings of how soft law instruments affect each other, (ii) an identification of gaps in increasingly fluid and disaggregated legal regimes, and (iii) research regarding the impact of specific anti-corruption measures.

International Criminal Court (ICC) President **Sang-Hyun Song** also discusses connections between law and development, but his think piece focuses on international criminal law. According to Judge Song, whereas references to social justice in the domain of development are not new, a more recent trend has emerged which increasingly recognises the interrelation between the rule of law and criminal justice on the one hand, and sustainable peace and development, on the other. International criminal justice supports peace and development through preventing mass violence, re-instating confidence in socio-political structures, and empowering victims to rebuild their lives. In turn, development supports international criminal justice since effective and capable national systems are crucial for the success of the Rome Statute system as a whole. Judge Song calls for more to be done to strengthen national jurisdictions to respond adequately to international crimes and he sees a key role to be played by the development community in this regard.

Multi-level challenges require a concerted effort of both national and international law. Sometimes these challenges are triggered by incidents and crises, as **Himamauli Das** illustrates in his think piece. He describes the unprecedented increase in the size of the financial backstop provided by the international financial institutions (IFIs), governance and institutional changes at the IFIs and other multilateral groupings, and an evolution in the political and institutional mechanisms of the international financial architecture. As efforts continue to support the global recovery and the implementation of reforms to the financial system, countries will need to resolve to what extent they wish to further elaborate on existing mechanisms. Decisions need to be made as to whether new, enforceable rules need to be developed, instead of standards. Countries also need to assess compliance mechanisms, such as peer reviews, assessments and sanctions.

Multi-level challenges are caused by multi-layered legal orders. These layers are not restricted to law created by States and public authorities. In his think piece, **Rik Torfs** shares the future trends he discerns in the relation between law and religion. He signals, for example, the disconnect between the ideas of the religious groups and the overall discourse in society. The role law plays in this development is that it further marginalises religion. While freedom of expression gains importance, the notion of religious freedom is narrowed to its individual form. Also, he sees a trend towards religion no longer being excluded from non-discrimination legislation, as discrimination of women is more and more qualified as a crime.

### 3.3. The Perspective of Technology: How is Technology Affecting Law?

Many think piece authors emphasise technological development as a main driver of legal change. Because of new technologies, rules sometimes become obsolete. But the impact of new technologies goes beyond rules and statutory legislation. Just as internationalisation raises some serious questions regarding basic legal principles and basic legal concepts, new technologies can render legal concepts that have been used for ages obsolete. Jacqueline Lipton and Rolf H. Weber both see the need of restructuring cyberlaw. **Jacqueline Lipton** points out that on the Internet everything is dependent on the intermediaries at work. The 'blackout protest', of among others Wikipedia and Google, against the Stop Online Piracy Act in January 2012, showed very clearly the power of online service providers, often missed in the discussions about the nature of cyber law. Therefore, there is the necessity of a law of the 'intermediated information exchange'. Unlike the case of many physical world interactions, the victims of online wrongs are more immediately attracted to legal action against an intermediary than against the primary wrongdoer (because of the anonymous global nature of the Internet and the interest of the intermediaries to be seen as safe). The cyber law of the future will therefore need to focus on the legal liability of online intermediaries. This has not been the case in past conceptions of cyber law. In the other think piece that deals with cyber law, that of **Rolf H. Weber**, informal law is presented as the best mode for regulation. An evolutionary approach should mainly encompass procedural models being better suited to comply with an uncertain future and allowing a reconciliation of conflicting interests. Key elements in this concept are organisation, governance, and dispute settlement. Thereby, civil society must be adequately positioned through a multi-stakeholder approach to determine what social impacts law should cause.

**David Eagleman** and **Sarah Isgur Flores** also find that a lot of work needs to be done to align law and policy with the current state of science – this time modern neuroscience. After showing how ineffective and inefficient current criminal justice policies are in terms of preventing new crimes, they propose a way to no longer base these policies on blameworthiness, but on biology. Currently, law does a very poor job in taking the genetics and the environment of the perpetrator into account, while these are exactly the reasons why someone committed the crime. This is very hard to do right, anyway. So that is why Eagleman and Isgur urge to shift the emphasis away from blameworthiness to a more forward-looking approach, based on a better understanding of the brain. This approach is the neuro-compatibility index, comprised of seven criteria to quantify how well a system of criminal law is compatible with the lessons of modern science.

While Eagleman and Isgur are making the case for bringing tested techniques of biology into the realm of law, **Albert Lin** discusses the largely untested method of geo-engineering. But there is good chance that it will materialise at some point, as it is gaining attention as a possible tool for ameliorating climate change. He uses the metaphor of a thermostat that will enable humans to fine-tune the Earth's climate. This highlights the dilemma that comes with the nature of this form of engineering: who should be in charge of this thermostat? Only States, or also other actors? How to incorporate the interests of future generations? And how to organise the compliance mechanisms needed?

Autonomous robots are dealt with in **Surya Deva**'s think piece. Robots are considered autonomous when they are capable of perceiving information delivered as language or, otherwise, are able to learn, reason and make decisions based on their experience, without direct human intervention or instruction. Deva zooms in on the implication of the presence of such robots for human rights. He asserts that robots can be 'holders' of human rights as much as human beings or corporations can be. What then needs to be done when autonomous robots violate these rights? This needs a new regulatory framework at international level in which (trustees of) robots should have a say as well. Deva concludes that robots should and could be hold accountable for their actions and that sanctions would be appropriate if they violate human rights. Robots could compensate their victims or pay fines, they could be confined, and ultimately be destroyed.

**Madeleine de Cock Buning**, **Lucky Belder** and **Roeland de Bruin** discuss a broader spectrum of legal consequences of the rise of autonomous robots. In six scenarios, they introduce a whole array of problems that might arise in terms of intellectual property, legal capacity, liability, and privacy. But differently from Deva, these authors stress that it would be wise to demonstrate restraint in developing a specific legal framework regarding robots. Many of the potential legal issues are already addressed in existing legislation. For instance, regulations surrounding corporate entities, ICT systems, motor vehicles, or even domestic animals could be relevant to evaluating the legal status of autonomous robots.

Finally, **Jim Dator**'s think piece focuses on the impact of communication (and communication technology) on the nature of legal and governmental structures. Dator's starting point is that in order to forecast alternative futures of law, lawyers, courts, and judges, it is necessary to understand their alternative pasts and presents, and to determine what aspects of the pasts and presents might continue to influence their futures, and what novelties might arise creating new conditions. Looking at the way judicial systems have been shaped by communication technologies in the pasts and might be shaped by current and emerging communication technologies in the futures, this think piece takes us on a fascinating and visionary journey that starts thousands of years ago and ends decades (or more) into the future.

### 3.4. The Perspective of States: What is Changing or Needs to Change?

In order to deal with the challenges of internationalisation, new technologies, and a multi-layered legal order, both law and justice systems have to innovate. Some think pieces focus on the way these innovations should be designed, whereas other think piece authors draw on previous experiences with innovating law and the justice system. According to the latter, legal pluralism affects both the chances to innovate and the way innovations should be designed. **Maurits Barendrecht** opts for a sweeping, but incremental change of State institutions. Dissatisfaction with the functioning of core organisations is widespread. What if we create a board of trustees for the State and have them start taking responsibility for the performance of its institutions? Most surely, they would come to the conclusion that the habits that Barendrecht lists should be rooted out one by one. Bad habits – such as trading with jobs in high government positions instead of letting the best person be selected or making agreements between parties forming a coalition government in secret negotiations limiting the issues that will be tackled by the government – should be replaced by good habits that make it possible to integrate innovative instruments for collective decision making and governing communities in a variety of State institutions.

**Ji Weidong** strongly argues against one such innovation in the case of the Chinese judiciary: excessive mediation. Ji sees the complexity that China faces in these times of transformation, globalisation, and financial crisis as a danger to society. Practices like 'big mediation' and 'active judiciary' lead to elasticity of rules. But that is the opposite of what is needed to steer China away from the uncertainties it sees itself challenged with. The judiciary should concentrate on the coordination function of law instead. Rule of law is more important than ever to ensure that money is earned and social wealth is distributed. And thus, more important than preoccupying oneself with people's satisfaction levels of court performance.

**Dacian Dragos** discusses another part of the world in which the State has undergone and is still undergoing major transformation: Central and Eastern Europe. He focuses on transparency. How has this, relatively recent, concept taken root in the public administration of these countries? Dragos concludes that regulating and implementing transparency laws is hard for many reasons. But again, innovations such as e-government tools can help. Institutionally, the preeminence of Ombudsman-type institutions will be the trend, and they will act both as mediators and enforcers of transparency.

In his think piece, **Daveed Gartenstein-Ross** makes the case to not have the controversies that surround the preventive detention of violent non-State actors (VNSAs) prevent States from making the right decisions. As it seems, the need for States to protect itself against VNSAs is here to stay and with it, the need for preventive detention policy. A more mature discussion is needed to acknowledge the values that have driven preventive detention, and seek to determine when detention is justified as compared to other options: prosecution in military or civilian courts, kinetic military action, or simple release of the individuals in question. If preventive detention is seen as an option that truly must be avoided, we must ask whether that will incentivise killing over capturing the opponent. Gartenstein-Ross is, however, not overly confident that this discussion will actually materialise: "The shame that Western countries feel about detention policy will probably shunt these questions to the side as everyone rushes to cleanse their hands of the matter—and, in so doing, most likely allows an even worse system to remain".

Finally, **Benjamin Odoki** shares in his think piece several trends that, from his perspective as the Chief Justice of the Supreme Court of Uganda, he sees influencing States, and particularly the administration of justice. The trends are 1) geo-political changes and the increasing regional integration; 2) legal pluralism; 3) the impact of technology on law and courts; and 4) specialised courts. These trends impact each other. The result will be even stronger regional networks in a world where the power shifts away from the West. Legal pluralism will be a distinctive feature of these networks, but with less emphasis on customary law, which will be deemed out of touch with modern society. As Barendrecht and Dragos, Odoki sees an important role for technology, both in terms of substance and process, in reshaping State institutions, most notably the judiciary.

### 3.5. The Perspective of Trade and Private Actors: How Are Trade and Commerce Driving the Future?

International trade and the behaviour of private actors make up the final theme addressed in the think pieces in this volume. The dramatic expansion of international trade may have been a major driver of the internationalisation of law but the regulation of international trade appears to still show some serious defects. Again, legal pluralism may hamper taking the next step towards true international trade law. Whereas legal pluralism is sometimes used to refer to different sets of values, it also appears that real interests are at stake. A next step toward international law thus requires that the old big powers (US and Europe) also compromise on their interests. **Gabrielle Marceau,** in her account of the future of international trade law, is asking the question: how best to deal with new trade and non-trade concerns? Marceau departs from the premise that while the rules of the World Trade Organisation (WTO) essentially intend to promote trade, these rules do not promote trade above all else, as trade interacts with issues other than trade. Marceau's piece offers a conceptual framework for categorising the different manners in which non-trade concerns are addressed in the WTO agreements. Employing this framework, she analyses how various non-trade concerns of contemporary and future significance for the WTO (which either impact or are impacted by the trade matters) might be addressed in international trade. Marceau demonstrates that where WTO rules have been introduced to regulate interactions between trade and non-trade concerns, they have generally been framed to promote trade. She also argues, however, that existing WTO rules do not fail to acknowledge the need for non-trade concerns (NTCs) to circumscribe trade on occasion, as evidenced in broadly interpreted exceptions.

**Imelda Maher**'s think piece is concerned with competition law. She argues that despite the globalisation of international trade, efforts to create an international competition law under the aegis of the WTO have failed, and to date, international competition law still does not exist as such. Instead, competition law is characterised by a proliferation of national regimes forming part of the web of rules, agencies, networks, agreements and institutions, with some shared sense of purpose predicated on the dominance of an economics-approach in this field in relation to private market behaviour. States have entered into enforcement agreements and enforcement networks have grown especially since the turn of the century, primarily with the aim of improving enforcement through policy learning, technical assistance, and provision of examples of best practice. According to Maher, with this focus on enforcement, there is limited debate as to the nature of competition policy and the question that finds less common purpose – that is, the extent to which States are subject to competition rules. In short, the relationship between competition and regulation is under-developed. The introduction of competition laws in Brazil, India, China and South Africa suggests that this question will become more significant in the next decade and beyond, with a re-calibration of the balance between international trade law and international competition law.

In their contribution, **Mary Footer** and **Andrew Forbes** draw attention to the challenge of China for international trade law. Acknowledging that the continued economic rise of China presents a range of challenges for international trade law, they argue that the only real certainty for the future of China is that its development will continue on a unique trajectory, influenced by ancient Confucian tradition and modern authoritarian ideology. This, in turn, presents a challenge for the multilateral trading system, as previously it had dealt with a largely ideologically homogenous group of States that take a similar approach to the rule of law. The authors discuss this changing reality and mention a number of areas where Chinese ideology is already affecting the way in which China interacts with the rest of the world. As they expect the coming decades to witness new interpretations of international trade law and new directions in trade governance, Footer and Forbes provide a number of suggestions as to how actors in the multilateral trading system may need to adapt to the changing ideologies in trade, technology, and development that China's rise is bringing about. Readers familiar with the first volume of *The Law of the Future and the Future of Law* will easily recognise many points of resemblance between Footer and Forbes' think piece and Randal Peerenboom's think piece from last year's volume.

Two think pieces in this section – one by **Severin de Wit** and the other by **David S. Levine** – provide a critical perspective on intellectual property law and its future. If future thinking about law is generally not quite common, intellectual property law is notably absent from such explorations. Daring to look forward, de Wit discusses challenges in the public and private domains that will shape the future of intellectual property law. After mentioning current disparaging themes around intellectual property (examples mentioned are: market failures; troubled access to medicine; impediments to free flow of information; copyright overextension; digital right protection; overkill and patents stifling rather than stimulating innovation), de Wit explores the main drives of such critique and how the law can change so as to restore confidence both in the public as well as in the private domain. He does not expect a major international treaty to solve all difficulties, but rather sees that change will come from domestic law (and case law), local legal initiatives, and common practices.

**David S. Levine**'s think piece is a call for intellectual property law without secrets. In a world where secrecy is on the wane, so he argues, archaic forms of law-making must similarly be reconsidered and discarded. He posits that international negotiations regarding intellectual property (IP) laws like the Anti-Counterfeiting Trade Agreement (ACTA) and Trans Pacific Partnership Agreement (TPP), and any future international IP law-making procedures, lessen the adherence to a theory of secret negotiations and embrace the inevitable and desirable need for the public to ask questions and offer meaningful input. Whether or not attempting to continue on the current course would be futile, the risk of doing so, Levine warns us, is erosion in the relevance of and confidence in IP law as a legitimate and effective form of regulation. On the other hand, the benefit of adopting a more open and participatory processes will be better, more balanced, and thoughtful law, for all concerned.

The issue of data protection is closely linked to intellectual property and the rise of new communication technologies. **Lokke Moerel**'s think piece is about data protection and how to best regulate and enforce it. Bearing some similarity to what was said above regarding competition law and intellectual property law, this provides yet another example for an issue that transcends borders and yet is regulated mostly at the national level (and only in a minority of States). As Moerel puts it, the digital era is characterised by an unprecedented continuous worldwide flow of data both within multinational companies as well as with their external service providers, but while large corporations operate internationally, State governments legislate nationally. Moerel explains that besides leaving gaps in the patchwork of national data protection regulations, this situation also leads to overlaps in applicable national rules that often deviate or outright conflict. This legal landscape provides a challenging background to test whether transnational private regulation of data protection can provide solutions where legislation fails to. Moerel evaluates a remarkable example of the emergence in the EU of a complex hybrid system of self-regulation (global corporate privacy policies) with public arrangements (the data protection authority of the EU headquarters of the multinationals validating such corporate privacy policies and providing support in the area of supervision and enforcement).

Next to international trade and intellectual property, some think pieces focus on the regulation of private actors and corporate social responsibility. **Christopher Bovis** writes about the regulation of public-private partnerships. He describes such partnerships as complex forms of cooperation between the State and private actors, which exceed the remit of traditional contractual interface, moving into a strategic sphere of public sector management. Public-Private Partnerships aim at delivering both infrastructure facilities and public services and are regarded as attractive and credible solutions to the *infrastructure deficit* of many developed and developing States. Bovis' think piece provides a conceptual forecast of the legal and regulatory mapping of Public-Private Partnerships. Bovis elaborates on the current and future legal trends within which the regulation of Public-Private Partnerships will be developed. Furthermore, and in conjunction to the emergence of legal trends, he reflects on societal needs which need calibrating in terms of expectations, but mostly perception, when faced with the modality of Public-Private Partnerships for the delivery of public services. Finally, he provides a conceptual map of the challenges for the development of the law in relation to Public-Private Partnerships, by depicting their interface as public services instruments, as investment instruments, and as growth instruments. Bovis concludes with recommendations for law and policy makers in relation to the law of the future for Public-Private Partnerships.

Two of the think pieces in this section deal with corporate social responsibility (CSR). **Austin Onuoha** looks at the relation between legislation and CSR and reflects on some of the areas law could be used in the future to ensure better and more impactful CSR. Focusing in particular on the situation in Nigeria, he examines the tension between the use of national legislation and the application of international law against the background of the push for soft law by the international community. Onuoha suggests that, whereas the debate around CSR is concerned with voluntary and mandatory initiatives, there are areas where law could in future be used to streamline the practice of CSR, and manage relationships between companies and communities. CSR aspects that are discussed in this think piece include community consultation/engagement, FIPC (Free Prior and Informed Consent by communities who own land), criteria for allocation and sharing of funds for CSR initiatives, professionalisation of CSR function, monitoring and evaluation, and the streamlining and strengthening of community governance structures. Onuoha concludes with the recommendation that in the future, law, on the one hand, and voluntary initiatives, on the other, should complement each other rather than compete.

According to **Martijn Scheltema,** a further increase in (international) private regulation in the area of CSR may be expected. He calls for a more profound assessment of the effectiveness of the plethora of private regulation that already exists. Assessing the effectiveness requires an integrated approach involving legal, economic, sociological, and psychological insights. He argues that additional research is required on hybrid enforcement systems and on the question in which cases public or private enforcement is effective. Regarding conflict resolution and prevention, he suggests that non-judicial mechanisms seem preferable, though stakeholders experience difficulties in finding the proper ones. More research and a global facility are needed to assist stakeholders in this respect. Scheltema further suggests that this trend has implications for the legal profession, and recommends future lawyers in this area to acquire additional skills: for example, on assessing effectiveness of international private regulation and its enforcement and on non-judicial dispute management mechanisms.

**S.I. Strong**'s think piece does not focus on any particular area of substantive law, rather on a procedural matter which has gained importance in recent years: alternative forms of collective redress in the cross border context. Her departure point is that despite the creation of a single global marketplace, most types of legal injuries are compensable only in national courts constrained by territorial boundaries. This is true even in the increasing number of cases involving large-scale injuries in the cross-border context. Rather than resolving the dispute at one time, in one forum, defendants are forced to proceed simultaneously in several different jurisdictions, with all the costs and risks associated with parallel litigation, while plaintiffs who are similarly situated in all other regards often hold different legal rights and remedies simply by virtue of their place of residence. Strong asserts that this situation seems neither fair nor desirable. Accordingly, in her think piece she considers whether any alternatives to litigation exist (for example, arbitration and settlement), and whether any of these other options offer a superior means of addressing injuries of this nature.

### 3.6. The Perspective of Law in its Context: Law as a Concept in the Past, in the Present and in the Future

As many think pieces show, the law of the future requires new rules and principles, new and improved legal institutions, and sometimes a re-definition of familiar legal concepts. As some think piece authors argue, the law of the future also requires re-thinking law, legal scholarship, and legal education. The think piece by **Edward Rubin** addresses certain assumptions about law (and the rule of law) which, so he argues, are rooted in a specific history rather than expressing truths about law *per se*. According to Rubin, when legal scholars and others speak about the law, particularly when they claim that the rule of law is violated in the modern regulatory State, they are relying on the idea that law should prescribe modes of action, should constitute a coherent system, should be generally stated, and should be generally applied. Rubin argues that these are not necessary features of law, as they only reflect the particular way that law was used as an instrumentality of governance in pre-modern Europe. The advent of the administrative State and democratic government renders that approach obsolete. According to Rubin, the new approach that is developing, and will constitute the law of the future, is that law should prescribe results, not procedures; that it need not possess any internal coherence; that it should address each policy issue on its own terms; and that it should treat firms and natural persons on an individualised basis. Those features enable it to serve as an instrumentality of governance for a modern State.

**Mauro Zamboni**'s think piece concerns the relations of law to politics, which he considers to be one of the major difficulties confronting today's practitioners and scholars of law. While legal actors are educated in the belief that law and politics are two distinct worlds, when faced with real issues, so he argues, they are forced to deal with the very responsibility of choosing a political course for an entire community. Seeing the transformational space of law-making as the space in which the values or ideas produced inside the political arena are transformed into legal categories and concepts, the primary purpose of this think piece is to look at the way forward with respect to the relations between law and policy.

The law of the future does not only require new concepts, it may also require new ways of teaching. **Clark Cunningham** would like to see legal education follow the same development that medicine went through some decades ago in terms of a powerful new model of education: the teaching hospital staffed by physician-scientists. But as **Miguel Poiares Maduro** points out in the last think piece, this looking beyond the borders of one's own field will not come naturally to legal science and education. According to him, on the one hand, the legal field does not 'authorise' any other social scientists to research the study of law (the presumption being that legal education cannot be understood or questioned by non-lawyers); on the other hand, there is a tendency to focus exclusively on what law itself is, and consider issues of education as unworthy the attention of lawyers.

## 4. An Outlook

So what does this eclectic collection of think pieces teach us about trends and challenges for the law of the future? This is a question that we must subject to a lot of exchange and debate – and we will, – so we cannot fully answer it. We can, however, venture a few, first conclusions.

A first trend, which will not come as a surprise, is internationalisation. Nowadays, it is a cliché to argue that internationalisation is a major trend, but the think pieces that address these processes show both the significant consequences of internationalisation and the fundamental nature of this trend. If a global law perspective is deployed, such as the perspective Twining advocates, law cannot be practiced and taught as it has been practiced and taught in the past. We see from this and the previous volume of *The Law of the Future of the Future of Law* that internationalisation touches upon many areas of law. This volume adds some quite fundamental questions and perspectives to processes of internationalisation.

The rise of new connections between different layers and sectors within the legal order should be mentioned as a second trend. A few examples: whereas Cisse, Biebesheimer and Nash observe new connections between security, justice, and development, Dumas, Scott, and Lawton emphasise connections between official law created by public authorities and processes of self-regulation. Trade law and intellectual property law are also increasingly affected by other issues than just trade and intellectual property, respectively.

The latter also point to a third trend. After a period of exponential expansion of international law, we are increasingly confronted with the limitations of international law. It appears difficult to change the behaviour of legal actors with international law only. The international and the local need to be linked. Citizens, large corporations, public organisations, and even governments may be confronted with international law, but this does not mean that they comply with it. Social, cultural, political, and economic incentive structures appear persistent and not apt to change.

A fourth related trend that should be mentioned is connected with the limitations of international law. As international law further evolves, it appears to be confronted with legal pluralism that does not automatically converge. The case of China is mentioned in several think pieces, but the think piece of Dragos shows that even convergence of legislation does not mean that legal practices have also converged.

A fifth pervasive trend concerns new technologies. The internet, autonomous robots, geo-engineering, and connected bio-, neuro-, and nanotechnologies do not only compel governments to create new regulation but these technologies also question some of the basic principles on which law has been built (for example, property and intellectual property).

To those who have heralded internationalisation and the rise of international law, these trends may seem rather pessimistic. It appears that we have left the frontier phase of internationalisation (through the creation of international law) behind, a phase in which everything seemed possible. Instead, a more realistic picture of internationalisation emerges in which we observe a number of challenges.

A first challenge can be referred to as a true internationalisation of law. Even in highly internationalised areas of law such as competition law, it appears that national or regional law prevails. True internationalisation also means that more justice is being done to the needs of regions, countries, and actors outside the US and Europe. If their interests are better taken into account, the face of international law may change quite substantially.

A second challenge is related to the increasingly multi-level and multi-layered character of the legal order. This challenge may be referred to as creating connected law. The law of the future requires well-developed and sometimes surprising connections between different layers and areas of law and different levels of rule-making and law enforcement.

The third challenge is a largely conceptual challenge. In many areas of law, familiar legal concepts are increasingly out-dated or lacking: data protection, autonomous robots, geo-engineering, and the internet. Referring to this challenge as purely conceptual may be misleading. This challenge is not a mere theoretical or academic challenge. If new concepts are not created soon, the regulation of technologies worldwide will be undermined.

A fourth challenge for the law of the future relates to change management. Both ambitious and realistic strategies are needed to innovate legal and justice systems. A well-balanced strategy of ambition and realism takes both future challenges and trends, and the context in which implementation takes place into account. We must learn more about how to do this well.

Connected with this is a fifth challenge we see: the urgent need for mechanisms to cope with legal pluralism in a global context. If legal systems are not well understood within their social, cultural, political, and economic contexts, we run the risk of developing the wrong solutions for regulatory or legal problems. The think pieces in this volume demonstrate some of the confusion and misunderstanding that result from ignoring legal pluralism.

The trends we have derived from the think pieces may cause some pessimism among the pioneers of international law and internationalisation. In the realm of legal internationalisation, the discourse of utopianism or outright rejection is being replaced by a discourse of messy processes, long-term perseverance, and realistic strategies. This is not pessimism. It appears that both practices of legal internationalisation and the study of these processes are maturing. And that is a ground for optimism.

There is no doubt that more trends, challenges, and questions, can be deduced from the think pieces in this second volume of *The Law of the Future and the Future of Law*. We welcome you to the debate.

# CHAPTER I

## THE GLOBAL LAW PERSPECTIVE:

## TO WHAT EXTENT ARE WE MOVING TOWARDS A GLOBAL LEGAL SYSTEM?

# 1.1.

# Globalisation and Law: Ten Theses

**William Twining**[*]

This paper nails to the door ten theses about ways in which a global perspective challenges some widespread, but not universal, assumptions underlying Western traditions of academic law and legal discourse.

## 1. Introduction

William Twining,
"The Ship",
Station Rd,
Nr. Vacoas,
Mauritius,
Indian Ocean,
The Southern Hemisphere,
The World,
The Universe,
*et cetera, et cetera.*

In our youth, many of us will have indulged in this childish conceit. It suggests two things about how we think. Firstly, that it is easy to depict our world in terms of concentric circles neatly organised in a single hierarchy: global, regional, national, provincial, local, and so on. Secondly, a child may think that the centre of the universe is where one happens to be. However, maybe there is no centre for the phenomena and the issues we are discussing. This paper suggests that when thinking about the future of law from a global perspective, we need to try to break free of such simplicities. In order to be succinct and mildly provocative, I shall advance ten theses that challenge some widespread assumptions in Western discourse and scholarship about law. Much recent literature about globalisation and law, including the "think pieces" produced for the Hague Insti-

[*] **William Twining** is the Emeritus Quain Professor of Jurisprudence at University College London.

tute for the Internationalisation of Law (HiiL) conference in The Hague 2011, suggest that we are starting to move away from such assumptions, but that our leading thinkers have not yet liberated themselves from all of them.

| **Ten Theses** | |
|---|---|
| 1. | On the whole, we lack concepts, well-constructed hypotheses and reliable data to make many reliable evidence-based generalisations about law in the world as a whole. |
| 2. | We need usable conceptions of non-State law that enable us to make some differentiations, appropriate to context, between the legal and the non-legal, and we should not expect such concepts to carry much intellectual weight. |
| 3. | Many of the most significant patterns relating to law are sub-global. |
| 4. | Accepting a conception of non-State law leads to recognising legal pluralism as a social fact. |
| 5. | There is a danger in romanticising legal pluralism: many non-State orders are oppressive, unjust, inefficient, corrupt, *et cetera*, and incompatible with the ideal of the Rule of Law. |
| 6. | Patterns of diffusion of law are more complex than is commonly supposed. |
| 7. | Insofar as talk and claims about diffusion, harmonisation and convergence of laws tend to be text-oriented, they mainly tell us about surface phenomena. |
| 8. | From a global perspective, we live in an age of religious revival and pluralism of beliefs. To talk of this as "a secular age" is misleading and dangerous. |
| 9. | One of the main challenges facing the human race in a situation of increasing interdependence is how to construct institutions, processes and rules that promote co-existence and co-operation between peoples and groups with very different cosmologies and values. |
| 10. | Western traditions of academic law are vulnerable to charges of ethnocentrism. |

**Box 1:** Ten theses.

Let me begin with a word on so-called "globalisation". Let us isolate two usages, a broad one and a narrow one. Firstly, economic globalisation is typically depicted in terms of the increasing domination of a putative single global economy by the forces, institutions, and ideology of free market capitalism. This domination is now under challenge. Globalisation in this narrow sense is what the "anti-globalisation movement" has been against. A second, broader view is that "globalisation" refers to complex processes of increased interaction and interdependence in rela tion to all kinds of human relations and conditions: climate, communication, transport, disease, war, security, migration, crime, governance, and entertainment. In this broader view, "globalisation" is not necessarily restricted to processes that are genuinely worldwide, but is extended to include many examples of increased transnational interaction or interdependence that are quite limited geographically. For example, the practice of Muslims in Britain seeking *fatwas* by e-mail, the attacks on cruise ships by pirates, or the Wikileaks episode have been loosely attributed to "globalisation". Here I shall adopt the broader view, but I shall be cautious about using the word "global" in relation to phenomena that are less than worldwide. For example, I shall not talk of global lawyers, global law firms, global legal education, the global legal order, and only very hesitantly about global law.

All legal scholars, practitioners and reformers need to consider the implications of globalisation for their own work, both now and in the future. Adopting a global perspective can be useful not only in considering genuinely world-wide problems but also for constructing broad overviews and setting a context for more particular enquiries. However, a global perspective has definite limitations in dealing with immediate practical problems.

Elsewhere, I have identified some assumptions underlying mainstream discourse of Western traditions of academic law that are challenged by adopting a genuinely global perspective. These assumptions are widespread, but not universal. The ten theses advanced here deal selectively with five of these that are especially relevant in the present context.

***Western traditions of academic law*: *some simplistic assumptions*;**

(a) That law consists of two principal kinds of ordering: municipal State law and public international law (classically conceived as ordering the relations between States) ("the Westphalian duo");

(b) That nation-States, societies, and legal systems are very largely closed, self-contained entities that can be studied in isolation;

(c) That modern law and modern jurisprudence are secular, now largely independent of their historical-cultural roots in the Judaeo-Christian traditions;

(d) That modern State law is primarily rational-bureaucratic and instrumental, performing certain functions and serving as a means for achieving particular social ends;

(e) That law is best understood through "top-down" perspectives of rulers, officials, legislators, and elites, with the points of view of users, consumers, victims, and other subjects being at best marginal;

(f) That the main subject-matters of the discipline of law are ideas and norms rather than the empirical study of social facts;

(g) That modern State law is almost exclusively a Northern (European/Anglo-American) creation, diffused through most of the world via colonialism, imperialism, trade, and latter-day post-colonial influences;

(h) That the study of non-Western legal traditions is a marginal and unimportant part of Western academic law; and

(i) That the fundamental values underlying modern law are universal, although the philosophical foundations are diverse.

In short, during the twentieth century and before, Western academic legal culture has tended to be State-oriented, locally focused, secular, positivist, "top-down", Northo-centric, unempirical, and universalist in respect of morals. Of course, all of these generalisations are crude and subject to exceptions – indeed, none has gone unchallenged within the Western legal tradition – and issues surrounding nearly all of them constitute a high proportion of the contested agenda of modern Western jurisprudence. However, at a general level this bald 'ideal type' highlights some crucial points at which such ideas and assumptions are being increasingly challenged.

**Box 2:**. Assumptions in Western traditions of academic law.[1]

## 2. Ten Theses

### 2.1. Thesis One: Global Generalisations about Law

Thinking about globalisation encourages us to adopt a broad global perspective in order to think in terms of broad overviews and total pictures. However, it also tempts us to generalise about law beyond our capacity. On the whole, we lack concepts, well-constructed hypotheses, and reliable data to make many evidence-based generalisations about law in the world as a whole. A central theme of my recent writing has been: beware of false, misleading, exaggerated, and superficial, as well as illusory, meaningless, reductionist, and biased or ethnocentric comparisons and generalisations about legal phenomena or a combination of these.

There is a simple explanation, and part-justification, for our limited ability to generalise about law in the world as a whole. We lack concepts,

[1] Source: William Twining, *General Jurisprudence: Understanding Law from a Global Perspective*, Cambridge University Press, Cambridge, 2009, pp. 5–6.

hypotheses, data and other requisite tools because – with only a few exceptions – for the last two centuries or so, our Western traditions of legal practice and academic law have focused almost exclusively on the domestic or municipal law of particular industrialised or industrialising sovereign nation States. For example, until recently, almost all lawyers were qualified to practice in a single country, sometimes only a part of that country, such as England or California. I am told that the Florida Bar examinations are still exclusively focused on Florida and Federal law, without a single element of foreign or transnational law, even though Miami is an extraordinarily cosmopolitan city and aspires to be not only "the capital of Latin America", but also a leading centre of transnational and regional commercial and financial activity. Similarly, nearly all "mainstream" Western legal theorists – Bentham, Weber, Kelsen, Hart, Raz, Rawls, Dworkin, including sceptics such as Legrand and Duncan Kennedy – have focused almost exclusively on municipal or State legal systems. The major exceptions have been uneasy attempts to accommodate public international law narrowly conceived and some leading theorists of legal pluralism, such as Santi Romano, Ehrlich and Harold Berman.

The "think pieces" for the 2011 conference provided ample evidence of how rapidly things have changed in legal scholarship and theory over the last 15 years or so: amongst the salient themes are the erosion of sovereignty, human rights, multinational corporations, and regional as well as multi-layered governance, comparative and supranational constitutionalism, the fragmentation of international law, and the appearance of new actors on the world stage.

## 2.2. Thesis Two: Non-State Law

My second thesis is that if one adopts a global perspective, a picture of law cannot sensibly be confined to the Westphalian duo of municipal State law and classical international law concerned with relations between sovereign States. This is far too narrow. A picture of law in the world that leaves out religious law, customary law, transnational commercial law, new forms of regional and supranational ordering, and various forms of "soft law" at different levels simply leaves out too much. We need usable conception(s) of non-State law that enable us to make some differentiations, appropriate to context, between the legal and the non-legal. The late Neil MacCormick's conception of law as normative institutionalised order, Brian Tamanaha's radical pruning of Hart's concept of law, and my own modification of Karl Llewellyn's law jobs theory in terms of 'thin functionalism', all claim to do this job. However, we should not expect any conception of law to do much work.

### 2.3. Thesis Three: Sub-Global Patterns of Law

Some of the most significant patterns relating to law are sub-global. These do not fit neatly into geometrical or geological metaphors: concentric circles, vertical hierarchies, horizontals or diagonals. Our heritage of law is much messier than that. Many of our inherited patterns of law in the world are related to empires, diasporas, alliances, language spread, trading blocs, trade routes, and legal traditions. Think of the Islamic world, the British Empire (and its surprising survival, the Commonwealth), North Atlantic Treaty Organisation (NATO), Association of Southeast Asian Nations (ASEAN), Organisation of the Petroleum Exporting Countries (OPEC), and the civil law world. All of these are sub-global. Some are geographically contiguous, some not. Their internal and external relations are complex. They coincide, overlap or disaggregate in many different ways. We talk of English as a global language or the Arab world or the Islamic world in much the same way as we talk about the Cricket World Cup or the Baseball World Series. This is just hype. None of these are genuinely worldwide and they are decentralised in many ways. These historical legacies will strongly influence the development of State law and other forms of law in the next 30 years.

### 2.4. Thesis Four: Legal Pluralism

Accepting a conception of non-State law leads to accepting legal pluralism as a social fact, not only in far-away places, but in every country in Europe and the West. Legal and normative pluralism occurs at all levels of ordering, not just within particular countries – transnational, supranational, national, regional, networked, diasporic, *et cetera*. Legal pluralism raises an agenda of issues conceptually, empirically and normatively, including difficult policy questions about recognition, jurisdiction and integration.

### 2.5. Thesis Five: Legal Pluralism and the Rule of Law

Socio-legal writers on legal pluralism launched a powerful attack on "State centralism" – the tendency to assume that the sovereign ("nation")

State is the only legitimate source of legal authority and the most powerful, most efficient, technically superior, and just form of ordering. Many of the think pieces and the Law of the Future documents explicitly focus on municipal law and the national lawmaker. Even scholars of legal pluralism find it difficult to break away from (often subtle) forms of State-centric thinking. There is, however, a danger in romanticising legal pluralism: legal pluralism is an important social fact, but many non-State orders are oppressive, unjust, inefficient, corrupt, *et cetera*. Some people believe that the best, perhaps the only, hope for achieving and preserving democratic values, the rule of law, good governance, human rights, and distributive justice rests with strong liberal democratic States. What are the prospects for the rule of law in situations where the State is no longer the only or even the main form of governance?

## 2.6. Thesis Six: Diffusion of Law

Adopting a global perspective highlights the pervasiveness and the complexity of diffusion of legal ideas – sometimes referred to as reception or transplantation. Throughout history, legal traditions and legal and normative orders have interacted with and influenced each other – sometimes unidirectionally, sometimes reciprocally, or in more complex patterns. Sometimes it has been assumed that the main agents of reception are either governments and officials or legal elites – for example, a colonial ruler imposing its municipal law and institutions on subject peoples or Turkey, Ethiopia or Japan "voluntarily" importing legal models and ideas. However, it is now recognised that the processes of diffusion are more varied and more complex than such naïve models of reception suggest. Religious legal traditions have interacted for centuries; a human rights case in Germany can affect human rights in the United Kingdom either via Strasbourg or the writings of jurists, or transnational human rights databases; indigenous peoples struggling for recognition in their traditional homes in New Zealand, Canada and Australia are now in direct touch with each other, sometimes networking by e-mail, as are many kinds of social movements. Perhaps most significant is the recognition that government officials are not the only, or even the most important, agents of legal change: migrants, merchants, and missionaries have carried their law with them; law travels with armies and aid workers; legal ideas are spread transnationally by legal education and scholarly writings; and, law is diffused as much by literature as by legislation.

## 2.7. Thesis Seven: Surface Law

The pervasiveness and complexity of processes of diffusion highlight some other points. Bruno Latour's striking phrase "no transportation without transformation" may be an overstatement, but we can never be sure that what has travelled has remained the same – that what was imported was identical to what was exported. It may superficially look the same, but is that only a surface similarity? That is one reason why we have to be cautious of talk about convergence, harmonisation, and unification of laws. There are questions about when and why homogenisation of law is desirable; but in addition we have to be able to assess whether claims to convergence or unity only refer to surface phenomena. The issue is mainly about information. Formal legislative texts or agreements or expositions of doctrine tend to be very uninformative. Western traditions of legal scholarship have been largely text-and-doctrine oriented; they mainly tell us about surface phenomena. Typically they tell us little or nothing about how or whether a given principle, rule or law is or will be interpreted, adapted, applied and implemented, enforced, used, manipulated, or ignored. In short, from information provided merely by legal texts and expositions of doctrine, we do not know to what extent they make any difference in practice, let alone transform economic, social or other relations and behaviour. Surface law is not law that is merely on the surface; rather it is that aspect of law that is only visible on the surface, and with that information we are unlikely to be able to tell how it interacts with its immediate context and how it operates, if at all, in practice.

## 2.8. Thesis Eight: Belief Pluralism

Closely related to sub-global legal patterns is the social fact of belief pluralism. There are strong strains of universalism in the Western traditions of ethics – as exemplified by natural law, Kantianism, utilitarianism, and some versions of human rights theory – which have to confront the social facts of differing belief systems, cosmologies, cultural values, ideologies, *et cetera*. This is not the place to enter into profound philosophical issues about universalism and relativism, and complex issues about the relationship of beliefs to identity. It is important, however, to be aware of our biases. Continental European and Anglo-American traditions of academic law may be quite confident about the nature and problems of legal phenomena in their own geographical spheres, but when they venture out to other places, or the world as a whole, they are vulnerable to charges of parochialism or ethnocentrism. One of the main challenges facing the human race in a situation of increasing interdependence is how to construct institutions, processes and rules that promote co-existence and cooperation between peoples and groups with very different cosmologies and values.

## 2.9. Thesis Nine: A Secular Age?

We must be wary of talk of "a secular age" – for example, the suggestion that human rights are now a sort of irreligious, even atheistic, substitute for liberation theology. "Secular", of course, is sharply ambiguous: it can mean non-religious or even anti-religious; or it can mean independent of or transcending religion, for example, in relation to tolerance and freedom of religion. Demographers of religion (for example, Philip Jenkins) tell us that from a global point of view, we are experiencing a period of religious revival – illustrated by non-Christian immigrants in Europe, Christianity in Uganda, or the spread of the Yoruba religion in the Americas. It is mainly in some parts of the West that we have experienced religious decline, and it is quite parochial, even ethnocentric, to think that this reflects global patterns. On the other hand, the idea of the secular State as a bastion of religious tolerance, holding the ring for people with different belief systems, is a crucial idea in a period of greater interdependence and migration. Being clear about this is, for example, crucial for human rights theory. As Abdullahi an-Naim has eloquently argued, it is a mistake to try to promote ideas of human rights solely or even mainly as a non-religious doctrine. If Muslims are to be persuaded that the international human rights regime is for them, they have to find its justification and support in Islamic premises. Insofar as different belief systems, including religions, have doctrines that support tolerance, although in different ways, we may still hope for workable solutions to problems of co-existence and cooperation, but these solutions cannot be based solely or even mainly on non-religious ideas of secularism associated with our Enlightenment.

## 2.10. Thesis Ten: Ethnocentrism

Ethnocentrism is the projection of ideas derived from one's own culture and background onto others – because these ideas are assumed to be universal, or essentially the same as, or more advanced than, or superior to those of others. Ethnocentrism may often be based more on ignorance than arrogance. Our Western traditions of academic law and legal practice, parochially focused on the municipal laws of our own societies, have exhibited very little interest in non-Western legal traditions and cultures. The few legal scholars who have taken an interest in Hindu law, African law or Islamic law – at least before 9/11 – have been treated as marginal, esoteric, even eccentric. Also they have, of course, been open to accusations of one form of ethnocentrism, *viz.* "orientalism". Sometimes these charges are unfair. Collectively we – Western legal scholars – have been largely indifferent to, unaware of, and fundamentally ignorant about non-Western legal ideas and practices, and the concerns and interests underlying them or the languages in which they are expressed. We should not assume that we have nothing to learn from other traditions and cultures – Islamic ideas on commercial morality, Confucian ideas on harmony and probity of leaders, and Chthonic ideas on ecology. So are we qualified to prescribe global solutions?

## 3. Conclusion

Adopting a global perspective highlights a number of challenges to some widespread assumptions in our Western traditions of legal scholarship and legal practice. A global perspective can help us to recognise the diversity and complexity of systems of ordering human relations in the world and to realise that we are not uniquely at its centre. The Hague is not the centre of the world and "we" – mainly a bunch of Western jurists – cannot on our own prescribe solutions for the world's problems. Although we can and should think about how the complex processes of globalisation bear upon our own situations and ideas and what we can bring to the table to negotiate stable and acceptable responses to transnational, supranational, and genuinely global issues. A global perspective is not a view from nowhere; rather it aspires to be the recognition of views from almost everywhere.

## 4. Sources and Further Reading

An Na'im, Abdullahi, *Islam and the Secular State: Negotiating the Future of Shari'a*, Harvard University Press, Cambridge, MA, 2008.

Berman, Harold, *Law and Revolution: The Formation of the Western Legal Tradition*, Harvard University Press, Cambridge, MA, 1983.

Berman, Harold, *Law and Revolution II: The Impact of the Protestant Reformations on the Western Legal Traditions*, Harvard University Press, Cambridge, MA, 2003.

Benton, Lauren, *Law and Colonial Cultures: Legal Regimes in World History 1400–1900*, Cambridge University Press, Cambridge, 2002.

Buchanan, Allen, "Rawls's Law of Peoples: Rules for a Vanished Westphalian World", in *Ethics*, 2000, vol. 110, no. 4, p. 697.

Glenn, Patrick H., *Legal Traditions of the World: Sustainable Diversity in Law*, 4th ed., Oxford University Press, Oxford, 2010.

Jenkins, Philip, *The Next Christendom: The Coming of Global Christianity*, Oxford University Press, Oxford, 2007.

Latour, Bruno, *Aramis or the Love of Technology*, Harvard University Press, Cambridge, MA, 1996. Tranlsated by Catherine Porter.

MacCormick, Neil, *Institutions of Law: An Essay in Legal Theory*, Oxford University Press, Oxford, 2007.

Muller, Sam, "The Law of the Future and the Future of Law", in Sam Muller *et al.* (eds.), *The Law of the Future and the Future of Law*, Torkel Opsahl Academic EPublisher, Oslo, 2011.

Muller, Sam *et al.*, *Law Scenarios to 2030: Signposting the Legal Space of the Future*, The Hague Institute for the Internationalisation of Law, The Hague, 2011.

Sen, Amartya, *The Idea of Justice,* Harvard University Press, Cambridge, MA, 2009.

Tamanaha, Brian, *A General Jurisprudence of Law and Society*, Oxford University Press, Oxford, 2001.

Tamanaha, Brian, Sage, Caroline and Woolcock, Michael (eds.), *Legal Pluralism and Development: Scholars and Practitioners in Dialogue*, Cambridge University Press, New York, 2012.

Taylor, Charles, *A Secular Age*, Harvard University Press, Cambridge, MA, 2007.

Twining, William, *General Jurisprudence: Understanding Law from a Global Perspective*, Cambridge University Press, Cambridge, 2009.

Twining, William, "Globalisation and Legal Literature", in *Osgoode Hall Law Journal*, 2012 (forthcoming).

Twining, William, *Globalisation and Legal Scholarship* (Montesquieu Lectures, 2009), Wolf Legal Publishers, Nijmegen, 2011.

Twining, William (ed.), *Human Rights: Southern Voices,* Cambridge University Press, Cambridge, 2010.

Twining, William, "Normative and Legal Pluralism", in *Duke Journal of Comparative and International Law*, 2010, vol. 20, p. 473.

# 1.2.

# The Future of Law and the Enviroment: The Emergence of Global Enviromental Law

**Elisa Morgera**[*]

Using international biodiversity law as a testing ground, this think piece will argue that "global environmental law" represents the future of law in the environmental arena. Global environmental law is a concept emerging from the promotion of environmental protection as a global public good through a plurality of legal mechanisms relying on a plurality of legal orders. It emphasises the functional role of States as protectors of the environment, as a common interest of humanity, and with respect to the considerable role of global institutions in international law-making and compliance monitoring. Global environmental law further underscores how international environmental law increasingly affects individuals and groups in society, and private operators, within and across national boundaries. It also points to the growing role of international private law in the environmental arena. Global environmental law emphasises the inter-relations and mutual influences between international, regional, national, sub-national, and transnational law for the protection of the environment, thus pointing to the increasing usefulness of comparative legal methods to understand environmental law.

## 1. Introduction

Environmental law is a fast developing, pioneering and increasingly sophisticated area of regulation. As Neil Gunningham aptly summarised:

> Environmental law is characterised by a creative combination of pluralism and pragmatism: it presents different combinations of traditional regulation, market-based instruments, incentive-based approaches, risk management, voluntary instruments and procedural approaches, while enabling local or indigenous communities, NGOs and the private sector to col-

[*] Dr. **Elisa Morgera** is a Lecturer in European Environmental Law, School of Law, University of Edinburgh, UK.

laborate with authorities in, or even relieve them of, environmental management tasks.

Against such a rich and relatively recent past, environmental law in the likely future will be characterised by more recent trends: specialisation, globalisation, and the return to bilateralism. Private actors and instruments will also be of ever increasing relevance. This piece will discuss in turn how these trends contribute to the character of 'global' environmental law, with a view to suggesting how lawyers should prepare themselves to fully understand the environmental law of the future.

## 2. Increasing Specialisation

There are currently over 500 international treaties and other agreements relating to the environment. Within many of these multilateral environmental agreements, law-making is continuously undertaken, and on average 300 days per year are spent in intergovernmental negotiations to further develop and enhance the implementation of international environmental law. As a result, international regimes have become increasingly specialised. A growing number of soft law instruments and, exceptionally, of new treaties (mostly in the forms of protocols) are adopted, while the practice of monitoring or managing subsidiary institutions is increased. The ultimate goal is to see to the development of more targeted approaches to global environmental challenges, and identifying new and emerging environmental threats. Notwithstanding the form and legal force of these developments, they all contribute to more sophisticated and unprecedented legal and quasi-legal approaches to environmental protection and management.

Consequently, there remain fewer and fewer *generalist* international environmental lawyers, while the number of specialists is on the rise: international climate lawyers, international biodiversity lawyers, and international chemicals lawyers, to name but a few examples. And within each category, further specialisations are developing: in the case of climate law, lawyers specialising in emission trading, the Clean Development Mechanism, or Reducing Emissions from Deforestation and Degradation; or in the case of international biodiversity law, lawyers specialising in conservation, biosafety, or access and benefit-sharing. The need for a broader understanding and a comparison of different international environmental regimes, and their mutual interactions, is, however, not diminished. But it has become a team effort rather than a task for an individual expert, in order to garner and build upon in-depth understanding of the specificities of, and specialist legal solutions within, each international environmental (sub)regime.

"Global" environmental law is thus a concept that can capture the increasing interactions and reciprocal influences between different regimes of international regulation, which have in common the focus on issues of common interest to humanity as a whole. This common trait led to a shift from a discretionary to a functional role of States (as protectors of the common interest of humanity) that is visible, but emerges in different forms, across multilateral environmental agreements. As a result, individuals and groups are identified as "beneficiaries" (not as "addressees") of international environmental law: that is, international environmental law "formally addresses States" but it assumes a global dimension in crucially "affect[ing] States and individuals and groups in society".[1] For instance, under the Convention on Biological Diversity (CBD), institutional proliferation has resulted in a continuous and evolving interpretation of the Convention text, through the development of thematic and crosscutting programmes of work, and the adoption of guidelines and principles aimed not only at affecting national implementation, often through reforms of national laws and administrative practices, but also at influencing the conduct of private operators, particularly in their relationships with indigenous and local communities.

"Global" environmental law also calls attention to the increasing role of international organisations in the making and implementing of international environmental law. International institutions have become more and more significant players in setting the international agenda, influencing intergovernmental negotiations with expertise and administrative services, monitoring and guiding the conduct of States in implementing and complying with international instruments, and interacting with non-State actors and occasionally directly influencing private behaviour. A glaring example is provided by the Convention on International Trade in Endangered Species (CITES) and its National Legislation Project, which has enabled the CITES Secretariat in the absence of an explicit basis in the Convention to determine whether State Parties' national legisla-

[1] See Ellen Hey, "Global Environmental Law and Global Institutions: A System Lacking 'Good Process'", in R. Pierik and W. Werner (eds.), *Cosmopolitanism in Context: Perspectives from International Law and Political Theory*, Cambridge University Press, 2010, p. 45.

tion adequately implements CITES. The project has increased the CITES Secretariat's work in assisting countries in developing or revising their implementing legislation, both at the international level through the involvement of CITES parties in the Convention's relevant subsidiary bodies, but also through on-the-ground workshops, projects, and expert missions. As highlighted by Ellen Hey, among the questions that emerge in connection with this dimension of global environmental law is that of the accountability of international organisations.

## 3. Globalisation

These on-going and increasingly specialised developments at the international level are paralleled by continuous efforts in the development and implementation of environmental law at the European, regional, national and sub-national levels. This leads to the creation of complex interactions and cross-fertilisation between different levels of environmental regulation, and between different specialised areas of environmental law. These multi-directional interactions are also captured by global environmental law, which refers to the promotion of environmental protection as a global public good through a multitude of legal mechanisms, relying on a plurality of legal orders.

Global environmental law thus places international environmental law in the context of interactions between a plurality of legal orders and creative patterns of interplay between international, national and local regulation. In that regard, global environmental law reflects the contemporary presence of international, national and transnational traits of environmental law and the contributions of a variety of international, translational, national and sub-national actors to environmental regulatory systems. It underscores the increasing regulatory influences exercised not only by international organisations, but also by transnational networks of experts providing legislative advice in the context of development aid, and other forms of international technical cooperation provided by non-governmental organisations (NGOs), and involving indigenous and local communities and private actors.

As Young and Percival illustrate, global environmental law can be seen as the result of transplantation: the borrowing of legal principles and tools from the national by the international level, in addition to the adaptation of legal principles and tools from one country to another. It can also result from convergence, that is, the spontaneous similarities in legal responses between different countries to similar external pressures and the linking of national systems. This can be explained by the growing constraints imposed upon States by international environmental law and the expectations international environmental law creates in terms of implementation by private entities.

Innovative instruments that quintessentially embody global environmental law are the 'biocultural community protocols', developed through a bottom-up approach. Through such protocols, indigenous or local communities articulate their values and customary laws, relating to its traditional knowledge and natural resources, against the background of international environmental law. These protocols therefore are an attempt to use international law in a national context, in order to support the local manifestation of the right to self-determination. Community protocols are the product of international and transnational networks of experts comprising State and non-State entities: they have already been developed through the involvement of networks of NGOs, intergovernmental organisations (the UN Environment Programme), and bilateral donors, with a view to prepare communities before engaging in contractual negotiations with private entities. A recent international environmental treaty, the 2010 Nagoya Protocol on Access and Benefit-Sharing under the CBD, specifically recognises this innovative instrument and requires State Parties to support the development of such protocols by indigenous and local communities. This is quite significant, as parties to the Nagoya Protocol are specifically called upon to respect the customary laws of indigenous and local communities at all levels of implementation of their international obligations. The Nagoya Protocol also provides for other avenues for bottom-up inputs into the international legal regime on access and benefit-sharing. For instance, it encourages the use of model contracts and codes of conduct to allow different groups of stakeholders and different sectors to experiment with more specific approaches to the implementation of international law. As a complement, it calls upon the protocol governing body to take stock of these stakeholder-led developments, thereby creating a formal opportunity for the international community to learn from experiences on the ground, and possibly insert some of the lessons learned and successful ideas into the international regulatory system.

## 4. Return to Bilateralism

While multilateralism takes the lion's share of international environmental law-making and compliance monitoring, bilateralism has recently been returned to and put to service for the realisation of the international community's environmental objectives, with implications for different levels of environmental regulation. Notably, this recent phenomenon is not aimed at circumventing or supplanting multilateral environmental initiatives, but rather at complementing them. It can either provide additional tools to ensure compliance with multilateral environmental agreements, or it can provide impetus and new ideas where the development of international environmental law, at the multilateral level, experiences delays or is uncertain.

While being undertaken outside a multilateral environmental framework (in the context of bilateral trade agreements or bilateral cooperation treaties), bilateral initiatives are thus increasingly utilised so that these may contribute to reaching multilateral environmental objectives: bilateral initiatives aimed at supporting the implementation of multilateral environmental agreements in partner countries. In addition, bilateral initiatives are also used to encourage regulatory convergence in other countries or build common ground or even joint positions in the context of ongoing multilateral negotiations. Notably, the European Union and the United States have created unprecedented links between their bilateral agreements and the implementation of CITES – and to a lesser extent also of the CBD – combined with trade incentives or trade sanctions, capacity-building support, and joint monitoring bodies that allow for multi-stakeholder inputs.

While these bilateral legal instruments may provide targeted cooperation and specific means to support compliance with multilateral environmental agreements according to a partnership approach, bilateral initiatives may still be largely and particularly dominated by one party, which imposes its interpretation of international agreements and of the findings of multilateral compliance mechanisms. The distinct United States and European Union approaches – the one sanction-based, the other incentive-based –to bilateral initiatives and their different selections of relevant multilateral environmental agreements certainly speak of their *de facto* dominant position in their partnership with other States, based on the partner countries' dependence on market access to the EU or US. These initiatives may thus lead, as Gregory Shaffer and Daniel Bodansky assert, to the 'migration' of legal norms from powerful States to other countries. Competitive interests, or the desire to realise one country's priorities in on-going multilateral negotiations, are also important drivers in this new wave of bilateral initiatives.

Once again, global environmental law provides an apt lens for fully appreciating this recent development. The implications of these bilateral agreements should be analysed not only in terms of black-letter compatibility between different international agreements, but also in terms of practice resulting at the multilateral level; the implications of national legal developments driven by bilateral agreements on the outcomes of multilateral compliance procedures; or bilateral efforts' influence on the outcomes of multilateral negotiations. Equally, these initiatives should be appreciated *vis-à-vis* their impacts at the national and local levels in terms of the adoption of domestic legislation, practices and approaches for the protection of the environment, and their impacts on the customary laws and claims of indigenous and local communities.

## 5. An Increasing Role for Private Actors and Instruments

As pointed out above, global environmental law also emphasises the role of the private sector in environmental regulation at different levels. International environmental instruments, such as the CBD guidelines, increasingly address private companies. In addition, the private sector has become an increasingly active player in the development and implementation of international environmental law by providing views and lessons learned in on-going intergovernmental negotiations. In addition, multilateral environmental agreements' secretariats directly engage in standard-setting or pioneering implementation with private companies. The CBD Secretariat and the UN Permanent Forum on Indigenous Issues, for instance, have partnered with an association of private enterprises to elaborate guidance to the aromatic, perfume and cosmetics industry interacting with indigenous peoples. Another example concerns the BioTrade Initiative that was initiated under the aegis of the UN Commission on Trade and Development to engage private companies to develop a verification framework formally to recognise their efforts towards conservation, sustainability and benefit-sharing. In that context, the CBD signed a Memorandum of Understanding with the Union for Ethical BioTrade (UEBT), a non-profit-making entity, the private-company members of which commit to gradually ensuring that their sourcing practices promote the conservation of biodiversity, respect traditional knowledge, and assure the equitable sharing of benefits along the supply chain, with a view to raising the awareness of cosmetic and food companies on access and benefit-sharing principles.

Meanwhile, outside multilateral environmental frameworks, other international organisations are increasingly relying on the objectives of multilateral environmental agreements and international environmental law principles in setting standards directly applicable to the private sector. This is the notable case of the International Finance Corporation, the private arm of the World Bank, which has developed Sustainability Performance Standards for private entities operating in developing countries, and is directly based on multilateral environmental agreements and notably on the CBD. Similarly, international bodies engaging in the monitoring of private companies' conduct have made recourse to certain CBD guidelines, particularly those on fair and sustainable interactions with indigenous and local communities, to promote environmentally responsible corporate conduct. This is the case of the implementation structure of the Guidelines for Multinational Enterprises of the Organisation for Economic Cooperation and Development, and also for the UN Special Rapporteur on the Rights of Indigenous Peoples. These initiatives therefore significantly amplify the impact of international environmental law on private operators.

Another trend concerns the increasing use of private law instruments for the implementation of multilateral environmental agreements. International climate change law in particular has seen a rapid and exponential growth in the use of contracts, mostly through its market-based mechanisms. As Kati Kulovesi explains,

> Contractual obligations under the Clean Development Mechanism are regulated both at the international level, through the procedures and (formally) non-binding guidance elaborated under the Kyoto Protocol and by private international law.

These developments at the multilateral level have also engendered parallel initiatives at the regional (in the case of the European Union) or sub-national (in the case of individual states within the US) market-based initiatives, which may also be linked through private international law. A similar evolution is bound to happen in the context of the international biodiversity regime, where the recent Nagoya Protocol on Access and Benefit-Sharing establishes international obligations for countries to ensure that "mutually agreed terms" – that is, private contracts – are established before access is granted to genetic resources from another State and the associated traditional knowledge of indigenous and local communities. The Protocol, as Claudio Chiarolla notes, may thus have a variety of implications relating to private international law, such as questions relating to the national law applicable to an ABS transaction and recognition of foreign judgments that are going to be critical for the Protocol's effective implementation.

## 6. Conclusions: Teaching and Researching Global Environmental Law

The concept of global environmental law can serve to pull together the above-described trends, by highlighting how the increasing specialisation of environmental law is thriving on the interactions between different levels of regulation; between different actors and between unilateral, bilateral and multilateral initiatives; as well as between public and private tools. So, what do these trends mean for future research and for the training of the lawyers of the future?

Global environmental law is a concept that can also be useful as a methodological framework and as a research and teaching agenda: it prompts the study of environmental law at the international, regional, national, and sub-national levels as inter-related and mutually influencing systems. It encourages the use of comparative methods in that endeavour, although this necessitates further reflection in order to define and overcome specific methodological challenges in that respect. Finally, global environmental law calls for systematic and multi-level analyses of the practice of non-State actors, particularly international organisations, international networks of experts providing advice on environmental legislation across the globe, international civil society, and the private sector, with a view to fully understanding their contribution to the making and implementation of environmental law at all levels.

## 7. Sources and Further Reading

Chiarolla, Claudio, "The Role of Private International Law under the Nagoya Protocol", in Elisa Morgera, Matthias Buck, and Elsa Tsioumani (eds.), *The 2010 Nagoya Protocol on Access and Benefit-Sharing in Per-*

*spective: Implications for International Law and Implementation Challenges,* Marthinus Nijhoff, 2012.

Ellis, Jaye, "General Principles and Comparative Law", in *European Journal of International Law,* 2011, vol. 10, no. 4, p. 949.

Gunningham, Neil, "Environment Law: Regulation and Governance: Shifting Architectures", in *Journal of Environmental Law*, 2009, vol. 21, p. 179.

Hey, Ellen, "Common Interests and the (Re)constitution of the Public Space", in *Environmental Policy and Law*, 2009, vol. 39, p. 152.

Hey, Ellen, "Global Environmental Law and Global Institutions: A System Lacking 'Good Process'", in R. Pierik and W. Werner (eds.), *Cosmopolitanism in Context: Perspectives from International Law and Political Theory*, Cambridge University Press, 2010, p. 45.

Jonas, Harry, Bavikatte, Kabir and Shrumm, Holly, "Community Protocols and Access and Benefit-Sharing", in *Asian Biotechnology and Development Review*, 2010, vol. 12, no. 3, p. 49.

Kulovesi, Kati, "Exploring the Landscape of Climate Change Law: Two Emerging Trends", in Erkki Hollo, Kati Kulovesi and Michael Mehling (eds.), *Climate Change and the Law*, Springer, 2012.

Marin Duran, Gracia and Morgera, Elisa, *Environmental Integration in the EU's External Relations: Beyond Multilateral Dimensions,* Hart, Oxford, 2012.

Morgera, Elisa and Tsioumani, Elsa, "Yesterday, Today and Tomorrow: Looking Afresh at the Convention on Biological Diversity", in *Yearbook of International Environmental Law* (online), 2011, vol. 21, p. 3.

Morgera, Elisa, "Bilateralism at the Service of Community Interests? Non-judicial Enforcement of Global Public Goods in the Context of Global Environmental Law", in *European Journal of International Law*, 2012 (forthcoming), vol. 23, no. 2.

Morgera, Elisa, *Corporate Accountability in International Environmental Law*, Oxford University Press, Oxford, 2009.

Shaffer, Gregory C. and Bodansky, Daniel, "Transnationalism, Unilateralism and International Law", in *Transnational Environmental Law*, 2012, vol. 1, p. 31.

Wiener, Jonathan B., "Something Borrowed for Something Blue: Legal Transplants and the Evolution of Global Environmental Law", in *Ecology Law Quarterly*, 2001, p. 1295.

Yang, Tseming and Percival, Robert V., "The Emergence of Global Environmental Law", in *Ecology Law Quarterly*, 2009, vol. 36, p. 615.

# 1.3.

# Judicial Review and International Rule-Making

**Frank Vibert**[*]

It is widely acknowledged that international rule-making is undemocratic. An increasing awareness has also grown that rule makers are far from infallible. At present there is no coherent system for the judicial review of the rule-making of international bodies and most operate without the possibility of judicial challenge to their policy-making decisions.

This think piece considers the contribution that judicial review at the international level might make in order to combat both the democratic deficit and the problem of functional failures – real or alleged.

The think piece outlines alternative approaches to constructing a system of judicial review at the international level and places such efforts within the broader context of global constitutionalism.

## 1. Introduction

This think piece looks at the absence of judicial review of the rule-making and policy-making activities of international institutions. It defines international rule-making institutions broadly so as to include not only bodies such as the International Organisation of Securities Commissions (IOSCO) and the International Accounting Standards Board (IASB) that have important regulatory tasks covering financial markets and accounting standards, but also the Bretton Woods organisations that attach policy conditions to their loans, the World Health Organisation (WHO) that advises and stipulates how members are to report, monitor and address health conditions, the International Panel on Climate Change (IPCC) that guides international policy-making in respect of climate change, as well

[*] **Frank Vibert** is Senior Visiting Fellow at the Department of Government of the London School of Economics and Political Sciences. I am grateful to comments received from Dr. Jan Kleinheisterkamp (Senior Lecturer, LSE, Law Dept) on an earlier draft.

as bodies such as the Financial Action Task Force (FATF) and Egmont Group that establish practices relating to money laundering.

The think piece considers the contribution that judicial review might, in the future, make towards addressing the two fundamental problems of international bodies – that their procedures are undemocratic and that their activities are prone to functional failure. It looks at what is involved in moving from judicial review in a national context to an international level and to the practical steps that might be involved. Finally, it places judicial review within the broader context of constitutionalising the international order.

## 2. Two Fundamental Problems

International rule-making, broadly defined, suffers from two fundamental problems. First, it is undemocratic in the way in which it is carried out. Secondly, the rule makers make mistakes of commission or omission that are more widespread than commonly realised. The democratic deficit has long been acknowledged – although views differ as to how severe the problem is. The problem of functional failure has come to attention more recently as the International Monetary Fund (IMF) failed to foresee the 2008 international financial crisis, the WHO has been accused of mishandling the outbreaks of avian and swine flu, and the IPCC has come under attack for its handling of the evidence on the human contribution to global warming.

The diagnosis of the democratic deficit is not straightforward. The conventional view has a strongly normative point of departure. In democratic theory, the voters are the principals in the system, and governments and official bodies, including international organisations, are their agents. The conventional view sees a kind of democratic 'two-step' taking place. Governments aggregate the views of their people and then reflect them at the international level in establishing the policies and rule-making activities of international bodies and in making international agreements. Under principal/agent theory, the democratic deficit arises because agents spring free of the control of the principals because of their superior knowledge and information and the influence of other incentives. This means that governments have a good deal of latitude in what they do, allegedly on behalf of their people and in turn international bodies acquire additional latitude in what they do as they interpret the wishes of governments. The end result is that the people are distanced from rule-making outputs that may no longer reflect their preferences.

An alternative diagnosis rejects this largely normative starting point that places people at the beginning of the chain. Instead, international rule-making is seen in reality as world dominated by professionals and experts who diagnose the 'problems' and propose 'solutions' to governments or government bodies. It is a top-down process where voters are largely unaware of what international organisations do, where rules are made, who makes them, and at the same time, have highly limited opportunities to influence them even if they did understand what was being done. Instead of the supposed democratic 'two-step' that rests on a large number of simplifying assumptions that are rarely spelt out in full, the top-down process is seen as one where experts and professionals in their field propose the content of rules, governments take a decision on expert advice, and the people are at the receiving end. To give a practical example, an individual asked for personal details when opening a bank account is unlikely to be aware of the recommendations of FATF which may underlie the request, or even to have heard of FATF.

Following this approach, the production of new rules and regulations at the international level can be modelled along the lines of models of other forms of diffusion of innovation where the recipients, the people, are takers of innovation and not the source. This model recognises that while States and their agencies may be the addressees of international rules and regulations, the targets are increasingly businesses and individuals within States, and the democratic deficit arises because people have no means of influencing decisions that affect them.

The diagnosis of functional 'failure' suffers from a multitude of possible explanations – from those offered by political science that focus, for example, on the mismatching of the scale of government structures to the scale of the problem and policy 'translation' problems in moving between different levels of government; to those offered by sociologists who look at cultural or organisational failure; and to those put forward by behavioural psychologists and economists who look at the behavioural and cognitive processes of those trying to understand the workings of complex social systems and to make the rules.

One well-established strand of theorising concerns 'epistemic elites'. This focuses on the key role of experts and professionals in rule-making – their shared principled beliefs, common views on causalities, and similar knowledge gained from practical experience in similar positions of responsibility. These characteristics provide professional groups with great strength in diagnosing policy problems and in devising responses. Those same strengths, however, also contain cognitive biases and sources of error that need to be guarded against. When failure is attributed to cognitive weaknesses, it is because the need for procedures to guard against the biases of professional groups and organisations is simply not recognised and the necessary safeguards are not in place. The IMF has attributed its own failure to foresee and respond to the 2008 international financial crisis to cognitive failure of this sort.

There has been very little empirical work done on the cognitive dispositions and biases of international rule-making groups, but in many ways, a diagnosis of cognitive failure fits the facts of the financial crisis and other alleged failures in international rule-making better rather than other possible explanations. The dispositions associated with cognitive failure, a tendency to over-generalise, to be unresponsive to new information, and to be over-ambitious, can all be recognised at the international level.

It has been fashionable to suggest that networks are the answer to weaknesses in international rule-making. They are not. Networks have many strengths. They are flexible and can introduce competing ideas and approaches. However, they can also be collusive and reject those they consider to be outsiders. They are composed of the same experts that contribute to top down rule-making and subject to the same professional sources of cognitive weakness. WHO and IPCC both make extensive use of networks of experts and professionals, as do many other international organisations. It has not shielded them from allegations of failure in what they do. Nor has it stopped the reality of top-down rule-making. How many employees facing the end of defined benefit pension schemes are aware that this may owe much to the 'mark to market' principles promulgated by IASB - a private networked international organisation - or are even aware of its existence?

## 3. The Relevance of Judicial Review As a 'Challenge System'

In the context of national regulatory systems, the practice of the judicial review of regulatory and policy-making decisions by agencies is well established, particularly in the US, Germany and the UK. What is immediately apparent at the international level is its virtual absence. However, the disputes settlement regime of the WTO might be seen as a partial exception to this.

There are dangers in assuming that practices at one level of government can and should be transposed to another. The settings are often different and the parallels misleading. What has been termed policy-making accountability at the national level takes place in democracies within a general setting where all those with authority, legislatures, executives, and executive agencies, can in theory be held to account and judiciaries play a key role in ensuring that this happens. At the international level, the branches of government familiar at the national level are missing and it is agencies that proliferate. It remains difficult to define the essence of this international rule-making space, characterise its institutions, and account for the huge variety of instruments and procedures through which rules are conveyed. Nevertheless, despite differences in the rule-making settings, the key question remains as to what judicial review at an international level might bring to help reduce both the top-down nature of international rule-making and to help strengthen procedural defences against the cognitive weaknesses of experts and professional groups.

The principles of judicial review in a national context are not entirely settled, but there appears to be a growing body of accepted practice that is common to many judiciaries despite other differences they might have in judicial doctrine, structure, tradition, or practice. Generally speaking, courts do not try to reopen the substance of a decision by a regulatory or rule-making body. Often, they do not possess the expertise to do so. They may rule on the legal basis for an agency's action, but they are likely to be cautious in so doing because law makers often provide for regulatory discretion when framing statutory terms of reference.

The key pillars for review are, first, a procedural requirement for regulatory bodies to show that they have allowed for all those who wanted to comment on a proposed rule the opportunity to do so, including the right to receive a reply to their comment. Secondly, there is a burden of proof requirement that requires the rule-making bodies to show that they have not omitted evidence that is material to the decision. Thirdly, courts may be under an obligation to check that the decisions of the rule makers are proportionate to the problem being addressed.

Leaving aside the unsettled or grey areas in the principles of judicial review, these three pillars are relevant both to top-down international rule-making and to the cognitive weaknesses of the expert rule makers. Allowing all those with an interest in commenting the opportunity to do so and the right to a robust reply, would present an opportunity for a voice at the international level. Yet, it would not be the voice of the people. Rather, it would be the voice of those affected by a rule and those who, for other reasons, may have an interest in it.

An insistence on the opportunity for comment would also require international bodies to consider alternative views on the way they have framed a problem and alternative ways of going about the analysis. In so far as the rule makers have to guard against accusations of material omissions in their analysis, they may also be encouraged to assess the reliability of the evidence they rely on, to trace their analytic steps and processes methodically, and to attach confidence weightings to their data, their models and their final assessments. A need to show courts that their actions are 'proportionate' would also work in the same direction as procedural and evidentiary standards by encouraging care when expert bodies draw inferences from the evidence.

In short, the pillars of judicial review translated to the international level could help reduce the democratic deficit by mitigating top-down rule-making and, at the same time, help bolster defences against weaknesses in the cognitive dispositions of expert bodies. Judicial review would put in place a 'challenge system' helpful for mitigating both the democratic deficit and epistemic weaknesses.

## 4. What Is Required and How to Achieve It

Practical arrangements to put in place a system of judicial review at the international level have to sidestep all questions to do with fundamental judicial philosophy and principles of organisation. It has long been acknowledged that there is no coherent hierarchy and structure of courts at the international level and little prospect for it any time soon. Setting in place a system of judicial review thus needs to acknowledge that there is no ready-made structure into which courts or tribunals could fit in the way (for example, in the UK, the Competition Appeals Tribunal could be slotted between the Competition Commission and an appeal to the High Court) and no prospect of an overall agreement that would govern relationships between courts. Similarly, while global administrative law has been recognised as emergent, there is no practical prospect in the short term of agreement on the principles and practices that would need to underpin the development of an internationally coherent doctrine of review, and the best that can be hoped for is the recognition of minimum standards of review.

Within these fundamental constraints, any practical step towards judicial review would have to decide whether judicial review across all bodies could be entrusted to a single general court or tribunal of review, or whether individual organisations would each have their own tribunal established under international law or would accept the jurisdiction in which they were headquartered.

Simplicity would suggest either accepting local jurisdiction or that of a single international court including the possibility of a special tribunal attached to the International Court of Justice in The Hague. The development of local jurisprudence would risk the emergence of varied and possibly conflicting approaches. On the other hand, international organisations guard their own turf and would be the first to complain that a single international court would not understand the specificities of their own environment. In Europe, the European Court of Human Rights (ECtHR) has come under criticism for accepting too many referrals and for arriving at judgments that fail to take into account national specificities. In the case of the International Court of Justice in The Hague, any specially instituted panel or tribunal would also need to be able to accept suits brought by non-State actors instead of being limited to actions brought by States.

Against this background, there appears to be four main options for establishing a system of review, in descending order of practicality.

## 4.1. Internal Virtual Review

One option for establishing a system of judicial review would be for the legal departments of the international institutions themselves to act as virtual courts – that is to say they would place themselves in the position of a hypothetical court of review and advise management and boards whenever a proposed action would be vulnerable to be overthrown by a court review, if there were one, on the grounds of either procedural or material defects. The weakness in this approach is that the voice of legal departments is not always strong within their own organisation. They would need to define their own standards for any review and would be seen by the external world to be judges in their own cause.

### 4.2. Agreement on Principles by the OECD

Organisation for Economic Co-operation and Development (OECD) has taken the lead among international organisations in establishing international regulatory and governance principles, and its latest set of Recommendations was issued in early 2012. Their practical force is not confined to the 34 members of OECD itself but have a world-wide impact. It would be consistent with this role for OECD to set out minimum principles for the international judicial review of international rules while leaving it to the organisations themselves as to how to put them into practice. In setting out the principles, OECD could also benchmark the procedural standards to which international organisations should work. The weakness in this approach is that the recommendations would need to gain world-wide acceptance after adoption by OECD. OECD would itself be an interested party.

### 4.3. Administrative Procedures Resolution by the UN

Another alternative would be for the United Nations (UN) to take action itself. An organ such as Economic and Social Council (ECOSOC) could. for example. pass a resolution along the lines of the US Administrative Procedure Act that would set out what is expected of international bodies and of courts of review, and would also propose how such courts (or a general court) would be established or recognised. The weakness in such an approach is the difficulty of getting agreement among all UN members on a system that would reduce their discretionary policy making powers. The difficulties would include getting agreement on setting up any new international court or recognising existing courts in local jurisdictions.

### 4.4. Addendum to the UN Declaration of Fundamental Human Rights

A fourth option would be to amend the UN Declaration of Fundamental Human Rights so as to include the principles of rule-making and judicial review within a wider perspective under an additional section on rights to administrative justice. The weakness in any such option is the fear of reopening the content of the Declaration more generally, as well as contaminating the principles and practice of judicial review of policy-making with the hypocrisy and power politics that surround the implementation of the Declaration.

## 5. The Global Constitutional Perspective

Any practical steps towards the judicial review of international rule-making would have to be pluralistic in the sense discussed above, of avoiding fundamental questions about a coherent international judicial structure or philosophy, or system of relationship between jurisdictions. The avenues identified above all represent, to varying degrees, partial approaches. Nevertheless, even working within the practical limitations of what can be achieved would still represent a large step for individual international organisations that in many cases have relied on their international privileges and immunities to shield them from legal action (except in the case of administrative tribunals that look at personnel actions). In addition, it would also constitute a small but significant step towards constitutionalising the international order.

The grand vision of a global constitutional order has been stalled for some time. It does not seem practical to think in terms of a global parliament and global government. The UN Declaration of Fundamental Human Rights represents one rights-based approach to constitutionalism that is common to modern national constitutional frameworks. Unfortunately, in the context of the UN, the Charter is a deeply flawed instrument – undermined by big power politics in the UN itself, and failing to recognise in its provisions that in a pluralist world there can be many different and opposing interpretations of basic rights, particularly in cases where rights have to be weighed against each other. The principle of judicial review of rule-making decisions would establish an important component of the rule of law in a less controversial and less highly politicised area. Even in a pluralist setting, it would make its own contribution to this longer term objective of a constitutionalised global order.

## 6. Conclusion

In future years, an increasing amount of policy-making and rule-making should take place at an international level in order to tackle the many problems that cross international borders. At present, such a movement can be resisted by democracies as well as by undemocratic States. The reasons are that the rule-making takes place in an undemocratic setting, accountability is lacking, and professional elites have shown themselves all too vulnerable to failure in their diagnoses and prescriptions. Judicial review at the international level could make a modest contribution to redressing this situation and provide a different path towards building a global constitutional framework. None of the possible approaches to judicial review outlined above will be easy for international organisations to accept. However, they are beginning to review their procedures. In addition, they have a reputation for evidence-based rule-making that they have to protect if their activities are to be seen as legitimate. They are also important proponents of principles of good governance worldwide. In order to maintain their credibility, they must not only talk the talk to others, but also walk the walk and apply the principles of good governance to themselves.

## 7. Sources and Further Reading

Benedict, Kingsbury, "The Emergence of Global Administrative Law", in *Law and Contemporary Problems*, 2005, vol. 68, no. 3–4.

Haas, Peter, "Epistemic Communities in Bodansky & Hey", in *Oxford Handbook of International Environmental Law*, 2007, pp. 792–806.

Rose-Ackerman, Susan, "Policymaking Accountability", in *David Levi-Faur Handbook on the Politics of Regulation*, Edward Elgar, Cheltenham, 2011, pp. 171–184.

Vibert, Frank, *Democracy and Dissent: The Challenge of International Rule-making*, Edward Elgar, Cheltenham, 2011.

# 1.4.

## A Meta-Regulatory Turn? Control and Learning in Regulatory Governance

**Colin Scott***

The steering of organisational and individual behaviour is a central challenge of contemporary governance. This is important not only for regulation of matters such as the environment, employment relations, and financial markets, but also for issues of fundamental rights concerning the behaviour not only of businesses, but also of government. Long experience suggests that highly prescriptive approaches to regulation are frequently ineffective or even counterproductive. One reason for this is that we show considerable ingenuity in turning demands to change our behaviour to suit our own interests rather than meeting the public interest. Other reasons include the limited knowledge about the behaviours to be steered and a limited capacity for governmental monitoring and enforcement. An alternative way to think about the problem of steering behaviour is to reduce the emphasis on top-down control and seek to exploit the capabilities of targeted individuals and organisations both to regulate themselves, to monitor each other, and to learn about how they may benefit from pursuing more public-oriented objectives. Corporate social responsibility initiatives provide only one example of such a process at play. This piece will evaluate this meta-regulatory approach to governance – both its potential and known shortcomings – as a basis for developing regulation which is both more effective and more efficient. It addresses also the legitimacy issues associated with a 'meta-regulatory turn' in governance.

### 1. Introduction

The financial crises which have enveloped much of the industrialised world since 2008 are only the latest incidents to cause policy makers and academics to question the effectiveness and desirability of dominant mod-

* **Colin Scott** is Dean of Law and Professor of EU Regulation & Governance at University College Dublin.

els of regulatory governance. Whilst there is widespread disenchantment, there is little consensus on either the causes of problems with regulation, nor on the possible solutions. It is more or less inevitable that in a crisis, vulnerable governments should assert the need for more stringent regulation and, at least implicitly, attribute responsibility for failures to weaknesses in control. This is not the only way to think about the problem. A precisely converse position would be that market actors deferred too much to the normative content of regulation to guide their behaviour ("unless it is prohibited, I can do it"), taking insufficient responsibility for knowing what they should do.

An alternative to more stringent regulation is to think about the problem of steering behaviour so as to reduce the emphasis on top-down control, and seek to exploit the capacity of targeted individuals and organisations to regulate themselves, to monitor each other, and to learn about how they may benefit from pursuing more public regarding objectives. Corporate social responsibility initiatives provide only one example of such a process at play. This piece will evaluate the meta-regulatory approach to governance, both its potential and its known shortcomings. The objective is to set out an argument for ways in which this technique might further provide a basis for developing regulation which is both more effective and more efficient, without losing sight of the need for legitimacy.

## 2. Regulation and Its Challenges

### 2.1. Regulation

The steering of organisational and individual behaviour is a central challenge of contemporary governance. Regulation is both a core solution and a core problem. As a policy solution, regulation is attractive because it is relatively inexpensive and transparent as a means to demonstrate that governments are being responsive to policy problems as diverse as environmental degradation, anti-competitive behaviour, dangerous products, misleading commercial practices, problems of employment rights, risky financial behaviour, and even the behaviour of governments themselves over matters such as human rights.

Regulation is a key instrument of contemporary governance involving the setting of norms, together with mechanisms of feedback and correction (see Figure 1 below). In the US system, these different elements were combined from the late 19$^{th}$ century in independent regulatory agencies with powers to make rules, to monitor compliance, and to enforce where they found breaches. Within Europe and other OECD member States, regulation experienced a policy boom from the 1980s, not only seeing a surge in the establishment of regulatory agencies, but also as a recognition of the significance of regulatory modes of governance which deploy monitoring and enforcement of compliance with rules as their core mode, with or without specialised oversight agencies. It became apparent that governance through rules and oversight was not novel in Europe in this period, though its deployment was growing. Rather, long-established institutions and practices had become identified as a distinctive regulatory mode of governance.

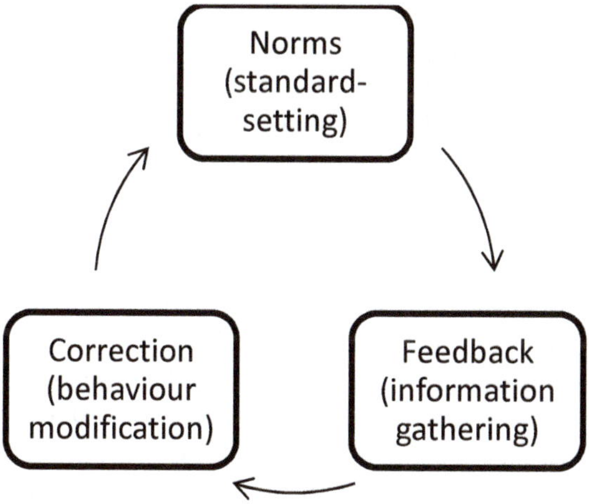


**Figure 1:** Key Regulatory Functions.

## 2.2. Challenges of Regulation

A core premise of regulation is that it is possible to steer behaviour in reasonably predictable ways. Long experience suggests that highly prescriptive approaches to regulation are frequently ineffective or even counter-productive. One reason for this is that we show considerable ingenuity in turning demands to change our behaviour to suit our own interests rather than meeting the public interest. It is difficult to set down in rules, with sufficient specificity, the behaviour or outcome that is required. Or, somewhat distinctly, the standard that can be set down in a rule has poor congruence to the outcome that is required.

A second reason of regulation being ineffective is that governments frequently have limited knowledge about the behaviours to be steered and limited capacity for monitoring and enforcement. Agencies have addressed these problems with prioritisation strategies and selective enforcement, which call into question the uniformity with which regulatory law is enforced. In the case of the global financial crisis, there is a significant debate as to whether the regulatory dimension of the failures was a product of regulation which was overambitious in the reassurance that it could provide as to the risks created in financial markets, or that regulation was insufficiently prescriptive, because it was based on principles rather than rules.

## 3. The Limits of Classic Regulation

### 3.1. Diffusion of Formal Regulatory Powers

A central idea in contemporary regulatory scholarship is that it is unrealistic and unhelpful to conceive of regulatory power being concentrated in independent State agencies. Even in those jurisdictions (including most of the OECD member States) where there is significant experience in delegating some powers to regulatory agencies, the capacity for action by those regulators is often limited. This is true in the first part because formal powers are often shared, with ministers and legislatures frequently retaining power to make or call in rules, and with powers to apply formal sanctions frequently requiring application to a court through costly processes of litigation. The existence of these shared powers, whether or not they are frequently deployed, clearly limits the capacity of agencies to act alone. The effects of diffusion of formal regulatory capacity are further accentuated by the powers to make regulatory norms and to monitor implementation held by supranational organisations, centrally the European Union (EU) institutions within the EU, but also within other international regimes such as that of the World Trade Organisation (WTO). The European Commission, in particular, acknowledges limits in its capacity, and seeks to foster engagement and learning in its regimes through the development of networks.

### 3.2. Diffusion of Informal and Private Power

The observation that power is commonly shared within regulatory regimes is further strengthened when we consider informal power. Informal power in regulatory regimes derives from the possession of key information and also financial resources by, amongst others, regulated organisations and also non-governmental organisations (NGOs).

Furthermore, State regulatory capacity is often not the only show in town. In many important areas of the modern economies, there is an implicit or explicit delegation to the private or self-regulatory capacity of firms, trade associations, standard-setting bodies, and so on. Such private regulatory capacity operates both at the national and transnational level. Whilst such capacity may be delegated in statute, it may also derive from varied forms of contractual arrangements, both bilateral and multilateral.

### 3.3. Regulatory Capitalism

These observations about the diffusion of regulatory capacity, referred to by Braithwaite, Levi-Faur and others as constituting 'regulatory capitalism', do not neglect the important trend towards the growth in the number of regulatory agencies across most OECD member States, and also the growth in rules in many sectors of the economy. Rather, regulatory capitalism locates the growth in regulatory agencies and rules within broader phenomena of diffused governance as a means to understand why we might expect classic regulation through agencies to be of limited effect, and to enable us to consider how it is, in practice, supplemented by other institutions and practices.

### 3.4. Learning in Regulatory Capitalism

Regulatory capitalism offers a diffused model of regulatory governance in which, for most regimes and policy domains, we should not expect one agency or organisation to be very powerful in what it can command others to do. Rather, relationships within regulatory regimes are often characterised as involving a high degree of interdependence, such that the capacity of one organisation to act effectively is dependent on the actions of others. Each organisation may feel it has a substantial degree of autonomy, albeit constrained by the capacity of others. This is most obviously true in respect of the classic relationship between a regulatory agency and a regulatee, where the outcomes of the regime are shaped by the conduct of both sets of actors, in response to each other and to varied aspects of the environment in which they operate.

If the capacity for control is limited for each of the various organisations involved, then they need to orient themselves around some other mode of action. I suggest that it is just as useful to orient action around learning as control. Learning here includes learning about the power and capacity of others, their incentives for action, their preference and motivations, and how one might key into these in order to stimulate an appropriate response. The imperative for learning applies as much to regulatees and third parties as it does to regulators, since each has the capacity to do things (such as supplying information) which will affect the others and secure a behavioural response.

## 4. Applying Meta-Regulation

### 4.1. Meta-Regulation and the Role of the State in Regulatory Capitalism

If it is correct that relationships within regulatory regimes are best characterised as interdependent, then this begs the question: what is the appropriate role of the State? If it is unrealistic to expect regulation to always exert detailed control over organisations targeted for regulation, then what role is left? Observations about regulatory capitalism suggest that State organisations should be more modest in their expectations as to what they can achieve through direct control. But these observations are also suggestive of a significant role for the State in steering or orchestrating activity within regulatory regimes. In some sectors, it may be possible to encourage the emergence or development of forms of self-regulatory or private capacity. This kind of activity, the regulation of self-regulation, has been termed 'meta-regulation' by Parker and others.

### 4.2. Meta-Regulatory Regimes

Private regimes offer the advantage of strong industry knowledge, support for the regime from the industry, and reduced cost for the State. The private actors might learn more about their preferences for regulation and the market advantages flowing from private regulation, such as the reassurance and confidence which it gives to users of their products and services. Risks of 'cartelisation', and pursuit of self-interest are often likely to be present. A key role for the State exists in overseeing private regulation, either implicitly, for example, through threats of legislation ('the shadow of hierarchy'), or explicitly through establishing a oversight regulator to oversee the exercise of delegated powers. Such oversight can be achieved through empowering the oversight regulator to request changes to private rules, or to challenge directly or through the court's decisions concerning the application of sanctions to regulated organisations found to be in breach of the rules.

## 4.3. Examples of Meta-Regulation

Numerous examples of regimes which deploy some form of meta-regulation can be found both at national and supranational level. These regimes are characterised by a central role for private organisations, such as firms and associations in establishing the regime, and/or setting the norms or standards, and/or monitoring and enforcing for compliance. The involvement of the State includes implicit encouragement or observation and more formal and institutionalised oversight. Examples include corporate social responsibility (Box 1), professional regulation (Box 2), advertising self-regulation (Box 3), and EU regulation of commercial practices (Box 4).

**Corporate Social Responsibility**

Moves towards encouraging businesses to engage in practices of corporate social responsibility (CSR) have engaged the State in the 'soft' encouragement to businesses towards more responsible business practices in respect of matters such as the environment and human rights. A somewhat harder mechanism sees States requiring companies to specify what they have done with respect to CSR (without necessarily requiring firms to undertake any particular actions). These soft and harder measures create an environment which encourages firms to learn about market advantages in engaging in CSR and to engage in surveillance and benchmarking against the activities of others in their sector, with the potential for laggards to learn from leaders.

**Box 1:** Corporate Social Responsibility.

**Professional Self-Regulation**

Strong traditions of self-regulation in professions such as healthcare and law have increasingly been challenged in many countries, partly in response to scandals, and partly as a result of a wider pattern of reduced deference to professional judgement. Changes which seek to provide stronger reassurance about professional regulation do not necessarily involve sweeping away self-regulation. A number of Australian states have introduced public regulators with a statutory role to oversee aspects of setting and enforcing professional codes by professional organisations in the legal sector. The UK has produced a meta-regulatory public body to oversee professional codes and complaints practices administered by professional councils in the health professions. Such developments retain many of the strengths of self- or professional regulation, whilst providing public reassurance

**Box 2:** Professional Self-Regulation.

**Advertising Self-Regulation**

Many industrialised countries incorporate some degree of self-regulation to address matters both of taste and accuracy in the practices of the advertising industry. Though regimes are varied they typically involve the setting of codes (often based on the Consolidated International Chamber of Commerce Code on Marketing and Advertising). The UK regime, administered by the Advertising Standards Authority (ASA), originated in market concerns about the reputation of the industry in the face of concerns about the legitimacy of the techniques deployed to sell products. However, successive UK governments have encouraged the ASA to develop both the content and processes in respect of codes and complaints so as to steer the regime in such a way that public objectives for advertising regulation can be met. Thus, there is an implicit delegation of public power, recognised as such by the courts. This confidence in the private regime for advertising was attested to by a decision to extend the ASA remit by supplementing its non-statutory powers over print advertising with the explicit delegation of statutory powers over broadcast advertising. Within the EU, the European Commission has been willing to engage with self-regulation of advertising and recognise its key role in providing reassurance over compliance with advertising standards. The legitimacy and effectiveness of self-regulation at national level is significantly bolstered by participation in the activities of a network coordinated by the European Advertising Standards Alliance.

**Box 3:** Advertising Self-Regulation.

**EU Regulation of Commercial Practices**

Many businesses within the European Union market their products with a claim to be a member of and/or to follow the requirements of a particular code of practice, typically set by a trade association. The EU Unfair Commercial Practices Directive includes amongst its listed misleading actions, 'non-compliance by a trader with commitments contained in codes of conduct by which the trader has undertaken to be bound', where the trader has undertaken to be bound by a code and its commitments are not simply aspirational (2005/29/EC, art 6(2)(b)). This measure requires member States to apply sanctions for such misleading actions. This oversight does not set any minimum requirements for self-regulatory codes, but rather holds businesses to their own commitments to follow them. For this reason, the technique is very much meta-regulatory.

**Box 4:** EU Regulation of Commercial Practices.

# 5. Conclusions

## 5.1. Policy Implications

### 5.1.1. A More Modest Role for the State

The analysis offered in this brief is suggestive of a more modest role for the State in the way it thinks about regulatory control. But, equally, it offers an enhanced role for the State in observing, learning about, and steering regulatory capacity, which is held by others. It creates a challenge to be creative about recognising how the capacity not only of businesses, but also NGOs and government organisations can be deployed to achieve public objectives, not through direct control, but rather through indirect steering. This may be done using formal powers of oversight and delegation, or the informal capacity of government to collect and deploy information. Such an approach raises challenges not only in demonstrating effectiveness, but also ensuring legitimacy of actions that involve both public and private action in regulatory regimes.

### 5.1.2. Assuring Legitimacy

Virtually any traditional or remodelled version of regulatory governance raises significant problems of legitimacy. In the case of the regulatory agency model, it is typically a key characteristic of the regime that it should operate at arms-length from elected government, with limited capacity for ministerial direction. This insulation is designed to permit agencies to implement efficient regulatory strategies without interference, which might be driven by short-term political concerns. An alternative which emphasises the capacity of regulated actors to set, monitor and enforce norms over themselves is perhaps even more vulnerable to questioning on the democratic grounds that elected government is not even responsible for such matters as key appointments and oversight. Accordingly, any discussion of 'meta-regulation', the steering of self-regulatory capacity as an alternative to traditional regulation must address the problem of democratic governance. The assignment of monitoring and steering capacity to public agencies or government departments may provide part of the answer. A more radical solution is to begin to conceive of regimes as creating their own community of stakeholders, within which a form of democracy, engaging all those affected, might be effectively developed. Examples of such democratic governance at the level of particular regulatory regimes are suggestive, but limited to date.

## 5.2. Implications for Research

### 5.2.1. Effects and Effectiveness

For researchers, there is much that is not well understood about the effects and effectiveness of regulatory regimes. Research should be undertaken to compare the effects of well-defined meta-regulatory regimes across sectors and across jurisdictions to better understand the conditions under which both primary regulatory activity, and steering and oversight, might be expected to be effective. Equally, such research might shed light on the kinds of conditions under which meta-regulation is unlikely to be effective, and where direct control by government through ministries or agencies, 'mega-regulation', might be more effective.

### 5.2.2. Legitimacy

A second set of challenges relate to better addressing the issue of legitimacy associated with regimes in which a good deal of power is delegated, implicitly or explicitly, to private actors. It is also important to understand the conditions under which a functional form of democratic governance for such regimes might emerge and be recognised as such. The potential pay-off for identifying a source of legitimacy for non-State governance at the regime level is that this might permit us to think of effective meta-regulation which does not engage the State in the oversight role, but rather deploys the techniques associated with market or community activity in giving regulated actors reasons to be effective in their setting, monitoring and enforcing of norms.

## 5.3. Implications for Training the Lawyer of the Future

Lawyers of the future will require fresh approaches to legal doctrine and a stronger understanding of the limits to their capacity as lawyers in order to better understand their role in this complex, interdependent regulatory environment.

### 5.3.1. Legal Doctrine and Legal Pluralism

At the level of doctrine, domestic public law must be located alongside contractual rules and practices which underpin many private regulatory arrangements and their dispute resolution mechanisms, and which are frequently transnational in effects. A key lens for understanding competing normative legal orders is offered by legal pluralism, with its questioning of the form and sources of law in regulatory governance and beyond. Such an approach assists not only in understanding the effects of law in regulatory regimes, but also in seeking the sources of legitimacy for regulatory governance which deviates significantly from traditional models rooted in administrative law.

### 5.3.2. The Regulatory Environment and the Sociological Citizen

It is of great significance that lawyers understand the limits to legal powers in regulatory governance. The ability to locate oneself and one's capacity for action, interdependent with respect to the capacity of others, requires us to stimulate a form of what Silbey and colleagues refer to as 'sociological citizenship' in those who are going to be effective at what they do. Being effective in an environment where powers are diffused requires lawyers to learn about what others can do and how that capacity can be harnessed. Tomorrow's lawyers will frequently deploy skills both of analysis and negotiation.

## 6. Sources and Further Reading

Black, Julia, "Constructing and Contesting Legitimacy and Accountability in Polycentric Regulatory Regimes", in *Regulation and Governance*, 2008, pp. 137–164.

Braithwaite, John, *Regulatory Capitalism: How It Works, Ideas for Making It Work Better*, Edward Elgar Publishers, Cheltenham, 2008.

Gilad, Sharon, "It Runs in the Family: Meta-Regulation and Its Siblings", in *Regulation and Governance*, 2010, vol. 4, pp. 485–506.

Gunningham, Neil and Sinclair, Darren, *Leaders and Laggards: Next-Generation Environmental Regulation*, Greenleaf Publishing, Sheffield, 2002.

Levi-Faur, David, "The Global Diffusion of Regulatory Capitalism", in *The Annals of the American Academy of Political and Social Science*, 2005, vol. 598, no. 1, pp. 12–32.

Parker, Christine, *The Open Corporation: Self-Regulation and Democracy*, Cambridge University Press, Melbourne, 2010.

Parker, Christine and Braithwaite, John, "Regulation", in Peter Cane and Mark Tushnet (eds.), *The Oxford Handbook of Legal Studies*, Oxford University Press, Oxford, 2003.

Scott, Colin, "Reflexive Governance, Regulation and Meta-Regulation: Control or Learning?", in Olivier de Schutter and Jacques Lenoble (eds.), *Reflexive Governance: Redefining the Public Interest in a Pluralistic World*, Hart Press, Oxford, 2010.

Scott, Colin, "Regulating Everything: From Megaregulation to Metaregulation", in *Administration*, 2012, vol. 60, pp. 57–85.

Silbey, Susan, Huising, Ruthanne, and Coslovsky, Salo Vinocur, "The 'Sociological Citizen' Relational Interdependence in Law and Organizations", in *L'Annee Sociologique*, 2009, vol. 59, pp. 201–229.

# 1.5.

# Integrating Healthcare and Legal Services to Optimise Health and Justice for Vulnerable Populations: The Global Opportunity

**Ellen M. Lawton***

The impact of social determinants like housing and income on health is now well-accepted and documented. Increasingly, the health and legal communities see access to civil legal services as a key intervention to reduce the effects of negative social determinants, improve health, and prevent disease. But to improve access to justice, the legal sector must look to the health sector for guidance on quality and evaluation metrics, capacity-building and sustainability.

Re-framing civil legal services for vulnerable populations as a critical facet of healthcare creates unprecedented opportunities for more efficient use of health and legal resources. If health is at the core of well-being for all vulnerable clients, then to reduce the dual burden of health and legal problems, the legal community – including *pro bono* resources in global corporate and private law firms – must closely align its activities and priorities with public health and healthcare partners, and invest in leaders who can innovate across both sectors and leverage scarce legal resources most effectively.

## 1. Introduction

The world is full of examples where health and law collide. A quick look at a local newspaper reveals some of the many connections between the health and legal sectors that permeate families and communities – the disabled veteran who needs a wheelchair ramp to get into his apartment building, the elderly woman who can no longer make healthcare decisions

---

* **Ellen Lawton** (J.D.) leads the National Center for Medical-Legal Partnership at George Washington University's Department of Health Policy and is the lead advisor for Walmart's signature *pro bono* medical-legal partnership initiative.

for herself, and the child exposed to environmental hazards in his community. Each of these situations implicates legal needs that would benefit from legal expertise, rather than being left solely to the province of medical care. Yet each also has immediate ramifications on the health of the individual and the family. For vulnerable populations – sometimes defined in the health community as groups that are not well-integrated into the healthcare system because of ethnic, cultural, economic, and geographical or health characteristics, and whose isolation from care puts them at risk – the link between health and legal needs is especially prominent, and grows demonstrably tighter all the time. This tightening link between health and legal needs must provoke and animate an urgent dialogue in the access to justice field about the goals and impacts of the access to justice system in relation to health, focusing on questions like *who should pay for justice? Does justice buy good – or better – health? Can society buy better health by paying for justice?* The link between health and legal needs also creates a meaningful opportunity for the legal community to absorb and utilise the substantial expertise of the health and public health communities regarding measurement, data-driven trend analysis and prevention priorities – all of which are notably absent in the legal community.

Early adopters of the medical-legal partnership (MLP) model in the United States are experimenting with measuring the impact of legal interventions on both health and the health systems – studying the return on investment for legal interventions for individuals, institutions and communities. MLP is a healthcare delivery model that integrates lawyers into the healthcare setting to address civil legal needs for vulnerable populations and promote system change. MLPs are attempting to answer the following questions: What if access to justice became so important to ensuring good health that the health sector is willing to pay for it? And how does the legal sector need to shift to respond to these opportunities?

## 2. Connecting Legal and Health Needs

Decades of research in the health care and public health sectors confirm that health status and disparities are deeply connected to social circumstances, or the conditions in which people are born, grow, live, work and age. Laws and regulations are important social determinants; they construct the environments in which individuals and populations live, influencing how and when people face disease.

Addressing these conditions as they relate to health is considered "primary prevention" in the medical context, and a main objective of public health practitioners. Using the unique skills and tools of the health sector, there is a robust capacity to depict – and *predict* – the health status and challenges of a wide range of population groups, including the disabled veteran, elderly woman, and chronically ill child referenced above. The legal community, however, is in the earliest stages of thinking about how to first collect, then aggregate and analyse data that describe the legal needs of vulnerable clients. The vast literature describing the social determinants of health offers a wealth of methods and strategies to help the field accomplish this task.

If public health researchers can correlate health outcomes with specific social determinants, the legal field should have the capacity to correlate health outcomes with specific legal needs and interventions. If health is a core part of human well-being, then it should be at the centre of the outcomes tracked in the pursuit of justice. Indeed, is it possible that the justice community could see health status as a proxy for justice? If so, there may come a time when the health sector – in recognition of the tight connection between legal needs and health status – tracks legal problems as assiduously as it tracks blood pressure and weight gain.

**Legal Needs: A Working Definition**

A legal need is an adverse social condition with a legal remedy – that is, an unmet basic need such as housing, food or healthcare – that can be satisfied via the application of laws, regulations, and policies. Unmet legal needs, which can lead to poor health outcomes, are critical social determinants of health

**Box 1:** Legal Needs: A Working Definition.

As the public health and health sectors in the United States, Canada and Australia begin to arch toward integrating legal services to address adverse conditions that impact health, it is clear that the global legal community can learn a lot from their peers in medicine and public health. For example, one can look to tools, frameworks and studies in medicine and public health to help *define* legal needs, *describe* the prevalence of legal needs, and *design* sustainable interventions and systems.

The legal community can also analogise, wherever possible, between and among the health, public health, and legal fields, to broaden audiences who understand the role and need for civil legal services. For example, is it fair to assume that the prevalence of legal need is similar to the prevalence of health risk/need? That, like health problems, the lower one's socioeconomic status, the worse one's legal problems? And that, like health problems, some legal problems can be prevented with "early screening and treatment"? What other analogies might help elevate the cause of justice such that it is on par with health as a societal value as expressed through allocation of resources?

| **Basic Needs with Legal Remedies, for example Legal Needs** | **Examples of Legal Needs That Affect Health** |
|---|---|
| Income/Insurance | • Health Insurance access and benefits<br>• Access to Public Benefits (disability, Social Security, *et cetera)* |
| Housing and Utilities | • Shelter access<br>• Access to Housing Subsidies and Sanitary Housing Conditions<br>• Access to Utility Services |
| Education/Employment | • Compliance with legal protections for children and adults with special needs, including disability or veteran status<br>• Protection from Discrimination<br>• Education Access for disabled children |
| Legal Status | • Clear and fair immigration procedures<br>• Help when criminal record issues arise<br>• Availability of identification (birth certificates, *et cetera*) |
| Personal/Family Stability | • Effective guardianship, custody and divorce procedures<br>• Availability of capacity, competency, and advance directives<br>• Availability of estate planning |

**Table 1.** Legal Needs that Affect Health.

## 3. More Lessons from the Health Sector

First and foremost, the legal community – both public and private – needs to better understand and honour the unique perspective, role and access that healthcare providers traditionally have in a community. Governments and funders tend to prioritise health services over access to justice, and hospitals and health centres constitute a vital part of any community. And while health services may fail to efficiently meet the healthcare needs of vulnerable populations, health services vastly outnumber legal resources. As a result, health organisations tend to have infrastructure, leadership, and capacity available at the local level to leverage alongside smaller-scale legal resources.

At a broader level, one could argue that the legal community ought to model all facets of best practices – from dissemination of information, to professional training, to the development of evidence-based practices – on the healthcare field, for the simple reason that the infrastructure, financing and implementation strategies for serving vast populations of vulnerable people in healthcare tend to be more advanced than in the legal community. Specific domains where the health sector offers important experience and frameworks include:

- how to measure impact and quality;
- how to anticipate and respond to trends using data; and
- how to strategically invest in legal interventions with a focus on prevention.

A recent report by the Australian Attorney General that described strategic frameworks for access to justice is replete with language traditionally associated with the healthcare sector, including "triage", "early intervention", and "resilience". For the legal community to successfully leverage the existing infrastructure of the healthcare system, it would do well to adopt the language of healthcare wherever possible. Other examples of key strategies and tools:

### 3.1. The Team Concept

People do not generally have legal, social, economic, or health problems – they just have problems that have multiple impacts on their lives. The healthcare sector prioritises training members on how to work as a team, understanding their role, and working at the top of their profession. Alas, the legal profession is historically ill-equipped to partner with other professionals, especially in the public interest sector, and there are few incentives to promote inter-professional team work. But as the legal profession begins to contemplate the role of non-lawyers in expanding access to justice, it will find that the healthcare setting has a ready team of "extenders" to train, and a system of triage and treatment in which to practice newly acquired advocacy skills.

### 3.2. Investing in Prevention – The Shift from Individual to Systemic Solutions

The health sector is decades ahead of the legal profession in terms of thinking about prevention. A helpful analogy likens surgery to litigation – both call for the intensive, yet inefficient allocation of resources focused on a single individual. Both surgery and litigation will always be necessary in some cases, but prevention can ensure that reliance on surgery or litigation is lessened by reallocating resources towards prevention activities. In the health context, the classic example is cardiac health: a public health campaign to improve cardiac health by promoting tobacco cessation, exercise, and weight loss has, as its ultimate goal, improved health and the reduction of cardiac surgery rates.

While it appears that the legal community is reaching consensus that the practice of individual representation for vulnerable populations is too intensive, inefficient, and costly, it has not yet coalesced around a set of prevention strategies. The public health field holds substantial experience in documenting the impact of prevention as well as shifting professional and community culture towards prevention.

Paediatrician and public health expert Megan Sandel of Boston University School of Medicine and the National Center for Medical-Legal Partnership describes the opportunity of *preventive law* as helping to move from individual legal interventions to broader systemic impact at the institutional and community level, where individual cases identified in the health setting act as diagnostic tools for failed policies – which are then more effectively addressed together by an integrated health and legal team. But it is an axiom of legal service provision that by the time a client realises that he has a legal problem, it is likely so far along that prevention is impossible. The healthcare setting, above virtually all other community settings, can provide the access, expertise, and atmosphere for preventive law practice. In order to provide early, preventive legal services, lawyers must practice civil law where clients frequently visit and where the idea of prevention already carries weight: healthcare sites. Indeed, legal services can only be accessed preventively in a setting where clients are seen routinely and can be screened for legal problems.

### 3.3. Leadership and Innovation

The health sector routinely makes explicit investments in leadership and innovation, celebrating leaders who nurture bold innovations that challenge the status quo. Health care leaders routinely look to other sectors – engineering and business – to invigorate standards and practices, which are evaluated using common metrics in the healthcare field. In contrast, the legal sector struggles to foster and scale innovations in access to justice. Why? Both the health and legal sectors confront limits on their resources due in large part to the disproportionate need of vulnerable populations. What is it about the healthcare field that supports a culture of innovation and leadership?

One possible, albeit simplistic, answer lies in the financing and sustainability mechanisms for healthcare – a complex mingling of private and government funds that support the goods and services distributed at the local level. Pharmaceutical and other profit-driven healthcare-related entities participate in the healthcare delivery system, and spark/support innovation for many reasons. In the legal sector, the only real commodity is information and advice provided by trained experts.

## 4. Medical-Legal Partnership: A New Standard of Care

As evidence on the impact of social determinants of health builds, an increasing number of healthcare, legal, and public health providers in the United States, Canada and Australia are teaming up to address these factors. Medical-legal partnership is a healthcare delivery model that integrates legal assistance as a vital component of healthcare. The power of the MLP model lies in its cross-disciplinary, *leveraging* nature, which aligns the legal community with a range of stakeholders and professions that are unified in seeking to improve health conditions and systems for vulnerable populations.

**Figure 1:** Medical-legal partnerships.

MLP is built on the understanding that social determinants of health often manifest in the form of legal needs; and that attorneys have special tools and skills to address these needs. MLPs revolutionise both the legal and healthcare settings that they touch, because the integration forces a shift in the dominant paradigms in the health and legal sectors.

| | Prevailing Model | MLP Model |
|---|---|---|
| Legal Assistance | • Service is crisis-driven<br>• Individuals are responsible for seeking legal assistance at right time<br>• Primary pursuit is justice | • Service is preventive, focuses on early identification of and response to legal needs<br>• Healthcare team works with patients to identify legal needs<br>• Aims include improved health and well-being |
| Healthcare | • Adverse social conditions affect patient health but are difficult to address | • Adverse social conditions with legal remedies are identified and addressed as part of care |

| | | |
|---|---|---|
| | • Healthcare team refers patient to social worker/case manager for limited assistance<br>• Advocacy skills are valued, taught, and deployed inconsistently | • Healthcare, social work, and legal teams work together to address legal needs, improve health, and change systems<br>• Advocacy skills are prioritised as part of the standard of care |

**Table 2:** Comparison of prevailing model and MLP model.

MLP practice has multiple impacts for patient-clients and communities, and for the professions and the legal and health institutions that partner together. A key outcome is the improved capacity of both legal and health professionals to screen, triage, and resolve problems that overlap legal and health domains, resulting in a vastly improved professional satisfaction and sense of efficacy.

## 5. The Global Opportunity for Medical-Legal Partnership

Like microenterprise and microloans, which started in Bangladesh and spread horizontally across countries around the world, including both developed and developing countries, the MLP model can apply in a range of different policy and legal environments – both resourced and under-resourced.

MLP can bridge the demonstrated gaps in the provision of health and legal services – providing a dynamic, multi-stakeholder team that serves the poor and disadvantaged, and supports justice and better health.

Nascent international experiences of medical-legal partnership, like those supported by Open Society Institute in Kenya, demonstrate both the universality of the MLP model, as well as its flexibility.

Civil legal aid, after all, is first and foremost about promoting the enforcement of existing laws that protect vulnerable populations. Thus, one can connect the rule of law to the health status of a nation, whereby identifying and addressing violations of laws that emanate from human rights frameworks will not only promote health, but will promote the rule of law.

## 6. Conclusion: Re-Framing Justice as Health

As the legal community struggles to find and scale solutions to the pervasive legal need that exists for vulnerable populations, integrating legal aid into the health care rubric makes sense from an implementation, sustainability, and financing perspective. Indeed, what if the business case for justice is actually improved health?

The emergence of medical-legal partnership as a leading innovation in the legal community is a positive step towards the twin goals of improved access to justice and improved health. As MLPs shift the dominant paradigm of legal aid service delivery and integrate perspectives and practices from the health care world, the team of trained non-lawyer advocates grows in both size and strength. The legal community – historically insular – will also benefit from the increased transparency and accountability that a partnership model demands, thereby hastening the move toward more efficient, less siloed access to legal services and expertise.

Conversely, as the health community begins to understand the pervasiveness of legal need, it becomes apparent that unresolved legal needs tend to ultimately wash up on the shore of the healthcare system in the form of disease sparked by, or exacerbated by, the social determinants of health. Health systems will begin to pivot toward integration of legal interventions alongside traditional healthcare and public health activities, and become committed to ensuring that health care institutions have the training and capacity to understand, screen, triage, and where appropriate, treat social determinants that have a legal component. They will realise, in fact, that there is a key partner missing from the health care team: the lawyer.

In the United States, the federal department of health is experimenting with funding legal aid lawyers to support their mission of improved health; at the same time, the federal departments that serve elders and veterans are considering investments in MLPs, with a goal of improved health for their target population. These early investments, matched by philanthropic investments from leading health care foundations including The Robert Wood Johnson Foundation and others, signal a new perspective on the capacity of the legal community to participate in creating and ensuring healthy communities. The legal community owes it to our new healthcare partners – indeed, champions – to place health front and centre in our mission to empower communities, and to demonstrate that commitment by collecting key data and training legal leaders to make the most of our shared priorities.

## 7. Sources and Further Reading

Braveman, Paula A., *et al.*, "Broadening the Focus: The Need to Address the Social Determinants of Health", in *American Journal of Preventive Medicine*, 2011, vol. 40, no. 1S1.

Johnson, Robert Wood, "Foundation Commission to Build a Healthier America", in *Beyond Health care: New Directions to a Healthier America*, Princeton, New Jersey, 2009.

Sandel, Megan and Hansen, Mark *et al.*, "Medical-Legal Partnerships: Transforming Primary Care by Addressing the Legal Needs of Vulnerable Populations", in *Health Affairs*, 2010, vol. 29, no. 9, pp. 1697–1705.

Shin, Peter *et al.*, "Medical-Legal Partnerships: Addressing the Unmet Legal Needs of Health Center Patients", in *Geiger Gibson/RCHN Community Health Foundation Research Collaborative*, 2010.

Tyler, Elizabeth and Lawton, Ellen *et al.*, *Poverty, Health and Law: Readings and Cases from Medical-Legal Partnership*, Carolina Academic Press, North Carolina, 2011.

Tyler, Liz Tobin, "Aligning Public Health, Health Care, Law and Policy: Medical-Legal Partnership as a Multilevel Response to the Social Determinants of Health", in *Journal of Health and Biomedical Law*, 2012, vol. 8, no. 120, p. 211.

National Center for Medical-Legal Partnership, available at http://www.medical-legalpartnership.org, last accessed on 6 August 2012.

The Hague Institute for the Internationalisation of Law, Towards Basic Justice Care for Everybody: Challenges and Promising Approaches, 2012, available at http://www.hiil.org/data/sitemanagement/media/TrendReport_Part1_020412_DEF%20(2).pdf, last accessed on 28 August 2012.

# CHAPTER II

# THE PERSPECTIVE OF CONNECTIONS:

## WHAT CONNECTIONS WITH GLOBAL ISSUES ARE EMERGING?

# 2.1.

# Toward Greater Justice in Development

**Hassane Cisse**[*], **Christina Biebesheimer**[**], **and Richard Nash**[***]

Development equated solely with "growth" at all costs, is no longer viewed by many around the world as the optimal means for a country's path towards prosperity. Indeed, all these terms – development, growth, and prosperity – have over the years expanded to become broader and generally more inclusive. Around the world, more and more indications seem to point towards a more vocal and powerful demand from various quarters for more equitable and inclusive growth at the macro, meso and micro levels. A key element of this is ensuring that social injustices are mitigated when they occur in order to avoid conflict, but also to ensure that appropriate socially just policies are put in place initially. Development organisations, including the World Bank, will have to adapt to this new trend and be able to respond to it adequately if they are to provide the services that countries and people demand. A critical component of this is likely to be more support for social justice interventions through a variety of stakeholders, which will have to inform a new global development pact more aligned with the needs and demands expressed by the people.

In the World Bank, we notice an incipient trend in development projects - in sectors such as health, infrastructure, mining, and natural resource management – to embrace justice as a necessary part of the development equation. This has created a burgeoning environment of different actors bringing multiple perspectives, skills, and insights into this field, which is pushing the boundaries of thinking around it. This think piece imagines this trend forward, sketching out the challenges it is likely to encounter and the potential it holds, and developing some recommendations for how the trend might be made most productive.

---

[*] **Hassane Cisse** is Deputy General Counsel Knowledge and Research, Legal Vice Presidency, The World Bank.

[**] **Christina Biebesheimer** is Chief Counsel, Justice Reform Practice Group, Legal Vice Presidency, The World Bank.

[***] **Richard Nash** is Counsel, Justice Reform Practice Group, Legal Vice Presidency, The World Bank.

## 1. Introduction

Predicting trends several decades forward in the fields of justice reform, development, and justice and development represents an exciting opportunity and a significant challenge. Had we written this essay in 2007 prior to the financial crisis, we might have written confidently about an expansion of assistance to develop open markets in support of domestic and foreign investment free from overly interventionist measures by the State. Had we written this essay prior to 11 September 2001, we would probably not have thought about the dramatic impact that global terrorism would have on citizens' relationships with the State, or predicted significant direct military assistance in the field of justice reform and dramatically increased spending on security and law enforcement efforts. Prior to the Arab Spring of 2011, we might not have dared to imagine the explosive potential of a call for justice, and might not have considered the transformative and revolutionary effect that social media could have on the process of change in public institutions.

These changes represent a dynamic and challenging continuum that impacts on development institutions and justice institutions, and that shapes the demands of citizens for justice. This essay looks at some of the recent trends in the field of justice reform – as we define it in the World Bank, the field that works to strengthen the formal and informal institutions that address breaches of law, and facilitate peaceful contests over rights and obligations – and imagines a future in which changing demands for justice change the shape of development.

## 2. A Changing Demand For Justice

While predicting the future is difficult, it is reasonable to hope that the future will see more countries becoming "middle income" countries. Governments may find themselves held accountable by increasingly empowered and articulate middle classes demanding more and better services. There is also a trend, particularly in some developed countries, towards increasing difference in wealth between the richest in a society and the rest. We have seen increasing wealth and power being accumulated by global corporations, many of which have significant impact on the lives and well-being of people around the world. These trends, too, may lead to changing demands for fairness.

Around the world, indications point towards a more vocal and powerful demand for more equitable and inclusive growth at the macro inter-State level. For example, the rise of the BRICs and G20 in international decision-making; at the meso level, multi-national companies adopting more environmental policies and promoting corporate social responsibility; and at the micro level, individuals seeking justice from other individuals and *vis-à-vis* the State and companies to reduce barriers to opportunity. The global financial crisis and the conditions which gave rise to the Arab Spring have brought about an increasingly strong and articulate voice for justice. This was conceived of both in the broadest sense encompassing the notions of equity and fairness of opportunity for the individual in each society, and thus the negation of entrenched societal injustices; and also in the narrower sense of ensuring that fair decisions are arrived at and enforced through legitimate institutions. Development equated solely with growth at all costs is no longer viewed by many around the world as the optimal means for a country's path towards prosperity. The "Washington Consensus" model of development from the 1990s onwards is well known, as are the criticisms. Indeed, all of these terms – development, growth, and prosperity – have expanded to become broader and generally more inclusive. Development is viewed not as solely the provision of financial and technical assistance from richer to poorer countries. Rather, it involves a process of change within societies across the economic, political, and social spectrums that may be influenced by internal factors such as population growth, natural resource development, increasing GNP per capita, or institutional development, as well as external factors such as climate change, trade flows, and global financial forces including financial and technical assistance factors. The early 1990s also saw the beginning of the World Bank's justice reform work, with an initial focus on reforming institutions to support the development of effective market economies. As the consensus around the "Washington Consensus" has dissolved, the Bank's work in engaging with the justice sector has expanded in new and innovative ways. There are many government institutions, non-governmental organisations (NGOs), and donor entities participating in the reform processes of justice institutions, directing them, carrying out analytical work to support better reform, or providing technical assistance to guide that work. We lay out here what we perceive as some emerging trends in the field of justice and development.

## 2.1. Justice as a Key Component of Development Thinking

The Bank's flagship annual publications, the World Development Reports, have increasingly stressed the importance of justice and equity in the context of development. The 2011 World Development Report (WDR) on "Conflict, Security and Development" points out how justice must be a priority if conflict is to ease, identifying justice as one of the three pillars, along with security and jobs, to help countries out of conflict and violence. The 2012 WDR on "Gender Equality and Development" shows that women's access to justice is key to their agency at work, in the family, and as members of the polity, and thus important in ensuring gender equality. The essential element of the various human opportunities indices being developed by the Bank and other agencies is that all individuals should have the same possibilities and chances, such as getting a job, going to school, and accessing health services. In society, an essential element of the concept of equity was discussed in the WDR 2006 on "Equity and Development". The WDR 2011 advanced these themes to recognise that justice is a broad and integrated area of development and thus, in order to achieve justice in a society and assist in its development, a holistic approach to a broad range of legal issues including land law, family law, and business law is needed.

In September of this year, the United Nations (UN) General Assembly convenes a High Level meeting on the Rule of Law to discuss the report of the Secretary-General on "Delivering Justice" (2012). This report, too, focuses on the importance of respect for the rule of law for delivering just outcomes in the daily life of all individuals. Just as the WDR 2011 stipulated that justice must be seen in the wider, rather than narrower, sense, the UN report states that "the equitable and transparent administration of housing, land and property based on rule of law principles is key to economic, social and political stability". We therefore see a converging trend within the international community with regard to how the rule of law and the justice sector can support more inclusive and equitable development around the world.

## 2.2. More Justice Interventions in Development Operations Across Many Fields

Perhaps partially in response to the trend towards conceiving of justice as a requisite for economic and social development, we see a visible upswing in the number of justice reform-related components in Bank development projects in fields such as health, mining, education, and natural resource governance. Infrastructure projects, for example, include mechanisms for grievance redress that build on local- or country-level justice practices and institutions, or pay attention to ways in which the project can strengthen policies and processes for negotiating investment projects between affected communities and large investors, or look to strengthen legal actors' ability to hold the project accountable for service delivery.

Private sector investors, too, are becoming increasingly concerned with the human and social rights impact of their actions, not only as a result of the increasing pressures from civil society, but also because it is being increasingly recognised as "good business". Large foreign investors are recognising that they need to become effective conflict analysers and mitigators, and will increasingly seek the assistance of civil society organisations with effective local expertise in these areas. In the Bank, we are engaged in work to support the development of "durable deals" in the context of development – that is, agreements based on a locally owned sense of equity – in the area of mining concession agreements and large scale land sales, to ensure that such deals benefit the local community as well as the society as a whole and do not become points of conflict. The Bank's focus on good governance has evolved to include the demand for good governance, which supports civil society actors in their efforts to hold governments accountable.

The growing interest in aspects of justice such as grievance and accountability mechanisms among development actors in fields outside justice has created a burgeoning environment of different actors bringing multiple perspectives, skills, and insights to the field of justice and development, which is pushing the boundaries of thinking around it.

## 2.3. Greater Focus on the Needs of Those Who Use Justice Services

A trend is visible in both the developed and developing world towards supporting justice systems that focus on users' needs and problems. Pioneered at the end of the 1990s and used with increasing frequency in many jurisdictions, legal needs assessments are giving greater insight into the strategies that people actually employ to resolve their disputes across the spectrum of dispute resolution possibilities that are open for them. The majority of individuals faced with a 'legal problem' (in the broadest sense of the word) may not turn to lawyers and judges for dispute resolution –

they are likely to turn first, or instead, to administrative decision-makers, to someone who can help mediate the problem, to family, community or religious leaders (the broad 'informal' or non-State sector of justice services). This recognition has encouraged formal justice institutions to pay greater attention to understanding and meeting the demands of their users. Thus, we see judiciaries beginning to employ interesting mechanisms to identify needs of potential users of their services – court user committees, user surveys, *et cetera*. And we see a recent explosion in innovative mechanisms of cheaper delivery of legal services to individuals (for example, through public access to case information, standard form document compilation on websites, websites providing direct access to legal advice, increasing use of paralegals, outsourcing documentation analysis to cheaper jurisdictions, and alternative funding arrangements for litigants) by courts and lawyers around the world.

The recognition that people employ myriad strategies to resolve disputes and seek justice has also helped to expand development actors' focus beyond courts, police, and prosecutors, broadening it to consider many possible centres of dispute resolution within a competitive landscape. Donors and countries seeking to respond to the justice needs of people are examining ways in which they may support community-level organisations that mediate disputes or monitor government services, administrative law entities, paralegal organisations, and customary justice entities.

### 2.4. And a Corollary Focus on Accountability to Those Users

Much of the discussion regarding rule of law and justice sector interventions has focused on promoting the independence of the judiciary as a means to ensure impartiality in judicial decisions and accountability of the executive. By the mid-2000s, however, significant consideration started to be given to the other, complementary, side of the coin – that of accountability of the judiciary to the citizens it serves. While the judiciary must be sufficiently independent from interference from public and private sector actors to be able to consider the cases before it with impartiality, it must also, like other government institutions, be able to demonstrate effective use of public funds to provide citizens with justice services. The focus on the accountability aspect of projects relating to the justice sector has grown in recent years, in terms of both an increased focus on the accountability of justice institutions to the citizens they serve, and an increased focus on the role of justice institutions in ensuring accountability of the government to provide essential public services to its citizens. Thus, while early efforts to improve justice institutions sought to measure inputs to those institutions (improvements in training, for example, or better IT systems and infrastructure to support the institutional function), recent justice reform projects are more likely to seek to measure outputs likely to affect the service rendered to users of the system – and justice institutions are encouraging citizens and NGOs to become directly engaged with monitoring their performance.

## 3. What Role May Justice Play in a Changing Paradigm of Development?

The World Bank has provided financial resources, technical assistance, and other support to assist countries in their development for over 65 years – though the content, focus and delivery mechanisms of that assistance have changed to reflect changes in the world as well as changing concepts of development. What would the development agenda look like if it took seriously the calls for justice of the type and nature we have outlined above?

Economic and material development will most likely continue to occur through the traditional mechanisms and institutions of countries creating competitive industries, moving up the value chain, with the government enabling the provision of relevant factor inputs and infrastructure (both hard and soft) (for example, roads, ports, education, health facilities, courts, laws and regulations) where necessary and appropriate. What if development lending in all of these sectors examined the justice implications of those projects, and analysed the way in which national and local justice institutions might be strengthened to address the most pressing justice needs of the people affected? In other words, what if the trends toward mainstreaming justice in development were to continue and gain strength? Just as environmental concerns and issues relating to gender equality are now mainstreamed in development projects, it would be possible consistently to incorporate justice in development lending. This might involve analysis and development of components that look to strengthen national and local justice mechanisms that encourage citizen participation in, or at least understanding of, the laws and agreements that underlie the project, and in monitoring project implementation, and mechanisms that ensure a process for hearing grievances. In some projects, this would mean formal State institutions such as courts, prosecutors, police, and legal aid offices. In some projects, it might mean non-State justice institutions, or hybrid institutions incorporating customary systems into a State system.

There would be challenges with mainstreaming justice across the development agenda. One area of concern of particular relevance to those working for the application of international human rights standards is that understandings of what constitutes justice vary across countries and cultures. Yet there are some values relating to justice that seem to be shared very widely around the world, and development actors are well placed to work on their implementation where large investment projects take place: values such as transparency and accountability of rules and rule-makers, equal application of rules to all, participation in development of the rules by those to whom the rules apply, and the rights of all to have grievances addressed when wronged.

Another area of challenge is that laws and justice institutions often reflect the interests of the powerful, protecting the *status quo*. Working to open up a debate about who benefits, who loses under a certain law or an agreement surrounding a development project, puts development actors in the thick of issues of power, politics, and hegemony. A vision of development that places justice at its core would need to seek to ensure that the poor have a voice and that social injustices are mitigated when they occur in order to avoid conflict.

## 4. Future Strategies and Research Agendas

What might strategies for mainstreaming justice as a necessary part of the development equation look like? In Sierra Leone, the government's bold health-care initiative for pregnant and breastfeeding women, and children under five, suffered leakage of up to 30 per cent of drugs before they reached clinics, and women were being charged improper user fees. Incorporating inexpensive methods of ensuring accountability of service delivery by local monitoring agents who act as investigators and assist individuals in launching claims, such as paralegals, has been shown to help individuals obtain benefits they were unfairly denied, and to create longer term deterrence effects and accountability of the State to deliver the services it has promised. In projects aimed at formal justice institutions, social accountability mechanisms such as the users' committees and user surveys discussed earlier could be encouraged and expanded on by courts to make their processes more transparent and accessible, and media and civil society organisations could be supported in efforts to ensure that police and prosecutors are acting diligently in collecting evidence and following up on cases, regardless of who the victim or claimant is.

An area in which there is a pressing research agenda starts from the WDR 2011's thesis that justice is a central concept to be addressed in working in fragile States, alongside jobs and security, to examine what the concept of justice means in such diverse contexts and how it interplays with the multiplicity of fragile relationships that restrict sustained growth. We need to better understand how development actors can address the notion of justice through the institutions and communities in such societies.

We also need better data regarding what a country stands to gain by investing in its justice institutions – in comparison to, say, its health or education institutions. Justice certainly has intrinsic value in a society, but it would also be useful to be able to measure its economic benefit more precisely. There is a good deal that is known about the economic impact of justice institutions. Research makes it very clear, for example, that crime and violence have a significant negative impact on economies, and justice institutions are a necessary part of the effort to address crime and violence. A recent study demonstrates that courts through their power of judicial review of executive (in)actions can play a powerful role in ensuring that resources devoted to health and education are distributed to those who need them most. But how can a middle-income country determine when and in what amount to invest scarce resources in justice institutions? There is need for a better understanding of the impact of investment in justice, as well as understanding of how justice institutions can most effectively use the resources at their disposal.

The sort of development assistance needed to help justice institutions respond to the pressing justice needs in their societies may shift in response to changing demands for justice. It may be that knowledge – knowledge about justice reform methodologies and also about how to analyse and work within local institutions, processes, and politics – will be needed more than financial assistance. Perhaps assistance in connecting people and ideas across justice institutions, private sector entities, NGOs, development actors, and local communities will take on higher importance.

The next decades may well present an opportunity for justice system institutions and the basic values inherent in those institutions to become a more mainstream, more explicit part of the development equation. Whether that happens will depend in significant part on the strategic demands that people make on their governments – and also upon the ability of governments, private sector actors, civil society, academia, and development agencies to strategically pool knowledge and respond expertly to requests for institutions that ensure accountability, enforce rules fairly, and facilitate peaceful contests over rights and obligations.

## 5. Sources and Further Reading

Delivering Justice: Programme of Action to Strengthen the Rule of Law at the National and International Levels: Report of the Secretary-General, UN Doc. A/66/749, 16 March 2012, available at http://www.unrol.org/doc.aspx?d=3141, last accessed on 15 October, 2012.

Ginsburg, Tom, "The Future of Law and Development", in *Northwestern University Law Review Colloquy*, 2009, vol. 104, p. 164.

Golub, Stephen, "What is legal empowerment? An Introduction", in Stephen Golub (ed.), *Legal Empowerment: Practicioners' Perspectives*, International Development Law Organization, Rome, 2010, p. 9.

"Making the Law Work for Everyone: Report of the Commission on Legal Empowerment of the Poor", United Nations Development Programme, 2008, available at http://www.undp.org/content/undp/en/home/librarypage.html?q=making+the+law+work+for+everyone, last accessed on 15 October, 2012.

Perry-Kessaris, Amanda (ed.), *Law in the Pursuit of Development: Principles into Practice?*, Routledge-Cavendish, New York, 2010.

Sen, Amartya, "What is the Role of Legal and Judicial Reform in the Development Process?", in *The World Bank Legal Review*, 2006, vol. 2.

Stiglitz, Joseph E., *More instruments and broader goals: Moving Toward the Post-Washington Consensus*, The World Bank, Washington, DC, 1998.

Stiglitz, Joseph E., "Is there a Post-Washington Consensus?", in Joseph E. Stiglitz and Narcis Serra (eds.), *The Washington Consensus Reconsidered: Towards a New Global Governance*, Oxford Scholarship Online, Oxford, 2008.

Tamanaha, Brian Z., "The Primacy of Society and the Failure of Law and Development", in *Cornell International Law Journal*, 2011, vol. 44, p. 209.

Trubek, David M., "The 'Rule of Law' in Development Assistance: Past, Present, and Future", in David M. Trubek and Alvaro Santos (eds.), *The New Law and Economic Development: A Critical Appraisal*, Cambridge University Press, 2006, p. 74.

Trubek, David M., "Developmental States and the Legal Order: Towards a New Political Economy of Development and Law", LANDS (Law and the New Developmental State) Working Papers, 2010, available at http://www.law.wisc.edu/gls/documents/developmental_states_legal_order_2010_trubek.pdf, last accessed on 15 October 2012.

Trebilcock, Michael J. and Daniels, Ronald J. (eds.), *Rule of Law Reform and Development: Charting the Fragile Path of Progress*, Edward Elgar Publishing, 2009.

"The World Bank: New Directions in Justice Reform", The World Bank, Washington DC, 2012, available at http://www-wds.worldbank.org/external/default/WDSContentServer/WDSP/IB/2012/09/06/000386194_20120906024506/Rendered/PDF/706400REPLACEM0Justice0Reform0Final.pdf, last accessed on 15 October, 2012.

*World Development Report 2006: Equity and Development*, The World Bank, Washington DC, 2005, available at http://web.worldbank.org/WBSITE/EXTERNAL/EXTDEC/EXTRESEARCH/EXTWDRS/0,,contentMDK:23080759~pagePK:478093~piPK:477627~theSitePK:477624,00.html , last accessed on 15 October 2012.

*World Development Report 2011: Conflict, Security and Development*, The World Bank, Washington DC, 2011, available at http://web.worldbank.org/WBSITE/EXTERNAL/EXTDEC/EXTRESEARCH/EXTWDRS/0,,contentMDK:23252415~pagePK:478093~piPK:477627~theSitePK:477624,00.html, last accessed on 15 October 2012.

*World Development Report 2012: Gender, Equality and Development*, The World Bank, Washington DC, 2011, available at http://econ.worldbank.org/WBSITE/EXTERNAL/EXTDEC/EXTRESEARCH/EXTWDRS/EXTWDR2012/0,,menuPK:7778074~pagePK:7778278~piPK:7778320~theSitePK:7778063~contentMDK:22851055,00.html, last accessed on 15 October 2012.

# 2.2.

# Combating Corruption in the 21st Century: Bringing the Babel of Voices into Harmony

**Claudia J. Dumas***

In this think piece, the law of the future is explored in the context of the rapid growth of the anti-corruption field. At the end of the 20th century, international efforts to constrain corruption started relatively narrowly, with a collective focus on preventing the bribery of public officials in transnational business transactions. Since then, numerous issues and goals have been grouped under the heading of anti-corruption, often with a common underlying assumption that greater transparency, accountability, and enforcement of the specified norms will constrain corruption in the applicable substantive arena and enhance the achievement of the broader substantive goal. The UN Convention against Corruption has added to the activity, with requirements and suggestions that ratifying States take various actions to prevent corruption, but with the Convention's articles setting forth its requirements in general terms. Governments, private sector, and civil society groups are increasingly promulgating new soft law initiatives and standards, which often layer on top of existing hard and soft law frameworks, rather than being tied to the implementation of specific standards of hard law.

Current trends – including the complex and transnational nature of grand societal challenges, the globalisation of commerce, and technological change – will likely cause a continued multiplicity of soft initiatives. This think piece suggests that reducing cross-border corruption and corruption within individual countries will require (i) an analysis of the assumed causal relationship between hard and soft law regimes and new understandings of how soft law instruments affect each other, (ii) a focus on both the performance of country level justice systems and closing opportunities for interna-

* **Claudia Dumas** is the President and CEO of Transparency International – USA.
The author gratefully acknowledges the research assistance of James Pagano, Intern at Transparency International – USA, in the preparation of this think piece.

tional money laundering, and (iii) increased research regarding the impact of specific anti-corruption interventions.

## 1. Introduction

Corruption, and legal efforts and mechanisms to constrain it, are not new to the 20th and 21st century. Some would assert that the temptation to benefit oneself improperly at the expense of others is part of human nature, thus explaining the focus on such areas as the duties and limits of rulers, government institutions, and codes of behaviour by philosophers and early governments since the earliest conception of nation States.

There is no uniformly accepted definition of corruption. Indeed, the United Nations Convention against Corruption (UNCAC) does not attempt to define the phenomenon and some scholars reject a unitary definition. Discussions around corruption in recent decades include reference to a variety of practices and terms, including bribery, solicitation, extortion, unfair advantage, nepotism, and embezzlement. A survey of the literature regarding definitions of corruption is beyond the scope of this think piece, as is a consideration of the circumstances under which varying definitions should be utilised and specific practices included. A frequent conceptualisation of the term corruption, however, is the "abuse of public office for private gain" with a broadening to "abuse of entrusted office for private gain" in order to extend the term to include behaviour by commercial interests and other persons who do not serve in a governmental capacity. References to corruption in this essay may generally be understood as referring to the latter phrase using "entrusted office".

While there is no consensus on a unitary definition of corruption, it is incontestable that there has been an explosion in the last 50 years, and especially in the last several decades, of discourse, conventions, laws, policies, standards, initiatives, technical assistance, academic research, and tools focused on eliminating or constraining corruption and various specific corrupt practices. It is this development – and particularly the promulgation of numerous soft law[1] standards and other initiatives to which na-

---

[1] The terms 'hard law' and 'soft law' as used in this think piece will utilise Abbott and Snidal's formulation. 'Hard law' refers to legally binding obligations that are precise (or can be made precise through adjudication or the issuance of detailed regulations) and that delegate authority for interpreting and implementing the law. 'Soft law' begins once legal arrangements are weakened along one or more of the dimensions of obligation, precision, and delegation.

tion States and entities within nation States are expected or encouraged to adhere – that has prompted this think piece. Is there an organising framework among these standards; is the trend toward an increasing number of disaggregated standards likely to continue; and what should be done to constrain corruption effectively in the future?

## 2. The Emergence of the Anti-Corruption Field

The United States passed the U.S. Foreign Corrupt Practices Act (FCPA) in 1977, following numerous investigations by the U.S. Securities and Exchange Commission (SEC) into the making by U.S. companies of questionable or illegal payments to foreign government officials, politicians, and political parties. Broadly speaking, the FCPA makes it a crime for any U.S. person or company to directly or indirectly pay or promise anything of value to any foreign official to obtain or retain business. The 1998 amendments expanded the FCPA to foreign companies and nationals if they cause, directly or through agents, an act in furtherance of the corrupt payment to take place within the territory of the United States. The FCPA also contains accounting provisions which require companies to maintain books and records that accurately and fairly reflect the transactions of the corporation, and to devise and maintain an adequate system of internal accounting controls.

The FCPA became the template for the Organisation for Economic Co-operation and Development (OECD) Convention on Combating Bribery of Foreign Public Officials in International Business Transactions, which was adopted in 1997. The Convention, currently with 39 parties, requires each State Party to make foreign bribery a crime. The Anti-Bribery Convention is overseen by the OECD Working Group on Bribery, which conducts a monitoring process on each ratifying country, focused on implementation and enforcement, and the steps which the country has taken to implement the working group's recommendations from prior reviews.

The late 1990's saw the introduction of numerous international conventions addressing corruption. These include: the Inter-American Convention against Corruption, the first multilateral anti-bribery initiative adopted one year prior to the OECD Anti-Bribery Convention; the Convention on the Fight against Corruption involving Officials of the European Communities or Officials of Member States of the European Union; and the Council of Europe Criminal and Civil Law Conventions on Corruption. This proliferation of conventions continued through the start of the 21st century, with the African Union Convention on Preventing and Combating Corruption and the UNCAC, which became effective in 2005. None of these conventions is self-executing, and each requires or urges the parties to take various actions to render illegal and deter various transnational and domestic corrupt practices. Progress of countries in implementing their commitments under these conventions is assessed through periodic review mechanisms specific to each convention.

A purely linear focus on multilateral conventions, however, misses the multitude of other initiatives and actors working to constrain corruption from the passage of the U.S. FCPA to where we presently sit in the first part of the 21st century. These include the founding in 1993 of Transparency International, the global civil society coalition fighting corruption. The Agreement on Government Procurement was signed in 1994, accompanying the signing of the Agreement Establishing the World Trade Organisation (WTO). Multilateral development banks and bilateral assistance providers seized on technical assistance to combat corruption in the late 1990's as a must-do, following the collapse of the Russian economy in part due to its informal economy and a growing recognition of the pervasiveness of corruption in both developing and formerly communist countries.

As has been noted by various commentators, including Slaughter, many issues requiring international cooperation are increasingly being addressed through more informal law-making efforts and groups. These include networks of government and non-government actors, such as regulators, professions, private sector businesses, industry associations, and non-governmental organisations (NGOs). The anti-corruption field is no stranger to this blurring of the roles between formal and informal networks and outputs.

Numerous international working groups and initiatives now exist, all with the common belief that decreasing transnational, nation State, and private sector corruption is essential to their respective goals. These include government driven groups, such as the G20 Anti-Corruption Working Group and the Financial Action Task Force; private sector and civil society groups identifying best practices and codes of conduct to support private sector compliance with anti corruption laws, and initiatives dedicated to ensuring that payments for the right to exploit natural resources end up in official public revenues. Table 1 provides an illustrative listing of some of the more prominent working groups and initiatives. The result is that combating corruption, including with approaches designed to increase transparency and accountability, is now viewed as an essential component of accomplishing a wide variety of global and national goals, including economic growth, poverty reduction, and re-building failed and weak States. Accompanying this is a steady cycle of assessment reports and convention reviews, action plans, new standards, and advocacy campaigns setting forth recommendations for an increasing number of areas of focus.

Conventions

- Inter-American Convention against Corruption (1996)
- OECD Anti-Bribery Convention (1997)
- Convention on the Fight against Corruption involving Officials of the European Communities of Officials of Members States of the EU (1997)
- Council of Europe: Criminal Law Convention on Corruption (1999)
- Council of Europe: Civil Law Convention on Corruption (1999)
- United Nations Convention Against Corruption (2005)
- African Union Convention on Preventing and Combating Corruption (2006)

Government Driven Initiatives

- Foreign Corrupt Practices Act (1977)
- U.S. Financial Action Task Force (1989)
- Stolen Assets Recovery Initiative (2007)
- G20 Anti-Corruption Working Group (2010)
- Open Government Partnership (2011)

Sectoral Initiatives

- Extractive Industries Transparency Initiative (2002)
- Publish What You Pay (2002)
- International Aid Transparency Initiative (2005)
- Construction Sector Transparency Initiative (2007)
- Publish What You Fund (2008)

Private Sector-Government-Civil Society Initiatives

- International Chamber of Commerce Rules of Conduct to Combat Extortion and Bribery (1996)
- United Nations Global Compact (2000)
- World Economic Forum Partnering Against Corruption Initiative (2003)

- Transparency International Business Principles for Countering Bribery (2009)
- Business 20 Anti-Corruption Task Force (2010)

Trade Initiatives

- WTO Working Group on Transparency in Government Procurement (1996)
- APEC Procurement Transparency Standards (2004)
- APEC Anti-Corruption Task Force (2004)
- Trans-Pacific Partnership (2006)

**Table 1:** Representative Anti-Corruption Measures

## 3. Progress in Combating Corruption?

Has the promulgation of laws and activity around these laws coincided with a decline in corrupt practices? While there have been stellar examples of anti-corruption reforms and progress in some countries, actual implementation of anti-corruption related reforms remains uneven globally. Indeed, concerns about rampant corruption and the absence of implemented standards appear to be fuelling recent initiatives, such as the highlighting by the G20 Anti-Corruption Working Group and the B20 Task Force on Improving Transparency and Anti-Corruption of steps for G20 countries to take that correspond to reforms recommended by the UN Convention against Corruption.

Transparency International's Corruption Perceptions Index (CPI), launched in 1995, ranks countries according to the perception of public-sector corruption. The Index lists countries on a scale of 0 to 10, with 0 being highly corrupt and 10 being very clean. Of 183 countries included in the most recent December 2011 report, 132 countries, constituting more than 72 percent of those listed, scored below 5. The absence of progress is further underscored in considering that 74 percent of the 159 countries surveyed in the 2005 CPI report also scored below 5.

The World Bank Institute's Control of Corruption data aggregation also presents a mixed picture. The aggregation, which utilises expert and survey data, is intended to capture perceptions of the extent to which public power is exercised for private gain, including both petty and grand forms of corruption as well as capture of the State by elite and private interests. While some country scores showed a net improvement from 2000 to 2010, other country scores decreased during the same period. It is also noteworthy that a number of countries had scores which improved from 2000 to 2005, but were followed by a decline in 2010, indicating that progress on combating corruption is subject to reversals.

Data aggregations and these two compilations can be critiqued on various grounds, including that broad references to corruption may not capture progress on individual reforms, perceptions may not accurately capture actual practices, and individual data sources may be from years prior to the years ostensibly measured. If one looks at enforcement of the 15 year old OECD Anti-Bribery Convention as one example of the status of a more specific reform, however, the picture also does not show marked progress. Transparency International's Progress Report on the Enforcement of the OECD Anti-Bribery Convention classifies parties into four enforcement categories, based on the number and significance of cases and investigations, taking into account the scale of the country's exports. The 2011 Report found little or no enforcement in 21 of the 37 countries surveyed, suggesting a lack of political commitment by government leaders toward enforcement and indicating that the impact of OECD monitoring reviews has been uneven.

## 4. The Future and Implications for a Disaggregated Regime

The emergence of numerous international agreements and standards intended to reduce transnational and national corruption has created an ornate web of hard law, soft law, and other standards without a clearly defined hierarchy. The vast number of substantive law areas and institutions targeted for reform by hard law mandates, hortatory language, and informal initiatives further complicates efforts to map the anti-corruption legal landscape. The landscape includes such varied matters as mechanisms for international cooperation in asset recovery investigations, whistle blower channels and protections, and public procurement practices.

This author believes that the recent trend toward the promulgation of international agreements and other standards, including by networks of governmental and non-governmental actors, is likely to continue for at least three reasons.

First, the globalisation of business, the conduct of international financial markets through which trillions of dollars flow daily, and the flow of people and natural resources, all cross national boundaries. Their cross-border characteristics and complex nature create complex challenges that require coordinated solutions and actions by public and private actors across national boundaries. Examples of these challenges include the tracing of funds illicitly appropriated by public officials, the ability of companies to conduct international business without being solicited for bribes, and minimising environmental damage caused by improperly issued emissions permits. It is noteworthy that the private sector has recently joined and is likely to step up its participation in anti-corruption standard setting. The opportunity costs to business of not participating in the global economy are too high to permit companies to focus on purely domestic markets and supply chains. The legal and reputational risks to long-term growth oriented companies of violating legal standards against corruption, however, are propelling business to participate in groupings and initiatives intended to facilitate compliance with anti-corruption laws and reduce corruption in rapidly growing markets.

A second reason for this continued trend is that measures that reduce corruption are not purely technical solutions, but produce winners and losers, and thus mixed incentives for reform. As in the case of the UNCAC, countries are frequently reluctant to agree to precise, binding anti-corruption undertakings. The existence of generally phrased and non-mandatory provisions, as well as the introduction of new broad undertakings, are likely to continue to propel the issuance of new standards and initiatives by governments, regulators, the private sector, NGOs, and civil society. As in the past, these standards and initiatives will be intended to support the implementation of generally phrased and non-binding provisions, including by prioritising specific reforms and adding new specificity through claimed best practices.

Third, information technology and social media are providing new abilities for those seeking to combat corruption to share information, compile data and press for reforms. As societies and upcoming generations embrace and move toward technology, it can be expected that new virtual communities and data will yield new communities of interest and approaches to combat corruption. The ability of sites such as India's Ipaidabribe.com to collect aggregate data on bribes paid by individuals, and the interest NGOs in other countries have expressed in its approach in combating petty bribery, is one example of how technology is facilitating new communities and innovations.

While new initiatives and collective action coalitions have the potential to assist in constraining corruption, the failure of efforts to date to reduce corruption on a global scale mandates some reflection. Several recommendations emerge in looking forward at the ability of law and the anti-corruption field to reduce cross-border corruption and corruption within individual nations.

## 4.1. Better Understand the Interaction between Soft Law and Hard Law Regimes

While there is a hope and assumption that new conventions and soft law standards will strengthen the anti-corruption playing field by raising national laws and practices, further research is needed to understand better how hard and soft law interact in varying circumstances in practice. States and other actors are not limited by a choice of whether or not to enact a new standard. Rather, they will often have the ability to choose their terms of cooperation, including how they will implement a generally worded standard and their choice of which measures to focus on implementing first.

Attention also needs to be paid to understanding the effects of multiple soft law regimes. For example, anti-corruption reforms espoused by a group with a relatively narrow substantive focus may positively alter how nations would otherwise implement reforms to constrain the same types of corrupt practices in other sectors and arenas by setting forth an adaptable, concrete approach. An additional scenario for examination is understanding the conditions under which re-bundling existing soft law provisions into new high profile initiatives enhance or deter from positive progress on the provisions. The inclusion in such an initiative of leaders with known limited support for particular reforms has the potential, for example, to create a positive drag or, alternatively, to impact negatively the country's longer term progress on the reforms if no significant progress is made under the initiative.

## 4.2. Include a Focus on the Performance of Country Justice Systems and Close Opportunities for International Money Laundering

Successfully combating corruption requires a number of complex laws and institutions. As an example, the United States included in its 2011 self-assessment under UNCAC statutes dealing with foreign bribery, bank fraud, mail and wire fraud, nepotism, procurement, whistle-blower protections, criminal and civil conflicts of interest, and misuse of public property. Adding international cooperation, and the roles of regional and international law bodies with lawmaking and adjudicatory functions, rapidly expands the laws and institutions involved in combating corruption.

Robust and fair enforcement of civil and criminal laws that combat corruption is essential for a meaningful reduction in corruption. Vigorous and fair enforcement of appropriate norms sanctions those who act improperly and also encourages compliance with law. Initiatives which advocate specific anti-corruption reforms may inadvertently shift the focus away from ensuring that national and sub-national investigatory, prosecutorial, defence, and adjudicatory functions have sufficient independence, competency, corruption safeguards, and resources to perform their roles both individually and as a system. Such initiatives may also adversely impact the provision of international financial and technical assistance needed for such justice system strengthening. All too often, justice system assistance efforts are uncoordinated, focus unevenly on differing parts of the justice system without a clear rationale for doing so, and ignore the junctures at which different bodies, such as judges and defence counsel, interact. In addition to strengthening enforcement within an individual country, stronger country level legal systems can both enhance international law enforcement cooperation and contribute to a more level playing field in that country to support greater economic growth.

The ability of political elites and organised crime to launder, conceal and enjoy the proceeds of illicit gains outside their home countries must also be curtailed for there to be any meaningful reduction in global corruption. In both developed and developing countries, corrupt and criminal interests are able to launder ill-gotten proceeds in financial accounts and shell companies without law enforcement being able to obtain information on their beneficial interest. In addition, the loophole and secrecy ridden regulatory systems of offshore financial centres offer safe haven for proceeds of crime and corruption. Until these practices and weak "know your customer" due diligence requirements for financial institutions are comprehensively addressed on a global scale, corrupt officials will be able to shelter funds and a shadow economy of corrupt payments will continue to flourish.

### 4.3. Increase Research on the Impact of Anti-Corruption Reforms

More research is necessary to understand the impact of specific anti-corruption reforms, the conditions under which they are successful, how they hold up over time, and their ability to catalyse further changes down the road. In short, much more study is necessary to understand whether various anti-corruption interventions actually alter the corrupt practices they are intended to reduce.

Effective anti-corruption reforms involve breaking down entrenched political interests, changing incentives, and transforming long standing patterns of behaviour. Recent research, for example, is providing a more nuanced picture of transparency's capacity to improve the performance of political institutions. In addition, new small-scale civil society initiatives developed in response to local conditions show important promise in reducing corruption, but their ability to scale up and long term impact are not yet known. This includes not only social media driven interventions, but more boots on the ground approaches such as organising village elders to oversee public procurement projects and publicly identify those contractors who utilise inferior construction materials. The importance of understanding the impact of specific measures is magnified by the ability of corrupt networks and individuals to adapt their behaviour, find new openings when one channel or practice is foreclosed, and engage in more subtle destructive behaviour. Furthermore, repeating ineffective interventions not only wastes resources and allows corruption to flourish, but, more destructively, can alienate already frustrated populations.

## 5. Final Thought

The complexity of tackling corruption requires a strong focus and collective action by governments, business, academics, NGOs, and civil society. The strong incentives which corrupt interests have against change, and an expectation that the current disaggregated legal regime will continue to evolve and grow, suggest that significant, sustained change will take time. A key actor in calling attention to the imperative of change, identifying priority reforms, and assessing their implementation is civil society. It is civil society that experiences corruption and its effects, and which also has a vested interest in the societal improvements which flow from cleaner political and financial systems.

## 6. Sources and Further Reading

Abbott, Kenneth and Snidal, Duncan, "Hard and Soft Law in International Governance", in *International Organization*, 2000, vol. 54, no. 3, pp. 421–456.

Anderson, Robert, “Renewing the WTO Agreement of Government Procurement: Progress to Date and Ongoing Negotiations”, in *Public Procurement Law Review*, 2007, vol. 16.

B20 Task Force Recommendations, 2012, B20 Organizing Committee.

Corruption Perceptions Index 2011, Transparency International, 2011.

Bellver, Ana and Kaufmann, Daniel, *Transparenting Transparency: Initial Empirics and Policy Applications*, IMF Conference on Transparency and Integrity, World Bank, Washington, DC, 2005.

Boswell, Nancy and Shah, Shruti, *UN Convention against Corruption Civil Society Review: 2011*, Transparency International-USA, 2011.

Downs, George W., Rocke, David M., and Barsoom, Peter N., “Is the Good News About Compliance Good News about Cooperation?”, in *International Organization*, 1996, vol. 50, no. 3, p. 379.

Grimes, Marcia, *The Conditions of a Successful Civil Society Involvement in Combating Corruption: A Survey of Case Study Evidence*, The Quality of Government Institute, 2008, p. 22.

Grundmann, Stefan, “The Future of Contract Law”, in *European Review of Contract Law*, 2011, vol.4, no.12, pp. 490–527.

Hechler, Hannes, Zinkernagel, Gretta, Koechlin, Lucy, and Morris, Dominic, *Can UNCAC Address Grand Corruption?*, CHR. Michelsen Institute, 2011, p. 2.

Heimann, Fritz and Dell, Gillian, *Progress Report 2010: Enforcement of the OECD Anti-Bribery Convention*, Transparency International, 2010.

Heimann, Fritz, Dell, Gillian, and McCarthy, Kelly McCarthy, *Progress Report 2011: Enforcement of the OECD Anti-Bribery Convention*, Transparency International, 2011.

Kaufmann, Daniel, Kraay, Aart and Mastruzzi, Massimo, *The Worldwide Governance Indicators: Methodology and Analytical Issues,* World Bank Policy Research Working Paper No. 5430, 2010, available at http://ssrn.com/abstract=1682130, last accessed on 6 August 2012.

Lindestedy, Catharina and Naurin, Daniel, “Transparency Is Not Enough: Making Transparency Effective in Reducing Corruption”, in *International Political Science Review*, 2010, vol. 31, no. 3, p. 301.

Mitchell, Ronald B., “Sources of Transparency: Information Systems in International Regimes”, in *International Studies Quarterly*, 1998, vol. 42, pp. 109–130.

Pauwlyn, Joost, "The Rise and Challenges of 'Informal' Law-Making", in *The Law of the Future and the Future of Law*, Torkel Opsahl Academic EPublisher, Oslo, 2011.

Peisakhin, Leonid and Pinto, Paul, "Is Transparency an Effective Anti-Corruption Strategy? Evidence from a Field Experiment in India", in *Regulation and Governance*, 2010, vol. 4, pp. 261–280.

Sampson, Steven, "The Anti-Corruption Industry: From Movement to Institution", in *Global Crime*, 2010, vol. 11, no. 2, pp. 261–278.

Shaffer, Gregory C. and Pollack, Mark A., "Hard vs. Soft Law: Alternatives, Complements, and Antagonists in International Governance", in *Minnesota Law Review*, 2010, vol. 94, pp. 706–799.

Slaughter, Anne-Marie, *A New World Order*, Princeton University Press, Princeton, 2004.

de Willebois, Emile van der Does, Sharman, J.C., Harrison, Robert, Park, Ji Won, and Halter, Emily, *The Puppet Masters: How the Corrupt Use Legal Structures to Hide Stolen Assets and What to Do About It*, Stolen Asset Recovery (StAR) Initiative, World Bank, 2011.

Zourdis, Stavros, "The Rule of Law in the 21st Century: Bridging the Compliance Deficit", in *The Law of the Future and the Future of Law*, 2011, vol. 11, p. 8.

# 2.3.

## Justice, Peace and Development

**Sang-Hyun Song***

There is a fundamental connection between international criminal justice and sustainable peace. International criminal justice – of which the International Criminal Court (ICC) is a small but central element – supports peace and development through preventing mass violence, re-instating confidence in socio-political structures, and empowering victims to rebuild their lives. In turn, development supports international criminal justice, since effective and capable national systems are crucial for the success of the Rome Statute system as a whole. However, more needs to be done to strengthen national jurisdictions in order to respond adequately to international crimes and the development community has a key role to play in this regard. Justice for mass atrocities is a concern common to both the development and the international justice communities, and the topic must be addressed in a concerted manner.

### 1. Introduction

For a long time, references to justice in the domain of development focused mainly on social justice. Recently, however, a trend has emerged which increasingly recognises the interrelation between the rule of law and criminal justice on one hand, and sustainable peace and development on the other. This think piece will discuss the potential for synergies between the two spheres, arguing that they are closely connected and should be treated as such by policymakers.

The sheer scale of the devastating effects of conflicts and large-scale violence on development has been recently emphasised by the World Bank in its landmark 2011 World Development Report. According to this Report, a civil war costs, on average, as much as three-decades of

* **Sang-Hyun Song** is an Appeals Judge and President of the International Criminal Court. For more than thirty years, he taught as a professor of law at Seoul National University Law School, beginning in 1972. He has also held visiting professorships at a number of law schools, including Harvard, New York University, Melbourne and Wellington.

GDP growth of a medium-size developing economy and, in addition, two decades are usually needed to restore trade levels after major outbreaks of violence.

As tragic as these findings are, they do not surprise me. I have personally witnessed how wars and mass atrocities tear communities apart, inflicting terrible physical and mental suffering, devastating social norms, and wrecking public institutions and infrastructure.

To enable the peaceful development of societies worldwide, the global community must enforce unequivocal norms prohibiting the illegal and indiscriminate large-scale use of armed force. In the long term, this requires both upholding relevant legal norms preventively and enforcing them effectively if atrocities do occur. These considerations should be fully integrated in the planning of international development aid and rule of law programmes.

## 2. Justice Supports Peace and Development

### 2.1. Emergence of the Modern System of International Criminal Justice

International crimes such as genocide, crimes against humanity, war crimes, and the crime of aggression, present one of the greatest threats to peace, security, and the well-being of the world. This recognition is reflected in the preamble of the Rome Statute of the International Criminal Court (ICC), which was adopted in 1998 by the majority of the world's nations.

The adoption of the Rome Statute was a historic achievement, the culmination of decades of work and negotiation by lawyers, diplomats, civil society groups, and individual citizens worldwide. States from all regions of the world agreed that joint action must be taken, relying on the force of international law, to ensure that the gravest crimes known to humankind will not go unnoticed or unpunished.

The ICC's Statute entered into force in July 2002. In its ten years of existence, the ICC has turned from a court on paper into a leading actor in the enforcement of international justice. As of 1 June 2012, 121 States, more than 60 per cent of the world's sovereign nations, have ratified or acceded to the Rome Statute, and the number keeps growing. Eight situations are currently before the ICC, and the Court issued its first judgement on 14 March 2012 in a case concerning the use of child soldiers in the Democratic Republic of the Congo.

One of the most significant features of the ICC and the wider Rome Statute system is the contribution it makes to the prevention of mass violence. No one is immune from accountability, as the ICC's arrest warrants for sitting heads of State demonstrate. The likelihood of punishment has increased for dictators, and the new generation of political and military leaders will be more cautious before deciding to murder or torture their political opponents or fellow citizens.

## 2.2. Justice as an Element of Conflict Recovery

More than a billion people on the planet live in areas of conflict, large-scale violence, or fragility. Millions of people have been affected by the crimes under the ICC scrutiny, among them countless victims of murder, rape, torture, forcible deportation, and other horrendous acts. In my capacity as President of the ICC, I have met with former child soldiers and others affected by war crimes and crimes against humanity. It is heart-breaking to sense the trauma that the survivors carry with them and the magnitude of the challenges they face in their efforts to restore stability and normality.

Large-scale violence does not only impact the direct victims, but also the surrounding communities. Studies have found that non-victims in the context of mass violations often have the sense that after what happened to the victims, no one can be safe, no one can really know what to expect. Furthermore, the fear and the deep sense of injustice caused by massive human rights violations can force victims to exclude themselves from public life and refrain from engagement with public institutions. These are just some of the major obstacles that those who wish to return to a semblance of their former lives are facing.

Consequently, justice and the re-establishment of the rule of law are an essential part of recovery and peace-building in post-conflict societies. Any efforts to help a society regain health, wealth, and capacity to profit from its own resources must include accountability for past atrocities and strengthening of the rule of law. Indeed, research suggests that countries that have held former leaders accountable for their crimes have, in most cases, come away stronger. If impunity is allowed to reign, it leaves a desire for vengeance among populations who have been victims of massive crimes, and provides fertile ground for the recurrence of conflicts. Transitional justice, including international criminal justice mechanisms, is one of the core tools to forestall the cycle of violence.

### 2.3. Victim Empowerment in the ICC

Where atrocities have already taken place, the acknowledgment of the suffering of the victims and the individualisation of guilt for the crimes helps to stabilise peace. However, attributing guilt to individual perpetrators is not sufficient. Therefore, to enable a more comprehensive process of justice, the founders of the ICC decided to introduce two very innovative approaches for the empowerment of victims.

The ICC is the first international judicial body to allow participation of victims in their own right, and not just as witnesses. People who were victimised by powerful criminals have now become actors in international proceedings designed to prosecute those crimes.

The second innovative feature of the ICC is the possibility of court-ordered reparations and the creation of a Trust Fund for Victims, which is equally without precedent in international criminal justice. Recognising both the rights and the needs of victims and their families, the Fund provides a restorative element alongside the retributive justice of the criminal proceedings. Currently, over 80,000 beneficiaries receive assistance provided by the Fund and its local and international partners.

In a sense, the Fund acts as a conduit between the principle of individual criminal responsibility for the most serious crimes and the commitment of the international community to address the multi-dimensional challenges that societies in post-conflict situations are facing. In responding to the particular needs of victimised individuals and communities in their quest for dignity, hope, and sustainable livelihoods, the Trust Fund for Victims complements other humanitarian or developmental initiatives in situation countries. As such, the Trust Fund is becoming an increasingly visible presence in the nexus between justice and development.

## 3. Development Supports Justice

There is no doubt that, in any society, the prospects of justice grow with socio-economic development. Quite simply, delivering justice always requires adequate resources and capabilities, such as courtroom and prison facilities, or well-trained legal and other professionals. A well-developed society is more likely to be able to secure these important features

This is particularly relevant for the system of the Rome Statute given its reliance on national judicial systems. Under the principle of complementarity enshrined in the Rome Statute, the national judiciary of each State retains the primary duty to investigate and prosecute grave violations of international humanitarian law. The ICC is a safety net that ensures accountability when the national jurisdictions fail in their task. Therefore, the domestic justice systems of States should be so well equipped to deal with ICC crimes that they can serve as the main deterrent worldwide and likewise provide justice for past atrocities, enabling a society to move on after large-scale violence. The Review Conference of the Rome Statute held in Kampala, Uganda, in 2010, recognised this as one of the most burning challenges for the further development of the system of international justice.

In a national setting, this requires a good legal framework and the necessary capacity in terms of skills and resources for investigations, prosecutions, and trials. This is no simple task to achieve, particularly in a post-conflict situation. In his 2011 Rule of Law report, the United Nations (UN) Secretary-General pointed out that there is currently no systematic way to foster the political will necessary for States to domesticate the Rome Statute and to bring those requiring assistance together with international actors willing to fund or provide such assistance.

To address this gap, a new movement has emerged under the shared leadership of States, civil society, the Assembly of States Parties to the Rome Statute, and the UN – bringing justice, development, and rule of law actors together to seek more synergies. A landmark event was held in October 2010 at the Greentree Estate in New York, which initiated discussion amongst relevant stakeholders. One of the outcomes of the second conference held at Greentree in November 2011 was the decision to form a group of actors aimed at developing strategies and country specific plans on the practical implementation of the principle of complementarity. The group will examine experiences of countries that have undertaken investigations and prosecutions of atrocity crimes. In order to know what kind of assistance States require from the international community to rebuild national infrastructure, it is also necessary to assess what expertise, capacity, and resources exist locally. The discussions are thus shifting to more tangible actions, aimed at strengthening national capacity to tackle atrocious crimes.

Another promising initiative is the Global Forum on Law, Justice and Development, established recently at the initiative of the Legal Vice-Presidency of the World Bank. The goal of the Global Forum is to provide solutions to global, regional, and national development challenges and to facilitate discussion and identification of issues related to law and development. It aims to promote a better understanding of the role of law and justice, and to strengthen legal and judicial institutions in the development process.

It still remains to be seen what precise roles various UN agencies, international organisations, NGOs, States and international donors can and should take. This will, of course, depend not only on the progress of the emerging development–justice alliance but also on the capabilities and broader strategies of each of the actors individually. The ICC itself, however, will have to, at least for the time being, confine its role to being a catalyst of different forms and sources of assistance. The ICC is, after all, merely a court and it has neither resources nor mandate of a development organisation or an implementing agency.

The role of the development agencies, however, is particularly crucial in this respect. Addressing the legacy of mass violence is currently not topping the agenda of development programmes. The World Development Report states, for instance, that it is much easier for countries to get international assistance to support development of their militaries than their police forces and judiciaries.

Development aid typically involves multiple actors – national, bilateral and multilateral – whose activities are closely related and frequently overlap. Securing justice for international crimes is politically a particularly sensitive area, and it is crucial that capacity building occurs in a coordinated and sustainable manner.

The world's legal systems and cultures are varied, and capacity building should always be adjusted to the circumstances and needs of each particular situation in a way that supports national ownership and empowerment from the very beginning. At the same time, there should be no deviation from universally accepted norms: such as the prohibition of torture or the prosecution of grave breaches of Geneva Conventions. We must persist in our efforts to incorporate these norms into a truly universal system of international criminal justice – one that resides locally but moves globally.

## 4. Conclusion

The development community and the international justice community share concerns about the impact of violence on human populations, and a desire to see nations affected by conflict move into a future where their citizens can thrive in safety. Forging new partnerships between these two spheres will take them both closer to their shared objectives. Lasting peace and prosperity in post-conflict societies can only be achieved if development challenges and justice enforcement are addressed in a coordinated manner.

The potential for synergy is significant. Those responsible for war crimes and crimes against humanity are often part of wider networks involved in corruption and organised crime. Helping societies dismantle these criminal structures represents a major step forward in the entrenchment of a culture of the rule of law. In this way, capacity building for addressing Rome Statute crimes supports the more general justice reforms and vice versa. These considerations are primarily relevant for policy-makers at national, regional and international levels. Specifically, justice for mass atrocities should become an integral part of development and rule of law programmes aimed at ensuring sustainable development as well as security in post-conflict societies.

For the individual lawyer engaged in a particular case before a national tribunal or an international court, the considerations discussed in this article bear little immediate significance. Criminal proceedings must always be conducted impartially and in strict compliance with fair trial norms, and decisions must be based on the applicable law and the available evidence – not on secondary considerations of the potential impact on development or otherwise.

However, law is not a stagnant matter restricted to courtrooms; rather it follows the needs of society, and lawyers participate in the process through law-making, diplomacy and treaty negotiations, civil society advocacy, and international cooperation. In this sense, the engagement of legal professionals in the strengthening of the system of international justice in its broadest meaning is a contribution to the peace and well-being of people everywhere.

## 5. Sources and Further Reading

De Greiff, Pablo, "Articulating the Links between Transitional Justice and Development: Justice and Social Integration", in *Transitional Justice and Development: Making Connections*, Advancing Transitional Justice Series, vol. 3, Social Science Research Council, New York, 2009 (*particularly relevant for the effect of large-scale violence on victims, non-victims and the affected communities in Section 2.2.*).

Sikkink, Kathryn, *The Justice Cascade: How Human Rights Prosecutions Are Changing World Politics*, The Norton Series in World Politics, W. W. Norton & Company, New York, 2011.

Sikkink, Kathryn, "Time, Making Tyrants Do", *New York Times*, 15 September 2011, available at http://www.nytimes.com/2011/09/16/opinion/making-tyrants-do-time.html, last accessed on 7 August 2012 (*particularly relevant for the benefits of holding leaders accountable in Section 2.2.*).

Strengthening and Coordinating United Nations Rule of Law Activities, Report of the Secretary-General, A/66/133, available at http://www.unrol.org/files/Third%20Annual%20Report%20of%20the%20Secretary-General.pdf, last accessed on 6 August 2012.

*World Development Report 2011, Conflict, Security and Development: Overview*, The World Bank, Washington, DC, 2011, available at http://wdr2011.worldbank.org/sites/default/files/WDR2011_Overview.pdf, last accessed on 6 August 2012.

# 2.4.

# Financial Markets – How is the Financial Crisis Changing the Global Legal Environment?

**Himamauli Das***

The international community responded to the financial crisis with a varying response that sought to reinforce multilateral cooperation, broaden representation, and deepen informal cooperative mechanisms. The result was an unprecedented increase in the size of the financial backstop provided by the international financial institutions (IFIs), governance and institutional changes at the IFIs and other multilateral groupings, and an evolution in the political and institutional mechanisms of the international financial architecture. As efforts continue to support the global recovery and the implementation of reforms of the financial system, countries will need to address the extent to which further elaboration of existing mechanisms is necessary. Decisions need to be made as to whether new, enforceable rules need to be developed, instead of general standards. Countries also need to assess compliance mechanisms, such as peer review, assessment and sanctions.

## 1. Introduction

The global financial crisis brought to light fundamental weaknesses in the resilience and integrity of markets, resulting in a need for a strong, coordinated policy response, and the need to develop new foundations for the international financial architecture. Amid the serious challenges to the world economy and financial markets, the United States convened leaders of the world's industrial nations to an initial meeting in Washington, DC, of the Group of 20 (G-20) Leaders on 14–15 November 2008. In its communiqué at the end of that meeting, leaders identified five common principles for reform and tasked finance ministers to complete a list of near- and medium-term concrete actions, drawing on the expertise of the International Monetary Fund (IMF),

* **Himamauli Das** is currently Assistant General Counsel for International Affairs at the U.S. Treasury Department. This article represents personal views of Mr. Das and does not reflect the views of the U.S. Treasury or other government agencies.

the then-existing Financial Stability Forum (FSF), and standard setting bodies. These five common principles included:

- Strengthening financial market transparency and accountability;
- strengthening national level regulatory regimes, prudential oversight and risk management, and, importantly, the transparent assessments of national regulatory systems;
- promoting the integrity of financial markets by bolstering investor and consumer protection, protecting against illicit finance risks, and promoting information sharing;
- enhancing and strengthening international regulatory cooperation and coordination across all segments of financial markets; and
- reforming the international financial institutions to better reflect the world economy and to enhance emerging and developing economy representation, and an expansion of the membership of the FSF and other standard setters.

By the Leaders' summit in Pittsburgh a year later, the G-20 leaders had designated the G-20 to be 'the premier forum' for international economic cooperation and had established the Financial Stability Board (FSB) as the successor to the FSF. The FSB, in particular, was to coordinate and monitor progress in strengthening financial regulation, and to act to make financial reforms to "rein in the excesses that led to the crisis". Through subsequent G-20 meetings, these recommendations and tasks have been elaborated and the close multilateral cooperation continues.

There has been significant progress on reforming the financial regulatory framework. From the initial detailed tasking to finance ministers to the robust work carried out by the FSB with the significant input of standard setters, the International Monetary Fund, and others, G-20 leaders have put in place a broad strategy for financial reform. Significant progress has been made regarding key elements, including the development of stronger minimum standards for bank capital and liquidity through the implementation of the Basel II, II.5, and III requirements, thus ending 'too big to fail' by means of strengthened resolution regimes and resolution planning for global systematic banks reforms, and changes to over-the-counter derivatives markets and compensation structures. In large part, the work of the FSB is moving from design to implementation by countries and monitoring progress in implementation. Some of the challenges at the national level are to seek convergence and consistency in the implementation of standards and principles across countries, to seek a level playing field and avoid discriminatory treatment, and to minimise unintended cross-border impacts.

Against the backdrop of reforms to the financial regulatory framework, the 2008 financial crisis brought new interest in and focus on the institutions and mechanisms of the international financial architecture and the ability of these international mechanisms to foster national-level implementation to forestall future crises. These efforts of the international community on these elements, which will be discussed below, point to an evolution in the global legal environment.

## 2. Global Financial and Macroeconomic Framework before the Financial Crisis

Firstly, some context is needed in order to frame the discussion. Prior to the financial crisis, the global financial and macroeconomic framework was roughly governed by the following:

- The Bretton Woods institutions – the World Bank, the International Monetary Fund (IMF), and the World Trade Organization (WTO);
- other international organisations, such as the Organization for Economic Co-operation and Development (OECD), the regional development banks (for example, the Asian Development Bank), with a role in economic and financial matters;
- regulatory standard setters such as the Basel Committee on Banking Supervision and the International Organisation of Securities Commissions (IOSCO); and
- informal multilateral groupings such as the Group of Seven (G-7) and Group of Eight (G-8) – and the Financial Stability Forum.

One can view the elements of the pre-financial crisis framework through the following legal or institutional prisms:

- *Organisations with legally binding commitments and compliance mechanisms.* The IMF and WTO impose legally binding commitments on their members, and, to a varying degree, an assessment and compliance mechanism.
    - Clearly defined rules negotiated between members and dispute settlement are central components of the WTO multilateral trading system. The institutional role of the WTO secretariat is primarily to supply technical and professional support to WTO bodies, provide technical assistance, to monitor and analyse trade develop-

ments, and to disseminate information, and to convene WTO conferences.

- The IMF Articles of Agreement imposes two sets of obligations on members – those regarding exchange arrangements under Article IV and general obligations of members under Article VIII. Two features distinguish the IMF framework from the WTO system. Many of the obligations imposed on members are framed in aspirational language – 'endeavour to direct', 'seek to avoid', and 'undertakes to collaborate' – but there are certain defined hard obligations. Unlike in the WTO, there is no dispute settlement mechanism to resolve disputes between members. While the IMF Articles create a mechanism to resolve 'any question of interpretation' between any member and the IMF or between members, it is rarely used. Rather, the IMF management (that is, its secretariat) is given the responsibility to "oversee the international monetary system in order to ensure its effective operation" and to "exercise firm surveillance over the exchange rate policies of members", which the IMF performed through periodic Article IV reviews of members. In this context, the IMF performs both soft law and hard law functions.

- *Organisations with limited or no binding commitments, but with international assessments and peer review.* A collection of international organisations provide financing, technical assistance, economic assessments, and a forum for countries to cooperate on economic and financial matters. These include the multilateral development banks, such as the World Bank Group; the various regional development banks, such as the Asian Development Bank and African Development Bank; and the OECD. While the main focus of the development banks is to provide financing and technical assistance to developing countries, they can perform economic and financial assessments (for example, the World Bank jointly with the IMF, conduct Financial Sector Assessment Programme reviews of countries). In serving as a forum for economic and financial matters, the OECD conducts peer reviews or assessments through which the performance of countries is monitored by peers, and serves as a forum for the negotiation of binding agreements (OECD Convention on Combating Bribery of Foreign Officials in International Business Transactions) or non-binding arrangements (for example, the Arrangement on Export Credits), as well as standards or models. The OECD also is host to the Financial Action Task Force (FATF) which, although not a formal body, serves as standard setter and a compliance mechanism to address money laundering and terrorist finance.

- *Formal, but non-binding, standard setters.* Regulatory standard setters established through various international efforts – including the Basel Committee on Banking Supervision, the IOSCO, and the International Association of Insurance Supervisors (IAIS), among others – played an important role in enhancing cooperation and the harmonisation of national-level regulatory standards. Standard setters generally do not possess any formal supra-national supervisory or regulatory authority, and their decisions or conclusions do not have any binding legal effect, nor do they have compliance or review mechanisms. Rather, these standard setters formulated broad supervisory standards and guidelines and recommended statements of best practices that, depending on the circumstances, national-level regulators were to take into account when developing national-level regulations. The standard setters also provided a forum for cooperation between members on banking, securities, insurance, or other such matters.
- *Informal, non-binding, mechanisms with primarily a policy role.* Prior to the financial crisis, the G-7 major industrial economies (and, later, the G-8) was a main economic policy coordination group at the finance minister level to monitor developments in the world economy and assess economic policies. The G-7 and G-8 addressed variously the challenges of a globalised economy, trade, debt, and development issues. Key steps were taken to enhance cooperation among the various national and international supervisory bodies, and international financial institutions, so as to promote stability in the international financial system, for example, the establishment of the FSF in 1999. Neither the G-7 nor the FSF had any formal status, secretariat, binding authorities, or any enforcement or compliance role.

## 3. Governance and Institutional Evolution Post-Crisis

The G-20 summit in Washington in 2008 initiated a significant effort to modify and strengthen mechanisms and institutions involved in international monetary and financial policy. One component of this effort was to bolster the financial capacity of the IMF and the multilateral development banks. Countries quickly responded by increasing the resources of the IMF and IMF borrowing facilities such as the New Arrangements to Borrow, and initiated a now-concluded and unprecedented round of capital increases at all of the multilateral development banks. Beyond enhancing the availability of financial resources to backstop the financial system, there were three key developments: to enhance emerging and developing countries' voices and representation, the evolution of the FSB as a key institution for policy coordination, and the role of the G-20.

In the Washington summit in 2008, the G-20 committed to advancing the reform of the Bretton Woods institutions to more adequately reflect the changing world economy, and to give emerging and developing countries greater voice and representation. By the Seoul summit in 2010, the G-20 had resolved to go further by pursuing additional reforms in the IMF, including further shifts in quota shares to dynamically emerging and developing countries and to under-represented countries of over six per cent, It also agreed on a reduction by two in advanced European chairs at the IMF Executive Board to facilitate greater emerging market and developing country representation, and a move to an all-elected IMF board.

- The Washington summit also emphasised the need for the FSG to expand its membership and for standard setters to review their membership as well. By the Pittsburgh summit in September 2009, the FSB was established as a successor to the FSF, with representation of all G-20 countries, FSF members, Spain, and the European Commission.
- The Toronto summit reaffirmed the FSB's principal role in the elaboration of international supervisory and regulatory policies and standards, and encouraged the FSB to identify ways to strengthen its capacity. By the Los Cabos summit in 2012, the G-20 had endorsed a revised FSB Charter for placing the FSB on an enduring organisational footing, with legal personality, strengthened governance, greater financial autonomy, and enhanced capacity to coordinate the development and implementation of regulatory policy, while maintaining strong links with the Bank of International Settlements (BIS).
- Finally, the G-20 was "designated to be the premier forum" for international economic and financial cooperation.

An initial Charter endorsed by the G-20 in 2009 established the FSB with clearly delineated operational components, a consensus decision-making process, and a permanent secretariat. The Charter itself was a step forward in imbuing the FSB with a more significant role and with a specific mandate and tasks. However, it was not a binding legal document and did not create a legal entity – there was no decision to establish either a national-level corporate form or an institution with international legal personality. As a result, the FSB did not have the capacity to enter into agreements or hire and fire staff, and had no privileges or immunities.

A revised Charter, endorsed by the G-20 in Los Cabos, went a step further in formalising the operational arrangements of the FSB. There are three salient features in the revised Charter. First, it continues to be a non-binding document and the FSB continues not to be a legal entity at this stage. The FSB report to the G-20, however, recommends creating the FSB as a Swiss association to provide it with legal personality, and further recommends that privileges and immunities should be conveyed to the secretariat (but not members) through an existing headquarters agreement between the BIS and the Swiss government. It will be of interest to see how the legal character of the FSB changes its operational modalities over time, including through the direct recruitment of personnel. While the Charter continues to reflect a consensus decision-making process, the FSB report notes agreement within the FSB to formulate rules of procedure to improve internal governance and to standardise internal processes. It will likewise be interesting to see if the FSB retains its flexible and informal operational arrangements in the context of a formal set of rules and expanded membership. Finally, the Charter continues the expanded FSB composition, set out in its 2009 iteration: national level regulatory and supervisory authorities, central banks, and finance ministries; international financial institutions; and international standard setting, regulatory, supervisory, and central bank bodies. Participation in decision-making by international groupings in their own right – including the IMF and the regulatory standard setters – is necessary to ensure coordination and full participation by entities with a significant stake in FSB deliberations, but is unique in that supranational bodies are viewed as representing their own interests in accordance with their own institutional arrangements distinct from those of national-level governments. Finally, the adoption of the G-20 as the premier forum for international monetary and financial policy coordination is also of note. As it recognised in Los Cabos, G-20 decisions have far reaching impact, and the informal and flexible character of the G-20 enables it effectively to facilitate economic and financial cooperation. Since 2008, the G-20 has considered a wide range of international economic and financial policies, including core elements to address the financial crisis – reform of the international financial architecture, macroeconomic stability, and financial regulatory reform – but it has also addressed a range of other important issues such as food security and commodity price volatility, fossil fuel subsidies, climate change, and the fight against corruption. As it broadens its scope, as it recognised in Los Cabos, the G-20 will have to address concerns about transparency and effectiveness, questions about formalising its processes and development of institutional capacity, and its role *vis-à-vis* the private sector and existing international institutions that have to date provided significant input to the work of the G-20.

## 4. Evolution of Accountability Mechanisms Post-Crisis

Much of the post-financial crisis effort focused not only on the improvement of standards, but also on evolving mechanisms to foster accountability in the context of soft law. Initial goals focused on monitoring and reporting on implementation of standards developed by the standard setters and have also moved towards greater assessment and peer review. There may be further interest in identifying mechanisms to ensure compliance and enforcement once assessment and peer review mechanisms are defined and begin providing results. Countries may need to consider the tension between a cooperative approach based on standards and soft law and a greater emphasis on compliance. In this context, countries may need to confront whether more binding legal mechanisms are required in the traditionally non-binding frameworks of the financial sector standard setters.

- Starting in London, G-20 leaders began to focus on accountability in order to bolster country commitments to refrain from raising new investment and trade barriers in goods and services. Leaders committed to notify the WTO of any such measures, and called on the WTO – together with other international bodies – to "monitor and report publically on our adherence to these regulatory undertakings". The OECD and WTO have subsequently produced reports on trade restrictive measures imposed by countries. In the financial regulatory reform area, finance ministers were instructed to implement the London decisions, and the IMF and FSB were asked to "monitor progress, working with the Financial Action Task Force and other relevant bodies, and to provide a report".
- Continuing this theme in Pittsburgh, G-20 leaders stressed a commitment to deal with 'non-cooperative jurisdictions' in three areas: on money laundering and terrorism finance in the context of FATF, in dealing with tax havens in the OECD context and expanding the scope

of non-cooperative jurisdictions (NCJs) on prudential standards, and information exchange in the FSB context.

- In Toronto, leaders established a 'fourth pillar' of the global financial reform agenda called "transparent international assessment and peer review". The Toronto communiqué pointed to two core elements of this pillar: the IMF/World Bank Financial Sector Assessment Process and robust and transparent peer review through the FSB, including through the "adherence to prudential standards". In an annex to the communiqué, leaders welcomed the implementation of the FSB's evaluation process on adherence to prudential information exchange and international cooperation standards in all jurisdictions.
- Carrying this mandate forward, in a paper from March 2010, the FSB laid out a framework to encourage adherence by all countries and jurisdictions to international financial standards, including by identifying NCJs, which in large part were modelled on the work of the OECD in the tax area and FATF for standards on combating money laundering and terrorism finance. FSB member jurisdictions were asked to "lead by example" by first committing to implement and adhere to international cooperation and information exchange standards in the financial regulatory and supervisory area. The paper laid out an evaluation mechanism through a process of dialogue and evaluation. Lastly, the FSB paper noted possible consideration of "a toolbox of possible measures" – both positive and negative – to promote adherence. The 2010 paper holds out the possibility of sanctions, including a list of sanctions that potentially include restrictions on financial institutions, restrictions on transactions by international financial institutions, and restrictions on cross-border financial transactions.
- In November 2011, the FSB made a public statement on the initiative to promote adherence and identified three categories of adherence: jurisdictions demonstrating sufficiently strong adherence, jurisdictions taking the actions recommended or making material progress towards demonstrating sufficiently strong adherence, and NCJs.

Regulatory standard setters in the financial sector have traditionally used a model to achieve international goals that departs from the international law model where an international organisation or group of countries seek to define internationally binding standards with possible compliance measures or regimes. The efforts of the regulatory standard setters such as the Basel Committee and IOSCO have been characterised by the issue of standards or principles with the goal of establishing a harmonised international regime through national level implementation of regulatory standards as domestic law. The standard setters, with support from participating members, have used peer pressure to foster implementation of standards defined at the international level. The FSB effort to promote adherence to the principles and standards laid out by the standard setters (IAIS, Basel Committee, and IOSCO) through peer review and assessment is consonant with this approach.

The FSB approach, however, also contemplates the possibility of negative measures. The March 2010 paper notes that if jurisdictions fail to make sufficient progress towards adherence, "FSB members would call upon its members to take further measures". It goes on to note that the implementation of any such measures will be subject to "any legal constraints that member jurisdictions might face", and prudential carve-out provisions included in many trade and investment agreements that permit countries to take measures in the financial services area for prudential reasons or to ensure the integrity and stability of the financial system. In effect, the FSB seeks to mesh its soft law approach with a hard law component at the international level. Whilst the principles and standards defined by the standard setters do not have legally binding effect, and neither the FSB nor the standard setters can directly effectuate compliance, the model proposed by the FSB would indirectly use national law regimes to "enforce" compliance. As such, the practical model being carved out by the FSB is in some respects distinct from the regimes established by the WTO and IMF (hard law compliance) and the soft law approaches of the standard setters.

## 5. Conclusion

In conclusion, the FSB and G-20 represent different facets of reforms in the legal architecture and their development will continue to be of interest. The FSB evinces a trend towards institutional capacity and compliance, necessary to design and implement the significant measures sought by countries to stabilise the international financial system. It is, however, premised on a distinct legal model and with a compliance mechanism that relies on national-level implementation, rather than internationally mandated legal direction. The G-20 continues the longstanding approach of the G-7, and G-8, by providing direction and guidance to international mechanisms – the international financial institutions and standard setters – but without significant movement towards an institutional structure or binding mechanisms.

# 2.5.

# Law and Religion: Likely Trends in the Coming Decade

**Rik Torfs***

Law and religion issues are confronted with two new trends. Firstly, certain religious ideas and practices are drifting away from mainstream thinking in society. Secondly, religious freedom will be exercised in a setting hostile to religion. Both trends may lead to restricting freedom. Moreover, one should not forget that they emerge in a global picture, including a more moralistic approach of legal principles and an increasing inclination to use religion as a weapon in class conflicts. All these elements will influence the degree of religious freedom individuals and groups enjoy.

Specific problems at stake are freedom of individuals faithful *within* religious structures, gender and sexuality issues creating new fields of tension between religion and State, as well as the legal place of upcoming forms of spirituality no longer controlled by traditional religious groups and their leaders.

## 1. Introduction

My field is double. I am both a secular lawyer dealing with law and religion, and a canon lawyer focusing on the internal law of the Roman Catholic Church. Although this contribution will concentrate on the first issue, a look at the second one facilitates a deeper insight in the upcoming discussion.

## 2. Religion, Truth and the Perception of Religious Freedom

Thought and ideas within religious groups are increasingly disconnected from the overall discourse in society. This can be illustrated by the following paradoxical idea: religions stick to the notion of truth, yet at the same time, they deny any scientific or even argumentative technique of falsification with regard to their viewpoints. Consequently, the truth they

* **Rik Torfs** is a professor of law and canon law at the Universities of Leuven and Stellenbosch.

refer to is no longer a metaphysical or ontological truth, as competition with science is impossible, but a place offering certainty and stability, an alternative house to live in. The content of religion will increasingly influence the way in which religious freedom is perceived. Two elements should be taken into consideration. The first one has a long tradition, while the second one is rather new.

## 2.1. Religious Freedom, Human Rights and Radicalism

Human rights, including religious freedom, are truly operational on an intermediate level of unusual, but not radically deviant behaviour. They do not protect conformist behaviour, as acting the same way all others already do will be riskless and does not require extra-legal support. Yet human rights are also unable to protect strongly deviant behaviour. Here, penal norms and the maintenance of public order will set limits to pervasive claims for additional legal protection of religious freedom. Given this starting point, it cannot be excluded that many religious norms slowly move from the intermediate level to the sphere of radically deviant behaviour. For instance, penal norms and procedures in internal Roman Catholic canon law traditionally are covered by protection of free internal organisation that religious groups enjoy as part of religious freedom. However, this freedom could be controlled or restricted as a consequence of sexual abuse cases. Inadequate inner Church action may lead to intervention by secular authorities and thus, to a more restricted religious freedom. Another example comes from Islam. Wearing the burqa, and in a previous stage wearing headscarves at school, only became an issue after religious motives for doing so were partially eclipsed by political ones. To sum up, religious freedom as such will remain protected, but will lose force as a consequence of the application of a key human rights principle: unusual behaviour enjoys protection, radically deviant behaviour most of the time does not.

## 2.2. Religious Freedom in a Hostile Environment

Religious freedom weakens in a society hostile to religion. Religious freedom was given shape in a religious context. The basic picture used to be that a majority religion dominated the scene, while members of religious minorities were persecuted or hampered in their religious practice. The paradigm is clear: the central question concerns the place minority religions occupy within the overall religious landscape. Conversely, religious freedom was not meant to function in a non-religious or anti-religious context. Nevertheless it did so, at least to some extent. In communist regimes, religion was an official enemy, that is, the enemy of the system and not of the majority of the population. In the meantime, the existence of such a church hostile context is scientifically relevant: religious freedom was not guaranteed. The choice religious people were confronted with was between collaboration and resistance. Examples are the choice between the official and the patriotic Roman Catholic Church in China, or the dilemmas in the former German Democratic Republic. Perhaps, in that context, there was also a third choice, with the current president of Germany, Joachim Gauck (1940), being an example: churches could offer a space for relative freedom. The novelty of the coming decades may be the presence and practice of religion in a hostile atmosphere. Of course, the latter is not and will not become a world-wide phenomenon. However, in certain countries, including several Western European States, such a configuration is already present or is growing quickly. Although research remains elusive as a result of the difficulty to ask the right questions, there is a clear trend among the population of certain countries that shows a move from faith over to hesitation and indifference to scepticism and hostility. The idea that religion is intellectually inferior to atheism, and is just a consolation for human mortality, is gaining field among large groups of the population, not only among intellectuals. This phenomenon entails some questions, especially the following one: how do concrete human rights survive in a hostile context? Unlike religion, freedom of expression will most probably remain rather popular in the coming decades. Shall this lead to a more generous legal interpretation of free expression, and a more restrictive one of religious freedom? I suppose so, as certain indications of this trend are already present today: some authors advocate narrowing the notion of religious freedom to its individual form, thus omitting deliberate collective and organisational freedom.

## 3. The Evolution of Law, Ethics and Guilt

Law and religion will also be affected by an upcoming trend with regard to the evolution of law in general. It is clear that a more formal approach, as characterised by the human rights catalogues, will be strongly amended by a more emotional method, which will be defined by its followers as a more ethical one. Certain longstanding legal notions, such as formal procedural norms or the principle of prescription, are under pressure. This trend finds itself translated into very concrete points with regard to procedures. Many people ask the question whether crimes should remain unpunished as a result of technical mistakes during the process. All the more, as far as prescription is concerned, the idea that time takes away guilt is increasingly challenged. Prescription is seen as unjust. The cleavage between law and ethics is no longer taken for granted. Generally speaking, I am not in favour of this trend, as a mixing up of law and ethics may lead to a celebration of feelings of revenge disturbing equilibrium in society. Yet, the evolution seems to be continuing, probably partly as a result of the sober but technical human rights catalogue, which was often seen by the *vox populi* as a skeleton without content. In any case, the evolution will have consequences in the field of law and religion. This is because religious groups themselves formulate ethical norms, values and guidelines, without still disposing of the moral authority to make them universally credible. The result will be that the behaviour of religious groups, their leaders, their ministers, as well as faithful claiming to be religious, will be analysed along the lines of the ethical standards they formulate for others. In that regard, it is far from impossible that in penal cases, such as fraud or child abuse, religious people will be punished more severely than others. It is imaginable that religion will be seen as a circumstance aggravating guilt.

## 4. Religion as the New Face of Class Conflict

Law and religion may increasingly become a field in which the class conflicts of the past will be dealt with in the future. In the 20$^{th}$ century, the idea of class conflict found a translation in political thinking, as brought into practice by communist regimes in Europe and post-colonial governments in other continents. After the defeat of communism, symbolised by the fall of the Berlin Wall in 1989, new battlegrounds with regard to what were formerly known as class conflicts emerged. For instance, in the Balkan wars resulting from the splitting up of former Yugoslavia, religion was often used as a cover up for less respectable war motives. In any case, Croatia was seen as a Catholic country, whereas Serbia boasted its Orthodox roots. In other words, whereas in previous times social inequality was invoked as a reason for struggle, religion partly replaced it as a catalyst of grief, enriched by a flavour of dignity. Along the same lines, Islam as understood and practiced by many, especially young people, does not always mean that religious revival is nearby or taking place. It is very well possible to explain the success of religion from the perspective of class conflict. Very often, and of course abstraction made of the Gulf States, Muslims are not among the winners in our late capitalist world. In that regard, Islam can be both a tool to organise the world differently and a consolation for those who are not materially successful. The first goal is more difficult to achieve than the second one. Capitalism remains the overall framework people are living in. Yet the other function of religion continues to be available: even poor Muslims can argue that whatever the distribution of wealth may be, their God is the best. It will be interesting to see how invoking religion in a more global struggle will be used. Judges will have a hard time denouncing abuse of fundamental rights. Indeed, whereas abuse of rights in a private atmosphere, for instance in a real estate conflict between neighbours is generally accepted, qualifying certain forms of use of fundamental rights as abuse may in itself be a violation of fundamental rights.

## 5. Rights of the Faithful and Freedom of Religion

Another trend will be the degree of freedom that the faithful enjoy within their religious groups. The emancipation of individuals will probably continue along with higher overall education achievements in various countries. This will lead to new types of questions with regard to religious freedom. What will the rights of the faithful be *vis-à-vis* their religious leaders? This question will be asked at two different levels, namely at a doctrinal and at a practical level.

### 5.1. Rights of the Faithful at the Doctrinal Level

In the field of doctrine, the question is to what extent religious leaders will still be able to disqualify faithful as heretics, apostates, and schismatics. In the case of an entanglement between religion and State, like for instance currently in Iran, traditions can be continued, because religious norms can be enforced physically. Yet in more separation oriented systems with religious leaders only enjoying moral authority, the success of concepts such as heresy and apostasy is very doubtful.

### 5.2. Rights of the Faithful at the Practical Level

With regard to the practical level, questions will rise as to labour relationships including compulsory legal protection required by the State, as well as to the possibility of religious leaders and systems aiming at the control of the private lives of ministers and faithful. There are more binding State norms than in the past. Will religious groups be or remain exempted from some of these norms?

## 6. Religious Freedom and Discrimination

Conflicts between religion and the State will increase in the field of gender and sexuality.

### 6.1. Gender Discrimination

Equality between men and women is increasingly seen as a key value in a democratic society as governed by the rule of law. This is not always the case within traditional religions. One could even argue that the older religious groups are, the higher the risk will be that hostility *vis-à-vis* women and their position will be included in their tradition. Many religions do not only refuse women as ministers, but are also opposed to their equal position within civil society. Discrimination of women finds itself more and more included as a crime in penal norms. An important question will be whether these penal norms will also apply to religious groups. That is a matter of balancing. Which right prevails, religious freedom or non-discrimination? Although today religion remains very often excluded from non-discrimination legislation, it is very doubtful that this will remain true in the future.

### 6.2. Religion, Secularism and Homosexuality

Also with regard to sexuality, the tension between religious requirements and secular standards may increase. In the Roman Catholic Church, the official teaching on sexual ethics lost its credibility among Christian faithful as a result of the famous encyclical *Humanae Vitae* issued by Pope Paul VI in 1968, in which the use of non-natural contraception was denounced. Yet, more fields of tension between religious and secular standards exist, including the debate on homosexuality, although differences between religions remain very present in this field. In the Roman Catholic Church, the Magisterium still holds that practising homosexuality is a grave sin, although many Catholics strongly disagree with this view and accept or even foster legal State stipulation improving the situation of homosexual unions. Also, some Muslims accept homosexuality, yet here scepticism seems to be more widespread. More extreme Muslims put prostitution and homosexuality on the same level. The question is where the line will be drawn. My guess is that Western countries, after a short moment of hesitation, will nevertheless opt for complete equality between homosexual and heterosexual unions.

## 7. Spiritual Revival and Scientism

It is far from impossible that in the coming years, some 'real' spiritual revival will take place. By 'real revival', I mean a comeback of spiritual and religious ideas as such, and not merely as a result of a search for identity or as an expression of class conflict. It seems to be hard to live in an ideological and spiritual vacuum.

### 7.1. Institutionalised Religion and Scientism

Today, we are experiencing in certain countries a true revival of scientism in the style of Auguste Comte. The reasons for this phenomenon are hard to unravel, but most probably elements such as the decline of institutionalised religion, play a larger part than an increased credibility of science as such. If this hypothesis turns out to be true, the belief in science is more a form of belief than a scientific statement about science. Again using the same hypothesis, it is likely that this faith will also experience some form of decline and may give way at some stage to, sometimes intelligent, sometimes less intelligent, forms of faith.

### 7.2. Spiritual Revivalism and the Internet

Another possible cause for spiritual renewal is the information society. As a result of the Internet and the modern forms of communication linked up with it, people find themselves confronted with an almost unlimited number of stimuli, open to all forms of reaction. A new selection seems to be inevitable. Already today people are choosing for less information, for cutting the sources they are confronted with. A more sober information pattern may lead to new forms of spirituality, yet not always connected to traditional, organised religions. An important question will be about the legal protection that will be given to new forms of spirituality. Will it come close to the protection of religious freedom today? Or will new legal structures be more in line with privacy protection, as spiritual life will become a shelter similar to the house one is living in?

## 8. Conclusion

With regard to the three main questions that a law of the future approach includes, the following answers can be given:

At the policy level, politicians should refrain from regulating trends and tendencies before they clearly emerge. They should stick to the old principle that, in case there is no need to issue a law, there is a need not to issue one. Indeed, law and religion issues fit in the rather abstract fundamental rights debate. The latter leaves enough room for allowing local accents without betraying the hard core of what human rights really are. Case law will be essential when it comes to the protection of religious freedom, which also means that international judges, especially, should understand the mind of the local legislator without complying too easily with his less noble motives.

Topics for research are numerous. They include human rights within religious groups; the religious status of religion without faith yet expressing one's identity; the consequences of a society hostile to religion for the content of religious freedom; the question whether religion should adapt to modern standards including human rights or, conversely, should use human rights to criticise modern standards; and the question about the role of the individual within religious traditions, having themselves the inclination to highlight the collective dimension and the power position the latter entails for its leaders.

Lawyers of the future will only be good lawyers when they are not just lawyers. They should be educated people with a broad cultural background and a keen interest for underlying philosophical problems. This will help them to accept ambivalence in life without becoming relativists, because the protection of human rights can never be abandoned.

# Chapter III

# The Perspective of Technology: How Is Technology Affecting Law?

# 3.1.

# Cyberlaw 2.0

**Jacqueline D. Lipton***

When Wikipedia, Google and other online service providers staged a blackout protest against the Stop Online Piracy Bill in the United States in January 2012, their actions inadvertently emphasized a fundamental truth that is often missed about the nature of cyberlaw. In attempts to address what is unique about the field, commentators have failed to appreciate that the field could – and should – be reconceptualised as a law of the global intermediated information exchange. Such a conception would provide a set of organising principles that are lacking in existing scholarship; nothing happens online that does not involve one or more intermediaries – for instance, the service providers facilitate all digital commerce and communication by providing the hardware and software through which all interactions take place. This essay contemplates a future reconceptualisation of the cyberlaw field towards a law of the global intermediated information exchange. The author explains the benefits of such an approach in developing a more predictable and cohesive body of legal principles to govern cyberspace interactions in coming decades.

## 1. Introduction: The Nature of Cyberlaw

In January of 2012, a group of major online services providers – spearheaded by Wikipedia – staged a blackout protest against the bill in the United States for the Stop Online Piracy Act (SOPA). This legislation, had it been enacted, would have imposed onerous burdens on online service providers based on the liability of their customers for various intellectual property infringements. The outcry over this proposed legislation demonstrates what is often missed about the history and the future, of the field of law that we have come to know variously as cyberlaw, cyberspace law, and Internet law.

* **Jacqueline Lipton** is Baker Botts Professor of Law and Co-Director of the Institute for Intellectual Property and Information Law, University of Houston Law Center.

This area of law developed in the 1990s to reflect the challenges posed by the Internet for lawyers in different fields, including defamation and privacy law, intellectual property law, the law related to free expression, antitrust or competition law, and various aspects of corporate and commercial law. Since that time, debate has waged about the appropriate contours of the field and whether, in fact, cyberlaw is appropriately conceived as a distinct legal field in its own right. The alternative to accepting cyberlaw as a legal field is simply to include Internet issues within the areas of law for which digital networked technology has caused specific challenges, such as those listed above.

What has been missing in the past discourse relating to cyberlaw, and what the SOPA debates bring into sharp relief, is the fact that cyberlaw has been, and in coming decades probably should be, conceptualised as the law of the globalised intermediated information exchange. In other words, the central unifying thread for the field is the role of global online intermediaries – such as Wikipedia, Google, Facebook, Yahoo!, America Online – and their potential to attract liability for the misdeeds of their users.

Online intermediaries face the most unique challenges of any cyberspace actors. They are generally entities attempting to innovate in aspects of online information exchange. Wikipedia, for example, is a collaborative source of information. Google innovates in search engine technology. Facebook innovates in terms of online social interactions. Electronic payments systems and online businesses innovate in electronic commerce. Each of these areas of enterprise attracts customers who may engage in questionable as well as legitimate activities. Online actors utilising these intermediaries may engage in intellectual property infringement, defamation, privacy incursions, cyberbullying and harassment, electronic theft and fraud and the like.

Unlike the case of many physical world interactions, the victims of online wrongs may be more immediately attracted to legal action against an intermediary than against the primary wrongdoer for a number of reasons. It is often difficult to identify or locate an online wrongdoer because of the anonymous global nature of the Internet. Online wrongdoers are often impecunious or in foreign jurisdictions so it can be difficult to obtain and enforce meaningful legal relief against those actors. Additionally, intermediaries have a vested interest in cooperating with law enforcement in order to market and promote their services as safe for consumers. Thus, a particularly significant aspect to cyberlaw is the challenge to law- and policy-makers of achieving an appropriate balance between encouraging innovation in online services while at the same time protecting individuals from online harm. The legal liability of online service providers is the key to addressing this challenge. Laws focused on primary wrongdoers are less likely to have teeth than laws that account for the roles and responsibilities of those providing services through which harms may occur. Thus, the cyberlaw of the future needs to focus more clearly on the role of the online intermediary in the context of global information exchange. This has not been the case in past conceptions of cyberlaw.

## 2. Historical Conceptions of the Field

Cyberlaw teachers and casebook authors have typically struggled to provide such a unifying thread for the study of the challenges posed by the Internet to our current conceptions of the law. Such commentators have been plagued by debates surrounding Judge Frank Easterbrook's now infamous dismissal of cyberlaw as nothing more than a cyber 'law of the horse' that fails to illuminate the entire law in a meaningful way because it has no unifying features. A focus on the role of Internet intermediaries in the context of global information exchange would allow commentators to move the debate about the contours of cyberlaw away from the 'law of the horse' challenge and into something more meaningful.

The most often cited challenge to Easterbrook's categorisation of cyberlaw as a law of the horse is Professor Lawrence Lessig's follow-up piece in which he argued that what cyberlaw might in fact demonstrate is that law is not the only, or indeed primary, mode of cyberspace regulation. He emphasized that there are a number of regulatory modalities in cyberspace, law perhaps not being the most important. Both Lessig and Professor Joel Reidenberg argued that software code and system architecture are more important regulators of online interactions than law. This is because the code can effectively constrain online behaviours in a way that law cannot. Users cannot utilise software in a way that it was not intended to be used unless there is a problem with the underlying code or the user is a competent computer hacker able to reprogram the code. Law can never strive to be so effective in constraining behaviour. Outside the code-law debate, Lessig and others have additionally identified various other means of social regulation outside legal regulation. These additional regulatory modalities include social norms, market forces, and public education campaigns.

The state of cyberlaw today thus revolves around the axis of the debate established in the mid-1990s by commentators such as Easterbrook and Lessig. What is missing is a detailed examination of the role of law and a recognition that the law may play an important role in the regulation of cyberspace in years to come. The SOPA debate, taken in the context of recent case law developments about the role of online intermediaries in various legal fields, suggests that the cyberlaw of the future needs to focus squarely on the role of online intermediaries as its common unifying focus.

All online interactions – social, commercial, academic, artistic – are exchanges of information facilitated by one or more third party intermediaries. These third parties include search engines, payments systems, Internet service providers (ISPs), gaming platforms, social network operators, domain name registrars, and web hosting services. It is impossible for anyone to interact online without involving one or more of these intermediaries. Moreover, it is the struggle to address the legal role of these actors with respect to online wrongs that causes law and policy developments that are unique to cyberspace. It is therefore appropriate to characterise cyberlaw as the law of the intermediated information exchange transacted on a global stage. In the future, the cyberlaw field should revolve around the following issues: (a) delineating the legal rights and responsibilities of Internet intermediaries with respect to information exchange facilitated by their customers; and (b) investigating the impact of conflicts of law principles on the development of substantive legal rules in cyberspace. These aspects of the field derive from the two most distinctive features of cyberspace interactions – the fact that all interactions are intermediated by third parties, and the fact that interactions have the potential to cross jurisdictional boundaries.

## 3. Jurisdictional Challenges

With respect to the latter point, some may argue that jurisdictional challenges imposed on litigants by the Internet are not unique to cyberlaw, and are rightly conceived of within the field of conflicts of law or private international law. However, existing case law suggests that the there are certain ways in which the Internet skews the consideration of jurisdictional problems in ways not previously confronted by experts in the field of conflicts of law. For one thing, jurisdictional concerns are more likely to arise in Internet cases than in non-Internet cases because of the global nature of the communications medium. In other words, a greater proportion of Internet-related cases than of non-Internet cases will raise issues of extra-territorial reach of local laws and of the ability of the plaintiff's court to exert jurisdiction over a foreign defendant.

Because more courts will start by confronting these conflict issues in Internet cases than in physical world cases, there is a greater risk in Internet law that procedural determinations on jurisdiction or choice of law will effectively resolve an issue before the parties have a chance to argue their substantive cases. In other words, Internet cases run a greater risk of being resolved at a procedural stage, particularly if a court decides not to exercise jurisdiction over a foreign defendant. It may be that the cyberlaw of the future should call for more predictable *ex ante* rules on jurisdiction and choice of law to avoid an emphasis on procedural issues in Internet cases to the detriment of effective development of underlying substantive legal rules.

## 4. Role of Online Intermediaries

Jurisdictional issues aside, cyberlaw can easily be reconceptualised to focus on the role of online intermediaries with respect to liability for information exchanges initiated by their customers. Most current cyberlaw texts are divided in terms of familiar fields of law – constitutional law, conflicts of law, copyright law, trademark law, patent law, defamation and privacy law, *et cetera*. However, textbook authors and other commentators often miss the fact that so many of the cases over the last decade have revolved around common themes of online service provider liability for the activities of their users. The liability of online intermediaries for defamation is discussed in a chapter on defamation law while the liability of online intermediaries for copyright infringement is discussed in a completely separate chapter.

However, both questions raise similar issues about balancing the need to encourage innovation in the provision of online services with the need to protect existing legal rights, such as rights in an individual's reputation and rights to protect intellectual property. Even legislators are guilty of missing some of the major overlaps between questions of intermediary liability in different fields. Some commentators have attempted to justify the distinct approaches taken for intermediary liability for general tortious conduct under Section 230 of the Communications Decency Act with the approach taken for copyright infringement under Section 512 of the copyright legislation in the United States. However, such justifications are *ex post facto* rationalisations. Little thought was given at the time of the drafting of the respective pieces of legislation to the impact of adopting differing legal liability regimes for Internet service providers in different contexts.

More recently, American courts have struggled with the limits of secondary liability for copyright infringement with respect to different kinds of online service providers. In very similar cases involving the Perfect 10 men's magazine as plaintiff, American courts held that contributory liability for infringement was a possibility for the Google search engine, while the electronic payments systems were too far removed from the causal chain to attract secondary liability. Of course, these cases may be effectively reconciled – as the differing approaches to intermediary liability in the defamation and copyright context legislation may be reconciled. It may be that in the future the appropriate place for discussion of these kinds of issues should be within the field of cyberlaw reconceptualised as the law of the global intermediated information exchange.

One might argue that the key issues about intermediary liability have already been addressed by courts and legislators in most jurisdictions. From the mid-1990s to the dawn of the new millennium many courts and legislators around the world adopted new legal rules to deal with challenges posed by the Internet to existing legal fields. However, those rules were adopted in the context of specific fields of law such as copyright, trademarks, harmful speech, *et cetera.* There are few examples of laws that focus on the role of those who make the Internet what it is across multiple fields of law – the providers of online services. A few commentators in recent years have begun to focus their work more specifically on the role of service providers across different fields of law. In the future, more work needs to be done with this kind of focus so that the cyberlaw field can contribute something meaningful to the future regulation of online conduct outside debates about whether cyberlaw is an appropriate designation for a legal field.

## 5. Emerging Issues

### 5.1. Future Cyberspace Trends

It is important that the cyberlaw of the future take this focus because there are constantly new issues emerging online that raise challenges for the existing legal system. Some obvious examples of these challenges include: the future of online intellectual property protection; trademark and free speech issues under the newly expanded process for generic top level domains of the Internet Corporation for Assigned Names and Numbers; the regulation of online bullying and harassment; the challenges of finding an appropriate balance between freedom of expression and the protection of privacy and personal reputation online, particularly in the context of online social networking.

### 5.2. Cyberlaw as a Meta-Field

Suggesting a reconceptualisation of cyberlaw as a law of the online intermediary is not necessarily to say that distinct legal fields such as copyright, trademark, defamation, and antitrust should not continue to address Internet issues. Obviously, laws in specific pre-existing legal fields must accommodate the Internet such that, for example, digital copyright laws should continue to be placed within copyright legislation and not in some abstract Internet statute. A reconceptualisation of the kind addressed in this discussion is in a sense a meta-conception of a legal field. The cyberlaw of the future would be superimposed over, and at a higher level of abstraction than, pre-existing legal fields. This is really no change from what takes place in today's scholarly discourse on cyberlaw which confronts challenges from different fields within a more general 'cyberlaw' rubric. What this discussion is suggesting is that the notion of cyberlaw should have a unique central focus on the role of the online intermediary, rather than the distinct lack of focus it has maintained previously.

### 5.3. Practical Benefits of Reconceptualising Cyberlaw

An obvious advantage of such a reconceptualisation would be that it would allow commentators, judges and legislators to draw parallels across different fields of law to develop more cohesive and predictable rules for those who provide the backbone of the online experience – the online service providers. A focus on intermediaries may also assist in the global harmonisation of rules relating to the Internet if different jurisdictions adopted the same approach to reconceptualising cyberlaw. In turn, a more harmonised approach to substantive rules of intermediary liability for issues such as defamation, privacy and intellectual property infringement might lessen the pressure on jurisdictional questions such as choice of law. If global laws were relatively harmonised, choice of law questions would diminish in practical significance.

### 5.4. Harms and Remedies

Additional benefits may follow from adopting an intermediary-focused conception of cyberlaw in the future. If courts, legislatures and commentators were more focused on what is truly unique about the Internet, they could more meaningfully address other aspects of online harm that arise specifically from online interactions. For example, harms and remedies caused by online interactions tend to differ significantly from those in the physical world. Online interactions cannot cause direct physical harm, unlike, say, assault, battery, property damage and the like in the physical world. Online harms tend to fall into two categories – economic loss and personal humiliation. These are the kinds of harm that can be caused by wrongs based on information exchange as opposed to physical contact. Allowing for the development of a cyberlaw field that focuses on what is unique about online interactions, rather than spilling ink debating the 'law of the horse' issue, would create a conceptual space within which to address questions of harms and remedies that are unique to cyberspace.

## 6. Conclusions

The cyberlaw of the past has been something of a black sheep in law school curricula and in legal debate, never having its own clear boundaries and constantly battling the 'law of the horse' criticism. However, the cyberlaw of the future can and should move past these limitations. Legal developments in cyberspace over the past decade or so have demonstrated that there are a number of unique aspects of Internet communications that support a cyberlaw field. The key to the field is the role of online intermediaries; in particular, balancing the need to foster innovation in online services with the need to impose certain liabilities on intermediaries in order to prevent online harms to Internet users. If the global law and policy community can focus more directly on the role of the online intermediary, a more principled, predictable and cohesive set of cyberlaw regulations should emerge.

## 7. Sources and Further Reading

Easterbrook, Frank, "Cyberspace and the Law of the Horse", in *University of Chicago Legal Forum*, 1996, p. 207.

Grimmelman, James, "The Structure of Search Engine Law", in *Iowa Law Review*, 2007, vol. 93, no.1.

Lastowka, Greg, "Google's Law", in *Brooklyn Law Review*, 2008, vol. 73, p. 1327.

Lessig, Lawrence, *Code Version 2.0*, Basic Books, 2006.

Lessig, Lawrence, "The Law of the Horse: What Cyberlaw Might Teach", in *Harvard Law Review*, 1999, vol. 113, p. 501.

Moffat, Viva, "Regulating Search", in *Harvard Journal of Law and Technology*, 2009, vol. 22, p. 475.

Reidenberg, Joel, "Lex Informatica: The Formulation of Information Policy Rules Through Technology", in *Texas Law Review,* 1998, vol. 76, p. 553.

**Cases**

*Perfect 10 v Google*, 508 F. 3d 1146, 9th Cir. 2007.

*Perfect 10 v Visa International Service Association*, 494 F. 3d 788, 9th Cir. 2007.

# 3.2.

# The Future of Cyberlaw

**Rolf H. Weber***

Early cyberlaw perceptions (as an area without rules or as a code-dominated area) are not suited to survive in the future. Moreover, only information policy rules developed by civil society (in the form of soft or informal 'law', similar to customary law) meet the required legitimacy and design for cyberlaw. Thereby, an angle function is played by the information intermediaries; in a world of changing technologies, procedural rules must gain importance, in particular governance elements (multi-stakeholder approach), organisational elements (appropriate decision-making structures) and dispute settlement elements (imposing disciplinary and enforcement powers).

## 1. Early Cyberlaw Perceptions

### 1.1. Cyberspace as Area without Rules

In 1996 John Perry Barlow emphatically pronounced in his manifesto Declaration of Independence the belief:

> Governments […] You have neither solicited nor received ours. We did not invite you. You do not know us, nor do you know our world. Cyberspace does not lie within your borders

This concept assumes that cyberspace consists of a 'net nation', based on the analogy that most laws were conceived in and for a world of atoms rather than bits. In the meantime, netizens and scholars are less euphoric about the independence of, and particularly the lack of a legal environment, in cyberspace. Hectic legislative activity all over the world has shown that governments are indeed concerned about the 'legalisation' of cyberspace. Therefore, the concept of cyberspace as an area without rules cannot be a model for the future.

---

* **Rolf H. Weber** is Chair Professor for International Business Law at the University of Zurich, Switzerland, Visiting Professor at the Hong Kong University, Hong Kong, Director of the Center for Information and Communication Law of the University of Zurich, Attorney-at-Law in Zurich.

Equally, cyberspace law should not be regarded an ephemeral garden such as the law of the horse, having been (partly) controversially discussed by Judge Frank Easterbrook and Lawrence Lessig. As a result of this exchange of arguments, it can be said that cyberspace requires a new way of thinking and that law needs to shift its emphasis. In fact, cyberlaw seems to have become increasingly all-encompassing as well as a meta-field function.

### 1.2. Cyberspace as Code-Dominated Area

In the light of a perceived dissatisfaction with the regulatory models discussed in the early years of the Internet, Lawrence Lessig developed a more technically oriented approach, the so-called "code-based regulation", in 1999. Since technical elements play an important role in cyberspace, a technology-oriented theoretical approach seems more appropriate. According to Lessig, human behaviour is governed by a complex interrelation between four forces, namely law, markets, social norms and architecture. Code solutions, similar to legal rules, principally reflect 'information' that allocates and enforces entitlements. The design of the code materially influences human behaviour since architecture is one of the four 'regulators'; depending on the architecture, certain activities will be possible or difficult to carry out. Therefore, Lessig arrives at a world in which code can do much of the work that the law used to do, and far more effectively than the law did. Consequently, effective regulatory power shifts from law to code-based on an effective architectural framework.

However, Lessig's approach relating the code/architecture to the control paradigm has not remained uncontested: the aspect of established control structures has political impacts. Furthermore, courts should impose checks on the powers of private regulators where the respective regulation threatens important collective values. Consequently, the code/architecture model is not suited to replace a legal framework in whatever shape it might be developed.

## 2. General Foundations for Cyberlaw

The described legal perceptions show how difficult it might be to foresee the future legal environment in cyberspace, which is much more difficult than forecasting developments in natural sciences, as for example many drawings of Leonardo da Vinci or the science fiction books of Jules Verne show. Indeed William Gibson, who coined the term 'cyberspace', said in his novel Neuromancer (1984) that the future is always here, just unevenly distributed.

### 2.1. Legitimacy and Design of Legal Norms

Legal norms do not only need formal legitimacy in the sense that the norms are 'codified' through an acceptable law-making process, but also material legitimacy in the sense that people accept the necessity and/or the desirability of a given legal framework. In general, individuals and organisations tend to comply with rules and regulations and citizens are usually law-abiding. However, this kind of 'acknowledgement' might not be easily achievable in cyberspace. Therefore, lawmakers of whatever nature should keep in mind that legal norms will only be applied in reality if the addressees of the norms consider their imposition fair and adequate. In cyberspace, the concept of the 'social contract', leading to rules of behaviour through individual conviction and tacit consent, is difficult to realise.

Furthermore, the rapid technological developments in cyberspace do have important political and social consequences: (i) science and new technology, if developed in a future-oriented way, can question political structures and powers by causing an unsettling effect, as the examples of Galileo Galilei and the Arab spring revolutions have shown, and (ii) technologies need to comply with social expectations, namely their availability to the civil society, their social and commercial acceptability as well as their implementation in an appropriate way as seen from a cultural perspective.

As far as the design of legal rules is concerned, their creation makes sense if the application is likely to be effective. In practice, this legislative element means that legal norms should not try to follow a highly complicated path with many variables. A deep-rooted approach to law might be sophisticated, but not satisfactory in view of the need to have the legal rules accepted and applied in the (real) society.

### 2.2. Information Policy Rules

(i) In cyberspace, information policy rules designed by technology can be developed as *lex informatica*. Such a concept of *lex informatica* is comparable to the *lex mercatoria* established by merchants over the last few centuries, encompassing a legal body independent of local sovereign rules ensuring commercial participants a basic fairness in their relationships. Often, such a legal source is called soft law.

(ii) A first concept of *lex informatica* has been described by Joel R. Reidenberg, composed of a set of rules for information flows imposed by technology and communication networks which policy makers must understand. Reidenberg analyses three substantive topics, namely content, personal information, and ownership rights; thereby, the *lex informatica* follows an open approach as the systems configurations allow two types of substantive rules, namely immutable policies embedded in technology standards and flexible policies embedded in the technical architecture.

The strength of the *lex informatica* can be seen in the introduction of flexible standards, based upon the technological environment, enabling customisation of configurations. The flexibility and openness, however, is not without disadvantages: an adequate legal framework requires a minimum of predictability in order to establish reliable relations between persons; furthermore, the democratic legitimacy of 'policy makers' being in charge of setting the framework for technical solutions could be debatable.

(iii) In a similar way, Warren Chik analysed the disjuncture between the law and practices in cyberspace caused by the information technologies' developments including the socio-economic problems and proposed the framework of 'Internet-ional' legal principles based on the history of merchants' customs as a source of law. This approach underlines the suitability of customary international rules as a template for formulating cyberspace law-making rules by adapting customary rules to develop a set of determinants for cyberspace law.

(iv) Taking a social structure perspective Yochai Benkler has sketched a theory of social production in the information environment, which appears to be marked by collaborative forms of development being common-based (relying on a common goal of informational resources) or peer-produced (based on decentralised creative inputs). Thereby, Benkler intends to take care of the effects that law can have through the way it structures the relationships among people with regard to the information environment they occupy. Insofar, structural foundations are laid down in his approach optimistically designed as arising organically. According to Benkler the structure of the information environment is constitutive of the citizens' autonomy, not only functionally significant to it, leading to the assumption of trust in the empowerment of the individuals, rather than in the political system giving the structural contours of the environment.

(v) From the described concepts looking at information policy rules, the lesson that can be drawn consists in the assessment that the information intermediaries will play a crucial role in future cyberlaw. The intermediaries are the angle of the communication channels giving them a control function charged with the corresponding accountability and responsibility obligation. Therefore, the legal rights and responsibilities of the information intermediaries are becoming an important issue for future cyberlaw. Furthermore, due to the global character of the Internet, the impact of conflicts of law principles on the regulatory norms in cyberspace merits particular attention, at least to the extent that internationally accepted customary rules are not the prevailing states' norms.

## 3. Structural Elements for Future Cyberlaw

The description of the different scenarios that could lead to a legal order in cyberspace has shown that new approaches are needed for the future. In fact, it appears to be uncontested that normativity exists beyond States. Therefore, in a future-oriented perspective soft law and informational law should have an increased importance. An evolutionary approach needs to encompass substantive and procedural elements; in light of the rapidly changing technologies, any approach solely relying on substantive elements risks to loose material grounds within short time intervals. Therefore, procedural elements seem to be better suited to comply with the "needs" of an uncertain future. Three main issues in this respect are subsequently discussed, namely the governance elements, the organisational elements and the dispute settlement elements (following Weber, 2012).

### 3.1. Governance Elements

Future cyberlaw is designed on the basis of specific new governance principles; as typical assays of a more global governance, the following aspects are to be addressed:

- Governance should refer to an order, characterised in part by porous borders and power sharing amongst State, non-State actors, and geographic and/or functional entities.
- Governance must encompass collective efforts enabling the concerned persons to identify, understand and address worldwide problems going beyond the capacity of individual States to solve.

Consequently, future cyberlaw problems require by their nature a broader and more collective decision-making than in the past; the different interests and needs calls for the establishment of multi-level mechanisms ensuring that the voices of all concerned participants are heard and appreciated.

The absence of hierarchical structures and the fact that responses to new issues are complex should be acknowledged. Flat structures on different appropriate levels facilitate the decision-making by including the relevant persons and organisations at the actual point of their respective concern. In the context of Internet governance, the UN-formed Working Group on Internet Governance in 2005 identified a number of roles and responsibilities various stakeholders (governments, commercial world, civil society, academic and technical community) have; this definition still remains viable throughout the annual meetings of the Internet Governance Forum as well as in the context of the preparation of legal instruments by the Council of Europe.

An adequate governance approach should realise a participatory mechanism that reflects the view of the whole society. Therefore, future governance must be seen as a broad array of changes in the distribution of authority, legitimacy, accountability, decision-making and participation by individuals and organisations in ordering human society, in response to similarly broad changes to material, social, technological, and economic conditions. Consequently, in increased interconnectedness and complexity of life must be taken into account, leading to the formation of legitimisation of these aggregated networks of sub- or cross-State communities as rule-producing and rule-enforcing actors.

### 3.2. Organisational Elements

Whatever the quality of law will be in the future, organisational elements need to be addressed: a stable order will only be realisable if the degree of 'organisation' of the concerned persons is high, since in such a situation the implementation (and enforcement) of harmonised standards is facilitated. As past experience has shown, the implementation of autonomous soft law and non-State standards – based on the principle that they are considered by the concerned persons as the benchmark for behaviour – can lead to a gradual process of institutionalisation.

Therefore States, international organisations and inter-governmental bodies have increasingly recognised that soft law released by private persons is usually modern and dynamic; it also allows the implementation of appropriate decision-making structures. Sufficient coverage with adequate reputational and retaliatory tools can generate an acceptable degree of compliance. Reputational constraints are usually derived from the fact that illegitimacy itself creates 'costs', that is, members in standard-setting bodies must keep reputational discipline by refraining from overtly biased or self-serving decision-making.

If reputation is seen as an important factor in social life, civil society will act according to (aligned) incentives with the public interest; this is even more the case with market participants in business matters. In fact, neither regimes nor States have a fixed nature or self-evident objectives. This means that the degree to which rules are binding should not be conflated with whether they imply a formal legislative obligation; insofar, hard law and soft law are not dichotomous or qualitatively different forms of regulatory control. Lack in confidence in the organisational law and scepticism about the legal system is detrimental, and cannot be helpful in relation to the institution that provides a framework within which the civil society and commercial world should operate. Looking at the future of cyberlaw, it also seems to be unavoidable that new dimensions of global administrative law are to be explored, covering aspects of accountability, institutional differentiation and elaborated procedural techniques.

### 3.3. Dispute Settlement Elements

The establishment of an effective dispute settlement mechanism with the objective to complement and 'enforce' soft law is of major importance in order to attribute higher reputation to the respective new rules. Basic questions are: how should 'norms' be enforced? How can conflicts be resolved? As experience shows the possibility of invoking a dispute settlement mechanism tends to lead to better voluntary compliance with the rules. The term dispute settlement mechanism should be understood in a broad way, encompassing not only juridical 'proceedings' in a traditional form (such as state court procedures and arbitration), but also all thinkable forms of mediation. During the last two decades, different forms of alternative dispute resolution (ADR) mechanisms have been developed (such as the Uniform Dispute Resolution Policy of ICANN/WIPO); these models apply different forms of binding effects and range from negotiated solutions to clear recommendations and finally to enforceable judgments. The suitability of the manifold approaches depends on the given circumstances.

Dispute settlement mechanisms can equally be necessary to clarify which legal obligations are eventually incomplete or inadequate; insofar, the dispute settlement is able to establish the predicate for, and limit the scope of, retaliation. The availability of dispute settlement mechanisms also is a pre-condition for the introduction of (reputational or monetary) sanctions; examples could be the imposition of some sort of disciplinary and enforcement powers, attaching costs to the failure of complying with applicable rules. However, such a 'sanctioning' is only possible if adequate mechanisms allow the business world and the civil society to get hold of the relevant information constituting the basis for achieving redress.

## 4. Outlook

When designing future cyberlaw, legal scholars must take into account the function of law: what social impacts should be caused by law? The answer is that it should be founded on the expectations of civil society. For people to live together it is necessary to have meta-institutional structures that allow wide-spread participation by way of a multi-stakeholder model. Furthermore, governance elements are to be implemented, which encompass collective efforts enabling proper identification and understanding of worldwide problems needed for global solutions. In addition, organisational elements can provide for adequate procedural frameworks and dispute settlement mechanisms that are in a position to strengthen the accountability of all involved members of States' powers, commercial businesses and civil society.

## 5. Sources and Further Reading

Barlow, John Perry, "Declaration of Independence", available at http://www.eff.org/pub/Publications/John_Perry_Barlow/barlow0296.declaration, last accessed on 1 August 2012.

Benkler, Yochai, *The Wealth of Networks: How Social Production Transforms Markets and Freedom*, Yale University Press, The Haven/London, 2006.

Chik, Warren, "'Customary Internet-ional Law': Creating a Body of Customary Law for Cyberspace. Part I: Developing Rules for Transitioning Custom into Law", in *Computer Law and Security Review*, 2010, vol. 26, no. 2, pp. 185–202.

Easterbrook, Frank H., "Cyberspace and the Law of the Horse", in *The University of Chicago Legal Forum*, 1996.

Lessig, Lawrence, *Codes and Other Laws of Cyberspace*, Basic Books, New York, 1999.

Lessig, Lawrence, *Code Version 2.0*, Basic Books, New York, 2006.

Lessig, Lawrence, "The Law of the Horse: What Cyberlaw Might Teach", in *Harvard Law Review*, 1999, vol. 113, p. 501.

Murray, Andrew D., *The Regulation of Cyberspace: Control in the Online Environment*, Routledge-Cavendish, New York, 2007.

Reidenberg, Joel R., "Lex Informatica: The Formulation of Information Policy Rules through Technology", in *Texas Law Review*, 1998, vol. 76, p. 553.

Weber, Rolf H., "Future Design of Cyberspace Law", in *Journal of Politics and Law*, 2012, vol. 5, no. 4.

Weber, Rolf H., *Regulatory Models for the Online World*, Kluwer Law International, The Hague, 2002.

# 3.3.

## Defining A Neurocompatibility Index for Criminal Justice Systems: A Framework to Align Social Policy with Modern Brain Science

**David M. Eagleman*** **and Sarah Isgur Flores****

Criminal jurisprudence is often driven more by intuition and political needs than by evidence-based science. As a result, criminal laws frequently prove sub-optimal and inefficacious. As a guideline for improvement, we here define a neurocompatibility index: seven criteria to measure the degree to which a system of criminal justice is compatible with the lessons of modern science. These include: (1) understanding of mental illness, (2) methods of rehabilitation, (3) individualised sentencing based on risk assessment, (4) eyewitness identification standards, (5) specialised court systems, (6) incentive structuring based on psychology, and (7) a minimum standard of science education for policy-makers. As demonstrated in the ideas outlined here, a brain-compatible system prizes fairness and long-term crime prevention over harsh yet inconsequential punishment.

### 1. Introduction

While systems of criminal law have traditionally rested on intuitions about blameworthiness and punishment, the resulting policies sometimes result in low efficacy and high cost. Jails have become a prime recruitment point for gangs, and long prison sentences often leave the newly released with little ability to re-enter as productive members of society. These factors, along with many others associated with current norms in criminal justice, lead to high recidivism rates and increasingly high social and monetary costs to the communities in which they operate.

* **David Eagleman**, Ph.D., directs the Initiative on Neuroscience and Law (www.NeuLaw.org). He holds joint appointments in the departments of Neuroscience and Psychiatry at Baylor College of Medicine.

** **Sarah Isgur Flores**, J.D., is a graduate of Harvard Law School and a Research Fellow at the Initiative on Neuroscience and Law.

To improve this situation, criminal justice systems could draw great benefit from a deeper engagement with the lessons of modern science. In a biologically-informed, evidence-based system of law, criminals would continue to be taken off the streets – but with customised sentencing, new opportunities for rehabilitation, and more realistic incentives for pro-social behaviour. Alignment with the lessons of brain science suggests a new way forward for law and order – one that will lead to a more cost-effective, humane, and flexible system, benefiting both the convicted and the communities into which they are eventually released.

A basic starting point – one that is obvious in biology but not usually broached in legal or political circles – is the fact that individual brains are quite different. Along any axis we measure such as aggression, empathy, impulse-control, capacity to simulate possible futures, and risk aversion, we find that brains are distributed along a spectrum. While it is charitable to imagine that all adults possess the same capacity to make sound choices, it is a demonstrably incorrect assumption. In truth, brains are as individualised as fingerprints. We are each constructed from a genetic blueprint, and then born into a world of circumstances that we cannot control in our most formative years. The complex intertwining of genes and environment means that all citizens – equal before the law – possess different perspectives, varied personalities, and dissimilar styles of decision-making.

By allowing criminal laws to account for the deeply embedded neural programmes that steer our perceptions and behaviours, we can imagine a transition from blameworthiness to biology. This is because the assignment of blameworthiness demands the impossible task of untangling the hopelessly complex web of genetics and environment that constructs the trajectory of a human life. In place of this, we suggest that the assignment of blameworthiness is sometimes less important and should be subsumed by the larger assessment of what to do, moving forward. How likely are criminal actions to be repeated? Can this person be helped towards pro-social behaviour? How can incentives be realistically structured to deter crime?

There is no reason why social policy should not be designed as rigorously as any science experiment, leveraging a dispassionate view of the available data to optimise the utility of our money and efforts. The price of ignoring the science is over- and under-inclusive prison systems at high social costs to the larger communities they are designed to serve. Not all crime can be prevented, but when it happens, the perpetrators can be treated in a way that maximises their chance for re-integration into society instead of a process of enduring exclusion.

Before diving into the main argument, it is crucial to clarify one point: an improved biological understanding of human behaviour will not exculpate anyone; we will still remove from the streets lawbreakers who prove unable to conform their behaviours to the societal norms. In other words, an evidence-based system will not lead to excuses for anti-social behaviour or remove all the retributive elements that underlie criminal justice systems. It will instead place ideas of punishment and retribution in their larger biological context, improving the customisation with which we can respond to the vast range of criminal acts.

In the following section we will outline a neurocompatibility index. This measure comprises seven criteria to quantify how well a system of criminal law is compatible with the lessons of modern science. Measured against this neurocompatibility index, most countries in the world today fall short of a satisfactory score. Our future work will seek to rank all nations on this index.

## 2. A Neurocompatibility Index for Systems of Criminal Law around the World

### 2.1. Understanding Mental Illness

A criminal justice system informed by neuroscience will allow us to move beyond treating prison as a one-size-fits-all solution. To be clear, the authors of this paper are not opposed to incarceration. For many people, it provides both warehousing and future deterrence, to themselves and others. In some sense, prison is the original rewire-the-brain rehabilitation strategy.

But behavioural adjustment based on this sort of punishment works only for individuals whose brains are functioning in such a way as to appreciate the nature of the punishment as an effect of their actions. For those with various kinds of mental illnesses, exacting punishment has no utility because there is no way to tie it to their actions. Their brains are incapable of modifying accordingly.

Unfortunately, in many countries prisons have become *de facto* mental health care facilities. In America, for example, current estimates place the percentage of mentally ill at 35 per cent. This staggering number leads to an enormous strain on a prison system that has little to no hope of serving any kind of deterrence role in their future behaviour.

Despite recognition of mental illnesses going back to the Romans and Greeks, all modern societies have struggled with how best to deal with those guilty of a criminal act but unable to appreciate the consequences of their actions or conform those actions to societal norms. Many western countries still use an insanity defence that dates back to the mid-19th century. At the same time, studies have shown that of the less than one per cent of defendants who plead insanity in the United States, fewer than one in four are successful, and of those that are, 90 per cent have been previously diagnosed with a mental illness.

In large part, the United States' struggle to define mental illness in the 20th century highlights the difficulty inherent in this question, but also the need for such standards. And it exemplifies the need for all societies to understand mental illness, its causes, and what can be done to treat it or control its effects to be able to promulgate effective rules and standards in criminal proceedings. This translates into a need for the de-stigmatisation of mental illness and, resultingly, a meaningful insanity defence in every jurisdiction in the world.

A better understanding of mental illness comes with improved rehabilitative strategies for dealing with it, which leads to our next prong.

### 2.2. Methods of Rehabilitation

Worldwide, the most common method of dealing with law breakers appears to be incarceration. Beyond its physical costs, however, incarceration also comes with social consequences. First, it breaks an individual's social circles and employment opportunities. Especially for young people, the collateral consequences of jail time include an inability to earn a college grant, or, more generally, to optimise a career trajectory. Second, it introduces the incarcerated to prison social norms and social circles that are at odds with the interests of their community and often lead to drug use and gang membership both during a prison term and after.

A neurocompatible criminal justice system translates biological understanding into customised rehabilitation, viewing some aspects of criminal behaviour the way we understand conditions such as epilepsy, schizophrenia, and depression.

Although rehabilitation was previously seen as too expensive and politically unpalatable, many people now recognise the long-term cost effectiveness of rehabilitating offenders instead of packing them into overcrowded prisons. In California, for example, the prison system was required to release 30,000 inmates due to overcrowding, many of whom were incarcerated for non-violent drug offences. Without drug treatment, the chances of recidivism for these inmates are high and will create a negative feedback loop both for the prisoners and the taxpayers. But the challenge in this area has been the dearth of new ideas about how to rehabilitate.

A better understanding of the brain offers new ideas. For example, consider the fact that poor impulse control is a hallmark characteristic of the majority of those locked in the prison system. Whether as a result of anger or temptation, their actions override reasoned consideration of the future.

If it seems difficult to empathise with people who have poor impulse control, just think of all the things we all succumb to against our better judgement. Another martini? Late night pints of ice cream? Reality TV? It is not that individuals do not know what is best for them; it is simply that the frontal lobe circuits representing long-term considerations do not always win elections against short-term desire when temptation is present.

This line of reasoning suggests new strategies for rehabilitation to allow an individual to have better control of his behaviour, even in the absence of external authority. With Steven LaConte at Virginia Tech, we are developing a new approach, one that springs from the understanding that the brain operates like a team of rivals: a competition among different neural populations to control the single output channel of behaviour. Because it is a competition, the outcome can be tipped.

The basic approach is to give the frontal lobes practice in squelching the short-term circuits. To this end, we have begun leveraging real-time feedback to participants during brain imaging. This technique allows them to see when their brain is craving, and to learn how to control (in this case, to lower) that neural activity by strengthening other, long-term decision-making mechanisms. The approach leaves the brain intact – no drugs or surgery – and uses the natural mechanisms of brain plasticity to help the brain help itself. After training for better impulse control, a person may still crave cigarettes (or cocaine or someone else's wallet), but he will know how to win over the craving instead of letting it win over him.

This science of this 'frontal lobe workout' is at its very earliest stages, but we have hope that the approach represents the correct model: it is simultaneously well grounded in biology and libertarian ethics, allowing a person to help himself to better long-term decision-making.

At its most basic level, effective treatment options would help those who want to help themselves. Whether for those already in prison or for preventative treatment with individuals who are aware that they are at risk of anti-social behaviours, effective treatment methods offer people an opportunity to stay out of the system – a sort of voluntary preventative medicine that would reduce the burden placed on prisons and improve economic development in neighbourhoods devastated by drugs and drug-related crimes.

## 2.3. Individualised Sentencing Based on Risk Assessment

A neurocompatible criminal justice system provides for individual risk assessment. While no system should treat similarly situated individuals differently, neither should a fair system fail to account for the differences.

The common law in Western countries is already forward-looking in some respects. For example, it has long been the case that crimes of passion (for example, reacting violently when catching a spouse's lover) are subject to lower penalties than a premeditated murder. Those who commit the former are less likely to recidivate than those who commit the latter, and their sentences sensibly reflect that. Likewise, most systems of law draw a bright line between criminal acts committed by minors and those by adults, punishing the latter more harshly. This approach has low resolution, but the intuition behind it is sound: adolescents command different skills in decision-making and impulse control than do adults. It is appropriate to give lighter sentences to those whose impulse control is likely to improve naturally as adolescence gives way to adulthood.

Taking a more scientific approach to sentencing, case by case, could move us beyond these limited examples. Consider the important changes that are happening in the sentencing of sex offenders. Several years ago, American researchers began to ask psychiatrists and parole board members how likely it was that individual sex offenders would relapse when let out of prison. Both the psychiatrists and the parole board members had experience with the offenders in question, as well as with hundreds before them – so predicting who would go straight and who would come back was not difficult.

Or was it? The surprise outcome was that their guesses showed almost no correlation with the actual outcomes. The psychiatrists and parole board members had the same predictive accuracy as coin-flipping. This result astounded the research community, especially given the expectation of well-refined intuitions among those who work directly with offenders.

So researchers next tried a more actuarial approach. They set about measuring dozens of factors from 22,500 sex offenders who were about to be released. At the end of the study, they computed which factors best explained the reoffence rates, and from those data they were able to build actuarial tables to be used in sentencing.

As it turned out, when one compared the predictive power of the actuarial approach to that of the parole boards and psychiatrists, there was no contest: numbers won over intuitions to an astounding degree. In many courtrooms, these actuarial tests are now used in pre-sentencing to modulate the length of prison terms based on the risk offenders pose once released.

It will always be impossible to know with certainty what someone will do upon release from prison – a person's brain and experiences will never be fully quantifiable. But more predictive power is hidden in the numbers than people customarily expect. Statistically-based sentencing will be imperfect, but it nonetheless allows evidence to win over folk-intuition, and it offers customisation in place of blunt guidelines.

## 2.4. Eyewitness Identification Standards

A neurocompatible criminal justice system follows the foundational principle that the protection of the innocent trumps the prosecution of the guilty. No one is served when innocent defendants are convicted – not only is a productive member of society removed, but the guilty member is enabled to reoffend.

Television and popular culture tell us that DNA and fingerprints are used in nearly every case to ensure the conviction of the guilty. But in many cases eyewitness testimony is used as the main evidence against the defendant. This type of evidence is often persuasive because jurors, just like the witness, believe that their memories are like movies or photographs that can be recalled as objective truth.

In reality, memory can be highly unreliable, and eyewitness testimony is often plagued with errors. A victim is likely to be focused on the weapon being used against them and heavily affected by stress. The Innocence Project, an American organisation which uses DNA evidence to overturn wrongful convictions, reports that 73 per cent of their wrongful convictions were the result of mistaken eyewitness testimony and, of those, a third rested on the testimony of more than one mistaken eyewitness.

More needs to be done to curb the failures inherent in this type of evidence. While eyewitness testimony can never be eliminated from criminal proceedings, three decades of cognitive science literature suggest safeguards that can be put in place to ensure that these identifications are unbiased and put in their proper context during investigations and trials.

Several studies have confirmed a number of reforms that would drastically improve the reliability of eyewitness line-ups. For example, the police may give unconscious cues to a witness when reviewing a line-up. It has been shown that when the police officer administering the line-up is also not aware of who the suspect is, the rate of incorrect identification drops significantly.

New technologies will also continue to offer opportunities for improvement – for example, using iPads to display suspects' photos at the scene of a crime, before memory has moved too far along the forgetting curve.

### 2.5. Specialised Court Systems

Because some crimes are the result of inherently different impulses from others, a neurocompatible criminal justice system utilises specialised court systems that embed expertise with issues ranging from mental illness, drug addiction, and juvenile decision-making. By separating the courts in which these crimes are tried, the judges and lawyers involved are better able to address the specific needs of their communities and those on trial.

In many countries, family courts are already separated from other civil proceedings because of the level of expertise and uniqueness involved with divorce and child custody issues. The same is often true for purely statutory violations such as speeding or expired registration stickers. And yet, most criminal courts may only distinguish between felony and misdemeanour cases, meaning that the same judge tries murder and copyright violations. Relatedly, while some district attorneys' offices assign prosecutors to a specific division of crime, many do not – and the same prosecutor who tried a 17-year old gang member the week before may try a 50-year old paedophile the next.

By being forced to become repeat players in specific areas, judges and lawyers are more likely to understand that the intersection of an individual's motivations and capacities allows more refined treatment options, presumably with better societal and financial outcomes. After all, the same crime can be committed by very different brains for very different reasons.

Collectively, specialised court systems provide people with an opportunity to receive more informed sentencing, counselling, and rehabilitation, thereby enhancing their chances of staying out of the prison system.

## 2.6. Incentive Structuring

A neurocompatible criminal justice system is interested in tailoring incentives to have the greatest positive impact on behaviour. With a better biological understanding of how people actually behave (as opposed to general models of how they are hypothesised to behave, or should behave), there are several opportunities to optimise approaches in social policy.

To give one example, it has become clear that brains are more like a parliament of competing interests than a unitary executive version of the self. Just as in any parliament, some parties are prone to short-term decision-making while others are invested in the long term. These parties battle it out before reaching a decision, and we often find that the short-term party wins out more often in people that commit crimes.

As a result, people often appreciate the negative long-term consequences of their decision-making (prison), but find the impulses (wanting someone else's money) winning out nonetheless. In this light, one way to leverage this understanding is to build the incentive structure of a given penal system to help the long-term party win the day.

One approach, advocated by the policy scholar Mark Kleiman, is to ramp up the certainty and swiftness of punishment. For example, a drug offender may be required to submit to three-times-a-week drug testing and, if the test is failed, the offender is automatically sanctioned rather than simply facing the possibility of a future court date that would eventually lead to an uncertain sanction down the road. A similar program, Hawaii's Opportunity Probation with Enforcement, has led to a drop in re-arrest rates from 47 per cent to 21 per cent. By this same logic, economists have suggested that the drop in crime since the 1980s has been due, in part, to the increased presence of police on the streets: their mere presence shores up support for the parts of the brain that consider long-term consequences.

There are innumerable ways to tailor incentives to match our current understanding of the biological processes in the brain. A neurocompatible criminal justice system would find ways to decrease crime and recidivism by creating probation and parole systems that work with, rather than against, the decision methods offenders employ.

### 2.7. A Minimum Standard of Science Education for Policy-Makers

Nearly every state in America requires lawyers to spend some number of hours (usually around 15 a year) educating themselves on developments within the legal system. A neurocompatible criminal justice system would have a similar requirement for science education for judges, lawyers, law-makers, and parole officers who practise in this field.

Those involved in the day-to-day workings of our criminal justice systems should neither ignore nor exaggerate the relevant science. Just as the public once had to be educated on DNA evidence, parole boards should be equally aware of the social science relating to recidivism. At the same time, it is equally important for these repeat players to be told what science is not capable of telling us – for example, the idea that genetics would ever be able to tell us anything detailed about individual behaviour.

Changing the opinions and knowledge base of those involved in writing and executing our criminal laws is crucial to the full integration of successful treatment and sentencing options into the courts.

## 3. Conclusion

We have outlined a series of recommendations by which a criminal justice system could become more neurocompatible – that is, aligned with current knowledge about human brain science and psychology

Fundamentally, many issues relating to criminal justice systems around the world fall within the domain – or at least the penumbra – of a more refined understanding of human behaviour. A forward-thinking legal system informed by scientific insights into the brain will enable us to move beyond treating prison as a one-size-fits-all solution. From tailored sentencing to customised rehabilitation, these recommendations will allow a community to remove and isolate criminal behaviour while increasing the likelihood that those released from prison will return as productive and pro-social assets to the communities they are re-entering.

It should also be clear that today no country would score perfectly on the neurocompatibility index. Every criminal system has some distance to go before any can be said to be fully in line with modern knowledge about human behaviour and crime. The index here, however, can be viewed as 'best practice' standards based on a modern view of neurolaw. In other words, this neurocompatibility index sets up a series of guidelines by which governments and policy-makers can consider the inclusion of modern science into their criminal justice systems.

Finally, the issues outlined here mean that the lawyers and judges of the future will be handed a very different set of tools before entering their field. In addition to their current studies of legal history and concepts, these future practitioners will also possess a bedrock understanding of science, mental illness, eyewitness identification, opportunities for rehabilitation, and realistic ideas of how our brains process both the good and bad decisions each of us is faced with on a daily basis.

## 4. Sources and Further Reading

Bumann, Benjamin and Eagleman, David M., "Intuitions of Blameworthiness as a Heuristic that Evaluates the Probability of the Offender Committing Future Antisocial Acts", in *Thurgood Marshall Law Journal*, 2012, vol. 36, no. 2, pp. 129–155.

Chorvat, Terrence and McCabe, Kevin, "The Law and the Brain", in *Philosophical Transactions of the Royal Society Biological Sciences*, 2005, vol. 358, pp. 1727–1736.

Eagleman, David M., *Incognito: The Secret Lives of the Brain*, Pantheon, New York, 2011.

Eagleman, David M., The Brain on Trial, The Atlantic, 2011.

Eagleman, David M., Turning Our Minds to the Law, The Telegraph, 5 April 2011.

Eagleman, David M. and Correro, Mark A., Singh, Jyotpal, "Why Neuroscience Matters for a Rational Drug Policy", in *Minnesota Journal of Law, Science and Technology*, 2010.

Erickson, Patricia E. and Erickson, Steven K., *Crime, Punishment, and Mental Illness: Law and the Behavioral Sciences in Conflict*, Rutgers University Press, 2008.

Greely, Henry T., "Law and the Revolution in Neuroscience", in *Akron Law Review*, 2009, vol. 42, p. 687.

Hanson, Karl R. and Morton-Bourgon, Kelly E., "The Characteristics of Persistent Sexual Offenders: A Meta-Analysis of Recidivism Studies", in *Journal of Consulting and Clinical Psychology*, 2005, vol. 73, no. 6, pp. 1154–1163.

Jolls, Christine, "Behavioral Law and Economics", in Diamond and Vartiainen (eds.), *Behavioral Economics and Its Applications*, Princeton University Press, 2007.

Jones, Owen D., "Law and Behavioral Biology", in *Columbia Law Review*, 2005, vol. 105, pp. 405–502.

Sapolsky, Robert M., "The Frontal Cortex and the Criminal Justice System", in *Philosophical Transactions of the Royal Society Biological Sciences*, 2004, pp. 1787–1796.

Wellsk, Gary L and Quinlivan, Deah S, "Suggestive Eyewitness Identification Procedures and the Supreme Court's Reliability Test in Light of Eyewitness Science", in *Law and Human Behavior*, 2009, vol. 33, pp.1–24.

Note: A few sentences in this paper have appeared previously in David M. Eagleman, The Brain on Trial, The Atlantic, 2011.

# 3.4.

# Geoengineering's Thermostat Dilemma

**Albert Lin**[*]

Geoengineering is gaining attention as a possible tool for ameliorating climate change. These largely untested techniques are sometimes analogised to a thermostat that will enable humans to fine-tune the Earth's climate. Although overly simplistic, this metaphor highlights a fundamental dilemma that the capacity to geoengineer would raise: whose hand should control the thermostat? Unpacking this question exposes multiple issues warranting careful research and debate: (1) which nations should decide; (2) what role scientists and other expert communities should have in the decision making process; (3) what role non-State actors should have in the process; (4) how to account for the interests and preferences of future generations; and (5) what mechanisms should be in place to ensure compliance with decisions agreed upon. From the standpoint of organising collective action, geoengineering is relatively unproblematic because a single nation may have the resources and technical capacity to undertake geoengineering on its own. However, as the thermostat metaphor reveals, geoengineering will present extremely difficult challenges of law, policy making, and ethics for the international community.

## 1. Introduction

Geoengineering refers to a variety of unconventional and often controversial proposals for responding to climate change. These methods include: spraying tiny sulphur particles into the atmosphere to block the sun's radiation, fertilising the ocean to stimulate phytoplankton growth that might store carbon in the oceans, and the like. Geoengineering technologies are far from mature, as no geoengineering techniques are ready to be deployed, and thus no full-scale geoengineering projects have been undertaken. Moreover, even if some geoengineering techniques are perfected

* **Albert Lin** is Professor of Law at the University of California, Davis School of Law, where he specialises in environmental and natural resources law and also teaches evidence.

one day, they are unlikely to constitute a complete and permanent solution to climate change. Nonetheless, geoengineering proposals raise the prospect of choosing a climate for the planet. Accordingly, geoengineering is sometimes likened to a thermostat for the Earth, a metaphor that highlights a critical question: who should control the thermostat?

To be sure, the thermostat metaphor is overly simplistic. Similar to the term "global warming", the metaphor focuses too narrowly on average temperature rise. Climate change poses a grave threat not only because of hotter temperatures, but also because of rising oceans, more powerful storms, more frequent droughts, and other expected climate effects. The thermostat metaphor potentially trivialises climate change in suggesting that the problem is merely a matter of comfort. Furthermore, the analogy both overstates the degree of control that humans have over the Earth's complex climate systems and understates the technical difficulties of implementation. Geoengineering proposals involve various risks and uncertainties that we are only beginning to explore. These risks and uncertainties are magnified by the incomplete climate models on which we rely. In addition, adverse effects of geoengineering are likely to vary from one region to another, suggesting that no climate setting will be without objection. Finally, the thermostat analogy gives short shrift to the effects of climate change on other living things. The comparison encourages a utilitarian, anthropocentric mindset that obscures ethical consideration of other species and the environment. Ultimately, the thermostat metaphor represents a potentially dangerous framing of climate issues that could foster complacency and undermine more realistic and important responses to climate change.

Notwithstanding its serious shortcomings, the thermostat metaphor does capture a dilemma that looms over the geoengineering debate: who should decide whether and how geoengineering is implemented? In the discussion to follow, I assume that technically feasible methods of geoengineering could eventually be developed. Even under this assumption, geoengineering will raise numerous difficult issues for the international community. This essay uses the thermostat metaphor to explore some of the more prominent policy and legal questions at stake.

## 2. Collective Decision-Making

To what extent would a geoengineering thermostat pose a unique challenge for international decision making? On the one hand, ordinary international law-making procedures, though imperfect, may be sufficient to address geoengineering. State representatives could consider geoengineering governance through the United Nations or other multi-State organisations and address relevant concerns through treaties and other formal mechanisms. On the other hand, if geoengineering departs from other global concerns in significant ways, we may need new or modified decision making mechanisms that take those differences into account.

At least three aspects of the thermostat problem call for broader participation and input than is typical for international decision making processes. First, geoengineering decisions will have exceptionally far-reaching and concrete impacts. Geoengineering deployment could have potentially disastrous effects for millions, such as modification of the Asian and African summer monsoons. Governance of geoengineering thus must address a truly global concern, in contrast to relatively local fishery conflicts or transboundary pollution problems. Second, geoengineering would serve as a single thermostat for the entire world; for the most part, there is little realistic prospect for multi-zone climate control. This thermostat mechanism would allow little or no room for national variations on a global norm, in contrast with many other subjects of international regulation. Legitimate concerns thus would have to be considered in international fora if they are going to be considered at all. Third, and perhaps most importantly, a decision to implement geoengineering would require the resolution of contentious disputes rooted in deeply held values. People's views on geoengineering will depend on their underlying values and beliefs concerning justice, nature and tolerance for risk, and these values and beliefs will play an especially significant role amidst the substantial uncertainty surrounding geoengineering.

Granted, many problems addressed by international environmental law, such as climate change or ozone depletion, have involved disagreement over whether a problem exists and how to address it. However, once a problem is acknowledged, there is usually relatively little disagreement regarding the appropriate goal. With respect to climate change, for example, the international community agreed on a goal of stabilising greenhouse gas concentrations so as to avoid "dangerous anthropogenic interference" with the climate system. Similarly, recognition of the problem of ozone depletion led swiftly to a consensus to protect and restore the ozone layer. Geoengineering, however, presents a particularly thorny political problem because no obvious point of equilibrium is likely to command consensus support. Simply put, reasonable persons are likely to disagree on where the thermostat should be set. These circumstances suggest an especially strong need for open and deliberative decision making processes.

## 3. Issues to Resolve

The question of whose hand should control the thermostat actually involves multiple inquiries regarding: (1) which nations should decide; (2) what role scientists and other expert communities should have in the decision making process; (3) what role non-State actors should have in the process; (4) how to account for the interests and preferences of future generations; and (5) what mechanisms should be in place to ensure compliance with decisions agreed upon. This section considers each of these inquiries.

### 3.1. Which Nations Should Decide?

At first glance, it may appear self-evident that all nations desiring to be involved in setting the thermostat should have the opportunity to participate. Virtually every nation is a party to the U.N. Framework Convention on Climate Change (FCCC), which treats climate change as a matter of concern for the entire international community. A process inclusive of all interested nation-States is consistent with basic notions of fairness, and with the traditional international law narrative of equality and consent among sovereign States. Decisions resulting from such a process are therefore more likely to be viewed as legitimate than decisions made by a select few.

Processes that require formal international consensus as a prerequisite to action, however, can be slow and ineffective. Indeed, the complexity of negotiating comprehensive greenhouse gas emission reductions among the nearly 200 parties to the FCCC has led many to advocate that climate change negotiation processes be limited instead to a smaller subset of countries. Negotiations among the several nations responsible for the vast majority of carbon emissions, it is argued, can substantially reduce overall emissions without requiring commitments from non-parties to the negotiations. Geoengineering negotiations limited to a few States would offer similar advantages of relative simplicity and reduced vulnerability to obstruction by holdouts. Excluded parties would surely object, however, that it is presumptuous for a handful of countries to commit the entire world to a particular thermostat setting.

A bargaining structure akin to the World Trade Organisation's "green room" offers a hybrid approach that might facilitate consensus formation without excluding interested States. Under such an approach, a small group of countries participates in initial bargaining on a tentative agreement. Such agreement would still be subject to consensus approval by a larger membership. Undoubtedly, participants in the small-group negotiations could wield substantial influence on ultimate outcomes, and there would often be pressures in the large-group approval process to go along with tentative agreements. Careful attention to the selection of small-group participants is critical to reduce the danger of inadequate representation. Representation in geoengineering negotiations, for example, might include guaranteed seats for different geographic regions, on the assumption that geoengineering impacts will likely vary by region. Representatives of regions most vulnerable to the adverse impacts of geoengineering might even be given veto authority over decisions to implement certain types of geoengineering projects.

The fact that some geoengineering schemes could be carried out unilaterally complicates the question of which nations should decide. Unilateral geoengineering, even if undertaken with good intentions, surely would be denounced if it occurred without the sanction of the international community. Nonetheless, the possibility that a single nation could attempt to seize control of the thermostat or that several countries could engage in counterproductive geoengineering efforts is sufficiently serious to warrant concern about international conflicts that could result. A few countries, including the United Kingdom and Russia, have already expressed an inclination to move forward with geoengineering field tests in the absence of international approval. While such field tests are not equivalent to full-scale deployment, they still underscore the need for formal international attention to geoengineering. More generally, the possibility of unilateral action, collateral damage, and subsequent hostilities suggests that institutions relevant to international armed conflict, such as the United Nations Security Council, may ultimately have an important role to play in geoengineering policy making.

### 3.2. The Role of Scientists

A second issue raised by the thermostat metaphor focuses on the thermostat makers: what role should scientists play? Under a conventional understanding of scientists' role in policy making processes, while scientists are the ones generating data and recommendations, it is the democratically accountable officials who ultimately make policy choices. With respect to research activities themselves, the scientific community typically exercises broad freedom of inquiry and enjoys minimal external oversight. Knowledge is intrinsically valuable, so the argument goes, and external influences that might circumscribe or corrupt its pursuit should be avoided. Following the distinct roles of scientists and policy makers, few would advocate that scientists direct science-based policy decisions. In particular, determining where a geoengineering thermostat should be set is a value-based choice that lies beyond scientists' expertise and demands broader societal deliberation.

A strict dichotomy between research and policy, however, represents a gross oversimplification of reality. Research activities are not purely objective, as assumptions and models that underlie scientific research necessarily incorporate researchers' value judgments. Conversely, policy decisions often reflect significant influence by experts, whether resulting from their recommendations or their direct participation in decision making processes.

Science and policy issues are especially intertwined with respect to geoengineering. Firstly, as with other emerging technologies, early choices regarding research and development are likely to have outsized effects on subsequent technology adoption and use. Substantial investment in research can create and empower interests having a professional, financial, and psychological stake in promoting applications of that research. Secondly, the goal-oriented nature of geoengineering research means that efforts in the field will inevitably reflect policy preferences. Geoengineering does not involve a neutral inquiry into scientific "truth". Rather, geoengineering is more applied science than pure science in that it encompasses efforts to discover particular means of achieving a selected end. As such, research into geoengineering presumes at least some willingness to go forward with implementation in the future so long as certain conditions (of safety, risk-benefit analysis, or otherwise) are met. Yet geoengineering raises serious ethical questions of moral responsibility that demand careful reflection by society before committing to action. For example, is it morally permissible to cause further harm for the sake of ameliorating threats generated by our own past, present, and future conduct?

Ultimately, governance of geoengineering research cannot be divorced from governance of geoengineering deployment. Because geoengineering research may close off debate on the socially contested question of whether a geoengineering thermostat should be created in the first instance, the scientific community should not exercise free rein over the pursuit of geoengineering research. The need to involve non-scientists – political actors, nongovernmental organisations, and the general public – in the oversight of geoengineering research is critical and is gaining growing recognition. However, the form of that oversight and the nature of non-scientist involvement are yet to be determined.

Under one proposed option, scientists would take the lead in developing codes of conduct or other informal mechanisms of research governance. Bottom-up, non-governmental processes can be more immediate and flexible than those requiring State action. In theory, such processes can involve non-scientists, and they can lay the groundwork for more formal regulation. One danger in a bottom-up approach, however, is that the scientists whose research would be subject to any resulting norms may dominate the process. As a result, the option of not moving forward with research – an option that warrants examination because of the dangers of moral hazard and technological lock-in – is unlikely to receive serious consideration. Moreover, without the sanction of the international community, a bottom-up process and any norms generated by it will be lacking in political legitimacy.

### 3.3. The Role of Non-State Actors

The Westphalian conception of international law envisions little or no role for non-State actors in the creation of international law. That conception does not accurately describe international law today, however, nor does it set out an ideal for geoengineering governance. A system operating solely through the consent of sovereigns is unlikely to be fully representative. Sovereigns imperfectly reflect the interests of the people they rule, sometimes overlooking indigenous or minority concerns, and the political processes that lead to the formation of State positions may be exclusionary and opaque. Broader participation can increase the legitimacy of international governance and foster more informed deliberation.

In the abstract, the goal of creating more inclusive processes for global decision making commands widespread support. How to achieve this goal in practice, however, poses difficult questions. Sovereign States are reluctant to yield power, reasonable persons disagree as to who should be involved and in what capacity, and options for resolving fundamental conflicts in values are limited. Universal direct participation in setting any geoengineering thermostat, for instance, is hardly sensible or realistic. Even decision making along the lines of a representative democracy may be impossible, given the lack of political structures for democratically controlling international institutions. Indeed, the very concept of democratic representation on a global scale is problematic in the absence of a global public that shares a collective identity.

Notwithstanding the barriers to more inclusive governance, non-governmental organisations, community organisations, labour unions, and other civil society organisations have come to play an increasingly important role in international law. Such organisations are not democratically chosen and have no formal law-making authority. Yet they participate by framing issues, setting agendas, developing policy options, shaping State positions, and monitoring State commitments. Civil society organisations also function as pluralistic intermediaries between international legal regimes and the publics the regimes ultimately govern. These organisations can articulate citizens' concerns and channel them into international deliberative processes, while communicating to citizens the issues and decisions that are subject to those processes.

Civil society organisations could play an important role in raising public awareness of geoengineering and of the risks and uncertainties at issue. Their most critical task, however, may be to amplify the voices of those whom geoengineering would adversely affect. Whether working through formal law-making forums, less formal norm-setting arenas, or various media of general opinion formation, these organisations can remind the world that setting the thermostat should not involve the exercise of power by the few to advance narrow or purely domestic interests. Nor should setting the thermostat consist merely of a calculation that maximises benefits and minimises costs. Geoengineering – like climate change – will have victims, human and nonhuman. By giving these victims a name, face, and voice, civil society organisations can push the world toward making responsible decisions regarding any development or use of a geoengineering thermostat.

### 3.4. The Role of Future Generations

Incorporating the interests of future generations in thermostat-setting decisions presents an imposing challenge in light of political and economic pressures to respond to short-term concerns. To be sure, climate change is not unique among environmental problems in its enduring impacts. Geoengineering using solar radiation management (SRM) techniques has especially lasting implications, however, because of the so-called "termination problem" associated with these techniques. SRM techniques would ameliorate the warming effect of higher greenhouse gas (GHG) concentrations by reducing the amount of radiation striking the Earth. Because GHG concentrations are unchanged, the sudden cessation of these techniques would have catastrophic effects. Extremely rapid climate change would follow, leaving human societies and natural ecosystems little time to adapt. To avoid a catastrophe, SRM efforts, once deployed, would have to continue until GHG concentrations naturally decline. This process could take hundreds of years even if human societies drastically curb their GHG emissions. Deployment of SRM techniques, in other words, would commit future generations to continuing deployment for the foreseeable future, a politically and logistically daunting task.

Like the long-term storage of nuclear waste, the termination problem raises serious questions of intergenerational equity. Namely, what duties do we owe to future generations, and to what extent may we constrain their freedom of action? If intergenerational equity requires that each generation pass on the planet in no worse condition than received or that future generations have equivalent options for flourishing, it is not clear whether SRM would meet those requirements. Future generations would retain some ability to adjust any geoengineering thermostat, but the deployment of SRM would preclude the option of not using the thermostat at all. Obtaining the consent of future generations to such an arrangement is obviously not feasible, nor can we know in advance future attitudes that might inform our decisions.

Conversely, geoengineering might help us meet our obligations to future generations if it were to protect them from even worse climate consequences. It is critical to ensure, however, that geoengineering not become a self-serving excuse for present inaction. To ward off the temptation to shift the burdens of climate change to the future, legal mechanisms will be needed to represent future generations in deciding whether to go forward with geoengineering, and if so, with what techniques. These mechanisms might involve appointing a guardian or trustee to represent future generations in decision making processes or imposing fiduciary duties on decision makers to consider impacts on future generations. Giving an explicit voice to future generations does not guarantee a fair weighing of their concerns, but can prevent them from being completely ignored.

### 3.5. Compliance

Environmental subjects of international concern often present difficult collective action problems because their solution requires the aggregation of cooperative efforts to supply a global public good. The temptation to free-ride off of others' efforts has hindered agreement on significant reductions in GHG emissions, for instance. In theory, geoengineering faces lesser barriers to implementation than emission reductions insofar as it could be undertaken by a handful of nations, a single nation, or even a private actor. Because there can be only one thermostat for the entire world, however, geoengineering raises a different issue of global cooperation: ensuring that only authorised hands are on the thermostat. As already noted, there are likely to be strong disagreements regarding where the geoengineering thermostat should be set, if at all. Thermostat-setting disputes could lead to sabotage of geoengineering projects, countervailing efforts to manipulate the climate, or even armed conflict. These considerations suggest that compliance and enforcement mechanisms more typically associated with arms treaties may be needed. Mechanisms that may prove useful in enforcing a geoengineering thermostat include: verification regimes incorporating external monitoring and inspections, well-defined dispute resolution procedures, clear responses (such as sanctions) to treaty breaches, and export controls.

Non-State actors may have a particularly important role to play in monitoring geoengineering activity and bringing instances of noncompliance to the attention of relevant authorities. Ensuring long-term execution of an agreed-upon course will be particularly critical if SRM techniques are deployed. The institutions tasked with implementing SRM geoengineering must not only have the resources and technical capacity to carry it out, but also be designed to withstand economic and political pressures to compromise for the sake of short-term gain. At the same time, external oversight of such institutions, whether by a group of nations or by non-governmental organisations, can help assure that thermostat-setting decisions agreed upon are actually carried out.

## 4. Conclusion

The prospect of a geoengineering thermostat raises a host of difficult policy and legal questions. These questions cannot simply be ignored, as pressures to geoengineer will only increase unless we promptly and drastically reduce carbon emissions. Spurred by eager researchers, supportive wealthy donors, and industries seeking to profit from geoengineering contracts, geoengineering efforts are likely to move forward, and in doing so, to confront us with the conflicts embodied in the thermostat metaphor. Although the questions raised by geoengineering seemingly do not demand immediate resolution, inattention to the thermostat dilemma may limit subsequent options, commit us to less-than-desirable courses of action, and preclude careful and inclusive deliberation.

## 5. Sources and Further Reading

Barrett, Scott, *Why Cooperate?: The Incentive to Supply Global Public Goods*, Oxford University Press, Oxford, 2007.

Bodansky, Daniel, "Governing Climate Engineering: Scenarios for Analysis", Discussion Paper, *Harvard Project on Climate Agreements*, 2011.

Gardiner, Stephen M., "Is 'Arming the Future' with Geoengineering Really the Lesser Evil?", in Stephen M. Gardiner et al. (eds.), *Climate Ethics: Essential Readings*, Oxford University Press, 2010, p. 284.

Jones, Kent, "Green Room Politics and the WTO's Crisis of Representation", in *Progress in Development Studies*, 2009, vol. 9, p. 349.

Royal Society, *Geoengineering the Climate: Science, Governance and Uncertainty*, 2009.

Shrader-Frechette, Kristin, "Duties to Future Generations, Proxy Consent, Intra- and Intergenerational Equity: The Case of Nuclear Waste", in *Risk Analysis*, 2000, vol. 20, p. 771.

Victor, David G., "Towards Effective International Cooperation on Climate Change: Numbers, Interests and Institutions", in *Global Environmental Politics*, 2006, vol. 6, no. 3, pp. 90–103.

Wheatley, Steven, *The Democratic Legitimacy of International Law*, Hart Publishing, 2010.

# 3.5.

# Can Robots have Human Rights Obligations? A Futuristic Exploration

**Surya Deva**[*]

In the years to come, autonomous robots will play an increasingly important role in our lives and society generally. What implications does this scenario have for human rights? Can robots be 'holders' of rights as well as duties? This think piece will explore whether and how robots can bear human rights obligations. It will be contended that non-human entities like robots can (and ought to) be obligated to respect human rights. Here one can draw analogy with evolving jurisprudence concerning the human rights obligations of companies.

As far as the *modus operandi* of imposing such a duty on robots is concerned, one easy solution might be to hold their human masters accountable for human rights abuses resulting from robotic actions or omissions. This think piece will investigate whether this approach will be adequate or it might be desirable to attribute responsibility directly to robots as well.

## 1. Introduction

Robots have already become an integral part of our lives. In years to come, they are likely to play a more decisive and pervasive role in our lives everywhere – from homes to offices, hospitals, *crèches*, supermarkets, airports, factories, mines, disaster zones, battle fields, educational institutions, sport grounds and entertainment kiosks. This scenario will materialise faster when scientists are able to develop more sophisticated and autonomous 'social robots' – robots that have the capability to interact with humans, respond to requests made by humans/robots with ease, understand human emotions, and can operate without much human guidance. The invention of autonomous social robots is inevitable, because scientists keep on improving and testing the boundaries of existing gadg-

[*] **Surya Deva** is an Associate Professor at the School of Law of City University of Hong Kong.

ets. Moreover, robots would be more useful, at least in certain areas, when they behave like humans and do not rely too much on commands from humans.

Several factors will contribute to this increased robot-dependency. Economic efficiency will be a dominant variable furthering the cause of robots. Unlike factory workers, robots will not demand – at least in the foreseeable future – wages, lunch breaks, weekly holidays or maternity benefits. It is reported that Foxconn, the world's largest electronics manufacture and the key supplier of Apple, is planning to have one million robots working for it. It will not then be surprising if robotic factories may become a viable alternative to the current model of outsourced manufacturing. An ageing population and low birth rates should also encourage certain developed countries like Japan to push for a higher robot usage rather than relying on immigration to maintain a stable work force. The tendency to avoid or externalise risk is another variable that will promote the use of robots in dangerous activities. We already see this happening in terms of robots being used to fight wars. Last but not least, robots hold an edge over human beings in respect of performing tasks with speed, precision and uniformity.

This increased human-robot interaction will have many implications for legal and social norms. This think piece seeks to explore one such implication: the potential impact of robots on the realisation of human rights. Can robots violate human rights? If yes, how can they be made accountable for human rights violations? I argue that non-human entities like robots can, if necessary, be obligated to respect human rights. While traditionally States were entrusted with the duty to ensure the realisation of human rights, this position has undergone significant changes over the years. The evolution of human rights obligations of non-State actors such as companies is a case in point. The Guiding Principles on Business and Human Rights, which were adopted by the United Nations (UN) Human Rights Council in June 2011, acknowledge that business entities have human rights responsibilities independent of States. If artificial (and as compared to robots, somewhat invisible) entities like companies can be subjected to human rights obligations, there is no reason why robots cannot bear human rights obligations. In fact, the realisation of human rights requires that human beings can enforce duties against all centres of power – whether States, companies, terrorists organisations, robots or NGOs – that pose a threat to human rights.

This think piece also deals with the operationalisation of such a human rights duty *vis-à-vis* robots. One straightforward solution might be to hold the relevant human agents – for example owners, designers, programmers, manufacturers or sellers – accountable for human rights abuses resulting from robotic actions or omissions. However, since it is likely that human beings will form a company to programme and manufacture robots, this mode of accountability would be fraught with the same kind of challenges as experienced in making companies accountable for human rights violations. It might, therefore, be desirable to attribute responsibility directly to robots as well. Taking this path will of course imply devising sanctions that are appropriate and effective against robots.

## 2. Robots and Human Rights

### 2.1. Can Robots Violate Human Rights?

The basic premise that underpins the analysis in this think piece is that robots can be bestowed with independent personality, because in future they will evolve to have attributes like intentionality, rationality, free will and autonomy. If this premise is valid and reasonably foreseeable, one can then make a claim for robots having rights as well as duties as moral agents (though their moral agency might not be equal to that of humans). In this think piece, I only explore the possibility of robots as bearers of duties in relation to human rights. Similarly, while robots can also promote the realisation of human rights – for example, the use of robot jockeys in camel races has saved some poor children from slavery and sex robots might reduce human trafficking – I do not explore that dimension here.

Before conceiving human rights obligations of robots, one should ask whether and how robots can violate human rights. Robots can violate human rights in at least four ways. First, external actors such as humans, States and companies may programme or use robots to infringe human rights. Violations of this kind are more likely to take place in the context of current robots which rely significantly on human agents to perform the assigned tasks. The use of robots by States in war zones thus killing innocent civilians or by companies for collecting personal data illustrates this possibility. Considering that this type of robots might not command much autonomy, they should not be personally liable for human rights abuses resulting from their actions. Nor should they be denied the benefit of the defence that they were simply following the (unlawful) commands given by their human superiors. The situation should, however, be different in case of autonomous robots.

Second, sophisticated autonomous robots themselves can possess (or acquire) the capacity to trample human rights. Imagine, for instance, the possibility of a sales robot making racial comments to a serving customer, a caregiving robot touching inappropriately the body of an elderly person, or a security robot detaining a person unlawfully at the airport. Although it is difficult to predict at this stage, one cannot rule out the possibility of robots behaving like males and showing gender bias towards women.

Third, robots can also act in concert with other actors and thus become complicit in human rights violations. This is likely to happen only when we reach a stage of fully autonomous robots. Drawing analogy with various types of complicity of companies with State agencies, robots may participate directly in human rights abuses or merely benefit strategically by violations perpetuated by other actors.

The fourth and final possibility might arise in the form of a robot violating human rights of another robot. While this may sound too fanciful at this stage, it will not be inconceivable for powerful robots to abuse their position and power to infringe the interests of weaker robots if the humanity enters the age of a robotic society.

Assuming that robots can violate human rights in these diverse ways, questions will also arise as to the nature and extent of their human rights responsibilities. For instance, should robots be held liable for omissions as well? What about the indirect adverse impact of their actions on the human rights of others such as, for example, the impact of robot usage on unemployment.

## 2.2. Regulating Robots

Isaac Asimov had proposed 'Three Laws of Robotics': first, a robot may not injure a human being or, through inaction, allow a human being to come to harm; second, a robot must obey orders given to it by human beings except where such orders would conflict with the First Law; and third, a robot must protect its own existence as long as such protection does not conflict with the First or Second Law.

These Laws are precise but quite potent in safeguarding human interests. They are, however, premised on the vertical hierarchy between humans and robots in which the latter would serve the former. A related implicit assumption is that robots would not be completely autonomous from humans. The subservient nature of these laws, coupled with lack of legitimacy on account of robots not having a say in their drafting, makes them unsuitable to support a regulatory framework for a society in which robots may interact with human beings on a more horizontal level. Let me offer one illustrative example of the current asymmetry. Sex robots are being created to satisfy human urges and also make money in the process. But the dignity, emotions and sexual preferences of the robots providing sexual services do not seem to be taken into account at this point of time. This paradigm might have to change in future.

What is the way forward then? A new regulatory framework at the international level may be needed. One option may be for the UN to negotiate a framework convention dealing with various aspects of human-robot interaction – from licensing to agreeing a 'no-go-zone' (if any) for robots, their rights and responsibilities, the enforcement of rules, and potential sanctions. The framework stipulated in such a convention can then be used by States and non-State actors in regulating the robotic conduct. It is critical that there is a representation of robots in the drafting process of the convention, because States lack legitimacy to represent their interests. Even if robots possess the capability to participate in negotiations concerning their rights and obligations, it would be impractical for all of them to do so. Therefore, a selected number of trustees of robots, representatives of the International Robotics Society or representatives of robots should be invited to put forward the position of robotic community.

Under the current setup, States play a dominant part in drafting and enforcing international rules and regulations. They are likely to continue playing this part, though in decades to come, the formulation and enforcement of law might not remain as State-centric as it is now. This change will have implications for human-robot interaction as well. It should be possible for the Robotics Society to self-regulate and discipline deviant robots. Civil society is also likely to monitor the behaviour of robots locally and globally. Moreover, consumers and investors of robotics may play a role in setting and enforcing minimum acceptable rules.

## 3. Accountability Modes

There are two broad possibilities of making robots accountable for human rights violations. One can either go after humans behind robots (agency mode) or grill robots themselves (self mode). I explore both these options below and suggest that we should consider relying on both accountability modes to achieve an optimal level of regulatory efficacy. In fact, the existing principle of 'joint and several liability' can be employed to combine both the 'agency' mode and the 'self' mode of accountability.

### 3.1. 'Agency' Mode

Under the agency mode, robots can be treated as agents of humans who may programme, manufacture or put to use robots for harmful effects. If robotic actions result in human rights violations, we may rely on the product liability jurisprudence. Liability (both civil and criminal) can be based on negligence, knowledge or intention. Treating robots as products implies that such robots have no or minimal autonomy, rationality and free will.

In cases concerning autonomous robots which are controlled in certain respects by humans, one can invoke the principle *respondeat superior* ('let the master answer') to hold human agents responsible for the actions of robots. In other words, if the given conditions are satisfied (that is, a master-servant relation existed and the servant acted in the course of her employment), human masters can be held vicariously liable for human rights abuses committed by robots. It is also possible to employ the due diligence principle and attribute responsibility to a master who – despite having knowledge or reasons to believe that human rights violations can take place – failed to take reasonable steps to ensure that the robot did not violate human rights.

Although it is crucial to make accountable human beings who programme or use robots to infringe human rights, the sole reliance on the agency mode is likely to prove problematic for a number of reasons. First of all, implementing this approach entails identifying the human beings and companies behind a given deviant robot. This might not be easy or straight forward in all cases, as companies know well how to keep distance by design and insulate themselves from potential liability.

Another difficulty might be in establishing the master-agent or employer-employee relationship between human beings and robots. Even if such a relationship is made out, it may not be feasible to routinely rely on vicarious liability and attribute to their human masters the responsibility for human rights violations. For example, if a robot acted beyond the permissible scope of their programmed duties, modified its programme code or created other robots, human masters are likely to plead that the robot was on one's own 'frolic' and therefore, they should not be held responsible.

### 3.2. 'Self' Mode

The 'self' mode of accountability entails making robots directly responsible for their conduct. More specifically, in the context of this think piece, we consider responsibility for conduct that results in human rights violations. This mode will be especially relevant when we have truly intelligent and autonomous robots: the robots that are autogenous, possess the capacity to improve their knowledge, and can act without much guidance from humans.

One may ask how we could hold robots accountable for their actions. What sanctions could be invoked against robots and what purposes would they serve? Assuming that robots can and do own property, they can be required to compensate victims and pay fines for human rights violations. Robots can also be confined or injuncted to prevent future violations. In the worst possible scenario, the court can order a robot to be dismembered and destroyed. It is also possible to pass rehabilitative or reformative orders requiring robots to undergo remedial therapy and maintenance. 'Naming and shaming' should also remain a viable option, especially against those robots that have acquired public popularity.

These potential sentences against robots should serve several purposes – from vindication to retribution, deterrence and reformation. Victims of human rights violations feel vindicated when they see the visible perpetrator bear the consequence, whether it is a public apology or penal sanctions, of one's wrongful conduct. So, sanctions against robots should satisfy the legitimate expectations of victims. Assuming that robots of the future will be able to feel pain and experience shame/guilt, sanctions should have deterrent effect on the behaviour of deviant robots as well as other bystander robots. For the same reason, reformation and rehabilitation should also prove useful against robots.

## 4. Conclusion

Conceiving robots as independent moral agents who can bear human rights obligations will require a fundamental shift in how we have traditionally conceptualised human rights in the context of the 'State' versus 'individuals'. Such a re-conceptualisation is, however, necessary to ensure that the human rights discourse keeps pace with the changing times. Considering that the language of human rights has already been invoked to capture interests of non-humans and even non-State actors are being subjected to human rights obligations, extending human rights framework to robots would not be as radical as it might appear in the first instance.

While at this point of time we do not really have fully autonomous robots, it would be naïve, considering the technological innovations achieved so far, to assume that scientists would not be able to stretch or refine the robotic technology further. Human beings should debate and conduct research around multiple issues concerning human–robot interactions. This think piece, in which I have argued that robots can bear human rights obligations and that existing legal principles can be harnessed to achieve this outcome, should be seen in this context. Further debate and research is necessary not only for protecting the interests of humans but also for safeguarding robots against abuse by humans for commercial gains, social objectives or simply for pleasure.

## 5. Sources and Further Reading

Anderson, Michael and Anderson, Susan Leigh (eds.), *Machine Ethics*, Cambridge University Press, Cambridge, 2011.

Carpenter, Julie *et al.*, "Gender Representation and Humanoid Robots Designed for Domestic Use", in *International Journal of Robotics*, 2009, vol. 1, p. 261.

Deva, Surya, "Guiding Principles on Business and Human Rights: Implications for Companies", in *European Company Law*, 2012, vol. 9, no. 2, p. 101.

Enz, Sibylle *et al.*, "The Social Role of Robots in the Future: Explorative Measurement of Hopes and Fears", in *International Journal of Social Robotics*, 2011, vol. 3, p. 263.

French, Peter A. (ed.), *Individual and Collective Responsibility*, second edition, Schenkman Books, Rochester, 1998.

Herik, Herik Jaap van den *et al.*, "Understanding the Artificial", in *International Journal of Social Robotics*, 2011, vol. 3, p. 107.

Howlader, Daniel, "Moral and Ethical Questions for Robotics Public Policy", in *Synesis: A Journal of Science, Technology, Ethics, and Policy*, 2001.

Lin, Patrick, Abney, Keith and Bekey, George A. (eds.), *Robot Ethics: The Ethical and Social Implications of Robotics*, MIT Press, Cambridge, Massachusetts, 2012.

McNally, Phil and Inayatullah, Sohail, "The Rights of Robots: Technology, Culture and Law in the 21st Century", 2012, available at http://www.metafuture.org/Articles/TheRightsofRobots.htm, last accessed on 10 June 2012.

Simon, Stephanie, *Many Scans Make Light Work*, South China Morning Post, 8 April 2012.

Solum, Lawrence B., "Legal Personhood for Artificial Intelligences", in *North Carolina Law Review,* 1992, vol. 70, p. 1231.

Sullins, John P., "When Is a Robot a Moral Agent?", in *International Review of Information Ethics*, 2006, vol. 6, p. 23.

Wallach, Wendell and Allen, Colin, *Moral Machines: Teaching Robots Right from Wrong*, Oxford University Press, Oxford, 2009).

Wang, Kanglei, *Ushering in the Age of Robot*, South China Morning Post, 18 December 2011.

Yagoda, Rosemarie E. and Gillan, Douglas J., "You Want Me to Trust a ROBOT? The Development of a Human-Robot Interaction Trust Scale", in *International Journal of Social Robotics,* 2012, vol. 4 (forthcoming).

Yeoman, Ian and Mars, Michelle, "Robots, Men and Sex Tourism", in *Futures,* 2012, vol. 44, no. 4, p. 365.

Yu, Sherwin, "Machine Mortality: Computing Right and Wrong" available at http://www.yalescientific.org/2012/05/machine-morality-computing-right-and-wrong, last accessed on 10 June 2012.

Robots could Demand Legal Rights, BBC News, 21 December 2006, available at http://news.bbc.co.uk/2/hi/6200005.stm, last accessed on 10 June 2012.

# 3.6.

# Mapping the Legal Framework for the Introduction into Society of Robots as Autonomous Intelligent Systems

**Madeleine de Cock Buning*, Lucky Belder** and Roeland de Bruin*****

Autonomous Intelligent Systems (AIS) are the next step in the development of a more sustainable information society. Industries and governments around the world heavily invest in autonomous robots. The FET-Flagship Robot Companions for Citizens intends to develop sustainable autonomous robots that are able to interact with humans in order to provide care and companionship for the rapidly ageing society. Autonomous Intelligent Systems can perceive information, are able to learn, reason and make decisions based on their experience, without direct human intervention or instruction. Actions of AIS may have legal consequences, and for AIS that are unknown entities considering the current legal and normative framework this creates uncertainty on issues such as free-will, liability, privacy, consumer protection and ownership of (intellectual) property rights. These need to be addressed in order to optimise appropriate legal instruments for realising access to and acceptance of AIS-technology in society, thereby providing a unique opportunity for thinking about the future of law.

## 1. Introduction

Autonomous Intelligent Systems (AIS) are the next step in the development of a more sustainable information society. The European Commission acknowledges this in its policy documents on sustainable innova-

* **Madeleine de Cock Buning** is Chair of CIER and CAAAi, Professor of Copyright, Communication and Medialaw, and a member of the board of the Supervisory Authority to the Media.

** **Lucky Belder** is Assistant Professor, secretary of the CIER and co-founder of the CAAAi.

*** **Roeland de Bruin** is a Junior Lecturer and project researcher at CIER and CAAAi.

tion.[1] One of the challenges indicated in *Horizon 2020* (the financial instrument implementing the 'Innovation Union', aimed at securing Europe's global competitiveness) is: "cognitive systems and robotics". The aim is to develop "artificial systems that operate in dynamic real life environments, reaching new levels of autonomy and adaptability", [2] for "[t]here is a strong focus on advanced robotic systems, given their potential to underpin the competitiveness of key manufacturing sectors in Europe and a wide range of innovative products and services across the economy, from home appliances to health, security, space and leisure", whereby the target is to produce "systems that can operate autonomously in the real world through for example, scene and context understanding, anticipation and reaction/adaptation to changes, manipulation and navigation, as well as symbiotic human-machine relations".[3]

AIS can be envisioned as soft bodied, sentient and intelligent machines that are able to understand and communicate with humans and each other, equipped with predictive and decisional capacities, based on their own experience, being energy efficient and sustainable, in order to provide personal companionship and care assistance for the rapidly ageing EU-society, among other things.

In industry we can already see an increasing focus on robotics that is more or less autonomous. The global market for industrial robots was calculated in 2011 to comprise $12 billion, and industrial robot sales increased by 18 per cent that year. Russian entrepreneur Dmitry Grishin has recently announced to invest millions in the development of robotics in New York. The South Korean Government aims at a market share of 13 per cent in personal robotics to be achieved by 2013 and 20 per cent by 2018 and has therefore drafted the Robot Special Act, calling for large investments in robotics research and development. Corporations in Japan for instance, are known for their research and development in the field of robotics. Honda has been developing their humanoid robot ASIMO from 2000 onwards and predicts to sell as many robots as cars by 2020. Sony

1 Communication, Horizon 2020 - The Framework Programme for Research and Innovation, SEC(2011) 1427 & 1428 final, COM(2012) 808 final (Horizon 2020).

2 Forthcoming Annex 7 to the Decision, Work Programme 2013, Cooperation Theme 3, ICT[…], EC C(2012), draft available at http://cordis.europa.eu/fp7/ict/docs/draft-wp2013.doc, last accessed on 9 July 2012, p. 9.

3 *Ibid.*

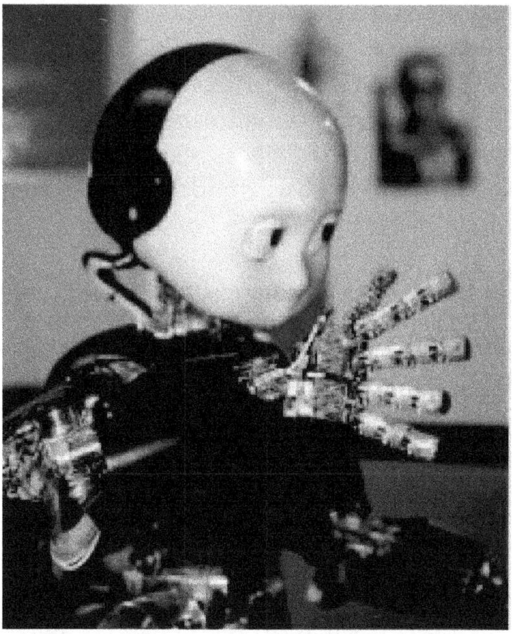

**Image 1:** iCub Robot, designed by the RobotCub Consortium. Photo by Lorenzo Natale, CC-BY-SA & GNU FDL 1.2 Licenses: http://en.wikipedia.org/wiki/File:ICub_sciencefestival_1.jpg

developed humanoid QRIO and the four legged commercial dog-robot AIBO.

## 1.1. Unique Opportunity for Law

The realisation of AIS in the forthcoming years will offer a unique opportunity to study the legal consequences and implications of the introduction of truly new phenomena into society. The fact is that autonomous systems are unknown entities in the current (European) legal and normative framework. This creates uncertainty on issues such as free-will, liability, privacy and consumer protection as well as ownership of intellectual property rights. It will lead to changes in the legal order and may even lead to the hypothesis that the development of AIS shall result in a partial paradigmatic shift in thinking about law. These are challenges that will have to be met in order to realise the access to and the acceptance of AIS technology in society.

After having given a definition of Autonomous Intelligent Systems, six scenarios will be presented in this contribution on the impact of the development of AIS on our society, which have been developed by the Utrecht University Centre for Access to and Acceptance of Artificial Autonomous Intelligence (CAAAi). These scenarios shall be key to the research into the legal and normative framework which will be developed by the CAAAi in the coming years.

### 1.2. Defining Autonomous Intelligent Systems

Autonomous Intelligent Systems consist of two elements. First, Autonomy, which relates to the level of human intervention. It can be seen as a spectrum, "in which the capacity of decision making by the system correlates with a proportional lessening of the degree of human intervention or interaction".[4] Less human intervention in the behaviour of a system implicates a higher level of autonomy. The second element of AIS is Intelligence, or the ability to think. Intelligence can be described as "the ability to adapt one's behaviour to fit new circumstances [which] encompasses [...] the ability to learn, to reason, of problem solving, perception and language understanding".[5] Intelligent agents are held to be able to collect and select information from whatever source, to make recommendations based on their own calculations, and to make and implement decisions without being instructed to do so. For this contribution AIS are therefore defined as non-human entities that are capable of perceiving information delivered as language or otherwise, that are able to learn, reason and make decisions based on their experience, without direct human intervention or instruction. 'AIS' and 'autonomous robots' are used as interchangeable terms in this contribution.

---

4 Royal Academy of Engineering, *Autonomous Systems: Social, Legal and Ethical Issues*, Royal Academy of Engineering, London, 2009, p. 2. See also Samir Chopra, and Lawrence White, *A Legal Theory for Autonomous Intelligent Agents*, University of Michigan Press, Ann Arbor, 2011, pp. 9–10; Ugo Pagallo, "Killers, Fridges, and Slaves: A Legal Journey in Robotics", in *AI and Society*, 2011, vol. 26, p. 349; and David Calverley, "Imagining a Non-Biological Machine as a Legal Person", in *AI and Society*, 2008, vol. 22, p. 532.

5 Colin R. Davies, "An Evolutionary Step in Intellectual Property Rights – Artificial Intelligence and Intellectual Property", in *Computer Law & Security Review,* 2011, vol. 27, p. 603, paraphrasing Jack Copeland 2000, via the Turing Archive. See also Lawrence Solum, "Legal Personhood for Artificial Intelligences", in *North Carolina Law Review,* 1992, vol. 70, pp. 1234–1238.

## 2. AIS in Society in Six Scenarios

From a practical perspective, the development and deployment of autonomous robots leads to questions regarding the normative framework for access to AIS-technology and the acceptance of the deployment of autonomous robots in daily life. These include legal questions such as whether or not AIS may enter into contracts in a way that is legally valid, and who may be held liable in case AIS inflict damage to people or property. Other indicated issues relate to the protection of private data collected by AIS, standardisation of AIS-technology and products, and the possibilities for protecting the intellectual property of AIS-generated works or inventions. These issues have future relevance upon the deployment of AIS in society, and are at the same time rather important for the development process itself. It can be argued for instance, that legal uncertainty concerning risk allocation and liability for damages inflicted by AIS – as well as legal uncertainty concerning rules for standards, consumer protection and privacy – may have slowing effects on innovation in this field. These issues form the basis for the six scenarios of AIS in society, some of which are well known in the field of law whereas others seem rather futuristic now but shall not be in the near AIS-future.

### 2.1. Scenario Access: Standardisation

A well-known issue in the field of innovation is illustrated in the first scenario, which is of great importance to the potential successful development and deployment of AIS in society:

> *British manufacturer S supplies lower leg parts for certain autonomous robots. These are shaped by melting metal alloys into a mould. S has agreed to deliver an X amount of lower leg parts to Dutch producer T, who assembles these into complete robot-legs. When S's mould cracks due to structural overuse he decides to buy a more robust matrix from a Japanese manufacturer. His new template however does not have the exact same curve as the broken matrix, which makes the lower leg parts unusable for producer T, who rescinds his contract with S and starts the search for a new supplier of compatible parts. Unfortunately, this leads to a temporary shortage of legs and therefore an undersupply of the specific robot.*

If the large majority of products or services in a particular business or industry sector conform to international standards, a state of industry-wide standardisation exists. This is currently certainly not the case for most AIS-technology. International standards safeguard consumers and users of products and services. Clarity on the quality of products and services that is created by conforming to international standards is not only beneficial to consumers, but also to all producers and manufacturers of AIS parts. Standardisation is voluntary and not legally binding unless national governments decide to incorporate the standards into their domestic legislation. Certain provisions in (intellectual property) laws, such as fair use and interoperability provisions for software allow research into the production of products that comply with technological standards. Discussions may arise as to whether such exemptions to IP rights should be stretched further or whether this would deter the leading producers of the standard technology too much.

## 2.2. Scenario Access: Intellectual Property Incentive

*A Dutch university's research centre closely collaborates with a major Dutch private corporation on the development of 'walking' robots. Two post-doctorate researchers in the group are programming the steering software. They exchange information with Italian computer scientists who have reached great results in programming the movement of joints in the feet of the robot. The corporate entity is eager to have access to this particular technology to apply it in their other production lines on adaptable wheelchairs in China. At the same time, another partner in the Dutch research centre is working together with British robot-designers and a team of academic psychologists, conducting research on the social functioning of robots and the effects of their appearance on humans. The work on the walking robot of the Dutch researchers is funded under the FP7 scheme of the European Union, which has specific rules on the open dissemination of research results.*

All research described above uses and produces information that may be protected by intellectual property rights. Robots are not only highly complex machines; they also are a large collection of intellectual property rights. The fundamental reason for protecting intellectual property is to create optimal conditions for innovation and creativity by safeguarding the exclusive exploitation thereof. Intellectual property protection implicates the creation of a temporary monopoly on the use of protected information, which means, by the same token, that this protection creates a limitation of access to and use of this information, which in turn may become an impediment to innovation. A second issue is that a significant part of this information is developed by publicly funded academic research centres, co-operating with private corporate entities. Most software is furthermore developed under open access models, whilst other software may be subject to patent rights. It is likely that the private corporations involved in research and development of software are eager to make the newly developed software that they have contributed to, profitable, and would therefore not be keen to disclose the software as research results, under open access conditions, which is likely to be required by public co-funding institutions.

### 2.3. Scenario Acceptance: Legal Capacity?

*Elderly Mr. X has poor health. His autonomous robot interacts in society and concludes simple agreements on his behalf. Mr. X instructs his AIS to purchase food or to buy his daily medicine.*

To function in society, fully AIS should be able to enter into some legal transactions. Law attributes legal capacity only to natural and legal persons. International instruments do not include provisions deciding who is rendered legally capable. Because AIS are legally defined as neither natural, nor legal persons, agreements that AIS would be party to would be null and void. Legal certainty could be achieved through conferring some kind of legal capacity to AIS, which is a big step to take. However, alternatives need to be considered and evaluated to indicate whether or not legal capacity is indeed required. Should AIS be granted legal capacity, the impact on society would be radical, since AIS would become an active, participating object in commercial society. One alternative to full legal capacity might be to consider AIS to be mandated by its owner for the conclusion of certain legal transactions. This alternative would imply that the owner of an autonomous robot, who instructs his AIS to conclude an agreement on his behalf, is solely responsible for his transaction. Another alternative could be to follow the rules for minors, which implies allowing AIS to conclude certain transactions that are common for minors, such as the purchase of groceries, music and DVDs. This would exclude the capacity to buy other goods such as luxury yachts, cars and houses.

In any case, when performing legal actions AIS should be built to also have basic knowledge with regard to the legal, economic and social rules and behavioural norms that apply when performing legal actions such as concluding purchase agreements. The legal and economic knowledge AIS are provided with can be tailored to the agreements that specific AIS will be making. AIS should furthermore be aware of the position that they fulfil when concluding agreements.

Conferring legal capacity on AIS brings other questions into play, for example regarding possible responsibilities that tie in with capacity, such as liability.

### 2.4. Scenario Acceptance: Liability

For the acceptance of AIS in society, allocation of liability is crucial. Should damage be caused to a person or an object through or by an autonomous robot, rules on liability should indicate who is to provide monetary security. Several currently existing liability rules could apply in case of AIS. The most relevant kinds of liability will be outlined below, accompanied by a short corresponding scenario.

> *An elderly robot-owner instructs her AIS to vacuum her living room. Whilst vacuuming, the autonomous robot suddenly stagnates, turns around five times and begins to move uncontrollably for a few seconds; long enough to knock over a Ming vase on the windowsill.*

According to current European Product Liability Law, the producer may be held liable for the damage to the vase. The Product Liability Directive (85/374/EEC) decides that all producers involved in the production process can be addressed for compensation insofar as their finished product, component part or any raw material supplied by them was defective.

> *The housecleaning AIS described above wrongly calculates the weight of the vase and the force needed to lift it, causing the AIS to shatter it.*

The damage may be attributed to an imperfection in the AIS software programme. There seems to be no technical impairment to the AIS, nor has the AIS-owner given an erroneous instruction. The damage is a consequence of a miscalculation of the AIS, generated by its self-learning software programme. With regard to strict liability rules, AIS-owners need to be well informed of AIS's imperfections and limitations. The liability for damages that are not the result of a defect in AIS can then be allocated. To this end, insurance by AIS-owners can be considered. Thus, allocation of liability and possibilities for new insurance systems are issues that need to be explored.

> *An AIS is going down the street while carrying a large bag of groceries. As it turns a corner it collides with a woman on a bicycle. The woman is injured and the bicycle damaged.*

Should the AIS be considered a legal entity, the autonomous robot can also be held liable according to rules of fault liability negligence. Otherwise the owner will be liable, as a consequence of the strict-liability rules.

General rules on tort law, dealing with strict liabilities and fault liability outside the realm of product liability have not yet been harmonised in the European Union. Therefore, the specific features of tort law differ largely between countries. Because of the great diversity in tort law, it should be considered whether or not it is desirable that certain actions of AIS are classified as tort.

Product liability and strict liability pose no specific requirements to the functionality of AIS. It is however important that every AIS that is distributed is accompanied by a user manual in which the limitations of AIS are explicitly mentioned and warnings are issued. It is also necessary that the AIS' log can be reviewed in order to trace technical errors and to recover the instructions that AIS have received.

## 2.5. Scenario Acceptance: Privacy

> *Mrs. A takes her AIS to a technical engineer for a periodic check-up. Besides checking the hardware, the engineer also checks the AIS software for inconsistencies and irregularities. During these activities, the engineer stumbles upon information that is stored on the AIS' memory. Amongst this information are Mrs. A's medical files, bank account number and her pin-code as well as her GPS-location information over the past 6 months.*

Personal information of AIS-owners and/or third parties will be saved in the memory of AIS software. In principle, this information should be accessible only to the person the data relates to. Effective security measures for the access of the data, for instance by putting in place login codes, can possibly form a first practical solution to this problem. However, it can for example be useful to extract medical data from the AIS memory by medical professionals. For such uses of stored personal data advanced tools based upon and aligned with at least the European Data Protection Directive (95/46/EC) should be in place. Should there be transatlantic use of personal data from the USA, the safe harbour principles are leading.[6] AIS should in any case be equipped with a technique that safeguards personal data stored in AIS memory against the use and abuse of personal data without the unambiguous consent of the data subjects, the owner of the robot and other people that have encountered the AIS, or without application of any of the other legitimate data processing criteria.

The risk of abuse of private information stored in AIS software is an issue that can potentially harm the acceptance and use of AIS in society. Securing personal information that is stored in AIS software can form a partial solution to this issue.

### 2.6. Scenario Acceptance: AIS-Generated Works

As an autonomous, sentient and learning system the AIS is involved in the creation of works of art, inventions or can be co-authors of miscellaneous designs:

> *The owner of an autonomous robot is a retired artist. His AIS is equipped with tailor-made software allowing him to create works of art together with his robot. The artistic output is partially dependent on the information (algorithm and database) the AIS-manufacturer has implemented into the robot. However, the AIS as a learning and sentient machine, is able to build upon this information through the experience that came from the instructions and examples the artist has confronted him with during their twenty years of cooperation. The AIS may therefore create new and marvellous works of art miscellaneous but original of character.*

6 2000/520/EC: Commission Decision of 26 July 2000 Pursuant to Directive 95/46/EC of the European Parliament and of the Council on the Adequacy of the Protection Provided by the Safe Harbour Privacy Principles and Related Frequently Asked Questions Issued by the US Department of Commerce, notified under document number C(2000) 2441, in the Official Journal L 215, 25/08/2000 p. 7–47.

Substantial investment or a certain amount of originality[7] can give rise to intellectual property protection to creative and innovative output. The copyright works created by or with the autonomous or semi-autonomous aid of the AIS, are referred to as AIS-generated works. Copyright is granted under the implicit assumption that the work is the expression of human creativity. Therefore utilisation of AIS in the creation process confronts copyright with new challenges. In the United Kingdom a specific regulation has been introduced for works created by computers under such circumstances that no human author can be designated. No other country has similar provisions in place. However, the necessity for specific regulation has not yet become evident. This will however change in the future when actual or partial autonomous creations by AIS will take place.

Depending on the extent of human-machine interaction, AIS-assisted or AIS-generated works will be independently created. The more autonomous the creation, which implicates the least human intervention, the more difficult it will be to find a form of investment protection for the works created in current legal systems. This scenario involves defining notions such as AIS-created art, creation in itself, and the anthropocentical requirement in copyright, which means that the creator of a work should be human, the mind-brain dilemma, *et cetera.*

## 3. Conclusions

To summarise, when AIS become active in our personal and social spaces, their acts will have legal impacts. For an AIS to fulfil its function as a companion for European citizens, it may need to enter into valid legal transactions, such as purchase agreements. Therefore it can be expected that some legal capacity will be required. On the other hand, if in the course of their activities material or personal damages occur, the question of who would be liable implies a range of potential candidates from com-

[7] Whether copyright is granted or denied depends on the applicable copyright regime. Copyright protection applies to works that are "original". In a common law country such as the UK there is a relatively low threshold for protection. A work is considered to be original if its creation required sufficient "skill, judgment and labour". A work thus requires a certain amount of creative intellectual activity and a certain amount of effort. This requirement is modest when compared to the thresholds in the civil law countries such as France, Germany and The Netherlands, all of which require creativity and individuality.

puter programmers, manufacturers involved in the production of AIS to the user of the AIS. At the same time, AIS with some self-awareness cannot be treated simply as things. Sentience, autonomy and the possible ability to experience frustration, or even suffering, raises issues of legal categorisation. The question arises as to whether and how degrees of sentience, autonomy and capacity for feeling could be assessed as a basis for assigning legal capacity to AIS. Another issue that will have to be addressed is the AIS in its capacity for creating and inventing robot-generated works or patentable inventions. This raises fundamental questions with regard to the objects of intellectual property rights, and to the ownership in general.

Therefore, there are significant legal issues that need to be addressed if AIS are to be deployed in European society including our personal and public spaces. In international literature there is a call for *sui-generis* regulation to avoid hurdles in the development of AIS. The first initiatives are already taken: A proposal for a European Commission directive is now being prepared.

Effectiveness of *sui generis*/technology specific regulations is however questionable, due to the unpredictable nature of technological development. Legal history also shows that hasty measures may be counterproductive. In this we can learn from the principle of subsidiarity as advocated by the European Union, for it would be wise to demonstrate restraint in developing a specific legal framework regarding robots. At the same time, new rules and norms should be subject to the principle of sustainability, and take the interests of all stakeholders into account, with an emphasis on the longer-term interests. Whilst AIS are unique in some respects it is also important to recognise that many of the potential legal issues surrounding robots are already addressed in existing legislation. For instance, regulations surrounding corporate entities, information communications technology systems, motor vehicles, or even domestic animals could be relevant to evaluating the legal status of AIS. Therefore it needs to be identified how and where AIS fit into existing legal and normative frameworks and where such frameworks will need to be extended to take account of AIS. At the same time, the potential of self-regulatory mechanisms need to be involved. By doing this, one should seek to develop appropriate legal instruments to both protect consumer interests (privacy, safety regulations) and to contribute to the innovation and acceptance of

AIS technology in society by finding a balance between protection, security and innovation.

## 4. Sources and Further Reading

Abbott, Kenneth W., "An International Framework Agreement on Scientific and Technological Innovation and Regulation", in Marchant, Gary E., Allenby, Braden R. and Herkert, Joseph R. (eds.), *The Growing Gap Between Emerging Technologies and Legal-Ethical Oversight – The Pacing Problem*, Series, The International Library of Ethics, Law and Technology, Springer Science and Business Media B.V., 2011, p. 127.

Ainoa, Juha, Hinkka, Ville, Huttunen, Anniina, Lechner, Lorenz, Siikavirta, Sebastian, Zhang, He and Sivunen, Anu, "The Digital Evolution – From impossible to Spectacular", in Neuvo, Yrjö and Ylönen, Sami (eds.), *Bit Bang: Rays to the Future*, Helsinki University Press, Helsinki, 2009, p. 8.

Asaro, Peter M., "A Body to Kick, but Still no Soul to Damn: Legal Perspectives on Robotics", in Lin, Patrick, Abney, Keith, and Bekey, George A. (eds.), *Robot Ethics: The Ethical and Social Implications of Robotics*, MIT Press, Cambridge (MA), 2011, pp. 169-186.

Askland, Andrew, "Introduction", in Marchant, Gary E., Allenby, Braden R. and Herkert, Joseph R. (eds.), *The Growing Gap Between Emerging Technologies and Legal-Ethical Oversight – The Pacing Problem*, Series, The International Library of Ethics, Law and Technology, Springer Science and Business Media B.V., 2011.

Bennett Moses, Lyria, "*Sui Generis* Rules", in Marchant, Gary E., Allenby, Braden R. and Herkert, Joseph R. (eds.), *The Growing Gap Between Emerging Technologies and Legal-Ethical Oversight – The Pacing Problem*, Series, The International Library of Ethics, Law and Technology, Springer Science and Business Media B.V., 2011, p. 77.

Boyle, James, "Endowed by Their Creator? The Future of Constitutional Personhood", in *The Future of the Constitution Series*, 2011, no. 10 of 14, 2011, available at http://www.brookings.edu/research/papers/2011/03/09-personhood-boyle, last accessed 15 October 2012.

Calo, Ryan M., "Open Robotics", in *Maryland Law Review,* 2011, vol. 70, no. 3, pp. 101-142.

Calverley David J., "Imagining a non-biological machine as a legal person", in *AI & Society*, 2008, vol. 22, pp. 523-537.

Carter, Ruth B. and Marchant, Gary E., "Principles-Based Regulation and Emerging Technology", in Marchant, Gary E., Allenby, Braden R. and Herkert, Joseph R. (eds.), *The Growing Gap Between Emerging Technologies and Legal-Ethical Oversight – The Pacing Problem*, Series, The International Library of Ethics, Law and Technology, Springer Science and Business Media B.V., 2011, p. 157.

Caudill, Maureen, and Butler, Charles, *Naturally Intelligent Systems*, MIT Press, Cambridge (MA), 1990.

Chopra, Samir and White, Laurence F., *A Legal Theory for Autonomous Intelligent Agents*, University of Michigan Press, 2011.

Copeland, Jack, "What is Artificial Intelligence?", Alan Turing Archive, available at http://www.alanturing.net/turing_archive/pages/Reference%20Articles/What%20is%20AI.html, last accessed on 15 October 2012.

Davies, Colin R., "An evolutionary step in intellectual property rights – Artificial intelligence and intellectual property", in *Computer Law & Security Review,* 2011, vol. 27, no. 6, pp. 601-619.

Cock Buning, Madeleine de, *Auteursrecht en informatietechnologie – over de beperkte houdbaarheid van technologiespecifieke regelgeving* (diss.), Otto Cramwinckel Uitgever, Amsterdam, 1998.

Geron, Tomio, "Not Science Fiction Anymore: Mail.ru Dmitry Grishin Launches $25M Robotics Fund", Forbes, 15 June 2012, available at http://www.forbes.com/sites/tomiogeron/2012/06/15/not-science-fiction-anymore-mail-rus-dmitry-grishin-launches-25m-robotics-fund/, last accessed on 15 October 2012.

Karnow, Curtis E.A., "Liability For Distributed Artificial Intelligences", in *Berkeley Technology Law Journal online*, 1996, vol.11, pp. 147-204, available at http://btlj.org/data/articles/vol11/Karnow.pdf, last accessed on 15 October 2012.

Levy, David, *Robots Unlimited*, A K Peters Ltd., Wellesley, 2006.

Nagenborg, Michael, Capurro, Rafael, Weber, Jutta and Pingel, Christoph, "Ethical regulations on robotics in Europe", in *AI & Society*, 2008, vol. 22, no. 3, pp. 349-366.

Pagallo, Ugo, "Killers, fridges, and slaves: a legal journey in robotics", in *AI & Society*, 2011, vol. 26, no. 4, pp. 347-354.

Rappert, Brian, "Pacing Science and Technology with Codes of Conduct: Rethinking What Works", in Marchant, Gary E., Allenby, Braden R. and

Herkert, Joseph R. (eds.), *The Growing Gap Between Emerging Technologies and Legal-Ethical Oversight – The Pacing Problem*, Series, The International Library of Ethics, Law and Technology, Springer Science and Business Media B.V., 2011, p. 109.

Smits, Jan M., *Elgar encyclopaedia of comparative law,* Edward Elgar Publishing, London, 2006.

Solum, Lawrence B., "Legal Personhood for Artificial Intelligences", in *North Carolina Law Review,* 1992, vol. 70, pp. 1231-1287.

Thaler, Stephen L., "'Virtual Input' Phenomena within the Death of Simple Pattern Associator", in *Neural Networks*, 1995, vol. 8, no. 1, pp. 55-65.

Turing, Alan M., "Computing Machinery and Intelligence", in *Mind*, 1950, vol. LIX, no. 236, pp. 433-460.

Van Dam, Cees, *European Tort Law*, Oxford University Press, Oxford, 2007.

Verschure, P. F. M. J., "Connectionist Explanation: Taking positions in the Mind-Brain dilemma", in Dorffner, Georg (ed.), *Neural Networks and a New Artificial Intelligence*, 1997, Thompson, London, pp. 133-188.

**Reports:**

*Autonomous Systems: Social, Legal and Ethical Issues*, Royal Academy of Engineering, London, 2009.

*Robotics and Autonomous Systems Industry* (Final Report), The Industrial college of the Armed Forces, National Defense University, Washington DC, 2011.

IFR Statistical Department, "IFR: All-time-high for industrial robots", 1 September 2011, available at http://www.worldrobotics.org/index.php?id=123&news_id=259, accessed on 15 October 2012.

**Policy documents**

European Commission, Communication from the Commission 'Horizon 2020 - The Framework Programme for Research and Innovation', SEC(2011) 1427 & 1428 final, COM(2012) 808 final (Horizon 2020), and the Forthcoming Annex 7 to the Decision, "Work Programme 2013, Cooperation Theme 3, ICT-Information and Communication Technologies", EC C(2012), draft available at http://cordis.europa.eu/fp7/ict/docs/draft-wp2013.doc, last accessed on 15 October 2012.

CA-RoboCom D.2.4: Robot Companions: Ethical, Legal and Societal Issues, 10 May 2012, Manifesto "More than Future, Robot Companions for Citizens: Enabling Technology for Sustainable Welfare", available at http://robotcompanions.eu/system/files/page-files/RoboCom%20OVERVIEW%20.zip, last accessed on 15 October 2012.

**Other online sources**

"South Korea aims to boost robotics", UPI, 17 april 2009, available at http://www.upi.com/Science_News/2009/04/17/South-Korea-aims-to-boost-robotics/UPI-83381240007065/, last accessed on 15 October 2012.

"Robot in our lives: Presentation of the Green Paper on Robotics and Law", available at http://www.europeanrobotics12.eu/news/robot-in-our-lives-presentation-of-the-green-paper-on-robotics-and-law.aspx, last accessed on 15 October 2012.

# 3.7.

# Communication Technologies and the Future of Courts and Law

**Jim Dator**[*]

In order to forecast alternative futures of law, lawyers, courts, and judges, it is necessary to understand their alternative pasts and presents, and to determine what aspects of the pasts and presents might continue to influence the futures, and furthermore what contingencies might generate new conditions. This paper looks at the way judicial systems have been shaped by communication technologies in the past and might be shaped by current and emerging communication technologies in the future.

## 1. Changing Communication Technologies and Changing Humans

For most of its existence, *homo sapiens sapiens* has existed as nomadic hunters and gatherers in small, face-to-face groups. We are biologically, and in many ways psychologically, evolved for that kind of life, and not for the world in which we now live. Agriculture and cities – civilisation – is only a few thousand years old. Industrial and information societies are mere recent eye-blinks in human history. Alfred North Whitehead said that civilisation is a race between education and disaster. It is also a race between biology and our constructed environment, and the cultures we have created within it, including the cultures of law. Many factors are responsible for the continuing, though uneven, transformation of humans over time and space. One of the most important factors has been changes in the way in which humans communicate. When we first emerged from the older *homo* line as *homo sapiens*, we could not speak. While we had big brains and helpful hands with opposable thumbs, our ability to think, to communicate thoughts, and especially to organise each other for group

[*] **Jim Dator** is a Professor and Director of the Hawaii Research Center for Futures Studies, Department of Political Science, University of Hawaii at Manoa. Research for this essay was supported in part by grant number 123-5830 from the University of Hawaii Foundation for the project entitled "Communicating Power: Technological Innovation and Social Change in the Past, Present, and Futures".

projects was limited. It was only later when changes occurred primarily in our jaw and larynx making it possible for us to produce meaningful sounds that *homo sapiens* transformed into *homo sapiens, sapiens*. That is when we really took off as a species.

## 2. Oral Societies

While powerful and transformative, speech was still a very limited mode of communication. It was extremely difficult to hold ideas 'still' in oral societies – to take them out of their immediate context and to ponder over them. It was not possible to go back and review what had just been said, much less what had been said and intended yesterday, or (if the concept even existed) a hundred or a thousand years ago. With speech, we could better organise ourselves for group projects, but typically only for immediate action. Planning and carrying out projects that ranged over years was very difficult (but not impossible, *vide* Jebel Faya, near the Persian Gulf, and the impressively large, geographically-separated, and successful Hawaiian kingdoms based entirely on the spoken word).

## 3. Before Writing

Then, only a few thousand years ago, some humans began using symbols, at first, not to convey ideas or emotions, but to designate items, identify who owned them, how much they were worth, perhaps where they were going. For about a thousand years or so, what eventually became writing was nothing but markers, labels, lists, tables. But these pale scratches made communication across time and distance easier than it had ever been before. Jack Goody notes that this began to enable forms of social organisation the world had never seen in Egypt, Mesopotamia, India, China, and central and western South America: institutionalised religion and priests in place of free-floating spirituality; formal education and teachers instead of amorphous beliefs, and skills based on observation and imitation; terrifying hierarchical authorities of many kinds including eventually, rulers, bureaucrats, judges and jailers.

## 4. Order Without Law

Before there was writing, there was order, but no law. As Stanley Diamond made clear,

> Custom – spontaneous, traditional, personal, commonly known, corporate [...] is the modality of primitive society; law is the instrument of civilisation, of political society sanctioned by organized force, presumably above society at large, and buttressing a new set of social interest [...] Law *and* order is the historical illusion; law *versus* order is the historical reality.[1]

## 5. Law and Rigidity

Literacy – hand writing and reading – became a profoundly transformative technology. Even though most people did not know how to read and write, formal life in scribal societies was for the first time based on written rules that were interpreted and enforced by power-wielding authorities. Wherever writing developed, rigid, rule-based, remote, enforceable government emerged in place of flexible, functional, direct governance. Most importantly, writing enabled thoughts to be frozen, codified, and made mandatory across time and space. Vast empires capturing huge numbers of people spread in large part because of the power of the written word and the power that the word gave to those who interpreted and enforced it.[2]

## 6. Colonising Time and Space

By preserving written law and religious scriptures, and by empowering scribes and priests charged with further preserving, interpreting, and enforcing legal and religious words, for the first time the past could effectively control the future, squelching spontaneous and easy adaptation to changing times and needs which the eternal present of oral societies made possible. While it might seem to one living in an oral society that norms and mores were eternal, in fact they were for the most part highly ephemeral and fleeting. Old norms were quickly forgotten when they proved dysfunctional and new ones easily adopted in ways that made them seem eternal.

---

1 Stanley Diamond, "The Rule of Law versus the Order of Custom", in Robert Paul. Wolff (ed.), *The Rule of Law*, Simon and Schuster, 1971, pp. 120 and 140.

2 Eric Havelock, *The Muse Learns to Write: Reflections on Orality and Literacy from Antiquity to the Present*, Yale University Press, New Haven, 1986; also D. R. Olson and N. Torrance (eds.), *The Making of Literate Societies*, Blackwell Publishers, 2001.

Jack Goody writes about law: "The very fact that laws exist in written form makes a profound difference, first to the nature of its sources, secondly to the ways of changing the rules, thirdly to the judicial process, and fourthly to court organization". Once written and enforced, rules are harder to change than they are in oral societies. Moreover, "legal norms no longer reside in the memory of each and every individual (at least of every elder) but may be literally buried in documents to be disinterred only by specialists in the written word".[3]

## 7. Law and Gutenberg's Printing Press

The next big transformative step in communication and governance was the printing press – and now we are approaching modern times and the kind of governance, law, and courts with which we are all familiar. Though printing was known first in China and Korea, and played a role in forming the legal systems of those cultures, it was the printing press (and auxiliary developments) of Gutenberg and others of the 15th and 16th centuries that enabled the spread and success of the Protestant Reformation, the flowering of old knowledge as new that energised the Renaissance, the creation of the Westphalian nation-State system, the cosmologies of Copernicus, Bacon, and Newton, and other ideas and technologies of the modern scientific-industrial revolution, culminating in the maturing of theories of 'democratic' governance of Hobbes, Montesquieu, Locke, Rousseau and others.[4]

## 8. The First New Nation

Fortuitously 'America' provided the *tabula rasa* upon which the fantastic idea formed of 'constituting' a new nation out of widely separated and diverse, artificially-created colonies by assembling a group of highly privileged men to come together, talk and then eventually write down a (handwritten!) Constitution for the United States. Informed by Greek and Roman Classics, and based on cutting edge ideas and technologies of the

---

[3] Jack Goody, *The Logic of Writing and the Organization of Society*, Cambridge University Press, 1986, pp. 134 and 143.

[4] Marshall McLuhan, *Understanding Media: The Extensions of Man*, McGraw-Hill, 1964; Elizabeth Eisenstein, *The Printing Press as an Agent of Change: Communications and Cultural Transformations in Early Modern Europe,* Cambridge University Press, 1979, S. Baron et al. (eds.), *Agent of Change. Print Culture Studies after Elizabeth L. Eisenstein*, University of Massachusetts Press, 2007.

day – especially Newtonian mechanics, Deistic theology, and the hand-powered printing press (steam-powered printing presses did not come into existence until about 30 years after the US did) – the US Constitution was a breath-taking social invention, brilliantly overcoming a host of design-challenges, though by no means all of them, while creating serious future problems as well. It was designed for, and fit for, a vast, overwhelmingly agricultural society with a small, widely-scattered, rural population of semi-illiterate farmers and plantation owners, many of whom wanted political independence from their mother country, far, far away.

## 9. 'Constitutionalism' and the Magic of Words

The fundamental principles of 'constitutionalism' have been widely copied. Since 1789, there have been very many opportunities for polities to envision and fashion new forms of governance – the governments of new American states themselves; the political revolutions in England, France and elsewhere in Europe in the 19th century; Russia in 1918; Japan, Germany and other 'Axis' nations after the Second World War; numerous former colonies in South America, Africa, the Middle East, and Asia, also after the Second World War; the collapse of socialist systems in the late 1980s and early 1990s; the attempt to create a European union; and most recently 'nation-building' opportunities after America attacked and destroyed existing governments.

And yet, people sat down and 'wrote a constitution', which, at the end, unreflexively imitated the Newtonian mechanistic and rationalistic assumptions of the late 18th century, ignoring the subsequent scholarship of Darwin, Freud, Einstein, Heisenberg, and Foucault. Moreover, they have acted as though the only communication technologies available for governance are still the printing press and the spoken word. In spite of the social revolution produced by electric and later electronic communication technologies that increasingly enable people to participate directly in governing so many aspects of their lives, all formal structures of government make direct involvement in government difficult to impossible. They still require 'representatives' physically to assemble somewhere in a central location, debate policies, and 'make law' by writing down their decisions, which are then administered by bureaucratised humans and enforced by officers of the law backed by the threat or use of deadly force. All of that made sense at one time. It is problematic now, and has been for quite a while.

Certain printed words (and those who wield and interpret them) have obtained over time a kind of arcane, magical, holy, super-human power vastly exceeding that of other printed words. When the power of these words seems to fail, instead of reaching beyond the logo-centric cosmologies and technologies that underlie them, and trying to base social order on newer cosmologies and technologies, most people – rulers and ruled alike, look for stronger words and more powerful, magical, phrases.

The situation in the United States is especially conspicuous in this regard. A stunning kind of logo-fundamentalism has captured both church and State. The US Supreme Court is currently controlled by people who believe that the original words of the US Constitution have an essential and unchanging meaning that is not only separate from, and superior to, what those words might have evolved to mean now (much less, how they might now be better interpreted to mean), but also have essential meanings separate from what even the Founding Fathers themselves might have intended the words to mean. The source of this kind of interpretation might be the fact that some of the most influential members of the Court were educated at a time when what was known as the 'New Criticism' was popular in departments of English in US universities.[5] According to the New Criticism, a work of literature must be interpreted on its own terms alone. An author's intentions, his experiences, or the historical period in which a work was written have no relevance. All that matters is the meaning of the words themselves as discovered by a close reading of the text itself.

## 10. The Word Is Out: The Image Is In

Some years ago, Ethan Katsch insisted that the Word was out – or soon would be – and that law, in form and practice, was about to be transformed by electronic communication technologies. Basing his argument on analogies of the role of the printing press as pioneered by the works of Marshall McLuhan and Elisabeth Eisenstein cited above, Katsh argued that law needed to, and would, find a new basis in electronics, and that new forms of governance would emerge. Many legal scholars seem not to have recognised the role that the printing press itself played over past cen-

5 Margaret Talbot, Supreme Confidence. The Jurisprudence of Justice Anton Scalia, The New Yorker, 2005, pp. 40–55.

turies in making 'law' the conservative, change-resistant agency that it is (or was) as electronic media began to play a new, more dynamic role.[6]

## 11. Consequence over Precedents?

The concept of 'law' thus may be shifting once again from being the fluid, adaptive, oral statements of judges in the old medieval courts, to fixed print documents (expressed in written 'constitutions' and 'positive' laws) in the recent modern age, and now to being fluid electronic bits. With the advent of the curiously-named 'word processor' 40 years ago, everything written has become a draft that can be 'cut and pasted' into other documents for numerous purposes. In the current 'Information Age', nothing written is ever final. Everything is fluid, flexible, temporary. 'Consequence' seems more important than 'precedents'. As we move beyond the information age, perhaps to a 'dream society', law may become as temporary as everything else in the society it seeks to regulate. Law might become a fleeting suggestion expressed in audio/visual/olfactory/tactile images in N-dimensional cyberspace.[7]

## 12. Social Media and the Law

Presently, social media and social networking are reshaping how people interact with themselves and with former 'authorities'. When sick, many people prefer to link-in and seek remedies from friends than to go to a doctor. When faced with a problem, they seek the advice of each other, and not that of a priest or a lawyer. When members of trial juries, they tweet about the case if they can get away with it. They only go to libraries if they want a quiet, safe, dry place to sleep. They have decreasing respect for formal authorities and more faith in the judgment of their friends.

---

6 Ethan Katsh, *The Electronic Media and the Transformation of Law*, Oxford University Press, New York, 1989; also Majid Tehranian, *Technologies of Power: Information Machines and Democratic Prospects*, Ablex Publishing, 1990.

7 Jim Dator, "Judicial Governance of the Long Blur", in *Futures*, 2001, vol. 33, no. 1; Jim Dator and Yongseok Seo, "Korea as the Wave of a Future: The Emerging Dream Society of Icons and Aesthetic Experience", in Susan Pares and J. E. Hoare (ed.), *Korea: The Past and the Present; Selected Papers from the British Association for Korean Studies BAKS Papers Series, 1991–2005*, Global/Oriental, Oxford, 2008.

## 13. Extraterrestrial Law?

Electronic communication technologies are also changing the practice of law with a clear movement from geographically defined 'law offices' and 'law libraries', to 'virtual communities' – and virtual courthouses globally dispersed. Though many patriotic jurists strongly protest, there are many good reasons to encourage the emergence of law beyond that of sovereign nations alone, and beyond 'international' law as well. By adopting 'best practices' from each other, a functional global law is emerging to address the challenges of our increasingly globalised humanity. But since settlements on the Moon, Mars, asteroids, and various L-5 locations are once again being seriously considered by China, India, Japan, Brazil, Russia, Europe – if not yet the United States – it is also time for future-oriented jurists to contemplate the emergence of law for the inner-solar system, which, being electronic – or 'post-electronic' – can be 'located' wherever intelligence is found throughout the universe.

## 14. Rights of Robots?

Indeed, electronic communication technologies have changed the 'persona' of law as well. Once upon a time, intelligence, such as it is, was considered a human monopoly. With the rise first of 'expert systems' and now of robots with artificial intelligence, we might embrace the rule not only of 'smart' legal and judicial software, but also of cyber lawyers, cyber judges, and bills of rights for robots.

In fact, it is not clear why humans need to be involved in routine judicial decision-making at all anymore. Of all social inventions (except mathematics itself), law is the most fit for computerisation of all but the most novel aspects of judicial decision-making. For 40 years, a major aim in most US legislatures has been to eliminate the discretion of judges by mandating determinant sentencing and other limitations on human judgment. It makes sense now to eliminate human error, fatigue, and bias altogether by eliminating humans wherever possible, relying entirely on judgments made by artificial intelligences. We do this in almost all areas of life already, why should judiciaries remain aloof?

## 15. Intelligent Law?

Marcel Bullinga has argued that "making rules and enforcing them are important government tasks. Right now, laws are written down on paper and enforced by individuals. In the future, all rules and laws will be incorporated into expert systems and chips embedded in cars, appliances, doors, and buildings – that is, our physical environment. No longer will police officers and other government personnel be the only law enforcement. Our physical environment will enforce the law as well". In his view, future governments will no longer write laws on paper that are interpreted and enforced by people. Instead, 'laws' will be open-standard software with authoritative algorithms that contain the appropriate regulatory information and protocols over the operation of all human activities. Intelligent devices will 'know' what laws or regulations apply and how to act upon them. They will make decisions and self-enforce them. They will resolve conflicts between them and conflicts of the laws among them. What were once called 'constitutions' will be composed of algorithms, describing processes by which they shall be distributed, protected, implemented, and revised, and new authoritative algorithms formulated. What were once 'courts', 'judges', 'lawyers' and the rest will be algorithms as well. No unaugmented humans need to be involved.[8]

## 16. Telepathic Law?

In the foreseeable future, biochemical processes may replace electronics and lead to brain-to-brain and source-to-brain transfer. Behavioural control may then move not only from humans to the environment, but also from the environment to the brain and central nervous systems. We may finally break through the limited interface of our biological input-output mechanisms. So far we cannot make screens smaller than we can see or buttons too small to push. If we can go beyond the input-output mechanism of eyes, mouths, ears, and fingers, and communicate directly brain-to-brain, or source to brain, we can do away with all 'media' and have direct mind-to-mind governance, either via electronic-like implants or direct mind transfer – 'mental telepathy'.

## 17. The End of Law and Order?

This kind of high-tech dream and post-dream society may not be realised as some of us have imagined. It may not be achieved at all. On the one hand our attachment to written words and to lawyers and judges who in-

[8] Marcel Bullinga, "Intelligent Government: Invisible, Automatic, Everywhere", in *The Futurist*, 2004, pp. 32–36.

terpret may be too resistant. On the other hand, looming and neglected environmental, energy, and economic challenges may make continued high tech societies impossible. We may effectively 'run out of oil' before we can develop and bring online viable alternatives. Long-deferred environmental challenges loom. Global population growth continues catastrophically at the same time that population is declining in some parts of the world. All economies are unsustainable to the extent that they are based on endless debt and endless growth in a finite planet. These problems are global, and yet we have no way to address them globally. Our obsolete nation-State system is powerless, and so the future of humanity on Earth is uncertain. It is entirely possible a way of life called 'development' that we have only known for a few hundred years is coming to an end. We may become farmers and hunters with their means of communication and conflict resolution once again. While I vastly prefer the high tech future I have outlined, the global trajectory seems to me to be largely heading in the other direction.

## 18. Sources and Further Reading


Baron, S. *et al.* (eds.), *Agent of Change: Print Culture Studies after Elizabeth L. Eisenstein*, University of Massachusetts Press, 2007.

Bullinga, Marcel, "Intelligent Government: Invisible, Automatic, Everywhere", in *The Futurist*, 2004, pp. 32–36.

Dator, Jim, "American State Courts, Five Tsunamis, and Four Alternative Futures", in Jim Dator and Yongseok Seo, "Korea as the Wave of a Future: The Emerging Dream Society of Icons and Aesthetic Experience", in Susan Pares and J. E. Hoare (eds.), *Korea: The Past and the Present; Selected Papers from the British Association for Korean Studies BAKS Papers Series, 1991–2005*, 2008.

Dator, Jim, "Futures and Trial Courts", in *Widener Journal of Law*, 2009, vol. 18, no. 2, 2009.

Dator, Jim, "Judicial Governance of the Long Blur", in *Futures*, 2001, vol. 33, no. 1.

Dator, Jim, "The Unholy Trinity, Plus One", in *Journal of Futures Studies,* 2009, vol. 13, no. 3, pp. 33–48.

Dator, Jim, "When Courts Are Overgrown with Grass: The Role of Courts in the 21st Century", in *Futures*, 2000, vol. 32, no. 2.

Eisenstein, Elizabeth, *The Printing Press as an Agent of Change: Communications and Cultural Transformations in Early Modern Europe*, Cambridge University Press, 1979.

Goody, Jack, *The Logic of Writing and the Organization of Society*, Cambridge University Press, 1986.

Goody, Jack, *The Power of the Written Tradition*, Smithsonian Institution Press, 2000.

Havelock, Eric, *The Muse Learns to Write: Reflections on Orality and Literacy from Antiquity to the Present*, Yale University Press, New Haven, 1986.

Katsh, Ethan, *The Electronic Media and the Transformation of Law*, Oxford University Press, New York, 1989.

McLuhan, Marshall, *Understanding Media: The Extensions of Man*, McGraw-Hill, 1964.

Olson, D. R. and Torrance, N. (eds.), *The Making of Literate Societies,* Blackwell Publishers, 2001.

Tehranian, Majid, *Technologies of Power: Information Machines and Democratic Prospects*, Ablex Publishing, 1990.

Talbot, Margaret, *Supreme Confidence: The Jurisprudence of Justice Anton Scalia*, The New Yorker, 2005, pp. 40–55.

# Chapter IV

## The Perspective of States:
## What Is Changing or Needs to Change?

# 4.1.

# Nobody Owns the State: How a Board of Trustees Can Help to Innovate Our Core Institutions

**Maurits Barendrecht**[*]

An intriguing feature of Western States is that no one is accountable for the core institutions. Take the parliament, the Cabinet of Ministers, the civil justice system, the Supreme Court, the law-making process or the Ministry of Justice, for example. There is no ultimate owner who is responsible for its performance. There may be convincing historical explanations for this. But why keep it that way? Countries may be able to achieve major improvements in the quality of life and economic growth if they expose their core institutions to the innovation processes that are common outside the realm of these core State organisations. Imagine if the State were to have a board of trustees. How would it monitor State institutions, get rid of bad habits and trigger innovation?

## 1. The Accountability Gap

Members of parliament and of the highest courts are passers-by. They struggle hard to make the best of the years in which they work in these positions. Even the leaders of the pack are more like the temporary occupants of a function, than the CEOs of organisations responsible for overall performance. A Prime Minister, the President of a Supreme Court or the speaker of a parliament can be criticised on how he performs his tasks. S/he is not supposed to take the lead in reorganising the cabinet, the court or parliament. So the working methods are left untouched.

This makes these organisations very special. Unlike other organisations, these institutions have no clear strategy, no targets, no visitation processes, no annual performance appraisals and no supervisory boards. There is no independent auditing of what these organisations do, they are hardly ever reorganised by consultants. They are almost immune to

* **Maurits Barendrecht** is a visiting Professor on the Rule of Law at The Hague Institute for the Internationalisation of Law and a Professor of Private Law at Tilberg University.

change. The formal rules governing them are set out in the constitution, or in other instruments that are very hard to adjust.

The ownership of the civil justice system or the law-making process is even more diffuse. A civil justice system critically depends on the quality of substantive laws, the design and financing of courts, civil procedure rules and the quality of legal services provided by the market. Law-making processes depend on the selection of the most urgent problems, the search process towards good solutions, bargaining with stakeholders, the quality of proposal-writing, the process of advising about laws, the scrutiny by parliaments, the options of challenging laws before courts and the way citizens are informed about new rules. These processes are hardly ever evaluated, let alone calibrated to make them work more effectively from input to ultimate outcomes.

## 2. Stability, Changing the Constitution and Quality through Checks and Balances?

Is this a serious flaw in design, or an implication of a choice for imperfect institutions that work through checks and balances? Most constitutional theorists are likely to argue that it is the latter. Democratic governance by these institutions may have many imperfections, but the mistakes made as a consequence of this can be corrected by public scrutiny or by other institutions. Gaps in laws can be filled by courts, and if necessary they can strike down the most inappropriate rules in a process of constitutional review. Bad laws can be replaced by better laws. Cabinet ministers who cannot find a way to work together under the existing rules can be replaced by politicians who know how to play the game.

Of course constitutions can be amended or replaced by new versions. Studies of these processes show that such change is slow and incremental, but also that core elements of constitutional design are correlated with economic growth and other desirable outcomes. On the other hand, we all know the examples of presidents manipulating constitutional change processes in order to grab power beyond two consecutive terms. So it may be better to seal off provisions regarding the number of terms a president can have or the way districts of members of parliaments have been defined. It may even be a good thing that institutions cannot be changed by their leaders. This protects them from being abused. By design, these leaders are doomed to be passers-by, the rule of law having freed us from the rule by men.

## 3. Run by Habit and Incentives of Participants

But what happens to an organisation that is not capable of changing its work processes if needed? A company run in this way would soon be out of business, perhaps after being plundered by the directors and the employees, at the expense of shareholders, the tax authorities and the customers. But State institutions are not exposed to competition, so they continue to exist. The way they work is very likely to be based on habits, good habits and bad habits, shaped by the incentives of participants. The following is a list of habits that have crept into the State institutions of some countries:

- Spending a good part of the time in a leading government job to raise funds and to campaign for re-election;
- Vicious advertisements, attacking competitors on the basis of a selection of facts, and a biased way of presenting them;
- Anti-competitive agreements always to follow the party line when voting in parliament;
- Agreeing with other incumbents to set boundaries of districts in such a way that re-election for all of us is more certain;
- Letting a vote for a proposal be bought in exchange for a specific benefit for your own constituency;
- Trading with jobs in high government positions instead of letting the best person be selected;
- Agreements between parties forming a coalition government in secret negotiations limiting the issues that will be tackled by the government;
- Ministries letting their agenda be determined by media and day-to-day political reality instead of by a list of long-term priorities for their area of government;
- Journalists interviewing politicians and trying to set them up against colleagues, because conflict sells;
- Polarised debates over proposals;
- Politicians not being allowed to collect information about issues from ministries directly but only through ministers answering questions in parliament;
- Limited capacity for legislation;

- Selecting simple issues with simple solutions instead of tackling the most important problems for a country;
- Holding officials accountable and firing them for the way they handled one specific problem instead of on their overall performance as leaders of their organisations;
- Writing rules that can only be understood by fellow lawyers;
- Buying or using television stations to advance the position of one particular party;
- Playing "chicken" with budgets and scaring the heck out of financial markets instead of responsibly managing the State coffers;
- Calling elections in order to advance the interests of own parties instead of serving the people with a good government until the end of the term;
- Highest courts selecting interesting moral dilemma cases such as "wrongful birth" instead of helping to develop guidelines for the most common and urgent conflicts people have;
- Letting people wait for years before issues are decided that have a huge impact on their lives or their businesses.

Nobody is to blame for these habits. Yes, some practise them more fanatically than others. But they have become part of the game everybody plays. Within the framework of the old State institutions, these habits work for politicians wanting to build their careers and achieve results, for media wanting to sell their wares and for judges who want to have good relationships with their colleagues in court.

Yet these habits have enormous costs. Without them, there would be more trust in government, less uncertainty and less squandering of resources. Good government is one of the surest ways to enhance economic growth. So why not innovate ourselves out of these habits?

## 4. Imagining a Board of Trustees

Let us imagine a board of trustees, with the mission to ensure that the working methods of our core State institutions are gradually improved and innovated. This is just a thought experiment. There may be many other ways to get innovation of the State going, but for the moment we will assume that an owner of the problem is needed.

Getting this done would be really difficult. Such a new institution would suffer from similar problems as the old ones. After a good start, bad habits would start developing and incentives of the participants would take over the steering wheel. The board would need to be selected, would need to agree on working methods, would need some powers, a budget and much more. All of this would cause headaches and political bickering, at least under the present rules of the game in most capitals in the world.

In a worst case scenario, such a board would develop into a Supreme Council of the Armed Forces such as the one in Egypt or Iranian Guardian Council of the Constitution. It might become just another of the world's 4,500 think tanks, soon to be branded as conservative, liberal or religious.

But not every new and independent institution is a disaster. Central banks, specialised courts, international regulatory networks and regulatory agencies can contribute to the common good if they have a specific task, such as using interest rates to keep inflation in check, dealing with all employment problems in a country or ensuring food safety. So why not an agency that monitors the performance of core State institutions and ensures that innovation takes place to improve them if necessary?

## 5. Monitoring Core Institutions: Are They Doing What Is Normal?

One of the problems when monitoring State institutions will be the benchmarks. Benchmarks for courts and for parliaments are now developing. However, they tend to codify the present rules of the game on a comparative basis. So, implicitly, they allow all the bad habits that developed within the framework of these rules to remain. That is not a good way to stimulate innovation. On the contrary, if new parliaments being set up in Arab countries follow these benchmarks they are likely to take over all our bad habits. Selling our institutions abroad without first updating them against the latest viruses is a sure way to lose the remaining trust in the Western type of governance.

The habits in the bulleted list in Section 3 suggest another way of monitoring what happens in State institutions. Many of them are habits that would be considered bad habits in other parts of life. A company is not allowed to mislead the public and to vilify competitors in an advertisement. Agreements to vote always with others would be considered a cartel in most places. In my institute, I am supposed to evaluate people on what they achieved on their tasks overall, not on how they handled one issue. Looking for dissent and then blowing it up would be called "gossip" in most communities, and engaging in it is a sure career stopper in corporations, as is hopping from problem to problem and never tackling the real issues. Not having a budget ready on time is unthinkable, as is intentionally and openly manipulating the processes for getting a job.

A board of trustees could prioritise these habits and address them one by one, by showing how they relate to norms of cooperation in communities, corporations and the market for goods and services. If the habits were out of sync with what happens elsewhere in society, adjusting the processes through innovation would be a good idea.

Most of these habits were never intended to be part of the game anyhow. The framers of the constitution and Montesquieu did not foresee them. They are the result of creativity of the participants. Rules have to be adjusted to weed out bad habits and to level the playing field. Markets need regulation (remember the financial crisis?). In cycling, there are now rules for the minimum weight of racing bikes and anti-doping rules the founders of the Tour de France never considered. Parliaments, the media, cabinets and courts need to adjust as well.

## 6. Ensuring Innovation

Innovation is mostly about integrating good habits. Since the 1800s, the options for collective decision-making and governing communities have broadened enormously. The following habits would be rather high on any nomination to be really integrated in a variety of State institutions:

- Methods for collective dialogue and facilitated interaction instead of debate;
- Collective decision-making by Analytic Hierarchy Process, democracy and many more;
- Opinion polls as tools to let people participate in prioritising problems to be solved by governments;
- Electronic voting on issues in a way that informs government decision-making;
- Cost-benefit analysis and SWOT analysis by experts and interaction with the broader public in consultation processes;

- Methods for deliberative democracy around issues where both specialised expertise and citizen participation are essential;
- Mediation and conflict management skills in courts and government decision-making;
- Complaint handling methods.

Innovation processes could be kick-started in many ways, for example leaders of State institutions could be asked about their reform programmes addressing issues. It would also be good to create some competition, inviting prototypes for new versions of institutions and to test them. For instance, one area of governance such as housing or health care could be addressed by State institutions following new rules or entirely new designs. Allocating funds for promising innovations, or engaging social entrepreneurs to do this would certainly also be part of the menu.

## 7. Conclusion

If institutions have no owners, we choose to be run by habit, good and bad. Relying on checks and balances between imperfect institutions, knowing that the game is increasingly manipulated by the participants, is not the only option that we have. Innovating our core institutions gradually is an alternative. We need to retake ownership of how we are governed. As a first step, governing our State should be brought in line with the way we – and the State – govern our own affairs.

## 8. Sources and Further Reading

Congleton, Roger and Rasch, Birgitta, "Amendment Procedures and Constitutional Stability", in Roger Congleton and Birgitta Rasch (eds.), *Democratic Constitutional Design and Public Policy: Analysis and Evidence*, MIT Press, Cambridge Mass., 2006.

European Parliament, Office for Promotion of Parliamentary Democracy, *Benchmarking for Parliaments: Self-Assessment or Minimum Criteria*, 2012.

Voigt, Stefan, "Positive Constitutional Economics II: A Survey of Recent Developments", in *Public Choice*, 2011, vol. 146, no. 1, pp. 205–256.

# 4.2.

## Definite Uncertainties and the Grand Design of the Legal System in China

**Ji Weidong***

The world has become much more complex as a result of globalisation, which on the one hand frees the market economy from territorial constraints, while on the other hand intensifies competition and conflicts of interests among countries. In the globalisation process, with incorporates the parallel and concurrent developments of uniformity-diversity and harmony-conflict, there have emerged certain complex structures. These global complexities and accompanying social uncertainties have further worsened since the financial crisis erupted in the United States in September 2008. Within this context, the Chinese legal system faces a dilemma: reducing external complexity and uncertainty requires rigid binding norms, while changing circumstances demand expediencies, which relativize the effects of rules.

Although fierce economic competition caused by globalisation enhances public awareness of the importance of the State, and China needs to continue the modernisation progress of building a more complete sovereignty and a legal community, the political reality today is supranational. Moreover, modern capitalist civilisation is at a dead end. The recent economic depression is just another vivid example of the unsustainable mode of overproduction-overconsumption and the collapse of the finance-driven development model. The future development pattern of China, therefore, is worth serious exploration and consideration, especially in regard to its fundamental elements and institutional structure.

---

* **Ji Weidong** is Dean and Presiding Chair Professor of KoGuan Law School, Shanghai Jiao Tong University, China, since 2008.

# 1. The Dilemma of Promoting Rule-of-Law and Paradigm Innovations

## 1.1. Uncertainties and the Role of Policy

The world has become much more complex as a result of globalisation, which on the one hand frees the market economy from territorial constraints, while on the other hand intensifies the competition and interests of conflicts among countries. Global complexities and social uncertainties have further worsened since the financial crisis erupted in the United States in September 2008. Under this unprecedented backdrop, the Chinese legal system is in a dilemma: reducing external complexity and uncertainty requires rigid binding norms, while changing circumstances demand expediencies, which relativize the effects of rules.

In general, uncertainties can be categorised into three types: 1. probabilistic uncertainties, which can be calculated and forecasted based on the probability theory (which may be termed 'risks'); 2. definite uncertainties, which lie completely outside of any rational calculation and prediction (which may be termed fate); and 3. uncontrollable uncertainties, that is, a violent and extremely unstable insecurity that undermines the structure and functions of the system (in other words, a crisis). From the perspective of legal order, the most noteworthy are definite uncertainties, because in such situations human behaviour tends to imitate and follow the majority, causing a one-sided trend and resonance phenomenon. Since legal techniques are diminished and marginalised when we consider definite uncertainties, the tendency of mutual imitation increases and definite uncertainties multiply. In this sense, preventing probabilistic uncertainties from deteriorating into definite uncertainties is the key policy priority of today's institution design. To state it in the positive, the rational first step is to transform definite uncertainties to probabilistic uncertainties.

## 1.2. Inherent Tensions of the Existing Legal System

In 2011, the socialist legal system with Chinese characteristics was officially declared "basically formed". A deeper analysis reveals that the Chinese legal system contains inherently diverse and conflicting elements. 'Chinese characteristics' connote local uniqueness and cultural regionalisms, which directly contradict the generality of modern legal systems, participation in global governance, and the contemporary mission of promoting civilisation change. The term 'socialist', in addition, embodies non-market factors and an anti-individual liberty disposition against the very fundamental concept of personality as the basis of a modern legal system. Entangled in confusing relationships of individual, collective, State and society, the ill-fated Chinese civil code has therefore been controversial for a long time. To a certain degree, the legal system is supposed to be a closed set of rules; otherwise, formal rationality and normative effects could not be achieved. In China, on the contrary, the tradition of emphasizing differentiated treatment in accordance with *QingLiFa* (a mixture of human feelings, natural justice and statutory rules), the conventional Chinese self-organising mechanisms, and the socialism of populist democracy reinforced by coercive power, display strong openness and elasticity. The tension therein manifests itself in the heated debates of amending three procedural laws, respectively the civil, criminal and administrative procedural laws, in which professionalism versus the mass line, the adjudicative power competing against the prosecutorial power are just the tip of the iceberg.

## 2. The Pitfall of Shirking Responsibility

### 2.1. Integration and Judicial Responses

In order to grease institutional frictions and resolve conflicts of rules, the focus of integration efforts should shift from continually strengthening the legislative function to effective enforcement and adjudication, especially techniques of interpretation which could bridge the gaps between rules and facts of individual cases, expanding the protection of rights, and fine-tuning or even creating special policies and jurisprudence with professional skills ingeniously applied in an indeterminate legal framework. The Chinese judiciary, unfortunately, has taken the opposite approach and has further pursued the openness and elasticity of rules. As the intrinsic consistency of the legal system diminishes, uncertainties increase and the problems of power-above-the-law continue.

A sympathetic inquiry into the logic behind the above-mentioned phenomenon reveals that the very reason that Chinese political-legal authorities promoted so-called 'big mediation' (*da tiaojie*) practices to handle social uncertainties lies in the impetus for flexibility in law. Within a rapidly transforming society such as China, conflicts intensify day by day, new controversies emerge endlessly and the fine line of legal-illegal gradually blurs. It is therefore very hard to make a definite decision under the prescribed statutory rules. Mediation and compromise come to adjudication's rescue. In the same vein, it is also understandable that the 'active judiciary' campaign, imbued with specific political connotations and administrative influences, was also launched to evade formal litigation and seek extra-judicial remedies.

### 2.2. The Paradox of the Criterion of People's Satisfaction with Court Performance

Recently in China there has been a popular idea that judicial performance should be evaluated by the degree of people's satisfaction. A hidden belief is that judges could adjust the application of law in accordance with mainstream attitudes; judges' discretion is therefore necessary and justified. Obviously, this active judicial policy will spur a flock of litigants to take advantage of the discretionary area carved out by this, greatly increasing communication between courts and the public. In practice, this judicial policy has caused Chinese courts trouble: disputants are encouraged to race to the courthouse, but judges are left with only outdated mediation techniques. As a matter of fact, it is impossible for courts to satisfy everyone. At least in most cases, half of the parties (the losing party) will be discontent with the unfavourable judgment. If courts attempt to please everyone, it is nothing but a shackling of themselves. To put it in another way, when people's satisfaction or people's feelings become criteria by which judicial performance is assessed, the administration of justice is then reduced to nothing but subjective prejudices and capricious feelings. The implied message is that judiciary is insignificant, and the legitimacy of judicial authority rests upon public opinion. This is nothing less than the deconstruction of the court system, a variant of legal nihilism.

### 2.3. Individual Responsibility and Nobody's Responsibility in 'Big Mediation'

The State is a certainty supplier in an uncertain world. From disorder to order, anarchy to government, the pivot of the evolution is the change from definite uncertainties to probabilistic uncertainty, that is, reducing uncertainties and increasing certainties.

When uncertainties increase, in addition to the resort to procedure as a solution, more emphasis should be placed on the responsibility regime, mainly the legal responsibility regime. The Achilles' heel of the current 'big mediation' and 'active judiciary' movements is that no meaningful responsibility or accountability system could survive. More than that, in the name of democratic politics on the basis of individual responsibility, we might find ourselves in the woeful predicament of no one being responsible for anything. Take the active judiciary movement, for example. Courts, supposed to be the last defence of State order, are now on the front line. The politicised judicial process draws attention to objective standards and firewalls in specific cases, exposing individual judges to unknown political consequences and risks. So judges tend to skirt their duties and dodge finger-pointing from the society.

In a well-functioning rule of law system, the legislative power is objective-oriented, policy-driven, and tolerant of political compromises; the executive power emphasizes hierarchy, efficiency, activism and expedience; whereas the judicial power is premised on law adherence, setting the bottom line of institutional fairness. In a specific case, the judiciary is only amenable to law and has the final binding say. This principle is the requirement of rules synthesis. It makes sure that the reasoning process of each judgment can be restored, verified and reproduced, substantiating the judicial responsibility system. Without sound, expounded reasons, judges cannot decline jurisdiction nor refuse to make decisions simply because of the lack of express statutory rules or a particular expertise. After an appellate procedure, judicial decisions are final and binding. Only in this manner can a decision-maker be responsible, and can the responsibility be clear and certain.

## 3. Ochlocracy Induced by Judicial Democratisation

### 3.1. Flexibility in Law Application Breeds Judicial Corruption

The primary side-effect of the 'active judiciary' and 'big mediation' movements in China is the ballooning flexibility of statutory rules, which gives free rein to executive power, thus changing probabilistic uncertainties into definite uncertainties. As judicial discretion also expands, it becomes quite normal that disputants imitate each other and deliberately put pressure on courts through persistent threats and demands, just as a popular saying vividly describes, "no fuss, no solution; small fuss, small solution; big fuss, big solution". As a result, it is the party agreement, instead of the general rule of justice, which serves as the legitimising basis of law.

The objective and neutral conception of justice eventually evaporates. This is the hidden logic of the so-called judicial democratisation.

Since judicial decision-making is turning into a consensus reached on the basis of mediation and settlement, it is difficult, if not impossible, to determine judge's responsibility: the higher the mediated settlement rate, the narrower the scope for accountability. There follows naturally an epidemic of judicial corruption. Under the responsibility and pressure of incorrectly-handled cases, more and more judges would be willing to evade their decision-making responsibilities. 'Big mediation' is a most convenient bypass. With extra-legal measures unbound, no matter how much the accountability system is stressed, judges can never be blamed for failing to justify their decisions. The line between legal and illegal is starkly vague. What we have is the resurgence of unbridled power.

### 3.2. The Danger of Judicial Deference to the Public

If the judicial power degenerates so that it yields to the sham democracy of manipulable popular opinions, the spirit of rationality and self-discipline will wither away, material desires and short-term acts of immediate interests will prevail, and populism and emotive public opinion will dominate the public sphere. It might not be long before society regresses to ochlocracy. It is the ochlocracy of 'bread and circuses' policy, extravagant social gathering in the Palace and bloody carnival at the Coliseum that hastened the decline of the Roman Empire. It is also the ochlocracy of generous annuity, bloated civil servants and indulging connivance of tax frauds and evasions that led to the budget failure and State bankruptcy of today's Greece.

## 4. Basic Dimensions of the Rule of Law: Sollen and Coordination

### 4.1. Concepts Explained

The principal cause of 'active judiciary' and 'big mediation' movements in China can be found in the misunderstanding of two fundamental dimensions of law. Generally, as rules of conduct, law deals with two types of issues: sollen and coordination. These two functions of law are respectively distinctive and should be clearly differentiated. In China, on the contrary, there is no explicit distinction, those two are intertwined, making impossible conceptual analysis and comparison. In particular, the coordination function of law has long been ignored, resulting in a chronic entanglement of ideology that institutional reforms have failed to shake off.

In this paper, sollen refers to the duty to do the right thing. It concerns value judgment, moral and legitimating elements, and also it relates to justifications of compliance. Sollen is closely associated with the cultural tradition and ideology of a society, in Friedrich K. Savigny's words, the 'national ethos'. As a country attaches great importance to its substantive ethical code and cultural identity, China always emphasizes core values. Thus sollen is a political priority and focal point of law. The rule of property ownership and domestic relationship, for instance, always involves the social conception of justice and moral order. The same applies for principles of public order and equitable responsibility. Undoubtedly, sollen commands everything, sometimes even against the facts. Disproportionate insistence on a single value or virtue brings out the dark side of the self-reinforcement of the said value or virtue, suppressing free and rational choices.

On the other hand, the coordination function of law refers to ordering on a technical level, favouring certainty and efficiency which has no direct and consequent relationship with value judgment. Traffic rules, for instance, are different from place to place, but they are all feasible. In itself, driving on the right as in China and the United States, could hardly be seen as more beneficial than driving on the left, as in Japan and Britain. As long as the traffic rule is clear and strictly implemented, the flow of vehicles is coordinated and traffic jams and collisions can be avoided. Of course legal processes contain sollen elements, but the major function is to coordinate conflicting claims, diverse interests and competing values on an equal footing, from which arises the best solution. The significance of legal procedure is, therefore, to an extent adapting a sophisticated sollen problem to a coordination issue and resolving the complicated value judgment on a technical and rational basis.

## 5. The Adjudicative Power Revisited from the Perspective of Coordination

### 5.1. Undo the Mishandled Problems

However, what we find in reality is always the opposite. Chinese people appear to prefer turning any simple dispute into a deep value contest, turning a coordination issue into a sollen problem, thus transforming technical issues into value-loaded wherein easy questions become complex. The dire consequence is the increase of social uncertainties. One cannot help thinking that this might be an intended situation that makes fishing in troubled waters possible. Equally interestingly, however, we have also witnessed incessant supervision drives, mass movements, and vindications of miscarriages of justice, as if the ruling party were determined to clear the muddy water and maintain social certainty. There might be good reasons behind these efforts. In any event, if sollen and coordination functions are confused, the latter certainly will be weakened. Once the coordination function of law is in doubt, the legal order itself is on the verge of collapse.

### 5.2. Highlighting the Coordination Function and Strengthening the Forces of Law

Besides overcoming defects of the current power structure, the key to weak law awareness and non-compliance problems in China is to differentiate the sollen function from the coordination function, give a full account of the coordination function, and make the law as effective as it should be, so that law contains both flexible structure and rigid binding effects. In essence, in order to unshackle the judiciary from such value judgments as morals, class wills, and State ideology, and make sure that judges are only subject to law and insulated from outside influences, we should commit ourselves to develop the coordination function of law. When the legislature's majority enacts its will, the courts can conduct constitutional review, safeguarding the certainty of the constitutional order and the coherence of the legal system. In this situation, law can have a coordination function. When the government abuses its power and infringes upon personal rights, administrative litigation balances the relationship of the State and the individual, which is also a coordination function of law. In these circumstances, had rules not been abided by and the judiciary not been independent, the inevitable coordination problems could not have been resolved and the social order would falter. Sollen then would fail too.

## 6. Legislative Sollen and Judicial Coordination

### 6.1. Distinguish Ends from Conditions

It is not difficult to imagine that so-called 'judicial democratisation' in fact not only twists justice and corrupts democracy, but also misunderstands some proper perceptions of democratic 'judicial participation'. In a modern rule of law State, democracy is supposed to concentrate on sollen issues, redesigning the institution through, as in Niklas Luhmann's terms a 'conditional programme', and expressing public wills through legislation. The judiciary should concentrate, in comparison, on coordination issues, redesigning the institution through 'goal-oriented programmes', and bridging individual claims and public wills through such systems and media as the principle of judicial independence and professional judging skills. Meaningful judicial participation is conditioned on the establishment of the procedural fairness principle and the formation of the legal community. In any event, it is not the negation of the legal system. In the real sense, the judiciary is democratic only when we can discover and build anew consensus through concrete trials, transforming reasonable demands of individuals, minorities and disadvantaged groups into legal terms through case law, and gradually pushing forward institutional reforms by way of responsive judicial interpretations different from the legislature.

### 6.2. Interaction between Sollen and Coordination

Considering the judicial function from the perspective of coordination, we find that judicial independence is no more than a legal yardstick by which power relations are in balance, an institutional brake to control the abuses of the legislature and the executive, and a prominent fortress of legitimate order and social fairness. It is exactly its independent and neutral status that enables judges to stand outside the factual power relations and fulfil the sollen function in the process of technical coordination. For judges, the right ideology is de-ideologisation; the correct value judgment is value-neutrality. As to those partisan values, they are better handled at the levels of government or law firms. When it comes to such sollen issues like political democracy, the people's congress should be the right forum for deliberations. Obviously the legislature should also perform the coordination function, especially on issues of determining taxes, tax rates, and re-distributional budget planning. Above all, the legislature should pay more attention to transforming sollen into positive rules in clear terms and to balancing or determining the appropriate sollen to coordinate and regulate social relations.

## 7. The Chart of Democracy and the Anchor of Rule of Law in the Financial Crisis

### 7.1. Uncertainties and Governmental Credibility

When conceiving the future legal order, we should never forget that the world is undergoing great changes. What we are facing is a global structural transformation.

The political domino has toppled – like the fall of the Berlin Wall – in North Africa and the Middle East since the Tunisian event in early 2011. Greater shock waves, however, came from developed countries. The US dollar devaluation, the EU debt crisis and the Japanese trade deficit have collectively triggered an epidemic of credit disturbances early this year, followed by a rapid gravitational shift of the global monetary system to the East and the South. Ever since the abolition of the gold standard in 1971, currencies have been guaranteed by governmental credit. But as the explosion of financial derivatives and futures trading on the exchange market, intervention and guidance measures adopted by government and central banks have all proven ineffective. Even government bonds become risky. It is therefore not surprising that the governmental credibility of developed countries is on the verge of breakdown. Moreover, representative democracy and constituency structure also make it hard for countries to cut deficits through higher taxes. Instead, as John M. Keynes pointed out, inflation as a disguised form of taxation becomes popular. Inflation, however, leading to local currency devaluation and relative appreciation of foreign currencies, has also become an alternative tool to adjust trade balances. All these increase social uncertainties.

### 7.2. The Rule of Law Should Take Priority Over Democracy, Especially Now in China

The megatrend has brought China unprecedented pressure, painful lessons from which to learn, and at the same time presented a significant and strategic opportunity. If, against this backdrop, we forecast China's development after 2012, it is important to realise that building and maintaining governmental credibility is the key point. In China, although the economy is relatively strong, the rich-poor divide widens further; improving investment environment and fairly distributing social wealth are now top priorities. Thus government credibility is more than ever dependent on efficient and equitable ordering, that is, rule of law and democracy. But in a country such as China where the local government debts now account for 30 per cent of the gross domestic product (GDP) and substantive appreciation of the Chinese Yuan can in no circumstances exceed 30 per cent, chaotic mass politics and 'big mediation' will probably twist the process of democratisation, increase social uncertainties and may even lead to the collapse of the system and social anomie. Thus, top-level design of the political reform should simply focus on coordination issues, prioritise rule of law (especially judicial justice), and clarify the detailed roadmap from rule of law to stable democracy.

As to the power structure in China, if the People's Congress and governmental departments could be viewed as representing the majority, it is equally important to recognise that the judiciary represents the minority, individuals and the disadvantaged. The majority's interests could be secured either through legislative procedures or in the name of the public interest protected through the executive implementation, but dissenting voices of the minority, especially of a common citizen, would hardly be reflected in the system even it is reasonable and correct. Only in court can every opinion be carefully heard and a way of incorporation into the framework of the system found. Especially in a relatively centralised government structure, judicial independence could clearly delimit the boundaries of power while providing institutional validity for the basis of power. Moreover, if judgments are made after considering special conditions and reasonable claims of the parties involved, it may as well remedy the loopholes of law and administrative measures. In and only in this sense, can the judiciary limit and correct the legislature and the executive to some extent, and be the lever for the minorities and individuals to promote social progress and institutional changes. This is the reason why the democratic process of legislation and the judicial independence are indispensable to each other.

# 4.3.

# Openness and Transparency in Central and Eastern Europe: Building Sustainable Governance?

**Dacian C. Dragos***

Very often, countries from Eastern Europe adopt state of the art legislation which is then difficult to implement due to factors such as limited administrative capacity coupled with differences between urban and rural areas, resistance to change within the bureaucratic machinery, passiveness on behalf of the citizens, *et cetera.* Implementation thus becomes the missing link in public administration reforms in these countries. Challenges remain as to the timing, accurateness and worth of the information disclosed, especially due to the fact that the experience of these nations had led to a genuine distrust of citizens in their governments. My think piece looks at trends in the foreseeable evolution of the practice of transparency in Central and Eastern European (CEE) countries, in the context of the ongoing debate on closing the gap between regulation and implementation of transparency laws. I believe that the culture of secrecy will be hard to overcome, but the trend of advancing transparency incrementally, through e-government tools, will continue. Institutionally, the preeminence of Ombudsman-type institutions will be the trend, and they will act both as mediators and enforcers of transparency. A sort of proceduralisation of transparency will be noticed also in the future, with different regulations brought together for increased clarity and effectiveness. The role of the media will continue to be strong; meanwhile a more active civil society will mark a shift in the effective oversight of transparency.

---

* **Dacian Dragos** is Jean Monnet Associate Professor of Administrative and European Law, and Vice Dean, Faculty of Political, Administrative and Communication Sciences, Center for Good Governance Studies, Babes Bolyai University, Romania. The author wishes to express thanks to colleagues and friends from CEE countries who have shared their views and provided national references on the subject: Polonca Kovac (Slovenia), Marton Gellen and Anita Boros (Hungary), Mariusz Swora (Poland), Sonia Skulova (Czech Republic), Vuk Cucic (Serbia) and Vedran Dulabic (Croatia).

## 1. Introduction

Europe has long had a tradition of practicing discreet and confidential administration (Sweden being an exception). Only around the 1960s the principle of openness of administration started to develop in Western democracies. Nowadays this principle has gained the status of the highest standards of administration; it is enshrined in constitutions and is even considered a fundamental right.

Transparency was expected to be among the first priorities of the new regimes from Central and Eastern Europe (CEE), in transition after the 1989 changes. However, transparency legislation was adopted only around year 2000 (Czech Republic 1999, Bulgaria and Slovakia 2000, Romania and Poland 2001, Croatia and Slovenia 2003, Serbia 2004, Montenegro 2005), with the exception of Hungary (1992). Fundamental laws either preceded this development by declaring the right to access public information (for instance, in Poland, Romania), or were amended after Freedom of Information Acts (FOIA) were in place, as recognition of the highest level of interest for transparency as a political freedom or right. The preoccupation of many Central European and former Soviet countries with reviving their own national legal traditions played a role here, while adopting and integrating international practices and trends were of secondary interest.

More difficult was the implementation of the new laws, as it is common knowledge that implementation is the 'missing link' of public administration reform in these countries. Questions remain about the timing, accurateness and worth of the information disclosed, especially due to the fact that the experience of these nations had led to a genuine distrust of citizens in their governments.

## 2. Implementing Transparency Laws in CEE: a (Insurmountable) Challenge?

The sole presence of the rules of transparency in a legal system does not guarantee their application and effectiveness. CEE countries have re-established pre-communist legal regimes inspired by Western ideals or adopted new regimes inspired by contemporary Western regulations. In any case, revered French, German and Anglo Saxon legal systems are used as models for this part of Europe. Against this background, it is noteworthy that resistance to change plays a very important role in CEE legal systems, and the fact that Western Europe is struggling as well to effectively implement transparency laws is not helping either. Governments from the new EU members feel encouraged in their secrecy by the fact that role-model jurisdictions like UK and Germany have only recently adopted FOIA legislation, and the implementation process is subjected to criticism everywhere. Even the country with the most developed regime of transparency, the USA, is struggling to get back on track after years of decline in the name of national security.

The development of transparency rules has stretched from being handled as part of human rights stemming from international treaties (data protection, access to public information), to being part of the principle of good governance.

The initial passive and minimal disclosure of information – basic data on public authorities – has been replaced gradually by pro-active transparency, the result of increased pressure for more relevant information about processes, procedures and outcomes. Specific regulations imposed by the EU have contributed as well – especially in areas like public procurement. A final stage was reached by adding civic participation to passive disclosure (Hungary, for instance, adopted a sunshine law only in 2010).

On the other hand, the process of developing norms of transparency was hindered by the development, alongside or even prior to that, of rules for protection of classified information and government secrecy. Thus, the FOIA in Poland has tailed the already (too) well designed laws about protection of personal data and of confidential information, while the Romanian FOIA was soon after adoption crippled by an extensive law on classified information. Such sequence gave rise to an unfavourable environment for the new legal culture being brought into light, that of openness in governmental dealings, and affected its effectiveness.

The evolution was markedly influenced either by strong Ombudsman type institutions (for instance in Hungary, Czech Republic, Slovenia and Poland) or by (constitutional) court rulings. Furthermore, the development of the regulatory framework of transparency granted new tools for political parties to compete on the public scene, by asking for public information and fighting in courts to get it – thus unintentionally assisting its dissemination.

An important challenge with regard to implementation is the existence of universal provisions for all public authorities, irrespective of their administrative capacity, existing cultural and social characteristics of public participation and communication in urban/rural communities as well as the relationship between the central and the local tiers of the government. Applying the same procedures to achieve transparency to central government and local government is sometimes a bad idea, as the results are quite different. The lack of administrative capacity at the local level of government entitles specific approaches towards how transparency is to be achieved.

The laws of transparency are considered one of the main tools to fight against corruption, which is both a plague that still impairs governmental performance in CEE countries and a catchword for the dialectic of reform in government. The role of the media is very important in this regard. Many legal systems have promoted special rights to information for representatives of media, with shorter deadlines and steeper penalties for non-disclosure. The idea behind this is to encourage mass dissemination in order to leave less room for individual encounters between citizens and administration. For instance, in Poland, the Press Law has played a distinct role in fostering transparency of governmental activities but also in shaping perceptions of citizens about governmental performance.

A general assessment of the implementation of transparency laws would come to the conclusion that practice is way behind regulations. Controlling mechanisms, when available, are based too much on the civil society as opposed to internal administrative control. Judicial review, although available, is not often effective due to the loopholes that can divert the final outcome – public authorities disregarding or resisting court decisions, finding ways to get around the imposed obligations, while lengthy court proceedings are a deterrent to possible litigants.

Public authorities often satisfy only formal requirements but do not provide essential information to interested persons. Aside from the ambiguities coming from the wording of FOIAs themselves, which usually do not benefit from supplementary enforceable guidelines, public offices regularly hide behind provisions of other specific statutes in order to explain the failure to provide an interested person with certain information. Public hearing is treated instrumentally by the government, and policy measures and regulations are adopted without prior consultations or only after formal ones (for instance, one practice is selecting participants to justify decisions already taken). In Slovenia, for instance, in spite of having procedures for impact assessment in place, two thirds of all draft regulations submitted to ministries, government and parliament are not subjected to transparency prior to adoption; the fact that there is a low demand for transparency and a low interest in public debates does not help either.

Scholars unequivocally agree that the explanation for resistance to implementation of transparency laws is the lack of a culture of openness, participation and the low esteem for public accountability as a concept.

However, the rhetoric of the governments in CEE countries is impressive: it shows commitment to transparency, initiative in assessing its effectiveness, and willingness to improve. Many policy papers and declaratory statements are evidence of this trend: the decision of many governments in the region (Czech Republic, Slovakia, Romania, Serbia, Montenegro, Macedonia, Croatia, Bulgaria) to join the Open Government Partnership initiative (initiated by Brazil, Indonesia, Mexico, Norway, Philippines, South Africa, United Kingdom and the United States in 2011) is meant to improve access to data, efficiency of the State administration and to encourage public participation in decision-making processes at national level. These aims involve further regulation but also, more importantly, implementation of existing regulations.

The gap between regulation and implementation is best showcased by the evaluation of transparency laws performed by outside experts. In September 2011, the Spanish-based organisation Access Info and the US-based Centre for Law and Democracy conducted a detailed analysis of the legal framework for the right to information in 89 countries around the world. The evaluation criteria included: the right to access, sending response procedures, exemptions, rejections, appeals, penalties and promotion of the law. Serbian law was ranked first, although the watchdog of its implementation, the Commissioner for Information of Public Importance and Personal Data Protection argues in its reports that implementation is faltering due to arbitrariness and abuse of public authorities when tagging information as confidential (which cannot be reviewed by the Commissioner), when refusing to comply with decisions of the Commissioner and when adopting a purely passive approach to transparency.

In spite of implementation deficiencies, a certain progress cannot be denied or overlooked. The result of court cases and pressure from NGOs has advanced the implementation process. There are more and more appeals to review bodies (administrative or judiciary) in matters of transparency, and the case law is aiding the development of best practices. The press (itself constantly evolving towards independence) has always revealed affairs of corruption using transparency inquiries. The proactive transparency has improved as well, due to the promotion of e-government. Generally, more and more public authorities are publishing reports online.

As a result of pressure from civil society (mostly NGOs), public sector organisations have become more responsive and aware of their responsibilities (this is true especially in the case of those organisations criticised in the evaluation reports drawn by NGOs). The motivating factor may have been in many cases the fear of being exposed by NGOs as being in non-compliance, but nonetheless, improvements are noticeable.

At their end, citizens have become more educated and aware of their rights in their relationship with public authorities. Citizens in urban areas are becoming more demanding and tend to hold public authorities accountable for how decisions are made at the local level.

## 3. The Future of Transparency Laws and their Implementation

Resistance to change will be an important reality in CEE democracies for the next 20 years, and it will constantly influence the way in which transparency laws are implemented. In this context, advancement of transparency is to be achieved by personal commitment of those holding public office. This regards both public authorities that apply the law and those that oversee the process.

Another factor contributing to the enforcement of transparency laws is the degree of involvement and the strength of NGOs or other representatives of civil society. CEE countries have yet to develop a culture of participation in public matters that would bear up a better involvement of citizens in administrative proceedings. This can be achieved through education, but also through effective enforcement of existing regulations, under the pressure of the civil society and media.

Watchdogs of transparency are very important for the enforceability of these laws. Some legal systems in the area have both Ombudsman-type institutions and courts to deal with litigation stemming from failure to implement transparency provisions. However, understaffing, underfinancing, politicisation and other shortcomings hinder the effectiveness of such (independent) institutions. This is the point where the lack of political will to subject public institutions to an effective scrutiny is the most obvious. It will always depend on the personal abilities and commitment of an officeholder (Ombudsman, Commissioner, Head of an agency) to make a dent in the secrecy of the government, as governments are hardly going to be initiators in the process of openness and transparency. The level of activism of the watchdogs is paramount for the success for implementation. This should be fading gradually leaving room for the development of more stable institutions, which would act in a consistent and linear manner, fulfilling legitimate expectations.

For some countries in the region (Serbia, Montenegro, Albania, Macedonia), accession to the EU can also be an incentive for better implementation of transparency laws, at least in the short term. Thus, lack of domestic political will for administrative reform and transparency could be replaced by external commitment to adoption of *acquis*, including the rule of law standards. For the rest of the countries in the region that are already members of the EU, a strong factor of development will be the process of Europeanisation of administrative law, and through it, of the transparency procedures.

Extensive legislative action on the harmonisation of other laws with the provisions of FOIAs should be undertaken. Effective implementation of transparency requirements could be enhanced by their inclusion in a general procedural administrative law, so as to form the day-to-day operating procedures for public officials, and not a special procedure, provided for by a special law. This codification can be part of the process of harmonisation envisaged above.

Large scale re-evaluation of information classified as secret or confidential should also be carried out. Clear guidelines on how to assess the public-private interest in disclosure and which information is worth keeping secret are necessary, both for those who apply the law and for those who enforce it.

Amended FOIA laws should take into consideration empowering, where not already the case, a Transparency (or Public Information) Ombudsman to look into the legality of classification decisions, in order to better advise petitioners about the likelihood of public information being wrongly withheld from disclosure. This would encourage the use of court actions against such administrative acts, which now are risky to take to court. I consider this institution-building to be a trend in CEE countries.

The interplay between freedom of information and data protection will be very important for the future of transparency as well. The use of personal data protection to justify non-disclosure of important public information is a preferred scapegoat for public bodies. With the increased use of internet in commercial transactions, the pressure to protect personal data will come more and more from the private sector, so I foresee a trend (at least in the near future) in giving pre-eminence to data protection over access to public information. The explanation is that data protection was neglected until recently, and there is the drive to catch up with the freedom of information, which sometimes intrudes in the personal life of persons. In the long run, an optimal balance has to be struck between the public access to information and data protection.

Implementation in local government (especially in rural areas which lack administrative capacity the most) could be enhanced provided that local authorities are given more discretion with regard to how certain provisions can be implemented (flexibility in the choice of policy tools); then, more discretion should be complemented by increased sanctions for non-compliance and their effective enforcement.

Transparency will be increasing inevitably due to technology and due to incremental professionalisation in public administration. The economic crisis has given opportunity for reform, and increased transparency is demanded due to limited public resources.

It is expected that public administration will be more and more forced to implement the emerging legal and policy standards regarding openness and accountability of public administration. Pressure from the media and civil society organisations should also be taken into consideration. They can serve as a tool for fostering and stimulating modernisation of public administration by putting pressure on public bodies to implement policies of transparency and accountability.

The constant development of e–government shall be the most obvious assistance to transparency, because it allows citizens to monitor the dealings of the government more easily and fosters participation in public affairs.

The Europeanisation of administrative law is a prominent issue in public administration, and it also covers many aspects of administrative law. National courts are engaged in shaping smooth paths for the application of good governance principles, including transparency in administration. The pressure of the European Commission in areas subjected to harmonisation will also be important for the overall advancement of transparency.

As part of various initiatives to promote the open government, a trend will be the attempt at uniformisation of databases in order to allow searches. A number of important data files will be transferred to systems that comply with open data standards, to ensure that anyone can freely incorporate this data in their work and publish it, particularly through automated computer processing. The laws of transparency are most likely to incorporate such requirements on the occasion of their amendment.

The concept of "open data" will be at the heart of future incentives for open government, both regulatory and operationally. This involves technical openness (data published electronically in a standard machine-readable format), legal openness (data published under an open license), availability and originality (individual data storages are published as a whole and unchanged; based on that statistics can be calculated) and structured data (the cataloguing of data in order to facilitate searching).

As for the legal education and training of future lawyers, the "law of transparency" will gain in importance both in initial education and in on-the-job training. It affects firstly public law but has far reaching consequences for the private law as well. Through field regulations, soft law and case law, the European Commission and the Court of Justice, respectively, will have an instrumental role in promoting transparency in government in this region, probably more evidently than in Western democracies.

## 4. Conclusions

The data shows that in countries which effectively implement transparency laws politicians are less likely to be corrupt, and those that are corrupt are more likely to be caught. A former judge of the US Supreme Court, Louis Brandeis, once stated that "sunlight is said to be the best of disinfectants". I fully agree with that, and this is the reason why I consider the issue of transparency as being at the core of any future reform of administrative law in CEE countries. However, in the near future, CEE countries will not encounter any far-reaching and spectacular developments that will significantly improve openness of government, for there are no social or institutional actors able to initiate such changes and to coordinate their implementation. Alternatively, at best, one may expect incremental reforms concerning particular problems (*exempli gratia* improving the quality of the law on access to public information and its implementation).

## 5. Sources and Further Reading


Birkinshaw, P., "Freedom of information and openness: Fundamental human rights", in *Administrative Law Review*, 2006, vol. 58, no. 1, pp. 177–218.

Boros, A., "Europeanisation of Administrative Law with a View to Hungary", in *Romanian Review of European Governance Studies*, 2010, no. 4, pp. 19–35.

Brandeis, L. D. (1913), available at http://www.brainyquote.com/quotes/quotes/l/louisdbra402349.html, last accessed on 3 June 2012.

Cardona, F., European Principles for Public Administration, in *SIGMA Papers*, 1999, No. 27.

Dragos, D. C., Neamtu, B., "Europeanisation of Administrative Law in Romania: Current Developments in Jurisprudence and Legislation", in *Review of European Administrative Law*, Europa Law Publishing, 2009, no. 1.

Dragos, D.C., Neamtu, B., "Reforming Public Administration in Romania: Trends and Obstacles", in *International Review of Administrative Sciences*, 2007, vol. 73, no. 1, pp. 699–721.

Dragos, D. C., Neamtu, B., "Re-using Public Sector Information – Policy choices and Experiences in some of the Member States with and Emphasis on the Case of Romania", in *The European Integration Online Papers*, 2009, vol. 13, available at http://www.eiop.or.at, last accessed on 1 October 2012.

Dragos, D. C., "Transparency in Public Administration: Free Access to Public Information. A Topical Comparative Analysis of Several Jurisdictions from Central and Eastern Europe", in *Transylvanian Review of Administrative Sciences*, 2006, vol. 17, no. E.

Dragos, D. C., Neamtu, B., "The rise and evolution of freedom of information legal regime in the European Union", in *Transylvanian Review of Administrative Sciences*, 2006, vol.1.

Dragos, D. C., Neamtu, B., Cobârzan, B.V., "Procedural Transparency in Rural Romania: Linking Implementation with Administrative Capacity?", in *International Review of Administrative Sciences*, 2012, vol. 78, p. 134.

Dunn, W.N., Staronova, K. and Pushkarev, S. (eds), *Implementation: The Missing Link in Public Administration Reform in Central and Eastern Europe*, NISPAcee Press, Bratislava, 2006.

Harlow, C., "Codification of EC administrative procedures? Fitting the foot to the shoe or the shoe to the foot", in *European Law Journal*, 2009, vol. 2, no. 1, pp. 3–25.

Hood, C., "What happens when transparency meets blame–avoidance?", in *Public Management Review*, 2007, vol. 9, no. 2, pp. 191–210.

Hood, C. and Heald, D. (eds), *Transparency. The Key to Better Governance?*, Oxford University Press, New York, pp. 47–58.

Makowski, G., *korupcją, Koniec walki z*, Newsweek, wyd. 5 December, 2011.

Piotrowski, S. J and Ryzin, GG Van,"Citizen attitudes toward transparency in local government", in *American Review of Public Administration*, 2007, vol. 37, no. 3 pp. 306–323.

Prechal, S and Leeuw, M De, "Dimensions of transparency: The building blocks for a new legal principle?", in *Review of European Administrative Law*, 2007, vol. 1, pp. 51–61.

Safjan, M., *Wyzwania dla państwa prawa*, Warszawa, 2007.

Suwaj, P. J., "Transparency as value and principle of the public affair management in a state under the rule of law versus public officials' duty to present financial declarations", in *Studies in Logic, Grammar and Rhetoric*, 2009, vol. 19, no. 32.

Access Info, Center for Law and Democracy, The Global Right to Information Rating – Results by Country, available at http://www.access-info.org/documents/6QC/RTI_Rating_Results.pdf, last accessed on 4 May 2012.

APADOR–CH (2007) Transparency in decision–making in Romania in 2007: Context, findings and future trends (in Romanian), Bucuresti, available at http://www.apador.org/publicatii/trans2007.pdf, last accessed 12 May 2010.

SIGMA Assessment Report Serbia (2011), available at http://www.sigma web.org/dataoecd/40/27/48970654.pdf, last accessed on 4 May 2012.

OECD, The Right to Open Public Administrations in Europe: Emerging Legal Standards of Administrative Transparency, SIGMA paper, no. 46, OECD.

Transparency International, National Integrity system Assessment Poland, 2012, available at http://www.transparency.org/whatwedo/pub/national_in tegrity_system_assessment_poland_executive_summary, last accessed on May 2012.

# 4.4.

# The Future of Preventive Detention Under International Law

**Daveed Gartenstein-Ross**[*]

This think piece will argue that fervent hopes to the contrary notwithstanding, policies relating to the preventive detention of violent non-State actors (VNSAs) will not end any time soon because the challenge posed by violent non-State actors will not end any time soon. What this think piece will not argue is that preventive detention of VNSAs is unproblematic. Rather, it will explore the line of argument that the issue of VNSAs that resemble a transnational military adversary in fact raises very specific problems. The preventive detention of VNSAs is undeveloped within international law, and has evolved only in the most *ad hoc* manner in US law. However, preventive detention by the United States or other Western powers is treated in mainstream discourse as though it is the worst of all options, when it is far from that, and this sanctimonious approach has helped give birth to a number of dangerous fictions with perverse second-order consequences.

## 1. Preventive Detention in International Law

Benjamin Wittes, a senior fellow in governance studies at the Brookings Institution, notes that "enemy combat detention is as old as warfare".[1] The reason is obvious: concern that a soldier or "unlawful combatant", if released, will return to the fight. Detention of combatants in armed conflict thus has a preventive rather than punitive function and has traditionally been uncontroversial within international law. The third Geneva Convention explicitly contemplates the detention of enemy combatants until "the cessation of active hostilities". However, following the attacks of 11 September 2001 and the wars against VNSAs that the terrorist attacks set in

[*] **Daveed Gartenstein-Ross** is a senior fellow at the Foundation for Defense of Democracies. He is currently a Ph.D. candidate in world politics at the Catholic University of America; and also earned a J.D. from the New York University School of Law.

[1] Benjamin Wittes, *Detention and Denial: The Case for Candor after Guantánamo*, The Brookings Institution, 2011, Washington, DC, p. 38.

motion, detention policy became highly controversial, so much so that Western countries are now clearly ashamed to utilise their power to detain. No Western nation-States other than the United States will do so in the course of "war on terror" operations.

The post-9/11 fight against al Qaeda and affiliated organisations has contained elements of anti-terror policing and also military force. After the attacks, the US Congress passed an act on the Authorisation for the Use of Military Force (AUMF), and in the US the idea that the country is at war has been affirmed by two presidential administrations of different parties, six different Congresses and the Supreme Court. In other words, no branch of the US government disputes that military force is one element of fighting al Qaeda and its affiliates. NATO partners similarly affirmed this by devoting troops to toppling the Taliban, the *de facto* rulers of Afghanistan who had sheltered al Qaeda, and undertaking stability operations thereafter.

However, the controversy over detention arose because this was a new kind of armed conflict, fraught with new problems. Several aspects of this new conflict made the traditional law of detention a poor fit, including the fact that al Qaeda operatives did not wear uniforms and confusion over what cessation of active hostilities means in this context. If al Qaeda really poses a generational challenge, as many observers claim, does that mean that individuals who supported al Qaeda and were picked up on the battlefield – even low level supporters – could be detained for a an entire generation?

These questions are difficult. However, the fact that formulating answers is hard does not mitigate the concern driving preventive detention: combatants who are released may well return to the fight. This can in fact be illustrated by recidivism amongst released detainees. In December 2010, the US's Director of National Intelligence released an unclassified summary of intelligence on recidivism, concluding that of 598 detainees transferred from Guantánamo, "81 (13.5 per cent) are confirmed and 69 (11.5 per cent) are suspected of re-engaging in terrorist or insurgent activities after transfer".[2] Though some analysts have questioned the reliability of these numbers, the fact that some percentage of released detainees have returned to the fight is beyond dispute.

2 Office of the Director of National Intelligence (DNI), *Summary of the Reengagement of Detainees Formerly Held at Guantánamo Bay*, Cuba, 2010.

Now, it is well known that no new detainees have been admitted to the Guantánamo Bay detention facility in years. However, this does not mean that the US and its allies will no longer need a detention policy. There remain broad geographic areas where the fight against al Qaeda, its affiliates, and fellow travellers resembles armed conflict more than a policing operation. These include Somalia, where al Qaeda's affiliate al Shabaab was until recently the dominant military force in the southern part of the country; Yemen, where al Qaeda until recently was so powerful that it could impose its harsh justice as the dominant force in the Abyan province; and Mali. Mali is perceived as of particular concern by Europeans. As a senior Western diplomat serving in the capital told a regionally-based journalist, "If Islamists continue to control vast areas of Mali where they can do what they like, then this will pose a direct threat to Europe".[3]

Military action to clear out al Qaeda strongholds in any of these areas will involve detention. Even if Western countries are not in the lead of military operations, preventive detention remains relevant. If Western countries refuse to engage in detention then, far from having clean hands, they are affirmatively choosing to let local partners shoulder detention responsibilities. After all, the alternatives to detention are simply unacceptable. One alternative involves an absolute preference for killing over capturing the enemy force. At the other end of the spectrum, catching and releasing enemy fighters rather than detaining them will result in a profusion of conflicts that nation-States abiding by the norms of international law cannot win.

## 2. Guantánamo Bay 2012

I undertook field research for this chapter at the Guantánamo Bay detention facility in July 2012. The last time I had been there was October 2006. During the previous visit, personnel were quick to point to positive aspects of the detainees' treatment, but I was left with a great many questions, in part due to recent incidents between the detainees and guards.

In May 2006, detainees had mounted a surprise attack on guards in Gitmo's Camp Four, which featured communal living. One detainee appeared to be attempting suicide, and when guards rushed in to thwart the

3 Afua Hirsch, *Mali Extremists 'A Threat to Europe'*, Mail and Guardian, Africa, 20 July 2012.

attempt, they were ambushed by inmates wielding fan blades and broken light fixtures as weapons. The following month, three detainees did commit suicide by hanging themselves with nooses comprised of sheets and clothing.

The changes in the intervening six years have been significant. Detainees can be divided into those whose behaviour is generally compliant with the rules, and those who are non-compliant. In 2006, about 80 per cent of detainees were non-compliant, a percentage that has basically reversed since then. Several independent interviews with Gitmo officials established that compliance rates at Camps Five and Six, the two remaining camps for conventional detainees, were now about 80 per cent (those dubbed "high-value detainees" are kept in Camp Seven, which is off limits to the media). The increase in compliance rates can be seen by detainees' living patterns. Today, Camp Six, which is modelled on a prison in Lenawee County, Michigan, is entirely comprised of communal living, while Camp Five, modelled on a prison in Terre Haute, Indiana, features both single-cell detention and also a communal wing. 80 per cent of detainees are held in communal living areas, which is seen as a reward for compliant behaviour.

I spoke at length with Zak, a senior cultural adviser of Jordanian origin at the detention facilities. He thought that much of the change in compliance was because detainees had been given a different incentive structure. "By listening to the detainees over the years, we have managed to understand how to give them something valuable", he said. When Zak first arrived in 2005, detainees were perhaps given one hour of recreation out of their cells; now they have 20 hours of access per day to the recreation yard at Camp Six. In addition to outdoor time, those in communal living facilities are given 24 hours a day of free movement within the block where they live (see Figure 1, illustrating communal living facilities in Camp Six).

**Figure 1:** Communal Living Facilities in Camp Six

Detainees have been given access to television, allowed to watch 20 different stations. Their library contains over 30,000 books; and they are provided with educational classes that include language classes, personal health and wellness, computer classes, art classes, and, most quixotically, courses on job interviews and resume writing. From Zak's perspective, expanding detainees' freedom of choice has been critical to increasing their compliance. "They want to go to class, we give them class", he said.

Further, although the Bush administration attempted to evade judicial review when it first set up its system of detention, various layers of review have developed. No new detainees have been admitted to Gitmo in years, so it is not clear if the Department of Defense would utilise the Combatant Status Review Tribunals (CSRTs) which are meant to determine whether detainees were properly designated enemy combatants. After all, the process provided by CSRTs was panned by the Supreme Court in its 2008 decision *Boumediene v. Bush*. Nonetheless, all current detainees have been through the CSRT process.

Detainees are then given *habeas* rights in federal district courts to challenge the legality of their detention. The district courts have reviewed detention decisions as original finders of fact, providing no deference to the CSRT determinations. Thereafter, an executive order provides a further layer of process both to detainees who are designated for continued law of war detention (there are 48 whom the Obama administration will not prosecute due to evidentiary issues, but will continue to detain because intelligence assessments conclude that they would be serious threats if released) and those who have been referred for prosecution. Under this order, detainees can challenge their detention before an inter-agency Periodic Review Board (PRB) that will determine whether detention remains "necessary to protect against a significant threat to the security of the United States". Detainees have a right to counsel before the PRB, which undertakes a file review every six months, and holds a full hearing before the board every three years.

Is this system ideal? Of course not. It was forged on an *ad hoc* basis, carved out primarily by US Supreme Court decisions holding that the legal processes provided for detainees were inadequate, as well as by a few executive orders. In some ways, the present system is designed to produce absurd results. For example, there are dual tracks for detainees whom the administration does not want to release outright, one punitive and one preventive. Because detainees who are treated punitively will be released when their sentences are up, this raises the strong possibility that detainees who have committed war crimes will be freed *prior to* those who have not.

There are also serious questions about the contours of preventive detention of VNSAs. In a conventional war, there is no real uncertainty about who the enemy is, while in the fight against al Qaeda, there is no clear and well-established definition of who qualifies for belligerent detention. This substantially increases the risk that someone will be detained long-term who should not be if there were clearer guidance. A second problem is that in conventional armed conflicts, the warring parties may not know when the conflict will end, but everyone involved can be relatively certain that the war will not last 30 years. There is inherently an end state that is far less than a lifetime. However, in the context of the war on terror, the principle that detention is justified for the duration of the hostilities produces a potentially very troubling result. A third problem, as Wittes notes, is that the present system of *habeas* review does not give either the detainees or the government what they need:

> The emerging system consistently fails to give the detainees what they really need from a system of review. For the detainees, after all, speed is of the essence. The innocent detainee rounded up by mistake has an abiding interest in getting before whatever adjudication mechanism there is relatively quickly and having a chance to make his case in a reasonable period of time.[4]

Needless to say, speed is not one of the present system's virtues. Moreover, from the government's perspective, Wittes notes that "certainty and predictability" are of key importance, and yet the *habeas* system is forging rules as it goes along, which is the very antithesis of certainty and predictability.

For these reasons, when I spoke with William Lietzau, the US's deputy assistant secretary of defense for rule of law and detainee policy, he said that the detention of VNSAs is an unsettled area of law. To Lietzau, clearly defined and developed rules govern the prosecution of VNSAs under the law of peace (*lex generalis*). The Geneva Conventions have forged a well-defined body of law governing the detention of privileged belligerents under the law of war (*lex specialis*). However, when it comes to unprivileged belligerents such as VNSAs, the applicable body of law is largely undefined. Lietzau has even designed a chart, which has become famous among his colleagues, illustrating the law's lack of development (see Figure 2 below).

## 3. Conclusion

The problems relating to forging a law of detention appropriate to VNSAs are many. However, the clear problems that exist do not mean that detention is the worst among a suite of hard choices for dealing with VNSAs. This is where the issue of perverse incentives becomes relevant. For one thing, if preventive detention is seen as an option that truly must be avoided, we must ask whether that will incentivise killing over capturing the opponent. As Wittes writes, "the increasing prevalence of kill operations rather than captures is probably not altogether unrelated to the fundamental change in the incentive structure facing our fighters and covert operatives".[5]

[4] Wittes, 2011, p. 62, see *supra* note 2.

[5] Wittes, 2011, p. 24, see *supra* note 2.

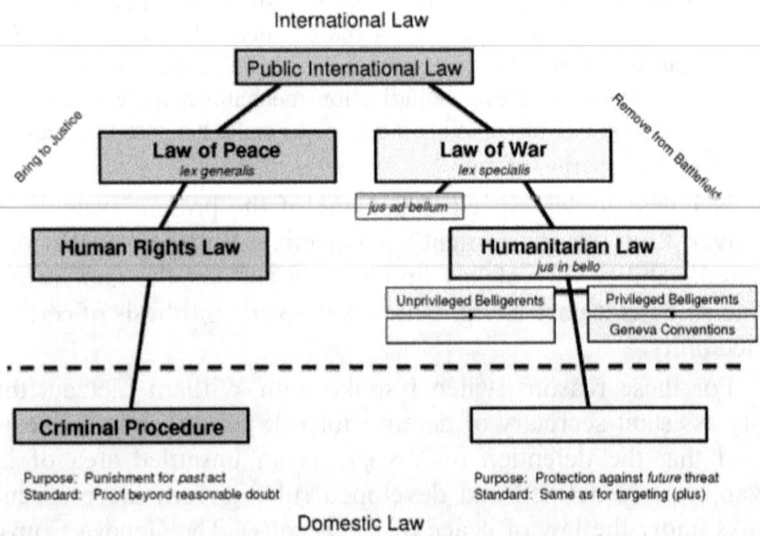


**Figure 2:** The law's lack of development, according to Lietzau

Second, there is the question of whether detainees will end up in worse conditions due to the stigmatisation of detention by Western governments. One overarching idea that has taken hold in our discussion of detention policy is that detention of VNSAs by Western governments is always unjustifiable and immoral, and local detention is preferable. However, when one compares detention conditions in Afghanistan or Somalia to those in Gitmo, the fiction at play here becomes apparent. As I stated previously, even if Western countries are not in the lead of military operations, preventive detention remains relevant, though it will be carried out not by Western powers, but rather by nation-States that will almost certainly have a far lower standard for detainee treatment. So the question must be asked whether the stigmatisation of preventive detention, rather than having a salutary effect on human rights, is in fact eroding them in important – but to international observers, somewhat invisible – ways.

In the foreseeable future, little is likely to change with respect to preventive detention policy. Obama indeed came into office determined to close down Gitmo, but his views on the matter evolved after he had dug more deeply into the relevant details. The claim that only "vehement congressional opposition" stands in the way of closing Gitmo is just one of the many fictions that dominates the debate over preventive detention.

Even if Obama had moved the detainees to Illinois, the actual problems attendant on detention would not go away.

And thus it will remain. There will continue to exist both the preventive detention that activists and the international community grumble about (Gitmo) and the detention that they ignore but is in fact significantly worse (Bagram, Somalia, and other local detentions). Unless our discussion of preventive detention matures significantly, the perverse incentives, absurdities within the law, and questions about legal protections will remain unanswered.

A more mature discussion would acknowledge the values that have driven preventive detention, and seek to determine when detention is justified as compared to other options: prosecution in military or civilian courts, kinetic military action, or simple release of the individuals in question. This discussion would acknowledge the second-order consequences of severely discouraging detention across the board, such as the potential for incentivising kills over captures or leaving detainees in worse conditions when they are held by ostensibly preferable local partners. From the recognition that detention will sometimes be justified, this discussion would attempt to alter the law governing it to remove aspects that do not make sense – such as the likelihood that war criminals will be released before those who have not committed war crimes – and truly address the hard issues. Those hard issues include establishing who qualifies for belligerent detention under a detention regime, and addressing the fact that cessation of hostilities may not occur during our lifetime. It would seek to build a system that includes speedy and predictable adjudication.

However, this mature discussion is exceedingly unlikely. The shame that Western countries feel about detention policy will probably shunt these questions to the side as everyone rushes to cleanse their hands of the matter – and in so doing, most likely allows an even worse system to remain.

## 4. Sources and Further Reading:

Elsea, Jennifer K. and Garcia, Michael John, *The National Defense Authorization Act for FY2012: Detainee Matters*, Congressional Research Service, Washington, DC, 2012.

Executive Order 13567, Periodic Review of Individuals Detained at Guantánamo Bay Naval Station Pursuant to the Authorization for Use of Military Force, 2011.

Hirsch, Afua, *Mali Extremists 'A Threat to Europe'*, Mail and Guardian, Africa, 2012.

Lake, Eli, *Somalia's Prisons: The War on Terror's Latest Front*, Daily Beast, 27 June 2012.

Klaidman, Daniel, *Kill or Capture: The War on Terror and the Soul of the Obama Presidency,* Houghton Mifflin Harcourt, Boston, 2012.

Melvin, Don and McGuirk, Rod, *Around World, Obama's Presidency a Disappointment*, Associated Press, 2012.

Office of the Director of National Intelligence (DNI), *Summary of the Reengagement of Detainees Formerly Held at Guantánamo Bay,* Cuba, 2010.

Wittes, Benjamin, *Detention and Denial: The Case for Candor after Guantánamo*, The Brookings Institution, Washington, DC, 2011.

**Cases**

Supreme Court of United States, *The Case of Boumediene v. Bush*, Judgment, 12 June 2008, 553 U.S. 723.

Supreme Court of United States, *The case of Hamdi v. Rumsfeld*, Judgment, 28 June 2004, 542 U.S. 507.

# 4.5.

## Changes in the Administration of Justice

**Benjamin J. Odoki***

The future developments of law will be as a reaction to many of the challenges that we are already facing today. Scarcity in terms of resources such as food, water and energy will both force States to look outwards in search of these resources and compel them to look inwards in order to build stronger relationships with neighbours for security purposes and convenience. This, combined with the disappointment of a divided and uni-polar international community, will lead to a growth in stronger regional networks. These networks will move to consolidate resources, economies and ultimately power, anchored by a common legal system, based on legal pluralism. The laws will be inspired by a common/civil law-based tradition with less emphasis on customary law which will be deemed out of touch with modern society. This modern judiciary will rely heavily on the advantages provided by technology in terms of both substance and processes.

### 1. Introduction

Law has always had to take account of the fact of change in order to remain relevant and continue serving a purpose In society. The way we live, interact and communicate is all subject to change, and the law which governs all of these aspects has to adapt to the constantly changing reality and the new challenges that it brings. Most of these changes will be precipitated by continuing globalisation, which has already changed considerably the actors in society, their respective interests, demands and expectations, their interrelations and the way they interact. The world is now connected in ways that would have been unimaginable three decades ago. The law has had to adapt in order to effectively address the numerous opportunities and challenges brought about by these changes.

One of the areas that will see changes will be in the administration of justice, more specifically in relation to judicial and court systems and

* **Benjamin Odoki** is Chief Justice of the Republic of Uganda.

processes. This will be impacted by changes in global governance and within the international order which will give rise to new superpowers that will shift the balance of power from the current dominance of Europe and North America. However, bottom-up pressures and the need to answer to the needs of the members of our society in an increasingly competitive legal sector will also impact the way justice is administered.

In this think piece, I have chosen to touch upon several issues that, from my perspective as the Chief Justice of the Supreme Court of Uganda, are particularly pertinent: 1) geo-political changes and the increasing regional integration; 2) legal pluralism; 3) the impact of technology on law and courts; and 4) specialised courts. Each one of these topics is hugely important. I could have focused my think piece exclusively on any one of them, but I have chosen to bundle them together, as I believe this can give rise to a broader perspective on the challenges that we face.

## 2. Between Legal Trends and Grand Societal Challenges

The legal trends mentioned above and further described below all relate in one way or another to grand societal changes and challenges.

One of the major societal challenges that impacts almost everything that we do and will have to be continuously dealt with in the future is scarcity. The growth of the world population to the estimated nine billion in 2050 will put great stresses on the resources that we have. States are therefore trying to find the most effective way of providing for their populations. For some States, acting as part of a regional community of a few States will enable them to pool resources together and use them more efficiently while also providing a stronger military and security might for their protection.

This scarcity of resources is also what will lead to a reform in the way that courts operate, as a means of using resources effectively, but also by taking advantage of available technologies.

The quest for better and more effective security will continue to provide an impetus for governments to focus on areas that they had previously side-lined. Recognising the global reach and networks of terrorism has forced governments to focus on those avenues being used by these groups to promote their agendas. One of the most important areas is the Internet. While it has provided great opportunities for communication, information gathering and interaction across borders, it has also been co-opted as a tool for procuring information on how, where and when to launch attacks as well as a recruitment tool particularly targeting young, frustrated and impressionable youth. Indeed, research indicates that hardly any terrorist operates entirely as a lone wolf – there is also a form of social and/or professional support in the background, which nowadays is often provided through online platforms. How we police the Internet to prevent these types of scenarios has become a fundamental part of governments' defence policies. It has led to more regulations both nationally and internationally with a broader definition of jurisdiction.

## 3. Emerging and Future Legal Trends

### 3.1. Geopolitical Changes and the Rise of Regionalism

There has in recent years been a drive towards more regional integration on the African continent. This trend is primarily driven, and will continue to be driven, by the need for greater security and influence due to the scarcity of resources and changes in global governance. Apart from the revival of the African Union, previously the Organisation of African Unity, the various regional blocs such as the East African Community (EAC) and Economic Community of West African States (ECOWAS) have expanded their scope and taken on a more proactive role than before. Within African States, the reality that only a strong community-based approach can yield enough influence to impact international policies will lead to greater regional integration and more deference to regional law and courts than to international law which will largely remain unbinding. Furthermore, regional blocs such as the EAC will take on greater prominence than continental blocs such as the African Union, because they will be more efficient and effective.

The countries comprising the EAC have already taken steps towards economic integration, with the intention eventually to have full political integration. The process towards economic integration will lead to the free movement of goods, people and services across the borders of the countries comprising this Community in the near future. This trend will only increase, with a greater move towards social, economic and also political, integration which could ultimately result in a single currency economy for the bloc. The EAC also has a Parliament as well as a community court (the East African Court of Justice (EACJ)) whose mission is to ensure adherence to the East African Treaty. It is envisaged that within 20 or 30 years there will be full political integration as well among the member States of the EAC. It is likely that this trend will be replicated across the other regional blocs in Africa and perhaps in other regions of the world as well.

Such regional integration will inevitably impact the law due to the convergence of the various legal systems within each bloc. All five East African States, for example, have different variations of African customary law within their systems, while two of them have a civil law-based legal tradition, although they are in the process of moving towards a common law one in order to align with the three other countries. Furthermore, we can expect that the EACJ, as the community court of the EAC, will play a role in bringing about such convergence of the respective legal systems. Indeed, this Community Court has already made rulings that have influenced the laws in the parent countries and we can expect more of this to come.

The trend towards regional integration will impact the global order as these organisations will have the economic and military strength to provide alternative paradigms to those created by the current superpowers. These regional blocs will form new power hubs which will be instrumental in creating new global systems as power moves from a predominantly national to a predominantly regional regime. This will lead to the creation of a legal environment with more binding force than is currently provided for in international law. It could lead to a fundamental reform of the UN system, or otherwise to the weakening or even complete dissolution of the United Nations and the creation of a Global Parliament, deemed more representative of the world's population.

Similarly, changes can be expected regarding the system of international criminal justice. Greater regional integration of and in Africa may very well impact the way in which African States handle international crimes such as genocide, crimes against humanity and war crimes. Ten years ago, the International Criminal Court (ICC) was considered a great promise in the global fight against impunity. Many African States ratified the Rome Statute. Today, many African States are frustrated and disappointed by the performance of the ICC in the first decade of its operation. They perceive it as a manifestation of the imbalance and unfairness of the global order. This may lead to a more localised approach to the fight against international crimes. States such as Uganda have already given local courts jurisdiction to try some of these crimes. Today, there are indications that regional courts such as the EACJ or the African Court of Human and Peoples' Rights (AfCHPR) could also be given jurisdiction over these crimes, thus shifting the focus from the ICC as a global court to local and regional venues. In summary, with the ICC being accused of selective prosecution, on the one hand, and with African States becoming stronger and more influential as a matter of greater integration in blocs on the other, in the foreseeable future we might see a shift towards prosecuting international crimes more and more at the national and regional levels, rather than by global institutions.

### 3.2. Legal Pluralism

In many African States, traditional forms of customary law exist either within or in parallel to the formal legal system. As regards to customary law, there is no blanket prescription for its criteria. Since customary law originated from different cultures, it is inevitable that there will be differences across the States. There is also no doubt that customary law has largely been side-lined as it is perceived to be archaic. The proliferation of the international human rights regime has further increased the anti-customary law rhetoric since it is perceived as being insensitive to gender equity and several other individual freedoms and rights guaranteed by modern constitutions and international human rights instruments. In order to accommodate it, in Uganda, customary law has continued to exist alongside statutory law, but the law has made it clear that it is only valid insofar as it is allowed by and does not conflict with the Constitution.

This marginalisation of customary law is expected to continue until it is fully absorbed into statutory law and there is no distinction between the two. A factor that will contribute to this is the increase in globalisation and in particular regional integration, which will necessitate the various national laws moving into conformity in order to have a regional law that is applicable to everyone.

### 3.3. Law and Technology

#### 3.3.1. Internet

Judiciaries in Africa and indeed the world over are still grappling with the new realities presented by the rise of technology and its constant advance. Technology has impacted virtually every imaginable field that can be legislated upon, whether health, agriculture, information, or defence, to mention just a few prime examples. While it has brought many advantages, there are many issues related to technology that have to be dealt with and regulated. Communication technology and the Internet in particular, are prime examples.

The Internet especially has connected the world in ways that were previously unimaginable. It has made it possible to communicate with someone in a different part of the world in a matter of seconds, transfer money to them, sign and e-mail a contract and exchange all kinds of data. These possibilities however have also created new avenues for crimes to be committed in the web sphere, whether it is online piracy where hackers are now able to infiltrate and secure secret government documents for their own use, or identity theft, which can then lead to fraud and theft.

There are two great difficulties with any attempt to regulate the Internet. The first is that technology, including internet technology, is developing much faster than it takes to legislate. The second is that the Internet, by definition, is a cross-border phenomenon.

Thus, while many laws have been created to try and tame these crimes, the law has still not been able efficiently to deal with it because the Internet is a rapidly evolving creature that can be difficult to anticipate. Many of the laws we still use are outdated, and because the Internet operates in a completely foreign way to the text- and rules-based approach of the law, the judiciary is always playing catch-up, so that by the time legislation has been approved and passed, the area you are trying to legislate has morphed into a different entity. The other difficulty with the legislation of the Internet is its cross-border nature. The Internet is a true reflection of globalisation, with its effects being more far-reaching than local jurisdictions. One person's actions in Uganda can have serious consequences for another in Australia. It makes using only national legislation highly ineffective. Truly effective legislation needs to be international in scope and policed strictly, and this will entail greater cooperation among States. This legislation will have to be reflected in all sectors. Interested readers particularly fascinated by this field are referred to other think pieces in this volume, such as the ones by Weber and by Lipton, who discuss the regulation of cyberspace in greater detail.

### 3.3.2. Virtual/E-Courts

The judicial process will also be dramatically influenced by technological advances.

The concept of a court today denotes a specified, physical, building or room in which a judicial officer sits with lawyers and their parties. This idea will have to change and adapt as technology makes it an increasingly unnecessary and expensive venture.

At present, in many African States there are simply not enough courts, and very few of them are located in remote areas. This creates one of the greater hindrances to access to justice in Africa, due to the distance that people have to travel in order to reach courts. So more courts are needed, but then there is the very high cost of setting up new courts, as well as maintaining and running them. Whether it is in the cost of construction of courthouses, or the amount of resources and personnel that have to be relocated for administering justice, this is a very expensive enterprise. The result is that there are fewer courts than needed, and their reach remains limited. One of the results of advancing with technology will be a move towards virtual courts which will allow judicial officers to cover larger areas, thus increasing access for people in distant locations, as the requirements will be far fewer and cheaper than they currently are.

Since technology is today more readily available and the cost continues to reduce, virtual courts have come to be viewed as a solution to this problem. Currently, the possibilities of a Video Conferencing System (VCS) which will enable in-court trials and hearings of defendants and witnesses who are in remote locations are being explored. The main goals are to increase transparency and to improve access to justice, by saving travelling costs for both parties. In 20 years, we may have to look to a completely virtual court system which would allow essentially paperless courts, largely or even entirely based on e-filing (with e-summons, e-pleadings *et cetera*).

The use of technology in the way court processes are conducted will lead to an almost paperless trial with more reliance on digital evidence, video relayed evidence *et cetera*. Not only will that technology increase efficiency, it will also be instrumental in the quest to improve access to justice, in particular to people in remote areas, who have hardly any access to justice.

### 3.4. Specialisation of Courts

Another recognisable trend that relates specifically to courts concerns the increasing role played by specialised courts. This is not an entirely new phenomenon and has been particularly prevalent in economic and business-related matters. Such matters require a certain level of technical knowledge from the judicial officers, without which procedures may become unduly long, inefficient and may even lead to unfair results. I expect this trend gradually to cover additional areas of expertise.

Uganda has seen an increase in efficiency and decrease in the backlog of cases as a result of introducing several specialised courts: the Commercial Courts, the Anti-Corruption Court, and the Land Division Court. As crimes become more sophisticated and areas of focus become too broad, courts will have to gain more technical knowledge and inevitably become more specialised. As new areas of civil litigation open up, courts will have to adapt to meet these new demands as well. We can therefore expect to see the specialisation trend continuing, with courts specifically dedicated to areas that were previously neglected, such as natural resources and the environment, as well as technology.

Somewhat linked to this, will be an increase in Alternative Dispute Resolution (ADR), in particular inasmuch as ADR will prove able to offer expertise through quick and relatively simplified and cheap procedures, as opposed to lengthy and expensive court processes.

## 4. The Most Significant Challenges for the Development of Law

There are two challenges that I would like to highlight regarding the further development of the law.

The first, continuing and persisting, challenge for the development of law relates to its intrinsic features: its reactionary nature and the lagging behind of slow law-making processes. The law needs to be more adaptable and able to anticipate changes in society and to regulate them proactively. It is possible to gauge global trends and legislate accordingly, and endeavours such as the 'Law of the Future' project will hopefully assist in this effort.

The second challenge is extrinsic, as it relates more broadly to geopolitical realities. Despite the interconnectedness caused by globalisation, it is still clear that States do not all have the same sphere of influence as others on the global stage. Countries in the developing world are still to a large extent marginalised, reinforcing the uni-polar order that has become significant over the past decade. The only way in which many of the challenges will be dealt with is if there is a greater partnership between the North and South countries. As the economies start to slow down in Europe and North America, the world will increasingly look to Asia and Africa as growing markets and providers of resources, and this will inevitably shift the balance of power.

## 5. Recommendations

With regards to policies and strategies for the future, it is clear that the global governance landscape has changed and will continue to do so. It is important that the current policies used in governing the world are reflective of these changes, as otherwise they risk becoming obsolete.

In order to anticipate major challenges brought by developments in technology, it is important for legal practitioners to conduct research in this field and constantly remain abreast of emerging trends thereby ensuring that the law is always evolving alongside them, rather than far behind.

[illegible] the world will [illegible] of [illegible]

## 5 Recommendations

[illegible] and strategies for the future [illegible] that the current policies used in [illegible] these changes, [illegible]

In order to address this major challenge, [illegible] this field in constantly [illegible] of emerging [illegible], ensuring that the law [illegible] evolving alongside them, rather than [illegible] behind.

# CHAPTER V

# THE PERSPECTIVE OF TRADE AND PRIVATE ACTORS:

# HOW ARE TRADE AND COMMERCE DRIVING THE FUTURE?

# 5.1.

# The Future of International Trade Law: How Best for Trade to Deal With (New) Non-trade Concerns?

**Gabrielle Marceau***

The precursor to the World Trade Organization (WTO), the General Agreement on Tariffs and Trade, was essentially about enhancing trade. Some of its provisions recognised, however, linkages between non-trade concerns and trade matters, including its famous Article XX which foresaw the possibility of non-trade concerns circumscribing trade promotion. The transition to the WTO saw WTO Members agree to expand the inclusion of some non-trade concerns, while keeping other non-trade concerns outside the parameters of the WTO agreements. Why has this happened, and can the WTO agreements' differential approach to addressing these non-trade concerns be understood? Perhaps on the basis that there is a need to bring certain non-trade concerns within the WTO system in order to further enhance trade; and to try to define when and how non-trade concerns can restrict trade. This piece offers a conceptual framework for categorising the different manners in which non-trade concerns are addressed in the WTO agreements. Employing this framework, this piece analyses how various non-trade concerns of contemporary and future significance for the WTO (which either impact or are impacted by the trade matters) might be addressed in international trade.

## 1. Introduction

The rules of the World Trade Organization (WTO) essentially intend to promote trade by reducing trade barriers on a non-discriminatory basis. These rules do not promote trade above all else, as trade interacts with issues other than trade. Such overlaps and intersections of interests and rules give rise to difficult questions. For example, should a country have

* **Gabrielle Marceau** is Counsellor in the Legal Affairs Division of the World Trade Organization, Associate Professor at the Faculty of Law at the University of Geneva and Visiting Professor at the Graduate Institute (HEID) Geneva.

the right to invoke religion as a basis for banning the entry of imports manufactured by persons of another religion? Should a country be allowed to refuse to export cotton to a country which fails to prevent the use of abusive child labour in manufacturing cotton t-shirts? Is it correct that a developed country can offer greater trade preferences to some developing countries over others on the basis that the former have ratified human rights (HRs) conventions?

These scenarios may illustrate the intersections of trade/non-trade concerns. It is very difficult to delineate between what constitutes a trade concern rather than a non-trade concern (NTC). Do all measures which promote non-discriminatory 'barrier-free' trade represent the furthering of trade concerns? Are the rationales offered in each of the foregoing scenarios trade or non-trade based, or both? In brief, what gives an issue its trade or non-trade character? Not everything that one might ordinarily attribute as a "trade issue" is regulated by WTO rules, but perhaps we can suggest that all matters covered by WTO rules are "trade" concerns? Economists, political scientists and lawyers may offer differing answers to these questions. This paper examines some issues relating to these questions from a legal perspective.

Trade remains important for a variety of reasons, as do non-trade concerns (NTCs). The future legitimacy and (legal) effectiveness of international trade law (ITL) depends on its capacity to address an increasing number of NTCs intersecting with trade. In the coming years, how WTO Members respond to calls to adopt more policies relating to NTCs will be critical. Compared to the days of its precursor institution, the General Agreement on Tariffs and Trade (GATT), legal landscapes are becoming increasingly complex; today they address more issues in more nuanced ways due to increased knowledge that translates to demands for new regulation. The WTO rules form part of these landscapes in which trade and non-trade regulations intersect. WTO law is only one (important) facet of ITL and only one component of the broader intricate web of domestic, regional, and international obligations which represent our global legal system. However, we need to understand which existing WTO rules regulate the intersections of trade/non-trade matters, to what extent, whether we should rethink them, or whether the status quo is appropriate.

The consequences for trade and NTCs will obviously differ depending on whether and how they are regulated (for example, inside or outside the WTO system) with resulting implications for (possible) conflicts within the WTO Agreement and between WTO law and other areas of international law. One might point to a plethora of contributories underlying countries' decisions as to whether and how to regulate matters. These may be economic, political or legal and this paper does not purport to address all or even the majority of them. Rather, this paper presents a legal perspective on the different ways in which existing WTO rules regulate NTCs. Of course WTO law is not static, and neither are other fields of law.

Section II finds that the WTO rules reflect different tools which co-opt the regulation of NTCs' interaction with trade to varying degrees. These tools are placed at different points on the WTO's spectrum of regulation. Some obligations traditionally considered as "non-trade" (id est intellectual property (IP) protection) are fully incorporated into the WTO by cross-reference. IP's place on the WTO spectrum is an example of where the non-trade subject of regulation is known and precisely regulated. Other NTCs are not represented on the spectrum because they are not specifically regulated by WTO law. In between these two extremes, NTC standards can serve as the basis for presumptions of WTO-consistency; while others are exceptions to generally applicable WTO rules. This paper shows that, while the WTO recognises that its rules cannot be read in "clinical isolation" from international law, where and how specific NTCs are placed within the WTO spectrum makes a difference. Notably, it affects the likelihood of, and the scope for unilateral regulation by Members for domestic non-trade objectives with extraterritorial effects.

## 2. Mapping the Different Legal Relationships between Trade and NTCs According to WTO Rules

Negotiations which preceded the establishment of the GATT (1944–47) suggested that the multilateral trading regime should address NTCs more deeply than the GATT eventually did. It was intended that, after World War II, the International Trade Organization (ITO) would be dedicated to regulating labour, employment and trade. In sum, it was on account of the impossibility of obtaining US Congress approval for trade and labour that the ITO never came into being. The GATT's provisional application continued until 1995, with a much narrower mandate than that envisaged for the ITO. Initially, the GATT essentially acknowledged NTCs only as trade-restrictive exceptions to the otherwise applicable rules prohibiting protectionism and promoting trade. In the context of goods trade, these trade-promoting rules ensured, and still ensure in current WTO rules, market access through the elimination of trade barriers, principally by reducing and binding tariffs and prohibiting quotas. However, recognising the intersection of NTCs and trade, Members gradually accepted the need to integrate NTCs in "trade rules" so as to explicitly allow NTC policy space while further eliminating other trade barriers. The 1970's brought a push for a trade-promoting harmonisation of standards used for regulations; some GATT parties agreed to base their domestic regulations on international standards.

History shows that how trade disciplines should address NTCs has always been a challenge but one that had to be faced, albeit sometimes more squarely than others, depending on the NTC and the moment in time. The following subsections demonstrate WTO law's current differential approach to regulating trade/non-trade interactions. It is notable that although non-trade/trade intersections are discernible in the application of essentially all WTO disciplines, there are few rules referring expressly to NTCs.

### 2.1. No Textual Reference to NTCs: WTO Rules Do Not Prevent the Non-Discriminatory Application of Regulations for Non-Trade Reasons

NTCs permeate the trading system. Products and services have qualities that are distinct from the fact that they are traded, and non-trade motivations may underlie trade-restrictive domestic regulations. For example, WTO rules do not prevent the non-discriminatory application of taxes and regulations to like products for cultural reasons.

### 2.2. Specialised WTO Agreement Fully-Integrating a NTC: Agreement on Trade-Related Aspects of Intellectual Property Rights (TRIPS)

WTO Members undertook, inter alia, to implement the provisions of pre-existing World Intellectual Property Organization (WIPO) conventions in the TRIPS. Members can resort to the WTO dispute settlement (DS) mechanism to ensure adherence to TRIPS, which also contains NTC defences (like public health, ordre public, the environment, and morality) for alleged failures to protect IP. This is the most WTO-integrated of NTCs.

### 2.3. Defences, Rights and New Presumptions: In WTO Legitimate Objectives Other Than Trade Can Be Invoked to Justify Trade Impediments Caused by the Promotion of NTCs

#### 2.3.1. Famous Article XX: NTCs as Defences to Trade Restrictions

Since GATT times, Article XX has permitted countries to maintain otherwise inconsistent trade-restrictive measures (TRMs) which are non-protectionist and materially contribute to achieving non-trade policies specifically listed in Article XX. In DS, responding WTO Members can invoke these exceptions as defences – the precise parameters of which are not set in stone. Once invoked, the DS employs a "balancing" test in order to determine WTO compatibility: this involves considering the value of the non-trade policy sought, the choice of measure, and the availability of less restrictive alternatives. It has been emphasised that the WTO Agreement's preambular reference to 'sustainable development'– not found in the GATT– demands an evolutionary interpretation that adds "colour, texture and shading" to the old exceptions' interpretation. Therefore, the future may see WTO DS interpret these terms to find other NTCs not explicitly specified.

Significantly, unlike during the GATT, multilateral support for the NTC measure defended is not necessary: an early WTO dispute concerning this recognised that all these Article XX exceptions allow responding Members to "unilaterally prescribe policies" for NTC purposes.

#### 2.3.2. The Right to Adopt Trade-Restrictive Regulations to Promote NTCs

The WTO era brought the refinement of some NTC regulation. In contrast to the GATT, where health measures were exceptions, the Agreement on the Application of Sanitary and Phytosanitary Measures (SPS) explicitly confirms Members' right to apply TRMs necessary to protect health. Such SPS measures cannot represent disguised protectionism and must actually protect against the identified health risk. The Agreement on Technical Barriers to Trade (TBT) also acknowledges Members' right to dictate product characteristics and related process/production methods through trade-restrictive "technical regulations". While they must be aimed at promoting "legitimate objectives", unlike the GATT exceptions, the list of permissible non-trade objectives is not closed, and the reference to 'sustainable development' as one of the WTO's legitimate objectives is important.

#### 2.3.3. New Presumptions of WTO Compatibility Given to International (Non-Trade) Standards

Harmonisation of the basis for TRMs: measures taken for health and other NTC purposes are now presumed consistent with the SPS and TBT where their implementation complies with "international standards". Such measures can be based on non-international standards (including those more stringent) where achievement of Members' legitimate objectives so require, but they do not benefit from presumptions of consistency.

### 2.4. Members' Control over the Interpretation of WTO Provisions:

There are a number of ways for Members to control the interpretation of WTO provisions. WTO law allows the membership to decide on the exact scope of WTO terms via various decision-making processes. Moreover, important substantive decisions have been adopted by the WTO membership further to SPS and TBT working committees.

### 2.5. Inhibiting Infringing a NTC Policy Cannot Be the Basis for a DS Claim (Except Under TRIPS)

Despite the increased breadth for NTCs to justify the circumscription of trade promotion, disputes cannot be initiated on the basis that the promotion of a legitimate non-trade policy concern has been prevented; in other words, there are no WTO obligations to protect the environment, health, human rights. Such policy defences or presumptions only operate to justify TRMs.

### 2.6. Governance Choices Reflected

For Members, the importance of regulating trade/non-trade interactions at the WTO varies. Nonetheless, for current and future NTCs, the central question remains where (if anywhere) they should be placed on the spectrum of WTO regulation. The ultimate placing generally reflects the balance between Members' social realities (policy space for trade and NTCs), international pressures, and Members' view of the current and future global legal order. States seem generally to favour specialisation reflecting the comparative advantage of different international organisations. For example, the presumption of consistency for measures which enforce international standards (pertaining to NTCs) confirms Members' respect for specialisation, as well as the efficiencies that such specialisation brings (harmonisation of standards reduces costs for traders). This respect was also reflected in WTO DS when Members were encouraged to consider resolutions of other international institutions in assessing whether the requirements of a WTO provision providing for exceptional preferential tariff schemes for development needs had been met.

## 3. New Trade and Non-Trade Connections

Exchange rates, freshwater sustainability, migration, and corruption are all important and their regimes' interactions with the WTO will certainly continue to present extremely complex ramifications. This section sets forth how each of these NTCs interact with trade and how WTO law applies to them. Section 3.2 relies on the framework set forth in Section 2 in assessing whether and how Members can regulate these interactions using WTO tools.

### 3.1. Examples of (New) Trade and NTCs Interactions

#### 3.1.1. Trade and Freshwater Sustainability

Freshwater is scarce and unevenly distributed across Members which have sovereignty over their territories. Tensions regarding access to water in foreign territories and water sustainability have already arisen between certain Members, and these tensions are set to heighten.

Although they do not specifically address water, WTO rules apply, to the extent that water is a commercial good. On-going trade facilitation negotiations could also affect water trade, as some of the issues it raises are similar to those of oil and gas trade. For example, WTO rules prohibit quotas but a Member might defend such an export water ban as required to conserve exhaustible natural resources or to protect health (both explicit Article XX exceptions). Moreover, products requiring large quantities of water in their production (virtual water) may soon be subject to measures applied for environmental or other legitimate purposes. No international standards for water sustainability appear to exist that could base a presumption of consistency under the SPS/TBT, but this could happen.

### 3.1.2. Trade and Corruption

Corruption is the misuse of public power for private gain. It negatively affects all Members' trading activities. While the word corruption never appears in the WTO agreements, many provisions have corruption-preventing effects by requiring transparency in the exercise of administrative discretion. The WTO's treatment of this subject is much narrower than other instruments. Indeed, the WTO rules do not address the supply side of corruption or provide for asset recovery or for the criminalisation of corrupt acts. However, the revision to the existing plurilateral Agreement on Government Procurement explicitly provides that one of its aims is to control corruptive practices and its Preamble explicitly references the UN Convention Against Corruption.

### 3.1.3. Trade and Economic Migration

Arguments abound that the abolition of restrictions on trade in goods/services should be matched by parallel action for the free movement of persons. Under the General Agreement on Trade in Services (GATS), Members may undertake to allow service suppliers (natural persons) to enter and stay in their territories temporarily (but not to enter the labour market). Adherence to these undertakings can be ensured at WTO DS (like TRIPS). Despite the fact that this form of temporary economic migration is much narrower than the larger migration debate (which also covers forced migration, such as sex trafficking, human smuggling, and refugees), commitments have been few and generally prefer highly-skilled service suppliers (often intra-corporate transferees), a reflection of the world as a "knowledge economy" where Members compete for skills and talents. This is not sufficient for developing Members who want broader commitments for other service suppliers. To this end, in December 2011, the membership made a (waiver) decision allowing the grant of preferential access to lower-skilled service suppliers from LDCs with which they share closer socio-cultural ties. Such preference for certain nationalities seems to be a (new) flexibility that will encourage Members to welcome LDC nationals into their societies.

### 3.1.4. Trade and Exchange Rates

Stable systems of exchange rates and trade are both global public goods. Significant challenges to the former have occurred at various points in history (notably since the 2000s). These have heightened attention on the dependence of trade on exchange rates. Moreover, while both the law of the International Monetary Fund (IMF) and WTO law contain provisions on exchange arrangements, a focus on the latter has resulted because of its binding DS system, which has no equivalent at the IMF and which some Members hope could be used to challenge alleged currency manipulators. Despite this recent attention, IMF law more specifically addresses exchange rates, and WTO law reflects this specialisation by emphasizing institutional cooperation. This division of labour and interconnectedness is evident in GATT Article XV which seeks to ensure that countries' actions, regulated by the two institutions, do not negatively affect the other. While this provision is not very clear, it seems to permit Members to bring WTO disputes on the basis that an exchange action (IMF's regulatory domain) impedes trade. Other WTO provisions may be relevant to tackle undervalued exchange rates, which might be considered an export subsidy, or dumping, or justify higher than agreed tariffs.

### 3.2. The Future of These Four NTCs

This subsection considers "whether and how" future WTO law might more specifically address these four non-trade concerns. It highlights some of the multitude of factors (of varying relevance depending on the concern) that might be considered in deciding whether to more specifically address these concerns. Then, bearing in mind the description in Section 2 of the existing tools used to regulate NTCs, some examples are offered on how these NTCs might be addressed.

#### 3.2.1. Whether to Address These NTCs More Specifically

*Extent of Appropriate Coverage?*

As a preliminary matter, one should note that each of the four NTCs described above has a much broader life than the common space they share with trade. Accordingly, if it is determined that they should be addressed more specifically by future WTO law, one must question how deeply into their spheres WTO regulation should reach. To date, it may seem that only the "trade-related" aspects of non-trade issues are addressed in WTO rules. This might be another emanation of the respect for specialisation and the expertise necessary to effectively regulate the full spheres of these NTCs. For example, oversight of the system of exchange rates requires specific expertise, surveillance and information from countries. The provisions relating to exchange rates in the current WTO rules do not extend to such systemic oversight, but only to the area of trade/exchange rate intersection. This seems appropriate, as seems the manner in which trade/migration is currently addressed (once optional commitments are undertaken, they reflect the extent of the intersection). Despite the foregoing, the great challenge remains the difficulty in definitively pointing to what constitutes a "trade-related" aspect of a particular issue or to where the frontiers between trade/non-trade concerns lie. The TRIPS purports to comprise only the "trade-related aspects" of IP, but some might argue that its protections go beyond this.

It might be argued that this is not the case for corruption. For example, although the GATS exceptions (similar to those in GATT Article XX) might allow Members to maintain otherwise inconsistent TRMs to combat supply-side corruption (such as service suppliers offering bribes), WTO rules do not impose obligations regarding supply-side corruption and disputes cannot be initiated on this basis.

*Are Clarity and Consensus Considerations?*

The integration of TRIPS by reference to existing conventions, previously under the auspices of another institution, shows at least prima facie a willingness to fully integrate NTCs in this manner. One might question, however, why IP protections were incorporated, while the minimum labour standards (individual rights like IP protection) of the International Labour Organization (ILO) were not? Is TRIPS' inclusion simply down to powerful US lobbyists? Could the unclear parameters of ILO obligations – subject to notorious divergence and disagreement among States – also be a factor? Did the clear-cut nature of IP obligations incline developing countries, which had not agreed to numerous TRIPS provisions in other fora, to accede to being bound at the WTO? If so, what are the implications for the four NTCs examined here? Given that there are no real functioning regimes for migration and water sustainability, one might suggest that they may not be candidates for full integration. Could other non-trade concerns be more apt to full integration? Suffice it to say that divergence and uncertainty as to obligations' exigencies might indispose Members from agreeing to full (TRIPS-like) integration.

*Treatment Outside the WTO*

The background as to why some NTCs are already WTO-regulated suggests the membership's consideration of both trade promotion and developments within and outside the trade sphere. For example, a WTO multilateral corruption agreement was proposed, but key proponent Members were eventually satisfied that the OECD Anti-Bribery Convention had achieved what they sought. Therefore, they did not lobby for its inclusion in the WTO.

### 3.2.2. How to Address These NTCs within the WTO Spectrum?

Different NTCs are more or less close to trade and WTO matters and thus call for different types of legal relationships through different mechanisms.

*TRIPS-like Approach?*

Members could decide to integrate (new) NTCs as WTO obligations but Members will presumably not treat all NTCs similarly. For example, it seems unlikely that WTO law will allow the initiation of disputes on the basis of alleged violations of water sustainability obligations in the near future. However, the legitimacy of trade-related regulation affecting water sustainability may be addressed by WTO law. One might imagine more specific, multilateral obligations covering corruptive practices in WTO law. Indeed, if additional obligations were being conceived, many questions would need to be addressed: should they be among all Members (multilateral), only among some (plurilateral), or optional (like GATS commitments)? For example, cross-references to existing conventions could be used for WTO to various ends (interpretations, obligations, defences or presumptions). Members could, for example, adopt decisions whereby illegal acts of private persons and enterprises could be attributed to them. Defences and justifications for maintaining export restrictions on water could also be negotiated as amendments or other forms of decisions and integrated into the WTO.

*Conditional Rights?*

As was done in the SPS and TBT, provisions could be drafted stating Members' right (subject to conditions) to adopt (restrictive) measures in order to promote any of these four NTCs so as to place the burden on the complaining Member to prove that such measures are not legitimate. WTO DS has allowed Members to maintain TRMs for the achievement of legitimate objectives, even if they have extraterritorial effects. Could the TBT also be interpreted, for example, so that its reference to preventing deceptive practices could include the right to ban particular imports on the basis of a need to combat corruptive practices in the country of origin or the specific foreign sector failing to comply with anti-corruption best practices?

*Defences and Justifications?*

Members can invoke the listed non-trade objectives of Article XX or other WTO flexibilities in order to justify TRMs. WTO exceptions and flexibilities have been interpreted in an evolutionary manner. For example, the exception in favour of "measures necessary for the protection of public morals" includes "standards of right and wrong conduct maintained by or on behalf of a community or nation". How broadly can these terms be interpreted? Could they include certain corrupt practices? Could they permit a Member to prohibit the entry of a service supplier on religious grounds? Could a scenario even be conceived where these terms could cover the promotion of sustainable water management? In the future, exceptions and justifications may be interpreted to include NTCs not examined to date, including some of these four specific NTCs.

Members might prefer not to wait for such DS interpretations and adopt consensus decisions, authoritative interpretations or amend existing provisions to ensure that they cover the NTCs they want, in the way they want.

*Presumptions in Favour of International Standards?*

Given that there are no real international standards for economic migration and water sustainability, the relevance of a WTO-consistency presumption appears moot today. However, Members may one day adopt a decision whereby TRMs maintained on the basis of guidelines issued by the IMF, or secretariats of institutions combating corruption, benefit from a presumption of WTO consistency.

*Treatment outside the WTO?*

Some NTCs may be best regulated uniquely outside the WTO. This may be the case for exchange rate or migration issues or other ""new"" NTCs. If it is, in recognition of their potential interactions, cooperative mechanisms between institutions might be established to ensure coherence and coordination.

## 4. Conclusion

This paper describes different types of relationships that exist between WTO trade provisions and NTCs. In particular, it highlights the extent to which interactions between some NTCs and trade have been more or less integrated into the WTO legal system. It demonstrates that where WTO rules have been introduced to regulate these interactions, they have generally been framed to promote trade, for example the harmonisation of standards is incentivised by presumptions of consistency. However, existing WTO rules do not fail to acknowledge the need for NTCs to circumscribe trade on occasion, as evidenced in broadly interpreted exceptions.

This paper surveyed the milestones in the trading regime's history where countries addressed the "whether and how" of NTC WTO integration. It appears that Members are spurred to do so where non-trade matters are either impacted by, or impact, trade. For example, increasing regulation of water sustainability outside of the WTO may eventually require reactions in WTO law. To date, the resulting approach of WTO law to various NTCs is a differentiated one. This paper does not suggest that the regulatory tools discussed are exhaustive or necessarily appropriate to regulate all interactions, or even the four "new" NTCs specifically explored. However, existing WTO law does have mechanisms whereby Members can experiment or gradually integrate NTCs as they see fit. Indeed, the membership may adopt decisions influencing the interpretation or application of existing provisions; or amend existing provisions; or fully-integrate NTCs (like TRIPS). Developments outside the WTO, including regional and preferential trade agreements, may explore experimentation in this regard. Such agreements have gone further in integrating NTCs as rights and obligations and have even given rise to disputes based on alleged labour violations.

Delineating between "trade" and "non-trade" or "trade" and "trade-related aspects" may forever remain an elusive task. However, the inability to delineate is not critical. It is not the identification of the delineation that is important, but the response. It is not critical but whether, and how, to deal with NTCs is nonetheless one of the biggest challenges for international trade law. ITL is here to stay. Will it manage to adequately address the complexities of trade-NTCs common spaces? Should it address these interactions? It seems that future collaboration and coherence which takes advantage of the efficiencies resulting from regimes' specialised mandates, but which focuses on potential synergies, will be essential for the sustainable development of the relationship between trade and NTCs in future international trade law.

I end with a final comment concerning a very live issue for the WTO: the power of trade is long-recognised and, with the establishment of the WTO, its strong DS system has ensured Members' adherence to their "trade" obligations. The conclusions of the WTO adjudicators are implemented, inter alia, for fear of retaliatory action. This makes WTO DS an attractive forum for countries wishing to enforce their "trade" claims, regardless of the fact that such a claim may put NTCs at stake. Once a claim is brought, WTO adjudicators are obliged to decide, and they can only make findings on the consistency of the challenged measure with WTO law. While WTO adjudicators have to date managed to avoid conflict with rights and obligations of other legal regimes, this may not always be possible in the future. Credit should be given to the highly effective adjudicative arm of the WTO, but it is no substitute for the input legitimacy that would come from a much needed consensus of the whole membership (one-hundred and fifty-five Members) directing how trade and non-trade concerns should interact. Unilateral actions on NTCs remain the second- and third-best alternatives to deal with these fundamental tensions between trade and NTCs. Only multilateral actions can offer sustainable and coherent solutions to the challenge brought about by NTCs which are at the heart of our human sustainable development.

## 5. Sources and Further Reading

Abbott, Kenneth W., "Rule-making in the WTO: Lessons from the Case of Bribery and Corruption", in *Journal of International Economic Law*, 2001, vol. 4, no. 2, pp. 275–296.

Abbott, Kenneth W. and Snidal, Duncan, "International Action on Bribery and Corruption: Why the Dog Didn't Bark in the WTO", in Daniel L. M. Kennedy and James D. Southwick (eds.), *The Political Economy of Inter-*

*national Trade Law: Essays in Honor of Robert E. Hudec*, Cambridge University Press, 2002, pp. 177–204.

Charnovitz, Steve, "The WTO and the Rights of the Individual", in *Intereconomics*, 2001, vol. 36, no. 2, pp. 98–108.

Charnovitz, Steve, "What is International Economic Law?", in *International Economic Law*, 2011, vol. 14, no. 1, pp. 3–22.

Hindley, Brian, "What Subjects Are Suitable for WTO Agreement?", in Daniel L. M. Kennedy and James D. Southwick (eds.), *The Political Economy of International Trade Law: Essays in Honor of Robert E. Hudec*, Cambridge University Press, 2002, pp. 157–170.

Hoekstra, Arjen Y., *The Relation Between International Trade and Freshwater Scarcity*, Staff Working Paper ERSD-2010-05, World Trade Organization, 2010.

Hughes, Valerie and Marceau, Gabrielle, "WTO and Trade in Natural Resources", in Boisson de Chazournes, Leb, Tignino (eds.), *International Law and Freshwater: The Multiple Challenges*, Edward Elgar Publishing Ltd, 2012 (forthcoming).

Kelsey, Jane, "How 'Trade in Services' Transforms the Regulation of Temporary Migration for Remittances in Poor Countries", in Meredith K. Lewis and Suzy Frankel (eds.), *International Economic Law and National Autonomy*, Cambridge University Press, 2010, pp. 269–294.

Mitchell, Andrew D. and Sheargold, Elizabeth, "GATT Art. XV: Exchange Arrangements", in Rüdiger Wolfrum and Peter-Tobias Stoll (eds.), *Max Planck Commentaries on World Trade Law*, 2010, vol. 5, pp. 352–364.

Lang, Andrew T. F., "Reflecting on 'Linkage': Cognitive and Institutional Change in the International Trading System", in *Modern Law Review*, 2007, vol. 70, no. 4, pp. 523–549.

Leal-Arcas, Rafael, "The GATS and Temporary Migration Policy", in Meredith K. Lewis and Suzy Frankel (eds.), *International Economic Law and National Autonomy*, Cambridge University Press, 2010, pp. 193–215.

Low, Patrick, Marceau, Gabrielle, and Reinaud, Julia, "The Interface between the Trade and Climate Change Regimes: Scoping the Issues", in *Journal of World Trade*, no. 35, 2012 (forthcoming).

Mercurio, Bryan and Leung, Celine, "Is China a Currency Manipulator? The Legitimacy of China's Exchange Regime under the Current International Legal Framework", in *The International Lawyer*, 2009, vol. 43 no. 3, pp. 1257–1300.

Marceau, Gabrielle, "Trade and labour: Rematching an old divorced couple?", in D. Bethlehem, D. Mcrae, R. Neufeld, and I. van Damme (eds), *The Oxford Handbook of International Trade Law*, Oxford University Press, 2009, p. 540.

Marceau, Gabrielle, "The WTO Dispute Settlement and Human Rights", in *European Journal of International Law*, 2002, Vol. 13, No.4, p. 75.

Marceau, Gabrielle, "The WTO is NOT a Closed Box", in *Proceedings of the 100th Annual Meeting, American Society of International Law*, 2006, pp. 29–31.

Marceau, Gabrielle and Doussin, Aline, "Le Droit du Commerce International, les Droits Fondamentaux et les Considérations Sociales", in *L'Observateur des Nations Unies*, 2009, vol. 27, no. 2, pp. 1–16.

Marceau, Gabrielle and Wyatt, Julien, "Trade and the Environment: The WTO's Efforts to Balance Economic and Sustainable Development", in Bovet, Peter, and Trindade Trigo (eds.), *Economie Environnement Ethique: De la Responsabilité Sociale et Sociétale*, Schulthess, 2009, pp. 225–235.

Panizzon, Marion, "International law on Economic Migration: A Ménage à Trois? GATS Mode 4, EPAs, and Bilateral Migration Agreements", in *Journal of World Trade*, 2010, vol. 44, no. 6, pp. 1207–1252.

Panizzon, Marion, *Trade and Labor Migration: GATS Mode 4 and Migration Agreements*, Friedrich-Ebert-Stiftung Occasional Paper No. 47, Geneva, 2010.

Trachtman, Joel P., *The International Law of Economic Migration: Toward the Fourth Freedom*, W.E. Upjohn Institute for Employment Research, 2009.

Trachtman, Joel P., "Trade and… Problems, Cost-Benefit Analysis and Subsidiarity", in *European Journal of International Law*, 1998, vol. 9, no.1, pp. 32–85.

U.N. General Assembly, 60th Session, Globalization and Interdependence: International Migration and Development, Report of the Secretary-General, A/60/871, 2006.

World Trade Organization, World Trade Report 2007 - Six Decades of Multilateral Trade Co-operation: What Have We Learnt? 2007, Geneva: WTO.

World Trade Organization, World Trade Report 2012 - Trade and public policies: a closer look at non-tariff measures in the 21st century, 2012, Geneva: WTO.

**Cases**

Appellate Body Report, Brazil - Measures Affecting Imports of Retreaded Tyres (Brazil – Retreaded Tyres), DS332, adopted 17 December 2007.

Appellate Body Report, European Communities – Conditions for the Granting of Tariff Preferences to Developing Countries (EC – Tariff Preferences), DS246, adopted 20 April 2004.

Appellate Body Report, United States – Certain Country of Origin Labelling (COOL) Requirements, DS384, adopted on 23 July.

Appellate Body Report, United States – Import Prohibition of Certain Shrimp and Shrimp Products (US – Shrimp), DS58, adopted 6 November 1998.

Appellate Body Report, United States – Measures Affecting the Production and Sale of Clove Cigarettes (US – Clove Cigarettes), DS406, adopted 24 April 2012.

Appellate Body Report, United States – Measures Concerning the Importation, Marketing and Sale of Tuna and Tuna Products (US – Tuna II (Mexico)), DS381, adopted 13 June 2012.

Appellate Body Report, United States – Standards for Reformulated and Conventional Gasoline (US – Gasoline), DS2, adopted 20 May 1996.

# 5.2.

# International Competition Law?

**Imelda Maher***

Competition law is characterised by a proliferation of national regimes and some shared sense of purpose predicated on the dominance of an economics-approach in this field in relation to private market behaviour. States have entered into enforcement agreements and enforcement networks have grown, especially since the turn of the century primarily with the aim of improving enforcement through policy learning, technical assistance and the provision of examples of best practice. All of these initiatives point to the continuing significance of national legal boundaries with some weaker recognition of challenges that global trade poses for competition enforcement. With the focus on enforcement, there is limited debate as to the nature of competition policy and the question that finds less common purpose is the extent to which States are subject to competition rules. In short the relationship between competition and regulation is under-developed. The introduction of competition laws in Brazil, India, China and South Africa suggests that this question will become more significant in the next decade and beyond with a re-calibration of the balance between international trade laws and international competition law.

## 1. Introduction

Despite the globalisation of international trade there is no international competition law. Efforts to create an international competition law under the aegis of the World Trade Organisation were dropped in the Doha Round with the working group on trade and competition disbanded in 2004. There has been a large increase in the number of States with competition statutes, over 100, with most enacted in the last fifteen years. This suggests that despite globalisation, when it comes to competition law national legal boundaries are fixed and impermeable. This however does not fully capture what has happened in the competition sphere or how it is

* **Imelda Maher** is Sutherland Professor of European Law, UCD School of Law, UCD Centre for Regulation and Governance.

likely to develop. Unilateralism, while a feature of competition law since the post-war era with the emergence of the doctrine of extraterritoriality and the tolerance and even encouragement of export cartels, is only a small part of the web of rules, agencies, networks, agreements and institutions that currently characterise international competition law.

Given the proliferation of national laws, can there ever be and should there ever be an international competition law? The answer to this question lies in part in examining to what extent competition law has been internationalised so far and the characteristics of that internationalisation. Thus, the first section will outline agreements that have emerged in the field. The second section will explore the emergence of networks. The final section will suggest what lies ahead, reflecting on the triggers of a global constitution, legal boundaries and legal internet before concluding.

Two preliminary observations that both point to the thick nature of national boundaries in this sphere are that first, the extraterritorial application of competition laws is a feature of the most influential competition regimes, that of the United States and the European Union. Second, unlike international trade law where the aim is to regulate the conduct of States as to what rules they can introduce and implement, competition law prohibits certain private behaviour and State conduct in the market where it acts as a private participant such as in procurement. Thus, debates and initiatives in this field are about how national competition regimes can prohibit certain conduct rather than having international rules prohibiting that conduct. The focus has been on two issues: the introduction of competition regimes at the State level and on improving transnational enforcement of national competition laws through cooperation across national boundaries. Thus, national boundaries remain a focus in relation to rules and enforcement with internationalisation indirectly seeking to shape private conduct through reliance on action on the national or regional level. Thus, in the absence of binding international competition norms the international competition regime will remain dense with national laws.

## 2. Agreements on Competition Law

The proliferation of national competition laws suggests that there is some common purpose between States to tackle anti-competitive conduct. This commonality arises from the importance of economics in the field and the prominence of an economic-based approach to enforcement. What is not clear is whether this leads to a common approach in enforcement. However, the emergence of agreements and networks to address this suggests that there is some concern to at least develop best practices.

## 2.1. Bilateral Competition Agreements

One of the most important tools an agency has is information on the market and the conduct of parties within that market. The sharing of such information across national boundaries especially given the globalisation of trade is important to ensure the effectiveness of competition regimes. If this information cannot be garnered at the international level, this would suggest it should be shared at the bilateral level. The legal difficulty with sharing such information is that only some regimes criminalise breaches of their competition laws, most notably the US, and more recently the UK. Thus, sharing information that may lead to criminal prosecution is not possible for those regimes that rely exclusively on civil law remedies.

Nonetheless, bilateral agreements are commonly directed mainly at cooperation in enforcement. The first agreement was entered into between Germany and the United States in 1976 and the EU and US entered into two such agreements. The most integrated agreement is that between Australia and New Zealand where the competition agencies can enforce each other's competition laws. The agreements provide mechanisms to assist the States when both are faced with the same competition issue or when one State needs the cooperation of the other to investigate an infringement of its laws because for instance, the evidence is available in the other State.

The extent to which such agreements can improve the effective enforcement of competition law is not clear. The EU/US reports point to deeper cooperation and there are some examples of the sharing of agency information, non-confidential but not necessarily in the public domain. The emphasis seems to be mainly on improving institutional understanding and support. In fact, bilateral agreements may not resolve difficulties or lead to a common response as can be seen in the approval of the GE/Honeywell merger by the US authorities and its disapproval by the EU authorities. This led to strong diplomatic exchanges, but ultimately to greater engagement between the agencies.

### 2.1.1. Extradition

Following 9/11, the UK and US entered into an extradition treaty. While primarily concerned with terrorist activity it has been used to extradite British company executives for competition-related offences. Where both regimes have criminal sanctions such cooperation on extradition is possible.

## 2.2. Trade Agreements

Competition provisions are often found in trade agreements, underlining the synergy between trade and competition. Where a trade agreement removes trade restrictions at the State level, there is a risk that private actors achieve market foreclosure through anticompetitive conduct. To mitigate such risk, some competition provisions are included in the agreement. There are two main forms, those that reflect mutual trading interests such as the US and Canada and those mainly entered into by the EU where the aim is to encourage harmonisation of competition norms, a form of competition law export. These agreements can be either bi- or pluri-lateral and there are examples with varying degrees of intensity on competition law from across the world, for example NAFTA, MERCOSUR, WAEMU, SADU, and ASEAN. The agreements range from those with a general obligation to have national competition laws and to cooperate on enforcement – for example, NAFTA – to the more common agreements which contain substantive provisions prohibiting certain forms of activity such as cartels. The scope of the substantive provisions vary with some only addressing private market behaviour and others extending to public procurement rules, mergers and even State aid to industry. The EU can be seen as the pinnacle of integration for regional trading blocs. It has extensive substantive competition rules binding on all member States and since 2003, all national agencies enforce the EU rules, assigning cases between them and the European Commission.

These agreements are the institutional response of the States to common problems and opportunities in the context of shared, if not global, markets. At the same time, national legal boundaries remain with those agreements that only address enforcement placing greater significance on national boundaries and laws than those with substantive obligations where the agreement penetrates further into the State and points to a greater sharing of sovereignty

## 3. Networks

The patchwork of agreements on cooperation and/or linked to trade has, since the demise of the WTO competition law agenda, been supplemented by a growing number of networks focussed on enforcement cooperation. These networks vary in nature. Some consist of agencies acting voluntarily and entirely outside the realm of formal law, such as the International Competition Network; some are part of international agencies, such as the OECD Global Forum on Competition, the UNCTAD International Group of Experts on Competition Law and Policy; while others are part of other regional groupings – for example, APEC and ASEAN. The common thread between them is the focus on improving enforcement of competition law through cooperation, shared learning, provision of best practice guides and technical assistance. Thus all the networks, albeit to a lesser degree than the more formal agreements and MOUs above, take the national boundary and State law as their starting point and seek to support national regimes albeit in the context of a recognition of common problems and global markets. In this instance, it is possible to say that the existence of these networks is recognition that the agreements are not sufficient to address the common challenges of competition law enforcement transnationally.

### 3.1. International Bodies

The role of international bodies in the development and support of networks and indeed in the creation of their own networks is significant with the OECD providing recommendations on best practices, reviewing national competition regimes at the behest of a State, and providing technical assistance through its competition programmes in South East Asia and eastern Europe, where it works in conjunction with a national competition agency in South Korea and Hungary respectively, to provide workshops and seminars on a regional basis. UNCTAD, like the OECD has an annual meeting of experts and also supports regional initiatives, notably in South America and Africa, with technical assistance being offered to national agencies. The relative 'new-ness' of many competition regimes means that there is a dearth of expertise and the networks provide support, information, knowledge and advice as required. The largest network is the International Competition Network set up following the collapse of the WTO agenda. It is now eleven years old having grown from fourteen members to one hundred and fourteen agencies, China being a notable exception. It has no offices, staff or budget. Instead, an agency volunteers each year to run the annual conference which has in excess of five hundred delegates. Matters of common concern are discussed with the main point of contact and content through the year being the excellent website. It is a self-governing body with effective competition enforcement as its main and only objective. The agencies are supported by non-governmental advisers who attend the conference following nomination by a national agency. These NGAs also participate in writing reports and other documents reflecting best practice. Smaller networks are also a primary vehicle for technical assistance allowing States to converge within particular regions such as Compal, the Nordic competition network, or around a common language such as the Lusaphone network.

The field of competition law now looks crowded with international bodies and a web of networks in operation with national agencies members of many. The challenge is to ensure that the multiple platforms do not fail by their very existence to meet their common objective. A plethora of fora runs the risk of diluting the already slim resources of agencies if they find themselves responding to more than one network. It is important to note in this regard that the networks may be seen primarily as sites of information and knowledge that do not demand active participation.

### 3.2. Why Networks?

The proliferation of networks with their emphasis on sharing best practice suggests first, that there is a common understanding of shared problems and a common discourse which is shared by the agencies and second, that there is a dearth of knowledge and that in some way these networks are responding to a common need. The networks operate primarily at the level of the agency and the emphasis on enforcement suggests general agreement as to what is being enforced and why. One critique of the networks is that the emphasis on praxis means that the question of the appropriateness of competition law and the different nature of markets receives limited if any attention. While the competition laws of different States bear often a remarkable level of similarity, with a well-nigh universal condemnation of price-fixing cartels, there are areas where similarity is not so marked such as the extent to which competition laws apply to State activity in the market, to mergers, to procurement and with regard to how far a market analysis is applied to activities that historically were offered by the State such as communications, water, energy.

The common thread in competition law seems to be in particular a common economics discourse, with economic analysis intrinsic to competition law. Economics transcends legal boundaries in ways laws do not, and the hegemony of the US economic thinking is apparent. While the ordoliberal tradition has been and remains an important influence in continental Europe in particular, it has not garnered the same level of recognition as the classic economics of the Harvard and Chicago Schools and behavioural economics.

### 3.3. Whither National Competition Laws?

In relation to a need for knowledge, this raises the question as to whether the rush to adopt competition laws at the national level is really the best response to the globalisation of trade. This is especially so given the practical problems of seeking to enforce competition norms that are national in nature in relation to conduct that can have a global impact, as seen in relation to international cartels. The extent to which competition policy needs to be integrated into national polities, and hence support and render meaningful competition laws, is a major issue. While competition law may be akin to a constitutional principle, for example, in the US, there remains ambivalence about it in many parts of the world. In developing countries there is a concern that developed countries did not introduce competition laws and encouraged cartels as a means of building economies for many years. Yet, they are expected to have competition laws in place. On the other hand, a competition law can be one aspect of good governance, acting as an anti-corruption mechanism provided it is enforced and applies to issues such as public procurement. It is also questionable whether competition law enforcement is an appropriate use of limited resources in States where the people have issues such as limited access to water, poor energy supplies and limited communications infrastructure. The response in part to this criticism is that an effective competition regime can allow such systems to develop and improve.

In other words, a key question that these networks and agreements do not – and are not designed to address, is the extent to which competition policy as articulated in the model UNCTAD law or the many national laws around the world, is perceived of as a public good, with a strong legitimacy predicated on public support both for the substantive measures, themselves, the scope of their application, how they are enforced and their relationship with other policy fields such as employment, environment and public service.

## 4. Conclusion

At this moment international competition law is a misnomer. Instead, competition law remains primarily a creature of national law with that law supported by overlapping and complementary networks of agencies focussed on enforcement and for developed economies primarily, more formal agreements dealing with competition enforcement or with competition provisions as part of a wider trade agreement.

A general competition law at the WTO level has been roundly rejected suggesting that fragmented national laws remain the only true measure with large economies, notably the US and EU having influence beyond their boundaries by applying their competition rules extraterritorially, by entering into agreements concerned with competition, and providing technical assistance to States without or with very new competition regimes. These entities remain highly influential in the OECD and the ICN. One argument as to why the UNCTAD model law for instance has not been as widely adopted as might have been expected is because the US and EU have not actively supported its initiatives as much as those of the OECD and the ICN.

The emergence of networks at the regional and international level suggests a flatter structure although it is not clear to what extent this is really the case. Given that the networks' main focus is on knowledge exchange and policy learning, rather than confronting difficult policy choices and given the implicit assumption of a common problem and common understanding of the economic rationale underpinning the competition regimes, this is possible. At the same time, it may mean that more intractable issues such as the relationship between competition rules and State involvement in the market are not addressed in these networks.

### 4.1. What Does This Mean for Policy?

At the policy level this means that States, who are not members of regional bodies with competition policy obligations such as the EU and ASEAN, are free to develop competition norms that take the best from the expertise and information provided by those networks or indeed to adopt no competition norms at all. Small open economies do not necessarily need any competition laws as competition is vibrant in any event. However, adoption of competition norms can be required by the IMF or World Bank or encouraged by the EU or the US or any other developed economy, which may provide assistance to facilitate it. For developed economies, soft influence can still be exercised through providing assistance and knowledge both on a bilateral and plurilateral level.

These trends suggest that having a competition statute per se says little about the nature of an economy and despite the rhetoric of commonality, there is a lot of difference between regimes. This suggests that it is for the State to articulate and to examine what can loosely be described as the limits of competition policy and law enforcement. What can competition policy achieve, how does it bed down with other regimes? What benchmarks can be applied to the national competition regime so that it can be evaluated? If competition policy is either poorly understood or not popular, should it be changed or should government or the competition agency lead from the front because it is the government's view that ultimately there is a strong case to be made that competition policy is a public good? The introduction of competition laws in Brazil, India, China and South Africa suggests that these questions will become more significant in the next decade and beyond with a re-calibration of the balance between international trade laws and international competition law.

## 4.2. What Are the Implications for Research?

What we know is that there is no appetite, for political reasons at least, for a transnational competition regime that can apply in particular to transnational corporations. Even if there was a move towards a global competition law, it has been stopped in its tracks. On the other hand, global markets remain and there are efforts to develop some sort of institutional framework both through articulating competition objectives in agreements and by developing governance structures and networks, to assist and support agencies. What we do not know and need to address is what are these networks doing and is there any empirical evidence of impact for what they do. It is necessary to articulate criteria against which to measure the effectiveness of these networks and for the ICN also to address its objectives given its size. One suggestion is that it will become a network of networks – it will be where the shape and scope of the patchwork of international initiatives are laid bare so it is at a minimum possible to see where gaps remain, what the on-going challenges are and to avoid unnecessary duplication.

### 4.3. What Does This Mean for the Lawyer of the Future?

What this means for the lawyer of the future, is that he/she needs to understand markets given that the law plays such an important role in their operation and hence he/she should be trained in some economics. As the relationship between the State and the market remains challenging, the need for the lawyer of the future to know the relationship between the market and the State, often articulated as competition and regulation, is important. This is important also for the citizen of any State. While competition law is so often cast as a prohibition designed to set as few limits as possible to the market cornerstone of freedom of contract, the key issue for developing the law and its application to international markets is the better understanding of the public dimension of competition law and how it can constrain inappropriate concentration of economic power, be it in the State or in private hands.

## 5. Sources and Further Reading

Bhattacharjea, Aditya, "The Case for a Multilateral Agreement on Competition Policy: A Developing Country Perspective", in *Journal of International Economics Law*, 2006, vol. 9, no. 2, p. 292.

Bode, Mariana and Budzinski, Oliver, "Competing Ways towards International Antitrust: The WTO versus the ICN", in *Marburg Economics Working Paper*, 2005, no. 3.

Brusick, Phillipe, Alvarez, Ana-Maria and Cernat, Lucian, *Competition Provisions in Regional Trade Agreements: How to Assure Development Gains*, 2005, UNCTAD.

Drexl, Josef, "International Competition Policy after Cancun: Placing a Singapore Issue on the WTO Development Agenda", in *World Competition,* 2004, vol. 27, no. 3, p. 419.

Elhauge, Einer and Geradin, Damien, *Global Competition Law and Economics,* Hart Publishing, 2007.

Ezrachi, Ariel, *International Research Handbook on Competition Law*, Edward Elgar Publishing, 2012.

Fox, Eleanor, "International Antitrust and the Doha Dome", in *Virginia Journal of International Law*, 2003, vol. 43, no. 912.

Gal, Michal, *Competition Policy for Small Market Economies*, Harvard University Press, 2003.

Galloway, Jonathan, "Moving Towards a Template for Bilateral Antitrust Agreements", in *World Competition,* 2005, vol. 28, no. 4, p. 589.

Geradin, Damien, "The Perils of Antitrust Proliferation - The Process of 'Decentralized Globalization' and the Risks of Over-Regulation of Competitive Behaviour", in *Chicago Journal of International Law,* 2009, vol. 10, no. 1.

Gerber, David, *Global Competition: Law, Markets and Globalization*, Oxford University Press, 2010.

Guzman, Andrew, *Cooperation, Comity and Competition Policy*, Oxford University Press, 2011.

Halabi, Sam, "Comity of Empagran: The Supreme Court Decides That Foreign Competition Regulation Limits American Antitrust Jurisdiction over International Cartels", in *Harvard International Law Journal,* 2005, vol. 46, no. 1, p. 279.

Hollman, Hugh and Kovacic, William, "The International Competition Network: It's Past, Current and Future Role" in *Minnesota Journal of International Law*, 2011, vol. 20, no. 2, p. 274.

Kronthaler, Franz and Stephan, Johannes, "Factors Accounting for the Enactment of a Competition Law – An Empirical Analysis", in *Antitrust Bulletin*, 2007, vol. 52, no. 137.

Lugard, Paul, *The International Competition Network at Ten*, Intersentia Press, 2011.

Maher, Imelda, "Competition Law Modernization: An Evolutionary Tale?", in P Craig and G de Búrca (eds.), *The Evolution of EU Law*, Oxford University Press, 2012.

Maher, Imelda and Papadopoulos, AS, "Competition Agency Networks Round the World" in A. Ezrachi (ed.), *International Research Handbook on Competition Law*, Edward Elgar Publishing, 2012.

Noonan, Chris, *The Emerging Principles of International Competition Law*, Oxford University Press, 2008.

Papadopoulos, Anestis, *The International Dimension of EU Competition Law and Policy,* Cambridge University Press, 2010.

Slaughter, Anne-Marie, *A New World Order,* Princeton University Press, 2004.

Sokol, D.D., "The Future of International Antitrust and Improving Antitrust Agency Capacity", in *Northwestern University Law Review*, 2009, vol. 103, no. 1081.

Sweeney, Brendan J., *The Internationalisation of Competition Rules*, Routledge, 2012.

Utton, Michael, *International Competition Policy*, Edward Elgar Publishing, 2006.

**Cases**

England and Wales, *The Case of the Norris v United States of America*, UKHL 16, 2008.

# 5.3.

## Changing Ideologies in Trade, Technology and Development: The Challenge of China for International Trade Law

**Mary E. Footer*** **and Andrew R. Forbes****

The continued economic rise of China presents a range of challenges for international trade law. The only real certainty for the future of China is that its development will continue on a unique trajectory, influenced by ancient Confucian tradition and modern authoritarian ideology. This presents a challenge for the multilateral trading system, which has previously dealt with a largely ideologically homogenous group of States that take a similar approach to the rule of law. A number of suggestions will be made as to how actors in the multilateral trading system may need to adapt to the changing ideologies in trade, technology and development that China's rise is bringing about. This will require increasing sensitivity in norm creation from policy makers. Future lawyers and researchers must prepare for the challenges that will come to permeate all aspects of international trade law as a result of China's long march forward.

### 1. Introduction

China has emerged to become one of the world's largest trading nations, becoming the second largest economy in the world in 2010. This is the first time since the Cold War that a nation has reached this size while maintaining an ideology that is fundamentally different to that of other major trading groups. This presents a challenge for the multilateral trading system that must now adapt to effectively include China within both law-making processes and systems of implementation.

* **Mary E. Footer** is Professor of International Economic Law, and Head of the Business, Trade and Human, Rights Unit in the Human Rights Law Centre, University of Nottingham School of Law.

** **Andrew R. Forbes** is a recent graduate from the School of Law at the University of Nottingham in Law LLB.(Hons) with a distinction in Chinese Law gained at the University of Hong Kong.

It is vital that this challenge is addressed effectively. China's cooperation is required to address all the major issues affecting global trade. Its continued use of the World Trade Organisation to carry out its trade policy will affect the status and importance of the institution itself. Any turn towards protectionism will have knock-on effects in other nations and conversely, China's continued support for free trade can promote the maintenance of open trade elsewhere despite the current impasse in the Doha Development Round. It is clear that as a large and active member of the multilateral trading system, it is vital that it plays by the rules agreed upon by all trading nations. This requires that the rules gain legitimacy for Chinese trade policy officials. In order to promote legitimacy, the interests of China must be seen to be sufficiently represented within the system and the rules to be applied in a fair and even-handed manner.

This contribution suggests that for this to occur, the ideological differences between China and other nations must be taken into account. Only then will the multilateral trading system be capable of maintaining the objectivity and impartiality that is needed for it to function effectively across different countries and cultures, including that of China. The focus of this contribution is on the identification of the areas in which these differences may have practical implications for the future of international trade law given the challenge that China presents for the multilateral trading system as an economic powerhouse. The three broad areas to be considered are trade, technology and development. In these key areas disparities in cultural and ideological perspectives between China and its trading partners will increasingly cause tensions and raise challenges for the multilateral trading system. By highlighting alternative perspectives it is hoped that more attention may be paid to promoting diversity in opinions and interests among China's trading partners, and thereby assist with meeting those challenges.

## 2. The Bases of Cultural and Ideological Differences

The root of such alternative perspectives stems from the combination of ancient Confucian tradition and modern authoritarian ideology. Until the economic opening up in 1978 under Deng Xiaoping, Chinese society had largely resisted the growing trend towards globalisation. This left the Chinese population with a markedly different perspective from much of the industrialised world. This is likely to remain the case even if more international influences do come to play an increasing role in Chinese culture.

It has recently been argued that Confucianism is returning to play a more prominent role in Chinese society as the ideology of Marxist communism fades from the rhetoric of the Chinese Communist Party (CCP). This can be seen in the use of Confucius Institutes for the projection of Chinese soft power. The fact that the CCP has embraced the Confucian tradition, as part of China's push to interact with the outside world, is significant. Through its selective interpretation of Confucian tradition the CCP has sought to steer a middle ground that appeals to the Chinese public without contradicting its continued use of official Marxist theory.

On the internal plane, the rise of CCP Confucianism is timely given the Party's need to deal with a rising tide of social unrest in China caused by growing income inequality, disquiet about environmental pollution and rampant official corruption. A return to Confucianism provides the Chinese Government with a broad platform to advance its narratives through a readily understandable message for its people while simultaneously underpinning the legitimacy of its system of governance. This can be seen in the CCP's continued focus on the promotion and maintenance of harmony in Chinese society, one of the core values in Confucian thinking, against the backdrop of an emerging pluralism. The difference between placing the highest value on harmony in the whole of society as opposed to the freedom of each individual within it should not be underestimated. It forms the basis of many of the most fundamental differences between Western and Chinese policies over the conduct of trade in a (non)market economy, the pursuit of technology and investment, and development.

Differences also stem from the more recent Communism experienced in China since the revolution in 1949. The Communist regime clearly consisted of a value system which was incompatible with the values of Western liberal democracies. Attitudes towards religion, property and freedom of expression differed almost entirely from the cultural values expressed in Western nations following World War II. By the end of Mao's time in power, the rule of law had been completely abolished and vilified in Chinese society and the 'unequal treaties' were portrayed as key to the century of humiliation experienced prior to the Communist revolution. While the regime has clearly adapted to an extent, particularly with regards to the property rights of citizens and the rule of law, differences in attitudes still remain.

China's governance system is very different to the liberal democracies in the Western world. Protection of rights and freedoms, which are deemed fundamental in the West, are often completely disregarded. The justifications for such actions are different to those used by Western governments. The recent National Human Rights Action Plan of China (2012–2015), issued by the State Council, provides a good example. The opening paragraph explains why the protection of human rights is important because "[i]t is of great significance to promoting scientific development and social harmony, and to achieving the great objective of building a moderately prosperous society in an all-round way".

In the Western world no such justification would be required for the protection of individual freedoms which are seen as intrinsically good. The concepts of scientific development and social harmony form part of the Chinese ideology and are valued more highly than freedom and protection of individual rights. The availability of these justifications in the Chinese discourse means that different policies such as increased State control over the economy, censorship of cultural materials and economic development are given priority over the development of civil and political rights. This poses a challenge for the multilateral trading system since many of these policies cannot be justified by other nations and give rise to charges of unfairness. The subsequent sections highlight certain areas in which the Chinese position has been challenged and demonstrate how Chinese ideology is affecting the application of trade law in these areas.

## 3. Changing Ideologies in Trade

Differences in ideology between China and other key players in the multilateral trading system may continue to cause problems in the creation and implementation of international trade law. The root of these differences between China and its major trading partners lies in the ideological disparity about market structure and economic governance.

China has clung on to its patrimonial sovereignty in the field of economic governance with its State-led socialist market-economy. State planning is an expression of an ideology that, in Pitman Potter's words, "draws on a reservoir of Chinese tradition derived from Confucianism and its assumptions about authority and hierarchy in social organization". Consequently, more emphasis is placed on the rule of technical experts over the views of individual members of society. This is scarcely reconcilable with the rest of the world's move towards the progressive endorsement of embedded liberalism in the multilateral trading system, based on free trade and a market economy, which is part of its freedom-centred ideology.

When joining the WTO in 2001 China agreed to be classified as a non-market economy (NME) for 12 years (and 15 years in anti-dumping disputes). Yet, the current Chinese leadership yearns for full 'market economy' status. To date China has been recognised as a market economy in bilateral treaties by 79 countries. However, its key trading partners, the US and the EU, have remained reluctant to grant it. Their aim in denying market economy status to China might be to encourage the Chinese authorities to complete economic and political reforms, which could lead to a more open and transparent economy, but the evidence suggests otherwise.

Despite its NME status, China is being treated sufficiently like a market economy already when it comes to the imposition of countervailing duties. This is illustrated by complaints involving dumping investigations, such as *EU – Footwear (China)*. In that case, an analogue country, Brazil, was used to determine 'normal value', with adjustments being based on world market prices. Had it been treated as a market economy, as China claimed it should have been, a determination of normal value would have been made by comparing export and domestic prices in the Chinese footwear industry.

More recently both the US and the EU have begun crying foul on unfair subsidies. Treating China as a market economy, rather than as an NME, in anti-subsidy complaints is economically and legally more significant than in anti-dumping because it goes to the heart of how a country regulates its economy. This can already be seen in *US – Certain Products from China* where a subsidy dispute was decided not on the basis of China's status as an NME but according to the Appellate Body's decision in *US – Softwood Lumber IV*, which involved two market economies, on the basis of out-of-country benchmarks. Thus, in *US – Certain Products from China*, in-country benchmarks for State-owned enterprise (SOE)-produced inputs, government provision of land-use rights and in-country interest rates set by State-owned commercial banks (SOCBs) were all rejected, as contrary to the relevant WTO rule on the matter. Significantly, China must constantly rebut the presumption that government ownership of an SOE (more than 50%) does not automatically result in its control of the enterprise; otherwise it would be a 'public body' for the purpose of

WTO anti-subsidy law. This is hurting Sino-American trade relations, as recent consultations between the two countries demonstrate.

The continuing failure to recognise these differences is damaging the legitimacy of the multilateral trading system. To China it seems unfair that anti-subsidy rules are being applied in this manner, especially when many of its major trading partners engage in similar practices in support of economically sensitive sectors such as agriculture, automobile production or the electronics industry, or else they have already chosen to grant it market economy status under a bilateral treaty. To some of China's key trading partners it seems unfair that Chinese industries and certain economic sectors are recipients of a wide range of subsidies in everything from iron and steel fasteners to wind-power equipment. At least in the matter of unfair trade practices, it appears that international trade law has so far failed to adapt to the ideologically different nature of China.

By not granting market economy status now China may be challenged through the WTO to comply with more open business practices, particularly in the matter of subsidies. For example, there is continued dissatisfaction (mostly from the US) over China's failure to revalue the renminbi (RMB), thereby aiding Chinese exports, as well as government subsidies for wind and solar power equipment.

Looking forward, it seems there is potential for the concept of market economy status to change, reflecting a shift towards increasing levels of State intervention in markets both in China and in the West. The recent bank bailouts in Europe have shown that even the most liberal economies may require intervention in times of crisis. Combining this with the pressure that China is increasingly putting on other economies to recognise its market economy status, the concept of market economy status is bound to undergo further change, possibly more rapidly than originally anticipated. This could have far reaching consequences for acceding WTO Members and perhaps influence anti-dumping and countervailing duty actions under WTO rules.

At the same time, China will continue to move along the path of State capitalism in support of SOEs, which even extends to SOCBs and other SOEs in the financial sector. Timely challenges to this policy, under WTO dispute settlement rules, may yet prove to be the most effective means of opening up the Chinese economy to greater foreign competition. In *China – Electronic Payment Services*, China's designation of the SOE China UnionPay, as the sole supplier of electronic payment services for all domestic RMB payment card transactions, was found to have violated its market access and national treatment commitments under the WTO Services Agreement.

## 4. Changing Ideologies in Technology

Ideological differences have already had an impact on the use of technology in China, as is clear from some recent trade disputes concerning the Internet, and censorship or content review mechanism. The Chinese approach towards censorship emphasises the maintenance of harmony within the Chinese society over and above the promotion of individual freedoms, both of expression and information. This is clearly an area in which, ideologically, Chinese and Western liberal perspectives differ.

Such differences have arisen in several ways. One example is the China-Google dispute, which arose in early 2010. It centred on an alleged cyber-attack by domestic computer hackers on the Gmail accounts of Chinese human rights activists and at least twenty other large corporations from different sectors in the economy. In retaliation, the American Internet giant declared that it would stop censoring politically and socially sensitive search results in China. Negotiations to resolve the dispute, in which Google sought self-regulation rather than censorship, failed. The corporation closed its Internet search service in China (google.cn) and began rerouting Chinese users through its uncensored search engine, based in Hong Kong.

Whereas direct attempts to deal with ideological differences arising from free speech may have failed, it has been suggested that “the WTO can play a role in opening up Chinese society”. Joost Pauwelyn has suggested that by making use of free market principles it may be possible to limit China’s public censorship and to “pry open markets”, and thereby “pry open [the] minds” of the Chinese people. This is misguided.

The case of *China – Publications and Audiovisual Products* clearly demonstrates the Chinese Government’s alternative perspective on culture, technology and trade, caught as it is between CCP Confucianism and the maintenance of its authoritarian ideology through censorship. Before the WTO panel and the Appellate Body, the Chinese Government argued on the basis of the public morals exception of Article XX (a) GATT 1994, that its content review of books, periodicals, electronic publications, and audiovisual home entertainment products was necessary to protect the Chinese people. It argued along Confucian lines that to do otherwise would jeopardise the nation's solidarity, destroy its social stability and endanger social morality. However, the challenge of understanding exactly how and why China's public censorship system operates on ideological grounds was swept away, amidst the subordination of its content review mechanism to the dictates of the free market.

The Appellate Body in *China – Publications and Audiovisual Products* upheld the panel's finding that China's WTO-plus trading rights commitments, forcing any importers of audiovisual products to be SOEs, was not 'necessary' to promote the aims of protecting public morals. Instead, this objective could be pursued by means of alternative, less trade-restrictive measures. One alternative was to have the Chinese authorities conduct all of the content review on imported material, following customs clearance, and thereafter grant the right to import and distribute such material to *all* companies, including foreign-invested enterprises (FIEs) under China's foreign investment regime.

While this action might make it easier for foreign material that passes the Chinese censor to be imported and distributed more effectively, it does not necessarily open up the Chinese market to cultural products nor does it lead to greater freedom of speech in the country. In fact, it might make it harder because China's substantive content review is left intact. It is noteworthy in this connection that China's Human Rights Action Plan (2012–2015), while reinforcing its adherence to a universalist doctrine of human rights, only endorses 'citizens' freedom of speech and the right to be heard *in accordance with the law* on its own terms. What the *China – Publications and Audiovisual Products* does not do is address the challenge that China, as a major trading partner which still sees itself as a fully functioning market economy with distinct "Chinese characteristics" and cultural values, poses for international trade law.

## 5. Changing Ideologies in Law and Development

China's unique ideology has had broad effects on the path of its recent, rapid development. The creation of legal institutions has come to play an increasingly prominent role in development theories. Development theorists have highlighted the importance of legal institutions as a way to attract investment and promote economic growth. The law has played a crucial role in China's development, forming the basis of the property rights vital to the new capitalism that has emerged, and providing the foundations for foreign investment in the country.

This contribution suggests that ideological differences have affected the way in which the rule of law has been interpreted and applied in Chinese governance. China's development of the rule of law is still in progress but it is clear that its approach is noticeably different to that in Western governance systems. We argue that the success of Chinese development without the existence of a rule of law system in the image of Western liberal democracies is affecting development paradigms. New conceptions of the rule of law 'with Chinese characteristics' will have a growing impact on development theories as other nations seek to emulate the rapid economic growth achieved by China in the past three decades.

China takes a unique approach towards the rule of law and it serves a different purpose to that in the Western world. It is not intended that the rule of law be used to promote democracy, liberal values or a liberal conception of human rights. Instead, law is seen as more important as a means of achieving social order. Additionally, China's recent history, culture and ideology affect how the rule of law is perceived and implemented.

Another influence is the role that Confucian principles play in the Chinese understanding of the rule of law, particularly the principle that rulers derive their authority to govern from their superior virtue. This suggests that they may be above the law by which they rule. CCP Confucianism can legitimise the broad discretion extended to decision-makers, and the view that 'morality trumps law', by appealing to these deeply rooted cultural beliefs.

China's unique approach to development challenges development paradigms. For example, there are clear differences between the Washington Consensus, which has held sway in the Western world since the early 1990s, and the alternative 'Beijing Consensus' applied by China. Instead of a sharp turn to free market reform and a liberal democratic system, the policies used by China have emphasised gradual export-led economic reform and the pursuit of State capitalism, constant innovation and experimentation, incremental governance reforms and authoritarianism. Although not expressed in a formal document, this approach has been labelled the Beijing Consensus because for China it replaces the widely-discredited Washington Consensus. A gradualist approach to development may have significant practical implications, particularly for sub-Saharan African nations that are now receiving increased levels of aid and infrastructure investment from China, which at the same time remains largely indifferent to, or else supports authoritarian regimes across the continent.

As Randall Peerenboom has pointed out the Beijing Consensus presents, from a development perspective, a different path where the integration of global ideas is "rigorously gut-checked against the demands of local suitability". It offers an alternative to the rapid exposure to liberal markets and ideas that were advocated and applied in the Washington Consensus, allowing broader policy space for governments to find their own best path to development and modernisation.

Ideology has had a great effect on the unique path taken by China in its development. At home and abroad, China's international interests follow directly from its domestic reform strategy and are managed by a strong party state that carefully balances domestic and global interests. China's official policy discourse, which still recognises the "Five principles of Peaceful Coexistence" (sovereignty and territorial integrity; mutual non-aggression; non-interference in internal affairs; equality and mutual benefit; and peaceful coexistence), is complemented by Confucian slogans advocating a "harmonious society" and a "harmonious world".

In the coming decades China's ideology may have an increasing effect on how other countries approach their own development. If the Beijing Consensus gains popularity, increased ideological pluralism may become the norm in the development paradigm. This will lead to a far more varied landscape than the one-size-fits-all approach advocated in the Washington Consensus. New conceptions of the rule of law could emerge, which while they lack the separation of powers and the array of civil and political rights that are contained in Western liberal systems, nevertheless maintain those existing structures so as to form a 'rule *by* law' system of governance.

## 6. Conclusion

This contribution has sought to highlight the new approach to international trade law that stems from the challenge that China's unique ideology and culture poses. At the same time, China's economic significance presents a direct challenge to the Western-centric system of law with its emphasis on the rule of law. How the international legal order and the multilateral trading system, which is bound by the rule of law, is affected by China's rise could set a precedent for the future as other nations with differing perspectives come to form a larger proportion of global economic activity.

There are a number of areas where Chinese ideology is already affecting the way in which China interacts with the rest of the world. This can be seen in its recognition as a market economy by some 79 countries even though there are others that still treat it as an NME but judge it by market economy standards. When it comes to technology Chinese ideological differences with its major trading partners appear to be narrowing. We can, however, expect China to continue to protect its unique traditions and culture, where necessary through new or existing forms of content review or by means of a public morals defence at the WTO. Finally, the unique Chinese ideological perspective can be seen in the recognition of a new discourse in development, typified by the Beijing Consensus, which demonstrates China's path to stimulating economic growth.

The coming decades will witness new interpretations of international trade law – be they in the field of WTO or preferential trading arrangements – and new directions in trade governance. The effect of Confucian ideology on the governance systems in ASEAN is already apparent and an expanded ASEAN + 3 Preferential Trade Agreements (PTAs), between ASEAN and each of China, Japan and South Korea, might also display such characteristics. Any new rounds of multilateral trade negotiations or international treaties, affecting the trading system as a whole, will need to reflect this new ideological pluralism or else it will be vulnerable to criticism by its membership for lacking legitimacy.

The implications of these developments for future policy makers, corporations and lawyers, active in the realm of international trade, are widespread. For policy makers, increased awareness of Chinese ideology could aid negotiations as it may lead to improved insight into the Chinese position in both multilateral and bilateral settings. For actors involved in trade disputes, their strategy may be affected now that the public morals defence, in support of cultural values, has received due recognition in the WTO dispute settlement system. For businesses and lawyers, an awareness of the cultural context may allow for an improved understanding of trends in international trade governance and provide a great opportunity to apply international trade law in a range of novel situations.

## 7. Sources and Further Reading

Bell, Daniel A., *China's New Confucianism: Politics and Everyday Life in a Changing Society*, Princeton University Press, 2008.

Dotson, John, *The Confucian Revival in the Propaganda Narratives of the Chinese Government,* U.S.-China Economic and Security Commission Staff Research Report, 2011.

Easterly, William, *The Elusive Quest for Growth: Economists' Adventures and Misadventures in the Tropics*, MIT Press, Cambridge, 2001.

Krever, Tor, "The Legal Turn in Late Development Theory: The Rule of Law and the World Bank's Development Model", in *Harvard International Law Journal,* 2011, vol. 52, no. 1, pp. 287–319.

Lai, Amy, "Sailing Toward a Truly Globalized World: WTO, Media Piracy in China and Transnational Capital Flows", in *UCLA Entertainment Law Review,* 2010, vol. 18, pp. 75–113.

Lim, Chin, "Trade Disputes: Is Europe Aiming at the Chinese Mothership?", Fung Global Institute, available at http://www.fungglobal institute.org/index.php?option=com_zrticles&id=192&view=publication &tmpl=component&print=1, last accessed on 12 June 2012.

Liu, Cynthia, "Internet Censorship as a Trade Barrier: A Look at the WTO Consistency of the Great Firewall in the Wake of the China-Google Dispute", in *Georgetown International Journal,* 2011, vol. 42, pp. 1199–1240, 1200–1201.

Luo, Changyuan and Zhang, Jun, "China Trade Policy Review: A Political Economy Approach" in D Greenaway (ed), *The World Economy: Global Trade Policy 2010*, Wiley-Blackwell, UK, 2011, pp. 52–75.

North, Douglass, *Princeton Economic History of the Western World: Understanding the Process of Economic Change,* Princeton University Press, Princeton, 2010.

Pauwelyn, Joost, "Case Note: Squaring Free Trade in Culture with Chinese Censorship: The WTO Appellate Body Report on China-Audiovisuals", in *Melbourne International Journal*, 2011, vol. 11, no. 2, pp. 119–140.

Peerenboom, Randall, "Ruling the Country in Accordance with Law: Reflections on the Rule and Role of Law in Contemporary China", in *Cultural Dynamics*, 1999, vol. 11, pp. 315–351.

Potter, Pitman, "Legal Reform in China: Institutions, Culture and Selective Adaptation", in *Law and Social Inquiry*, 2004, vol. 29, pp. 465–495.

Ramo, Joshua, *The Beijing Consensus*, The Foreign Policy Centre, London, 2004.

Rinaldi-Larribe, Marie-Jose, Lightfoot, William and Zhao, Zhongxiu, "Does China Deserve the Market Economy Status?", in *Journal of Chinese Economic and Foreign Trade Studies*, 2009, vol. 2, no.2, pp. 110–120.

Ruskola, Teemu, "Law without Law, or Is 'Chinese Law' an Oxymoron?", in *William and Mary Bill of Rights Journal,* 2003, vol. 11, no. 2, pp. 655–669.

Wang, Dong, "The Discourse of Unequal Treaties in Modern China", in *Pacific Affairs,* 2003, vol. 76, no.3, pp. 399–425.

Williamson, John, "Is the Beijing Consensus Now Dominant?", in *Asia Policy*, 2012, vol. 13, pp. 1–16.

Wu, Xiaohui, "Case Note: China – Measures Affecting Trading Rights and Distribution Services for Certain Publications and Audiovisual Entertainment Products" (WT/DS363/AB/R), in *Chinese International Journal*, 2010, pp. 415–432.

Information Office of the State Council, *National Human Rights Action Plan of China (2012–2015)*, 2012.

World Bank,"China, Overview", available at http://www.worldbank.org /en/country/china/overview, last accessed on 28 June 2012.

**Cases**

China, *Electronic Payment Services*, WT/DS413/R, Panel Report, 16 July 2012.

China, *Measures Affecting Trading Rights and Distribution Services for Certain Publications and Audiovisual Entertainment Products*, WT/DS363/AB/R, Appellate Body report, China Publications and Audiovisual Products, 21 December 2009.

China, *Measures Affecting the Protection and Enforcement of Intellectual Property Rights,* WT/DS362/R, Panel Report, China IP Rights, 26 January 2009.

China, *Measures Affecting Imports of Automobile Parts*, WT/DS339/340/342/AB/R, Appellate Body report, China Auto Parts, 12 January 2009.

European Union, *Anti-dumping Measures on Certain Footwear from China*, WT/DS405/R, Panel Report, EU – Footwear China, 22 February 2012.

United States, *Definitive Anti-dumping and Countervailing Duties on Certain Products from China*, WT/DS/379/AB/R, Appellate Body report, US – Certain Products from China, 25 March 2011.

United States, *Final Countervailing Duty Determination with Respect to Certain Softwood Lumber from Canada*, WT/DS257/AB/R, Appellate Body report, US – Softwood Lumber IV, 17 February 2004. United States, *Countervailing Duties on Certain Products from China – Request for consultations by China*, WT/DS437/1 G/L/988 G/SCM/D90/1, 30 May 2012.

# 5.4.

# Challenges in Public and Private Domain Will Shape the Future of Intellectual Property

**Severin de Wit***

Market failures, troubled access to medicine, impediments to free flow of information, copyright overextension, digital right protection, overkill and patents stifling rather than stimulating innovation are just a few of the disparaging themes around intellectual property. The main drives behind changes in IPR systems are growing discontent with the right to exclude, which is essential to most IPR systems, the diversity of IP policies between the West and the Developing countries, as well as digitalisation of information. The future of IPR will be shaped more by its users than by international IP legislative initiatives. This think piece explores the main drives behind a growing critical view on intellectual property and how the law can change so as to restore confidence in the workings of intellectual property systems.

## 1. Introduction

Intellectual property (IP) law practitioners are generally not known for their preoccupation with shaping the future of the law. Engaged with daily routines, IP law practitioners are more concerned with practical issues like the question in which EU country a new, unified, European Patent Court will be established and whether such a court, once in place, will maintain or change long held patent law concepts like "obviousness", and if so, whether common or civil law traditions will prevail.

## 2. IP Does Not Feature Prominently in International Law Publications

Literature on what intellectual property will look like in 2030 is scarce. Well-known writers seem more concerned with the possible future for different fields of law, ranging from criminal and environmental to constitu-

* **Severin de Wit** is a consultant at IPEG Consultancy B.V., The Hague, Netherlands.

tional and corporate law. Intellectual property is notably absent. When analysing the inconsistencies or inadequacies of current legal systems, intellectual property rights, also known as IPRs, do not attract the imagination of legal minds when they explore the challenges law systems face in the new millennia. Even a recent publication, *Realizing Utopia: The Future of International Law,* edited by a formidable legal mind in international law, Antonio Cassese, covered all imaginable areas of the law, except intellectual property.

The reason behind this is simply that intellectual property is not a subject that "translates" well into the mind of politicians, scientists, policymakers or even economists. IPR, however, is an important instrument in opening markets for knowledge, increasing Foreign Direct Investment and allowing innovation to spur (that at least still many believe). Therefore, IP should be included when we discuss about changes in the law today and consequently how the law of the future will look like with or without intellectual property.

*Realizing Utopia* is a collection of essays, written by a group of well-known international jurists, reflecting on some of the major legal problems faced by the international community. Remarkably, shaping an improved architecture of world society – or at a minimum, reshaping some major aspects of international dealings – does not seem to include what impact intellectual property laws have on these subjects.

## 3. Intellectual Property as a Historical Public Policy Instrument

The protection of intellectual property has a history that dates back several centuries. Christopher May and Susan Sell address this in their collaborative work on IP, "Forgetting History is Not an Option! Intellectual Property, Public Policy and Economic Development in Context", and note that the "[p]rotection of intellectual property has always been a form of public policy, an intervention in markets to transform their functioning". Tracing the development of IP policy as far back as the Middle Ages, May and Sell elaborate further on the topic:

> In the 1300's patents were grants of privilege awarded to those who brought new techniques into a sovereign's territory. British kings awarded letters of protection to innovators who developed new weaving techniques and various new industrialist processes. Rulers sought to attract and retain talented artisans in their territory, inspired by the mercantilist

> goals of limiting imports and promoting exports. Intellectual property rights emerged during the early mercantilist period as a means for nation-States to unify and increase their power and wealth through the development of manufactures and the establishment of foreign trading monopolies. The term patent, derived from the Latin *patere* (to be open), refers to an open letter of privilege from the government to practice an art. The Venetian Senate enacted the first patent statute in 1474 providing the maker of any 'new and ingenious device ... reduced to perfection so that it can be used and operated' an exclusive license of 10 years to practice the invention. Other nations followed suit and the granting of limited monopolies for inventions, and later to publishers and authors of literary works, became the dominant means of promoting innovation and literature.[1]

However, the question now is what has become of this romantic idea of IPRs stimulating innovation?

## 4. Property as the Leading Justification of IPRs

Over time, the predominant theme around intellectual property rights has been the right to a creation of the mind – to own this as if it is one's property – enabling the holders of IP to exclude others. As we will see later in this think piece, in the private domain the concept of "property" has caused many to argue that a right to exclude third parties from using such property should be altered into a compensatory liability regime.

Given the distributional consequences of the ability to own (and control, even temporarily) products of the mind and imagination (books, films, software, trade dress as well as technological innovations), intellectual property has frequently been an instrument of power and, once captured, the basis for further accumulation of power. However, unlike power that comes from the control of sparse material resources, the holders of intellectual property have had to construct the scarcity of property through legal instruments. The very process of defining what constitutes intellectual property effectively reinforces particular perspectives that may bene-

[1] Christopher May and Susan Sell, "Forgetting History Is Not an Option! Intellectual Property, Public Policy and Economic Development in Context", George Washington University, USA, paper presented at Intellectual Property Rights for Business and Society Birkbeck College, University of London, 2006, based on the authors' book, *Intellectual Property: A Critical History*, Lynne Rienner Publishers, 2005.

fit, some at the expense of others, treating some things as "property", while others remain "freely" available.

## 5. Intellectual Property Rights as a Source of Economic Power

Patented innovative ideas, copyrighted new creations of the mind, breakthrough product designs and the power of famous brands coincide with economic power as soon as these are exercised on the market. However, this economic power is not equally enforced or exercised. The right to exclusivity that is so quintessential to IP rights also creates asymmetrical economic power between the "have" and the "have not". As a matter of fact, asymmetrical economic power goes a long way towards explaining why semi-conductor chips are identified as intellectual property, whereas indigenous folklore is not. As Susan Sell and Christopher May describe in their "Moments in Law, Contestation and Settlement in the History of Intellectual Property",[2] the legal institutional development of IP shows significant difference from other forms of productive relations. In this sense, while other markets emerged prior to capitalistic models of organisation and were slowly integrated into the modern capitalist system, with products entering markets through production processes organised in a multitude of ways, this is not true of intellectual property. For markets in knowledge, the property had to be constructed through law, so that it could be allocated through market mechanisms; but those who sought this commoditisation were essentially nascent capitalists. Thus, unlike other forms of productive relations that were re-configured through the emergence of capitalism, intellectual property relations are the product of the great transformation of the sixteenth and seventeenth centuries.

Economic power has long been the leading force behind the pressure put on developing countries to accept Western intellectual property concepts that were previously alien to those countries. Chile provides a striking example. In 1990, an American-based private business association used its power not only to reject, but also actively to shape, the legislation of a foreign sovereign government. Until 1991, like many developing countries, Chile refused to grant patent protection for pharmaceutical products. This refusal was an effort to keep the prices of necessary medi-

---

[2] Susan K. Sell and Christopher May, "Moments in Law: Contestation and Settlement in the History of Intellectual Property", in *Review of International Political Economy*, 2001, vol. 8, no. 3.

cines affordable by placing public health considerations above property right concerns. Chile faced increasing pressure by a small group, called Pharmaceutical Manufacturers of America (PMA), to revise its laws to extend patent protection to pharmaceutical products. In 1990, Chile proposed a revised patent law, which was rejected by this small but powerful group, forcing Chile to go back to the drawing board and revise its patent law. This exceptional industry lobbying was basically a prelude to the related and even more far-reaching international agreement on IP, the 1994 Agreement on Trade-Related Aspects of Intellectual Property Rights (TRIPS), administered by the World Trade Organization (WTO).

## 6. Diversity of IP Policies Between Countries is a Function of Their Development Stage

As Susan Sell and Christopher May have shown, the diversity of intellectual property policies between countries is in part a function of their different stages of development. All other things being equal, a technological leader will prefer strong protection of its innovations, whereas a follower will favour access over protection. Strong economies will be served by expanding the markets for their goods, while weak economies are best served by cheap or free access to the technologies of advancement and development.

In the current world economic climate this is all the more true. In the public domain, India, due to its increasing economic power, allows its national pharmaceutical companies much more legal lenience in using proprietary processes and products, owned by foreign counterparts and covered by foreign owned patents, in order to protect national interests despite TRIPS: interests that collide with internationally recognised patent rights of third parties.

In the early 1960s, the first Indian drug companies came to the market. At that time, foreign multinational companies had mainly dominated the Indian drug market. This did not change until the early 1970s when domestic Indian companies were able to capture only about 25 per cent of the Indian market. The Indian government then decided to implement new legislation to allow its domestic companies to gain a greater market share. The motivation for that was to allow for a better and cheaper supply of medication. The Patents Act of 1970, which was later amended in 1972, 1992, 1995, and 1999, virtually abolished IPRs in the pharmaceutical sector using the following provisions: (1) product patents for pharmaceutical products were not granted; (2) the available process patents were very weak and offered only insufficient protection due to their restrictive five- to seven-year statutory term; (3) the equity share of foreign companies in Indian drug manufacturers was limited to 40 per cent; (4) price control was introduced to cut prices; and (5) a wide ranging system for compulsory licences was introduced. Of the above, the fifth is the most restrictive to the industry since it virtually eliminates all judicial reliance on the Indian IPRs. Over the years, mainly the production of generic drugs fuelled the growth of the Indian pharmaceutical industry. This was done through copying existing formulations of multinational companies and producing them in a larger scale after making slight process alterations. Since the weak IPR did not allow for litigation, more and more foreign companies ceased investment in the Indian market. Consequently, by 1991, Indian companies had turned market share numbers round in their favour and now served roughly 75 per cent of the market. However, after flourishing by means of the weak IPR for about 24 years, the regulatory framework changed for the Indian companies in 1994. In the process of joining the WTO, the Indian government had to sign the TRIPS agreement.

The case of India and its efforts to protect national generic industries is just one example of an intellectual property system that has come under increasing international criticism. Emerging economic powers, like those in BRIC countries, no longer tolerate a unilateral "dictate" on how to seek equilibrium between protecting national interests and protecting third party rights of foreign investors. Local indigenous knowledge, long ignored by Western pharmaceutical companies, is now at the heart of R&D projects in many developing countries, creating new challenges about who owns the intellectual property in knowledge derived from indigenous sources. The increased self-consciousness of those countries, caused by economic prosperity, provides them with the confidence that they can withstand international pressure to adapt their IP laws.

The overall theme behind the pressure by Western countries on developing countries to meet international TRIPS standards was that IPR strengthening would be a boon for increased Foreign Direct Investment (FDI). A further argument for developing countries to accept TRIPS was that the more importance was given to intellectual property rights, the better the behaviour of their economy would be: a proposition denied by many, among them Joseph E. Stiglitz. Stiglitz concludes that intellectual property regimes designed inappropriately not only reduce access to med icine, but also result in a lower economy efficiency and may even slow down the rhythm of innovations, with weakening effects, particularly serious in developing countries.[3]

The evolving trend of developing countries of showing economic growth where Europe and the US are lagging behind will only increase the number of occasions on which Western-originated pressure to adapt IPR regimes will be faced with scepticism and resistance, unless a fairer and more equitable IP system is put into place that allows those countries to develop their own IP legal systems. As Fink and Maskus point out in "Intellectual Property and Development, Lessons from Recent Economic Research",[4] future empirical work should look for natural experiments that explore within one country how economic variables have changed after a regime shift on a well-defined element of the intellectual property system.

## 7. Property and the Right to Exclude

At the heart of this growing discontent with the functioning of intellectual property systems are a number of developments. Firstly, there is the changing moral and social understanding on how property can be the legitimate reason for an IP right holder to exclude others even if this exercise of ownership has consequences on public health, security or public safety. Can a holder of patented AIDS/HIV medicines prevent countries from delivering generic copies of the patented version to open up a market that would otherwise be restricted to the rich and fortunate? As Susan Sell sets out:

> The history of intellectual property protection reveals a complex yet identifiable relationship between three major factors. First, it reveals shifting conceptions of ownership, authorship, and invention. These ideas denote what "counts" as property, and who shall lay claim to it. Second, this history reflects changes in the organization of innovation and the production and distribution of technology. Third, it reflects institutional change with these shifting ideational and material forces.

---

3 Joseph E. Stiglitz, *Making Globalization Work*, W.W. Norton & Company, New York, 2006, p. 106.

4 Keith E. Maskus and Carsten Fink (eds.), *Intellectual Property and Development*, Lessons from Recent Economic Research, World Bank Publications, 2005.

> Legal institutionalization of these changes in law alters power relationships and inevitably privileges some at the expense of others. Property rights both are situated within broader historical structures of global capitalism and serve to either reproduce or transform these structures. Particular historical structures privilege some agents over others, and these agents can appeal to institutions to increase their power.

Furthermore, the age of digital technology, the internet and the greater ease of reproduction have increased the demand for modifications in intellectual property practices. Young people have difficulty understanding why music, videos and other information kudos cannot be freely downloaded. Perceptions of "property" rights on information have undergone an almost revolutionary shift from the powered few having access to proprietary information and resources to a mainstream audience on all kinds of public internet platforms assuming and demanding information to be "freely available". This shift in perception of access to information has dramatic effects on the most core of traditional IP thinking: property and exclusivity.

The infinite information resources that the internet provides give further impetus to a shift in ideological views on who owns information materials, ranging from the concept that ideas and information should be completely free – unprotected and unrestricted – to the belief that intellectual property laws should remain the ultimate means of regulating who can and should get access to information, and at what price. It is this constant legal and societal battle that forces traditional providers of information, publishers and writers, composers, entertainers, film-makers and inventors alike, to change their business models over time. Again, this search towards the boundaries of private ownership where concepts of "property" and "exclusion" are the main themes will have serious implications on what intellectual property law will look like over time.

For advocates of the commons model[5], the legacy of the internet's development provides even further reason for questioning the durability of broad intellectual property protection as a means of spurring innovation.

[5] A model whereby multiple contributors ('commons') or authors share their work, without individual authors claiming copyright, yet providing the 'commons' to license the use of the entire work back to both the contributors and the general public.

## 8. Power Shift in IP Public Policy

Lastly, the shifting political power towards emerging economies in the BRIC countries, as discussed above, has a deep impact on legislative processes and global IP enforcement. As the history of TRIPS shows, a handful of powerful industries were able to force countries to adapt their IP laws so as to align them with Western concepts of intellectual property enforcement. Unilateral legislative initiatives use compulsory licensing to break patent monopolies on medicines deemed crucial for public health in developing countries. India's government, in May 2012, authorised a drug manufacturer to make and sell a generic copy of a patented Bayer cancer drug, arguing that Bayer charged a price that was unaffordable by most of the nation. Although the decision by the India Controller General of Patents, Designs and Trademarks was not the first time when a so-called compulsory licence of a patented drug had been granted in India, many believe that this opens the door to a flood of other compulsory licences creating a new supply of cheap generic drugs. This evidence of an increased self-consciousness is a clear sign of a power shift in intellectual property public policy.

## 9. Changes in the Private IPR Domain

In the private domain, it can be seen that intellectual property concepts – long held to be the cornerstone of the legitimacy of that part of the law – meet increasing criticism, questioning whether intellectual property has a future at all. It is undeniable that the form of intellectual property we have been taught at law schools and propagated by institutions, governments and multinational corporations and IPR practitioners – a system of complex statutorily-defined property rights – is in dire need of reconstruction. The future of intellectual property is at stake. No longer can the IPR establishment – current users of IP systems and law-makers who have been proliferating the advantages of IP – rest on their laurels and rely on fundamentals that have guided them for centuries: that patents reward inventors by granting them a monopoly for a limited time in exchange for the patentee disclosing his invention so that others can rely and build on his work, thus fostering innovation as a theme that slowly develops into anathema.

Criticism of the relationship between innovation and patents is increasing and certainly no longer limited to the academic world. As a result of modern technology, children of the information age hold different views on "openness" and "free (available) information". The general idea is simple enough, as Robert P. Merges describes in his recently published book *Justifying Intellectual Property*.[6] Digital media, driven by the internal logic of widespread availability and network effects, will flourish better and better serve the goals of the intellectual property system if digital content, and the platforms that carry it, are freed from property-based limitations. Merges' book is a legal and philosophical work in search of the best answers to these "openness" and "commonality" trends. He defends the idea that IP protection is in no way inconsistent with the promotion of a flourishing environment for digital media; quite the contrary: IP rights are essential to this goal.

## 10. Alternatives to Property-Based IPR Systems

Alternatives have been proposed to intellectual property as a right based on property that allows the owner to "exclude" and "control". IP laws that favour liability rules have been proposed as an alternative to exclusion. Property rules, as the name suggests, secure "entitlements" (like an injunction against a party that uses the patented invention or the trademarked sign or the copyrighted work, or monetary compensation – a royalty) as "property". To secure something as property, the rules must effectively prohibit others from taking or damaging the entitlement without first gaining the consent of the owner. Liability rules, on the other hand, neither seek to provide the security of a property rule, nor seek to force those who would take or damage an entitlement from first obtaining consent from the IP right owner. Instead, such rules create an obligation to remedy the usage of the property, for example by paying a reasonable price, or "rent" in economic terms. Failure to honour this obligation would in some cases constitute an infringement for which reparation could be sought.

Jerome Reichman is the leading proponent of using liability rules to address problems concerning the protection of traditional knowledge and sub-patentable[7] inventions. Under his proposed compensatory liability scheme, second comers will be required "to pay equitable compensation

6 Robert P. Merges, *Justifying Intellectual Property*, Harvard University Press, 2011.

7 'Sub-patentable inventions' are inventions falling below the conventional criteria for patentability.

for borrowed improvements over a relatively short period of time". As Reichman explains, such an alternative regime has several benefits. For example, it "could stimulate investment without chilling follow-on innovation and without creating legal barriers to entry". Such a regime "would also go a long way toward answering hard questions about how to protect applications of traditional biological and cultural knowledge to industry, questions that are of increasing importance to developing and least-developed countries".

## 11. Conclusion

Whatever the outcome of academic research into alternative IP systems, the future of intellectual property will be in large part dependent upon the actors in the IP field themselves. No remedy to a failing IP system can be found in new legislative initiatives, as is shown by the legislative process to create a new unified European Patent Court. As Jonathan Koppell shows in his book *World Rule*, Global Governance Organisations like WIPO, the WTO and other legislative bodies entrusted with international IP legislation, tend to face trade-offs between legitimacy and authority, often violating democratic norms, sacrificing equality and bureaucratic neutrality, to satisfy key constituencies and thus retain power. So it is not altogether that strange that no major new treaties on IP can come off the ground. As a result, inequalities caused by intellectual property "ownership" and "exclusivity" in the public domain will most likely in the future not be remedied by more internationally agreed legislation: for example, a change in TRIPS, but rather by domestic and case law, local legal initiatives and common practices. In the private domain, we have already seen the emergence of a new "openness" in intellectual property, evidenced by a "Commons" approach of Open Source in copyright and, in patent law, the Patent Commons Project initiative launched in 2005 by the Open Source Development Laboratories (OSDL). Furthermore, we will see a growing number of limitations in national case law around the world where the exercise of intellectual property-based ownership and exclusivity claims will make way for liability-based remedies. We can expect to get more differentiation between fundamental advances in knowledge and logical extensions of existing knowledge or incremental improvements that will, over time, receive a different kind of intellectual property protection. Societal needs to breach the "exclusivity" rule in intellectual property for the greater good (access to information, basic research, exemptions on patentable subject matter, resistance against overly long copyright term protection and other restrictions of IP exclusivity) will, as we expect, force the judiciary to allow much more room to exceptions to ownership and exclusivity in intellectual property in the future.

## 12. Sources and Further Reading

Boldrin, Michele and Levine, David K., *Against Intellectual Monopoly*, Cambridge University Press, Cambridge, 2008.

Calabresi, Guido and Melamed, A. Douglas, "Property Rules, Liability Rules, and Inalienability: One View of the Cathedral", in *Harvard Law Review*, 1972, vol. 85, p. 1089.

Cassese, Antonio (ed.), *Realizing Utopia, The Future of International Law*, Oxford University Press, Oxford, 2012.

Fink, Carsten, "Patent Protection, Transnational Corporations and Market Structure: A Simulation Study of the Indian Pharmaceutical Industry", in Keith E. Maskus and Carsten Fink (eds.), *Intellectual Property and Development, Lessons from Recent Economic Research*, World Bank Publications, 2005.

Hylton, Keith N., *Property Rules and Liability Rules, Once Again, Boston University School of Law*, Working Paper Series, Law and Economics, Working Paper no. 5-07.

Jaffe, Adam B. and Lerner, Josh, *Innovation and Its Discontents: How Our Broken Patent System Is Endangering Innovation and Progress, and What to Do About It*, Princeton University Press, 2004.

Koppell, Jonathan G.S., *Accountability, Legitimacy, and the Design of Global Governance*, University of Chicago Press, 2010.

Maskus, Keith E., *Intellectual Property Rights And Foreign Direct Investment*, Centre for International Economic Studies, University of Adelaide, Policy Discussion Paper No. 0022, May 2000.

May, Christopher and Sell, Susan, "Forgetting History Is Not an Option! Intellectual Property, Public Policy and Economic Development in Context", George Washington University, USA, paper presented at: Intellectual Property Rights for Business and Society Birkbeck College, University of London, 2006, based on the authors' book, *Intellectual Property: A Critical History*, Lynne Rienner Publishers, 2005.

Menell, Peter S., "Intellectual Property: General Theories", in Bouckaert, Boudewijn and De Geest, Gerrit (eds.), *Encyclopedia of Law and Eco-*

*nomics, Volume I. The History and Methodology of Law and Economics*, Edward Elgar, Cheltenham, 2000.

Merges, Robert P., "Contracting into Liability Rules: Intellectual Property Rights and Collective Rights Organizations", in *California Law Review*, 1996, vol. 84, p. 1293.

Merges, Robert P., *Justifying Intellectual Property*, Harvard University Press, 2011.

Merges, Robert P., Menell, Peter S. and Lemley, Mark A., Jorde, Thomas M., *Intellectual Property in the New Technological Age*, Aspen Publishers, New York, 1997, p. 122.

Müller, Benjamin, "Promoting the Role of Intellectual Property Rights Regimes in National Economic Development: Supporting Imitation to Foster Innovation", in *Scholarly Research Paper*, GRIN Publishing, 2008.

Porter, Eduardo, Tech Suits Endanger Innovation, New York Times, 29 May 2012, available at http://www.nytimes.com/2012/05/30/business/economy/tech-lawsuits-endanger-innovation.html, last accessed on 9 August 2012.

Reichman, J.H., "Of Green Tulips and Legal Kudzu: Repackaging Rights in Subpatentable Innovation", in *Vanderbilt Law Review*, 2000, vol. 53, no.6, p. 1743.

Sell, Susan, *Private Power, Public Law: The Globalization of Intellectual Property Rights*, Cambridge University Press, 2003.

Sell, Susan K. and May, Christopher, "Moments in Law: Contestation and Settlement in the History of Intellectual Property", in *Review of International Political Economy*, 2001, vol. 8, no. 3.

Stiglitz, Joseph E., *Making Globalization Work*, W.W. Norton & Company, New York, 2006, pp. 103–132.

Torrance, Andrew W. and Tomlinson, Bill, "Property Rules, Liability Rules, and Patents: one Experimental View of the Cathedral", in *Yale Journal of Law and Technology*, 2011, vol. 14, p. 138.

Xiang, Feng, "The End of Intellectual Property", in *International Critical Thought*, 2012, vol. 2, no. 1, p. 99, published on IPEG blog http://bit.ly/L1KxYg, last accessed on 9 August 2012.

Wit, Severin de, "Will the Patent Act Make It to 2110?", in H.W.A.M Hanneman (ed.), *A Century of Patents in the Netherlands*, Anniversary publication 100 year Dutch Patent Act, NL Agency, NL Patent Office, 2010.

# 5.5.

# Intellectual Property Law without Secrets

**David S. Levine***

Secrecy, particularly effective secrecy, is on the wane, and with it archaic forms of law-making must similarly be reconsidered and discarded. This think piece posits that international negotiations regarding intellectual property (IP) laws like the Anti-Counterfeiting Trade Agreement (ACTA) and Trans-Pacific Partnership Agreement (TPP), and any future international IP law-making procedures, lessen the adherence to a theory of secret negotiations and embrace the inevitable and desirable need for the public to ask questions and offer meaningful input. The risk of attempting to continue on the current course, futile or not, pretending that secrecy is desirable, causes an erosion in the relevance of and confidence in IP law as a legitimate and effective form of regulation, as already seen in the systematic problems associated with ACTA.

## 1. Introduction

The idea of secrecy is becoming quaint. Or, at least, the notion that one can maintain a secret for the period of time necessary to derive significant social value from maintaining a given piece of information as secret – what I call "effective secrecy" – is increasingly threatened. The threats to effective secrecy are many and varied, but operate at the nexus of technology and its intellectual property, and the human desire to innovate and change. Primary among the threats are the pervasiveness of powerful communication mediums like the Internet and hand-held computers like smart-phones and the resultant expectation that information will be free flowing and available in real-time; the advent of constant and pin-point surveillance whether in the form of Google Street View or United States civilian and military drones; the slow erosion of strong privacy values through the increasing utilisation and acceptance of social media; and an

* **David Levine** is Associate Professor of Law at Elon University School of Law and an affiliate scholar at the Center for Internet and Society at Stanford Law School, and founder and host of Hearsay Culture on KZSU-FM (Stanford University). More information at http://hearsayculture.com. Facts current as of July 2012.

ever-expanding belief that there is no real privacy or security online. The logical extension of this pincer attack against effective secrecy is that there are, in reality, fewer and fewer effective secrets.

At the same time, secrecy is attempting to forge new inroads. Governments are labelling information as secret, classified, and secret but not classified, in ever expanding numbers and related to topics, such as the creation of intellectual property law, that have never been secret before. Secret courts, secret warrants and secret tools like computer viruses and drone aircraft increasingly play a role in intelligence gathering, military attacks and national defence. The logical extensions of this attempt at increased secrecy are secret law negotiations encompassing vast substantive areas from financial regulations to intellectual property law, epitomised in the on-going negotiations of the Trans-Pacific Partnership Agreement (TPP). But these vestiges of the secrecy world of yore are increasingly futile attempts at maintaining effective secrecy, as the aforementioned technology, information architecture and activism trends converge to overwhelm these efforts: witness Wikileaks' public document dump of 250,000 US diplomatic cables and the public backlash against the secret negotiations of the Anti-Counterfeiting Trade Agreement (ACTA).

Thus, if you are keeping score, effective secrecy is losing the battle with openness. What is left is, not surprisingly, ineffective secrecy, whose hallmark is antagonism of the public, increased administrative morass and, in the case of IP law-making, imbalanced and poorly-drafted law – the very opposite of the assumed virtues of effective secrecy.

Thus, it is time to reconsider the theoretical underpinnings for secrecy in a technological age defined by unprecedented and unimpeded flows of information. Counter-intuitively, this think piece posits that the decline of effective secrecy must be embraced in intellectual property law not just because it is inevitable, but because it is also theoretically beneficial. Secrecy's very theoretical underpinnings have been proven unstable and unsustainable by examination of the creation and expansion of intellectual property law through the on-going negotiations of and tension surrounding the excessive secrecy attendant to the Anti-Counterfeiting Trade Agreement (ACTA) and Trans-Pacific Partnership Agreement (TPP).

Efforts to maintain effective secrecy, even if futile, have an unintentional consequence: they have made the procedure used in the creation of intellectual property law as important as its substance. The experience of ACTA and TPP leads to a counter intuitive suggestion that is the focus of this think piece: intellectual property law and law-making should embrace the trend towards less "effective secrecy" because it is socially desirable. By doing so, we will begin to harness the power and benefits of a world less governed by secrecy generally, which drastically improves the public's ability to offer meaningful, real-time input through the method of the under-valued question-and-answer format. We will, in sum, be able to reconceive our underlying theory about how IP law should be made. Because the way that IP law is made has a direct impact on the contours of the law itself, we will get better IP law.

## 2. There Will Always Be *Some* Secrets

Let us begin with a qualification: there will always be some secrets. Consider a few basic scenarios. At its core, a human being (as far as we can currently foresee) will always be able to keep information in her head that no other person will be able to access easily unless she begins to speak or write it on paper or in an electronic medium, or technology advances to the point where detailed mindreading is possible (and it might advance that far, although we are apparently decades from such a possibility). Plenty of secrets, like the outcome of most high-profile court cases, are kept secret this way. Two people will be able to go into a closed room, check for surveillance equipment and other people, and have a private conversation, subject to those individuals' ability to not share the contents of the discussion. Several people will be able to write down some information on a sheet of paper or electronic medium, place it in a locked safe or device, and maintain its secrecy so long as it remains securely there and everyone keeps their mouths shut. Or, as a recent story in The Huffington Post reported, nine grandmothers will be able to secretly pool their money to then use to make cakes and anonymously leave care packages for those less fortunate – and maintain their secret charity for 30 years until one of their husbands notices large withdrawals of money on a bank statement and asks questions. Most people would say that we want to be in a world where such secrecy is possible. Few people would want to live in a world where there were no secrets.

But is such secrecy always desirable? Note the threats to secrecy embedded in each of the basic scenarios identified above. In each scenario, technology, error and human nature operate to maintain a constant threat that a given secret will be revealed. Thus, putting a premium on maintaining the secret can cause enormous stress, both personal and professional, and in many cases will ultimately prove futile. Sometimes, the effort will be worth the payoff and social good will be maintained, as in the case of sensitive bilateral or multilateral negotiations to end an armed conflict.

However, increasingly and particularly in the creation of intellectual property law, Internet policy and other areas where collective and diverse interests are at stake, the effort, futile or not, is not worth the payoff and, in fact, is detrimental. For example, why should we slavishly maintain that such secrecy is necessary and warranted, much less possible, in intellectual property law-making? Why not embrace the uncertainty and foster a new governing paradigm that celebrates the fact that some information treated as secret, to paraphrase Stewart Brand, truly wants and needs to be free – particularly when the outcome will be positive?

## 2.1. Baby Steps: The Value of Asking Questions

The operative proposition of this think piece is that legislators and policymakers maintain adherence to regimes of secrecy simply because that is how it has always been done – control of information is the lever of power and influence – and, more perniciously, if no one knows what you are doing, the lack of accountability can keep you in office longer than the alternative. However, the effective power of such secrecy is increasingly becoming a figment of one's imagination or a wistful desire to return to a simpler time before secrecy was under pressure. As the ACTA backlash has shown, once the secret is effectively revealed, the sought-after power is usually severely diminished or eliminated for all but the few top-level decision-makers (like the lead trade representative or a leader of government) who are not at the actual negotiation table, but rather offer the top-level policy directives that are resident in their minds. For everyone else, including the staffers who actually negotiate the law and implement the policy, and who themselves may be victims of the same imperfect secrecy efforts that impede useful and timely public input, the inevitable leak renders them merely belligerent and unrealistic in the public's eyes if the continued perceived necessity of secrecy is asserted and pursued. The effort to protect the illusion of secrecy is, in a word, no longer effective, but rather counter-productive.

From a policy perspective, the continued adherence to the fiction of secrecy squanders opportunities to improve law-making. Thus, rather than view the current landscape as unfortunate and hopeless, law-makers should view it as offering a unique opportunity. The decline of secrecy and of the related control over information offers a unique opportunity to force experimentation in new, more inclusive and democratic forms of law-making, appropriate for a world where secrecy is not as respected, or perhaps needed, as it once was. At its most basic level, it allows for a heretofore unrealised use of questions as a form of offering public input and value into the intellectual property law-making process. Questions are an under-theorised form of public input, perfect as an initial first step towards public inclusion, for the new world into which law-makers are largely unwillingly being thrust.

In Hamilton Bean's ground-breaking study of the use of open source (read: public) information in current and future intelligence gathering and operations, he relates a comment from a member of the United States' 9/11 Commission that studied the events leading up to the terrorist attacks. He notes that, according to a 9/11 Commission staffer, questions from 9/11 victims' family members played a significant role in the substance of the Commission's investigation. The staffer noted:

> Most of [the family members'] influence was [in] the questions that they asked us that they wanted answers for. So, in the very beginning, we solicited from the families their list of questions, and every time they called us with another angle, or another thing to investigate, we kept [a list], and we made sure all those questions were answered in the commission's report, and we gave them an annotated version of where to find their answers, so that [the public] didn't have to go searching.

Of course, the predicate for being able to ask good questions is having essential information upon which to base questions. The 9/11 Commission was designed as a truth-finding commission that would ultimately offer suggestions regarding how the United States should respond legislatively so as to prevent future terrorist attacks, a topic that would have been normally viewed as highly sensitive, and therefore meriting a high degree of secrecy. But, in the structure and vision of the 9/11 Commission, the questions were welcomed (even if they were not always useful or on point) as a procedural device to further the mission of the 9/11 Commission and the collective interests of US citizens.

Current IP law-making, reflected in the on-going negotiations around TPP, adheres to the fiction of effective secrecy at the expense of more useful, modern law-making possibilities. For example, in the current climate pervading international IP law-making, such useful questions are not only generally unwelcomed, but they are impossible to ask. Because of procedural hurdles like the treatment of ACTA and TPP as a national security concern by the United States, public access to formal and current negotiating texts and proposals must clear the same procedural hurdles as a request seeking information about how to make a weapon of mass destruction, a nearly impossible hurdle to jump. And this secrecy, even if imperfect by virtue of leaks, nonetheless has an impact. In the case of ACTA, an official text was not released during the vast bulk of the negotiations, but several leaks occurred which formed the basis for rampant speculation and conjecture about ACTA's actual content. In the case of TPP, there has yet to be a formal release (although there have been a few leaks), even though the thirteenth round of negotiations have just concluded.

The result of this halting and imperfect secrecy: in the United States, only selected "cleared advisors", made up almost entirely of corporate representatives of the entertainment and pharmaceutical industries, have official access to portions of the draft texts. Thus, only they can offer meaningful input to the negotiators. Indeed, only they know what questions need to be asked. Similar situations exist in other negotiating countries. In the case of ACTA, the public, its experts, and everyone else were left asking shot-in-the-dark questions based on speculation, conjecture and fear, generating agitation against the process. When it was finally released, its every failing was perceived as the product of a corrupt process, and the ensuing protests rendered it all but dead. Given the equally closed nature of the TPP negotiations, the same fate likely awaits it once the secret is revealed, as must happen eventually. This is no way to make IP law in the 2012, and it benefits no one.

Aside from the strange reality that the 9/11 Commission focusing on terrorism and fundamental national security concerns, like the protection of life and borders, was more transparent than an international process for creating intellectual property law, this issue is troubling on its own because of its impact on the ability to ask knowledgeable questions. Under current conditions in the TPP negotiations, it is impossible to ask any questions, much less offer any input of significant detail and use, unless one happens to accurately speculate, based upon leaked drafts and/or conjecture based upon public statements, what might be an actual issue.

Indeed, at the San Diego round of the TPP negotiations, held in July 2012, civil society groups bravely attempted to offer detailed input based on a 16-month old leaked IP chapter draft text. Whether they were commenting on issues that had been resolved in the intervening 16 months is anyone's guess, but it was hard not to view their efforts as the idealistic part of a cynical charade. In other words, current IP law-making operates in almost the exact opposite fashion as the 9/11 Commission, with secrecy as the operative theory (and, given the leaks, imperfect secrecy as its reality), rather than a theory that embraces *making sure* that all public questions are answered with "an annotated version of where to find their answers, so that [the public] didn't have to go searching".

Intellectual property law and the public at large suffer from the continued adherence to secrecy despite all of the mounting obstacles to it, and the resultant eschewing of questions. As a body of law that increasingly encompasses collective interests like how information will be shared among individuals, be they German inventors or Egyptian protestors, and who will have the legal right to create new works of authorship and invention, IP law no longer has the luxury (if it ever did) of pretending that its issues are provincial or of concern to a small percentage of the population. Indeed, IP law is increasingly the body of law that regulates who will have access to information and who will be considered part of the global economy. To paraphrase Professor Eric Goldman, we are all both creators and consumers of IP, and IP law must recognise that fact lest it become disconnected with reality and eventually irrelevant.

Thus, administrative hurdles, such as equating intellectual property law-making with national security, have the basic impact of impeding questions. More broadly, it reflects the larger problem that intellectual property law faces: a continued adherence to the need for and sacrosanct theory of secrecy as a method of law-making. It is that staid adherence to the methodology of secrecy, which events beyond the control of intellectual property law and law-makers are rendering archaic, which is the trend that must be addressed if IP law is to remain relevant to today's innovators and creators. If effective secrecy is increasingly difficult to maintain, and if maintaining the secret proves more harmful than beneficial, then the operative theory underlying secrecy as a modality of law-making is under severe stress.

## 2.2. SOPA, PIPA, the Internet and Questions

To illustrate the value of questions at the expense of secrecy in the context of IP law-making, it is useful to consider the 2011 protests surrounding SOPA and PIPA and why they arose. The text of SOPA and PIPA, unlike ACTA (for most of the time that it was under negotiation) and TPP, were and are not secrets. They are bills, introduced in Congress and publicly available. The December 2011 web blackout, where dozens of websites, including Wikipedia, shut down for one day, reflected an awareness of the challenge in regulating Internet activities that goes back to its inception as a commercial medium. As explained in a letter authored by Mark Lemley, David Post and the author of this think piece, "The approach taken in [PIPA] has grave constitutional infirmities, [at least what we think would be the current PIPA] potentially dangerous consequences for the stability and security of the Internet's addressing system, and will undermine United States foreign policy and strong support of free expression on the Internet around the world". These three primary concerns reflect the interlocking challenges of regulating Internet activities. Specifically, the Internet, and the intellectual property law that often forms its rules and contours, implicates issues of commerce as well as personal and national security, globalisation and communication through free media between peoples whom, prior to the advent of the Internet, had no pervasive way to share information and ideas directly.

The protests may have brought home to many elected officials that it is no longer acceptable to profess ignorance of the technology underlying the Internet and the impact of regulation on it. By way of the protests, the public asked the basic question: do you, members of Congress, know or care about what you are doing to the Internet and what the impact will be of what you propose to do? In a very real sense, the protests epitomised what Hal Abelson, Ken Ledeen and Harry Lewis wrote in their terrific book *Blown to Bits*: "the entire social structure in which Internet protocols evolved prevented special interests from gaining too much power or building their pet features into the Internet infrastructure". The public applied that principle by asserting that no single industry or activity can (or should be allowed to) define what the Internet is, or how it should be regulated. The Internet is more holistic, and because of its pervasiveness as a medium to create, distribute and sell intellectual property, has taken intellectual property law along with it. Legislators were forced to reckon with that question because they could not hide the SOPA and PIPA texts, and in so doing were forced to table SOPA and PIPA. Whatever happens, we will all benefit from better law as a result.

However, in the international IP law-making arena, secrecy, effective or not, has become the procedural hammer used to violate this principle of holistic values, derived from the Internet but now impacting intellectual property law. Allowing only certain interests full access to the information needed to ask the right questions, while everyone else relies on leaked information, goes against the very basis of IP as a law designed to encourage innovation by all, not just a privileged few. That reality now threatens to fundamentally undermine not only balanced IP law, but its very legitimacy as a form of regulation. Thus, this think piece has addressed what secrecy means as a modality of regulation going forward, especially if the ability to maintain a secret – effective secrecy – is on the wane.

## 3. Conclusion

Unfortunately, the Internet's core value of eschewing special interests in the architecture is not as well-established in governments. Indeed, information flows to and from government are less sacrosanct as a governmental value than the similar value reflected in the architecture of the Internet. But if IP law is to find a middle ground that balances the competing interests of all involved, which is quite literally all humans, there has to be, as Yochai Benkler has described it, a space for such a middle ground to be found. But it cannot be discovered unless all stakeholders, not just the technology and content industries, are part of the discussion. It will not be found unless secrecy is made less paramount and all are able to ask intelligent questions.

IP law must embrace the Internet founders' core operating principle. The decline of effective secrecy and the under-appreciated power of the knowledgeable question means that if we are to find an IP middle ground, if we are to strike a balance, if we are to embrace the decline of effective secrecy and the rise of questions, then the technology and content industries, the USTR and the other negotiators of ACTA and TPP, and law-makers in all involved countries, need to embrace the public, or at least (in the near term) be open to meaningful questions from it. As Professor Bean has indicated, the very act of being allowed to ask intelligent and knowing questions is an enormous step in the direction of embracing new forms of intellectual law-making for a new century, and would provide heretofore unparalleled legitimacy to the on-going TPP negotiations.

Importantly, there are no technological impediments to allowing the positing of intelligent questions. Rather, the only impediment is vision and confidence in the public's ability to improve the process and create better intellectual property law by asking an intelligent question. It requires a theoretical reorientation away from secrecy as a means of efficiency and towards secrecy only where it is socially beneficial and where generally monolithic views are present. The recent miasma in international IP law-making has shown, to all but the very few "in" on what is left of the secrets, that secrecy is no longer a theoretically sound or practically useful prism through which to view all IP law-making. Effective secrecy as a tool of law-making may be nearing its death, and as that plays out, the vestiges of its attraction must be reconsidered.

## 4. Sources and Further Reading

Abelson, Harold, Ledeen, Ken and Lewis, Harry R., *Blown to Bits: Your Life, Liberty and Happiness After the Digital Explosion*, Addison-Wesley, USA, 2008.

Bean, Hamilton, *No More Secrets: Open Source Information and the Reshaping of U.S. intelligence*, Praeger Publishers Inc., Santa Barbara, 2011.

Benkler, Yochai, *The Wealth of Networks: How Social Production Transforms Markets and Freedom*, Yale University Press, 2006.

Castells, Manuel, *Communication Power*, Oxford University Press, USA, 2009.

Dreyfuss, Rochelle C., "Fostering Dynamic Innovation, Developing the Trade: Intellectual Property as a Case Study in Global Administrative Law", *Institute for International Law and Justice (IILJ), Global Administrative Law Series*, Working Paper No. 2008/4, NYU School of Law, Public Law Research Paper No. 08-66, available at http://ssrn.com/abstract=1316925 or http://dx.doi.org/10.2139/ssrn.1316925, lasted accessed on 28 August 2012.

Habermas, Jürgen, *The Structural Transformations of the Public Space: An Inquiry into a Category of Bourgeois Society*, translated by Thomas Burger and Frederick Laurence, MIT Press, 1991.

Hathaway, Oona A., "Presidential Power over International law: Restoring the Balance, *Yale Law Journal*, 2009, vol. 119, no. 2, p, 140.

Lemley, Mark, Levine, David S., Post, David G., "Don't Break the Internet", in *Stanford Law Review Online*, 2011, vol. 64, no. 34, pp. 34–38.

Lessig, Lawrence, *Code: And Other Laws of Cyberspace, Version 2.0*, Basic Books, New York, 2006.

Levine, David S., "Bring in the Nerds: Secrecy, National Security and the Creation of International Intellectual Property Law", in *Cardozo Arts and Entertainment Law Journal*, 2012, vol. 30, no.2, pp. 105–151.

Yu, Peter K., "Six Secret (and Now Open) Fears of ACTA", in *SMU Law Review*, 2011, vol. 64, pp. 975–1094.

# 5.6.

# Export of the Rule of Law: Corporate Self-Regulation of Global Data Transfers

**Lokke Moerel***

The digital era is characterised by an unprecedented continuous worldwide flow of data, both within multinational companies as well as with their external service providers. Whilst large corporations operate internationally, State governments legislate nationally. Besides leaving gaps in the patchwork of national data protection regulations, this situation also leads to overlaps in applicable national rules that often deviate or outright conflict. Further, the traditional territory-based enforcement tools are not adequate for States to force compliance. This legal landscape provides a challenging background for testing whether transnational private regulations (TRP) of data protection can provide solutions where legislation fails to do so. This think piece evaluates a remarkable example within the European Union (EU) regarding the emergence of a complex hybrid system of self-regulation (global corporate privacy policies) with public arrangements (the data protection authority of the EU headquarters of the multinationals validating such corporate privacy policies and providing support in the area of supervision and enforcement). In this manner, transnational supervision and enforcement is achieved not at the transnational level, but by granting the Data Protection Authorities (DPAs) and the court of the EU headquarters, global central supervision and enforcement powers. This leads to enforceable rights for individuals, even in jurisdictions where no (adequate) data protection laws are in place or where insufficient enforcement infrastructure is available.

## 1. Data Protection: The Regulatory Landscape

In the digital age, data protection is of increasing concern for governments, individuals and companies alike. Especially, the maturing of the internet led to a vast increase in cross-border flows of personal data both

* **Lokke Moerel** is a partner in the intellectual property, information, communication and technology department of De Brauw Blackstone Westbroek.

within and between groups of companies. Although all countries face essentially the same problem regarding the regulation of these vast flows of personal information, their governments have chosen substantially different solutions. Within the EU, the protection of individuals prevails, and the rights of individuals regarding the processing of their personal data have become a fundamental right and freedom, regulated by the EU Data Protection Directive (Directive). The wish to protect personal data of EU citizens when transferred outside the EU resulted in a "long arm" provision in the Directive, where it prohibited data transfers to countries outside the EU without an adequate level of data protection (EU data transfer rules). This extraterritorial provision prompted many countries outside the EU to follow suit in adopting comprehensive data protection legislation to facilitate on-going access by their multinationals to the EU market. Of the one hundred and ninety two member States of the United Nations (UN) about fifty to sixty of them currently have a legal framework for data protection. Many of these countries have imposed restrictions on the outbound transfer of personal data from their respective countries. Such outbound data transfer requirements are considered necessary by most countries, as there are still many countries with no data protection laws at all, as well as countries (most notably the US) with a limited regime, which mostly focus on the public sector and certain sensitive industries (most notably healthcare and telecommunications). As a consequence, the worldwide data protection regulatory landscape presently consists of (at best) a patchwork of very diverse national data protection laws which often deviate or outright conflict.

At present, the main tool applied by DPAs to try and solve gaps in applicable data protection laws and enforcement, is seeking cooperation with other DPAs in the event of cross-border data protection violations (that is, a network approach whereby each authority enforces in its own territory). However, until all jurisdictions have adequate data protection laws and supervision of these laws, this network approach cannot adequately solve all gaps in the applicable laws and enforcement issues faced by data protection regulators. As it is generally not expected that a global standard for data protection will be realised within the coming ten years, more creativity is required in order to solve the gaps in data protection, as well as in enforcement.

Solutions may only be forthcoming if DPAs are empowered to enforce on a cross-border basis rather than each DPA in its own territory.

Such central enforcement may be achieved if companies would be able to regulate their data protection by means of corporate self-regulation and make a choice of forum for central enforcement by one "lead" DPA (and its courts), preferably the headquarters of such a multinational. This will lead to enforceable rights even in jurisdictions where no (adequate) data protection laws are in place or where insufficient enforcement (infrastructure) is available.

## 2. Cross-Border Enforcement Issues in Data Protection Cases

The applicability, jurisdiction and enforcement of data protection legislation are generally based on a jurisdictional approach. These concepts are subject to limitations set by private international law (PIL). This is due to the fact that a key concept in determining the limits of State regulation is "sovereignty", which is a concept founded on the very existence of a territory. Cross-border data flows inherently challenge such sovereignty. In order to seek regulation of these cross-border data flows, States gave their laws a "long arm reach" (both in terms of the scope of applicability of their laws and of adopting outbound data transfer rules).

Although data protection regulation in many cases is of relatively recent times, the concepts of applicable law and jurisdiction are embedded in a long tradition of rules of PIL, where laws that over-extend their jurisdictional reach are considered an unacceptable form of "hyper-regulation", if they apply so indiscriminately that there is no hope of enforcement. Applicability regimes are therefore inherently delineated and cannot be instrumental in solving the present gaps in the protection of personal data and its enforcement. This automatically also applies to data transfer regimes, as these are only triggered if the relevant data protection laws are applicable in the first place.

Cross-border enforcement issues proliferate if (as is the case with data protection) the laws are highly varied across the globe or even lacking (as is often the case in developing countries). As a result, questions arise as to their enforceability within an international context. For example, are supervisory authorities of a country entitled (or obliged) to provide assistance to another supervisory authority regarding a breach of such authorities' national laws, whilst not constituting a breach in the country of the authority whose assistance is requested? Similar questions arise in respect of investigation powers and recognition or enforcement of foreign judgements, et cetera. This may entail that supervisory authorities have to obtain information on alleged breaches via the internet rather than relying on investigation performed in the relevant other jurisdictions.

From the perspective of individuals whose data are processed, the present jurisdictional approach does not provide effective protection. This is not for a lack of rights and remedies of individuals. For instance, the Directive provides for quite broad remedies and liabilities, and in principle allows individuals ample opportunity to ensure that a breach is remedied and compensation is obtained. However, to effectuate these rights and remedies through traditional judicial means is not viable in practice for a number of reasons. Data protection breaches in most cases involve relatively small levels of economic damages for individuals where it would be more costly to pursue a case through traditional judicial means. Due to the networked economy, even relatively simple breaches of data protection further present complicated cross-border jurisdictional and enforcement issues. The example below is for clarification.

A US consumer purchases a product over the internet from a Dutch company. The Dutch company involves one of its group companies in India for customer service purposes (help desk for installation of the product). The Dutch company has a privacy policy informing the consumer that his data are shared with the Indian group company for helpdesk services and the consumer provides his consent for this. The data of the consumer are hacked and the consumer becomes subject of identity theft. Here, as in all other cases, the consumer has to determine: (i) who is at fault; (ii) which laws apply; (iii) what are his rights under the applicable law(s); (iv) what are his damages; and (iv) where does the consumer seek redress? Even in this relatively straightforward case, answering each of these questions proves problematic and leads the consumer to effectively having no recourse.

## 2.1. Re (i) Who Is at Fault?

In this case, it will be difficult to establish which company is at fault (that is, the Dutch or the Indian company), as in practice it is often impossible to determine at which point in a network a hacker found entry. As a consequence, it will be impossible for the consumer to prove which of the two companies actually did not secure the data properly, in the absence of which each company can avoid liability.

### 2.2. Re (ii) Which Laws Apply?

The Federal Trade Commission Act (FTC Act) does not apply to a Dutch company doing business from the Netherlands, and the FTC has no jurisdiction. Dutch data protection law applies in respect to the data processing by the Dutch company. Supposing that the consumer can prove the security breach occurred in the systems of the Dutch company, the consumer could file a complaint with the Dutch DPA. Chances are slim that the Dutch DPA will take action based on an individual complaint of a US consumer in an isolated case. Instigating civil action in the Netherlands is too costly and not justified in light of the damages (if any) suffered by the US consumer. Language issues and time differences may also prove to be impediments. If the consumer can prove that the security breach occurred in India, chances are that the Indian company did not breach any provision of Indian law, as a result of which no recourse is available at all.

### 2.3. Re (iii) What Are His Damages/ Re (iv) Where Does He Seek Redress?

As long as the relevant identity theft has not led (yet) to any actual damages (like abuse of the credit card number of the US consumer), it will be difficult for the US consumer to prove actual damages and to establish whether these are recoverable under Dutch law.

This example shows that even if the questions can be answered, in practice still no effective resources may be available.

## 3. Thinking about Alternative Solutions for Enforcement

### 3.1. Self-Regulation Backed Up by Governmental Enforcement Tools

When looking at other forms of international ICT regulation of cross-border enforcement, these show few ideas about a more integral approach to enforcement. Initially, ICT regulators both at the national and the international level seemed to be united in their opinion that industry self-regulation and alternative dispute resolution (ADR) would prove a better alternative to solve enforcement issues in an international context than the traditional forms of jurisdiction-based government regulation, dispute resolution and enforcement mechanisms. However, as ICT law developed over the years, by now a preference can be discerned for co-regulation above pure self-regulation. The prevailing current thinking is that enforcement, in particular, cannot be left to the industry alone; self-regulation should be backed up by governmental enforcement tools. This can only be achieved by means of co-regulation rather than by self-regulation and ADR.

In the absence of more in-depth studies on cross-border enforcement of data protection, reference may be made to the general literature in respect of cross-border enforcement of consumer protection laws, which is shaped by ideas about what generally works in regulatory enforcement. This literature shows that the (by now) traditional forms of private enforcement, complemented by agency enforcement (as is also the current status under the Directive), are inadequate to force compliance. More creativity is required and also this literature points in the direction of self-regulation, backed up with governmental enforcement. Such self-regulation, however, does not materialise just like that and some of the alternative enforcement measures in the consumer protection arena are intended to work as an incentive for just that purpose. For instance, the imposition of disclosure obligations on companies has proven a stronger incentive for companies to achieve compliance (often by introducing self-regulatory policies) than the introduction of material rules. What I find instructive myself in this literature is that at first glance, the possibility of self-regulation and this particularly in an international context has a flavour of "leniency", of a soft approach to compliance and that in an area where human rights are at stake. The first thought is "who is going to monitor and enforce compliance"? It is instructive to realise that empirical research shows that government regulation and enforcement will not do the trick in a cross-border environment, unless such governmental regulation aims at regulating private regulation and some form of governmental enforcement of such private regulation.

### 3.2. Private Choice of Law and Forum in Global Corporate Self-Regulation

Solutions may only be forthcoming if DPAs are empowered to enforce on a cross border basis rather than each DPA in its own territory. This would solve some of the problems discussed above, most notably the potential requirement to address different courts under the application of different laws. The starting point of this solution is that, given the sovereignty of States, any such form of central enforcement will entail States relinquishing enforcement powers in some cross-border situations, in return for gaining central enforcement powers in other cases. As long as the instances, where central enforcement powers are obtained, are of more relevance to a regulator than the instances in which enforcement powers are relinquished, this would seem a viable option. Such central supervision and enforcement may be achieved if companies were able to regulate their data protection in transnational private regulation (TRP) and make a choice of forum for central supervision and enforcement by one "lead" DPA (Lead DPA) and the courts of the country of such Lead DPA, preferably of the EU headquarters of such multinational. As the headquarter has control of all data processing operations of such multinational, it is able to procure compliance on a global basis, and transnational enforcement is achieved.

## 4. Binding Corporate Rules (BCR)

### 4.1. Drivers for the Introduction of Global Corporate Privacy Policies

"Facebook has 900 million active users of which 7.5 are below 13"; "Wall-Mart handles more than 1 million customer transactions per hour, the equivalent of 167 times the books in America's Library of Congress"; "Every day, we create 2.5 quintillion bytes of data – so much that 90% of the data in the world today has been created in the last two years alone…"

**Box 1:** Some facts regarding data.

Group companies exchange employee and customer data as a course of business. Multinationals increasingly process these data in central IT systems, which are accessed by the group companies around the world. Due to innovations, such as dynamic routing and cloud computing, it is often no longer predictable how these data will be routed over the internet or where these data will be ultimately stored. The data transfers between group companies attract a multitude of applicable data protection laws. The existing overlap and conflicts in applicable data protection laws make one hundred per cent worldwide compliance by multinationals a practical impossibility. Furthermore, multinational companies largely ignore the EU (and other countries') data transfer rules as these lead to disproportionate administrative burdens. Practice shows that multinationals, rather than striving to comply with applicable national data protection laws on a country-by-country basis, implement worldwide self-regulation by introducing corporate privacy policies. Their corporate privacy policies provide for both company-wide data protection rules and for an adequate level of data protection throughout the group, and often ignore possible stricter national provisions. The territory-based enforcement tools of the DPAs have not been able to counter this continuing widespread disregard for data protection laws. The introduction of corporate privacy policies by multinationals has created bottom-up pressure on national legal orders. This is reflected in the growing number of beneficiaries who invoke these policies before national courts (so far mainly in the US). It is also reflected in the pressure exerted by multinationals on the EU DPAs to recognise their corporate privacy policies as a tool to comply with the EU data transfer rules (as their policies ensure an adequate level of protection of personal data when transferred throughout their group of companies).

### 4.2. The BCR regime

The EU Commission's advisory committee on data protection, Working Party 29, recognises the added value of transnational private regulation in the data protection area in light of the gaps and deficiencies of the present EU data transfer regime. In a series of opinions, the Working Party 29 set criteria for these corporate privacy policies, labelled Binding Corporate Rules, BCR, to provide for a minimum level of protection for the processing of data by a multinational on a worldwide basis. These BCR should (*inter alia*):

(i) be internally binding within the organisation (on all group companies and on employees) and externally binding for the benefit of the beneficiaries of the privacy policy (that is, must create third-party beneficiary rights for these individuals);
(ii) incorporate the material data processing principles of the Directive and the restrictions on onward transfers to third parties outside the group;
(iii) provide for a network of privacy officers for ensuring compliance with the rules;
(iv) provide for an internal complaint handling process;
(v) provide for an auditing programme covering all aspects of the corporate privacy policy;
(vi) ensure suitable training of the employees who process the data;

(vii) be enforceable by the beneficiaries of the corporate privacy policy (that is, the employees and consumers) via the DPA and the courts in the Member State of the EU headquarters of the multinational;

(viii) the EU headquarters should accept liability for paying compensation and remedying breaches of the corporate privacy policy; and,

(ix) group companies should have a duty to cooperate with the DPAs, to abide by their advice regarding the corporate privacy policy and to submit to their audits.

With BCR, the Working Party 29 introduced a complex hybrid system of self-regulation (corporate privacy policies) with public arrangements (the DPA of the EU headquarters of the multinationals validating such corporate privacy policies and providing support in the area of supervision and enforcement).

Empirical research, performed as part of a HiiL project[1], shows that the data protection compliance of multinationals that introduced BCR, doubled on all ten measured principles, comprising in total of seventy four indicators (see Figure 1 below).

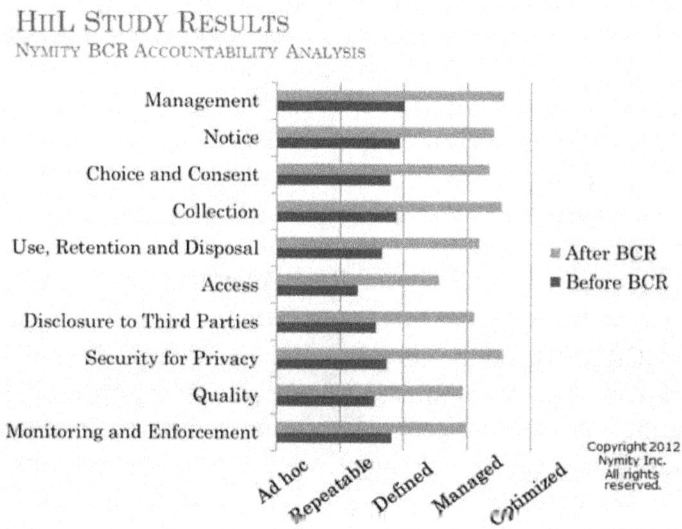


[1] The BCR case study was performed as part of the HiiL research project *Private Transnational Regulation: Constitutional Foundations and Governance Design*, see for scope www.hill.org. The empirical research has been performed by means of a privacy maturity tool which is developed by Nymity Inc, an international private-sector privacy compliance research firm.

**Figure 1:** HiiL Study Results: Nymity BCR Accountability Analysis.

Despite the evident benefits of BCR, some EU DPAs still oppose central authorisation and enforcement of BCR by one Lead DPA, for the reason that they do not have many of such headquarters in their territory, and therefore have not much to gain from such central authorisation and enforcement system. EU legislators are well advised to ignore this opposition and facilitate and encourage the adoption of BCR in the upcoming EU Regulation on Data Protection (Proposed Regulation).

### 4.3. Do BCR Provide for Adequate Redress Mechanisms?

A prerequisite for any form of redress is that BCR are enforceable. The requirement of enforceability is reflected in the first requirement of the BCR regime, which notes that the BCR should be "externally binding" for the benefit of the beneficiaries of BCR (that is, the employees and consumers whose data are processed under the BCR). BCR are in principle a unilateral undertaking by the multinational and not a contract. Many, but not all EU member States, take the view that rights may be granted to third parties by means of unilateral undertakings. If Lead DPAs in certain countries have doubts as to whether the BCR are externally binding (that is, legally enforceable) in their respective jurisdiction, a solution is to put a contract in place between the EU headquarters and, for instance, the group company in the jurisdiction of the DPA. In all member States it is possible to grant third-party beneficiary rights in a contract. However, rather than having to resort to legal solutions to ensure that BCR are externally binding, it would simplify matters considerably if European legislators could provide in the Proposed Regulation that BCR can be enforced as unilateral undertakings by third-party beneficiaries.

As BCR apply to the data processing operations of the multinational on a worldwide basis (that is, also to data processing operations not governed by the EU data protection laws), multinationals introducing BCR have a strong interest in including a choice of law and forum clause in their BCR. The main reason for this is that it is in the interest of the multinational that all complaints under the BCR are indeed ultimately dealt with by the Lead DPA (and the courts of the Lead DPA) as this DPA negotiated the provisions of the BCR under the applicability of the Lead DPA's own law (that is, the law under which the provisions of the BCR were drafted). This ensures for the multinational a consistent and predictable interpretation and application of the BCR. For the same reason, the multinational has an interest in the Lead DPA having central supervision over the BCR. Given the uncertainties under EU rules of PIL as to whether indeed a valid choice of law and forum can be made in respect of data protection, I recommend that European legislators ensure that in BCR such choice of law and forum may be made for the laws and courts of the member State of the Lead DPA.

To ensure that individuals have sufficient possibility of redress, the BCR regime requires that the multinational provides for an internal complaint and response facility. Many obstacles to cross-border enforcement of data protection, currently encountered by individuals, will be addressed by introduction of an internal complaints system. The individual will be able to file a complaint in his own language, with the group company with which he has a relationship, regardless of where the breach occurred or which of the group companies was responsible for the breach. The group company that receives the complaint will be responsible for ensuring that the complaint is processed through the complaints procedure of the multinational, and for ensuring that the required translations are provided. If the complaints procedure does not lead to a satisfying result for the individual, the group company will have to facilitate the filing of the complaint by the individual with the Lead DPA (or its courts). This procedure will lead to enforceable rights, even if damages of individuals are diffuse or too small to pursue through traditional judicial means, and where jurisdictions have no (adequate) data protection laws or if insufficient enforcement (infrastructure) is available. It further overcomes language-issues, time zone obstacles and minimises costs.

## 5. Conclusion

BCR, as an instance of Transnational Private Regulation, can do better than the present jurisdiction-based application and enforcement of the Directive:

### 5.1. Providing Material Data Protection to Individuals

BCR provide for more material data protection to individuals in practice than the current Directive and further provide data protection also to data processed by the multinational in countries where no or less data protection is provided for by State laws. Thus, gaps in data protection left by the regulations of nation States are no longer relevant.

### 5.2. Avoiding Gaps in Enforcement

The beneficiaries of BCR are provided with a central facility for complaints and the many obstacles to cross-border enforcement of data protection by individuals will be addressed. By granting central supervision and enforcement powers to the Lead DPA and its courts, transnational enforcement is achieved on a global basis.

### 5.3. Improved Regulation of Trans-Border Data Flows

BCR result in fewer administrative burdens for multinationals and simultaneously provide for more material data protection and redress to individuals. This is a vast improvement to the current situation, where trans-border data flows within multinationals are regulated by means of the EU standard contractual contracts to be entered into between the EU group companies and each and every non-EU group company, which lead to high administrative burdens for multinationals, while at the same time the data protection rights and remedies of individuals under these contracts, do not lead to meaningful data protection and redress in practice.

It is high time that the current uncertainties as to the validity and enforcement of BCR are solved; that the BCR authorisation procedure is streamlined; and that the enforcement powers of DPAs are harmonised and a common enforcement strategy for the DPAs is developed to ensure equal enforcement. This should not be achieved by way of further opinions of the Working Party 29, but by a revision of the Directive, which should preferably take the form of an EU regulation.

## 6. Sources and Further Reading

Cafaggi, Fabrizio, "Private Law-making and European Integration: Where Do They Meet, When Do They Conflict?", in Dawn Oliver *et al.* (eds), *The Regulatory State*, Oxford University Press, 2010, Chapter 10, pp. 201–228.

Hustinx, Peter, "The Role of Data Protection Authorities", in Serge Gutwirth *et al.* (eds.), *Reinventing Data Protection?*, Springer, 2009, Chapter 7, pp. 131–138.

Koops, Bert-Jaap, *et al.* (eds), *Starting Points for ICT Regulation. Deconstructing Prevalent Policy One-Liners*, TCM Asser Press, 2006.

Koops, Bert-Jaap, Miriam Lips, Sjaak Nouwt, Corien Prins and Maurice Schellekens, "Should Self-Regulation Be The Starting Point?", in Bert-Jaap Koops *et al.* (eds.), *Starting Points for ICT Regulation. Deconstructing Prevalent Policy One-Liners*, TCM Asser Press, 2006, Chapter 5.

Korff, Douwe, "New Challenges to Data Protection Study", Working Paper No. 2: Data Protection Laws in the EU: The Difficulties in Meeting the Challenges Posed by Global Social and Technical Developments, 15 January 2010. "European Commission DG Justice, Freedom and Security Report", available at SSRN http://ssrn.com/abstract=1638949, last accessed on 20 August 2012.

Kuner, Christopher, "Data Protection Law and International Jurisdiction on the Internet (Part 1)", in *International Journal of Law and Information Technology*, 2010, vol. 18, pp. 176–193.

Kuner, Christopher, *European Data Protection Law: Corporate Compliance and Regulation*, 2nd ed., Oxford University Press, 2007.

Kuner, Christopher, "Regulation of Transborder Data Flows under Data Protection and Privacy Law: Past, Present and Future". TILT Law and Technology Working Paper No. 016/2010, October 2010, Version 1.0, at 10, available at http://papers.ssrn.com/sol3/papers.cfm?abstract_id=1689483, last accessed on 20 August 2012.

Lips, Miriam, "Inventory of General ICT Regulatory Starting Points", in Koops, Bert-Jaap *et al.* (eds.), *Starting Points for ICT Regulation. Deconstructing Prevalent Policy One-Liners*, TCM Asser Press, 2006, Chapter 2.

Moerel, Lokke, *Binding Corporate Rules – Corporate Self-regulation of Global Data Transfers*, Oxford University Press, 2012.

Lokke Moerel, Case Study Report on Data Protection, Private Transnational Regulation: Constitutional Foundations and Governance Design, collaborative research project of HiiL and the European University Initiative, forthcoming, available at http://www.hiil.org/project/corporate-laissez-faire-or-public-interference-effective-regulation-of-cross-border-activities, last accessed on 1 October 2012.

Parker, Christine and Braithwaite, John, "Regulation", in Peter Cane and Mark Tushnet (eds.), *The Oxford Handbook of Legal Studies*, Oxford University Press, 2003, pp. 119–145.

Poullet, Yves, "ICT and Co-Regulation: Towards a New Regulatory Approach?", in Bert-Jaap Koops *et al.* (eds.), *Starting Points for ICT Regula-*

*tion. Deconstructing Prevalent Policy One-Liners*, TCM Asser Press 2006, Chapter 9.2.

Prins, Corien, "Should ICT Regulation Be Undertaken at an International Level?", in Bert-Jaap Koops *et al.* (eds.), *Starting Points for ICT Regulation.Deconstructing Prevalent Policy One-Liners*, TCM Asser Press 2006, Chapter 6.

Reich, Norbert, "Diverse Approaches to Consumer Protection Philosophy", in *Journal of Consumer Policy*, 1992, vol. 14, pp. 257–292.

Schellekens, Maurice, Bert-Jaap Koops and Corien Prins, "Conclusion", in Bert-Jaap Koops *et al.* (eds.), *Starting Points for ICT Regulation. Deconstructing Prevalent Policy One-Liners*, TCM Asser Press, 2006, Chapter 8.

Scott, Colin David, "Enforcing Consumer Protection Laws, UCD Working Papers in Law, Criminology and Socio-Legal Studies Research Paper No. 15/2009", available at http://ssrn.com/abstract=1441256, last accessed on 20 August 2012, also published in Howells, Geraint, *et al.* (eds.), *Handbook of International Consumer Law and Policy*, Edward Elgar, 2010.

Swire, Peter P., "Elephants and Mice Revisited: Law and Choice of Law on the Internet", in *University of Pennsylvania Law Review*, 2005, vol. 153, pp. 1975–2001.

Wugmeister, Miriam, Retzer, Karin and Rich, Cynthia, "Global Solution for Cross-Border Data Transfers: Making the Case for Corporate Privacy Rules", in *Georgetown Journal of International Law*, 2007, vol. 38, pp. 449–498.

"APEC Privacy Framework", available at http://www.apec.org/Groups/Committee-on-Trade-and-Investment/~/media/Files/Groups/ECSG/05_ecsg_privacyframewk.ashx, last accessed on 17 August 2012.

Centre for Information Policy Leadership, "Commentary in Response to the European Commission's Communication on 'A Comprehensive Approach to Personal Data Protection' 2011", available at www.huntonfiles.com, last accessed on 20 August 2012.

European Commission, Communication from the Commission to the European Parliament, the Council, the Economic and Social Committee and the Committee of the Regions, A comprehensive approach on personal data protection in the European Union, COM(2010) 609/3, 4 November 2010.

European Commission, White Paper on European Governance, 2001, COM 428 final.

European Data Protection Supervisor, "Opinion of the European Data Protection Supervisor on the Communication from the Commission to the European Parliament, the Council, the Economic and Social Committee and the Committee of the Regions – 'A Comprehensive Approach on Personal Data Protection in the European Union'", 2011, available at http://ec.europa.eu/bepa/european-group-ethics/docs/activities/peter_hustinx_presentation_(2)_15th_rt_2011.pdf, last accessed on 20 August 2012.

Inter-Institutional Agreement on Better Lawmaking concluded between the European Parliament, the EU Council of Ministers and the European Commission of 16 December 2003 (2003/C321/01), 2003, OJ C321/1.

Nymity Incorporated, BCR Case Study Empirical Research Results, Private Transnational Regulation: Constitutional Foundations and Governance Design, collaborative research project of HiiL and the European University Initiative, forthcoming, available at http://www.hiil.org/project/corporate-laissez-faire-or-public-interference-effective-regulation-of-cross-border-activities, last accessed on 1 October 2012.

OECD, *Privacy Online. OECD Guidance on Policy and Practice*, OECD Publishing, 2003, available at www.oecdbookshop.org, last accessed on 20 August 2012.

Rand Europe, "Review of the European Data Protection Directive, Technical Report dated May 2009", available at www.rand.org, last accessed on 20 August 2012.

"WP 168, The Future of Privacy, Joint Contribution to the Consultation of the European Commission on the Legal Framework for the Fundamental Right to Protection of Personal Data", as adopted on 1 December 2009, available at http://ec.europa.eu/justice/policies/privacy/workinggroup/wpdocs/2009_en.htm, last accessed on 20 August 2012.

WSIS Declaration of Principles, WSIS-03/GENEVA/DOC/0004, available at www.itu.int, last accessed on 20 August 2012.

# 5.7.

# The Regulation of Public-Private Partnerships

**Christopher H. Bovis**[*]

The notion of public–private partnerships reveals complex forms of cooperation between the State and private actors, which exceed the remit of traditional contractual interface, moving into a strategic sphere of public sector management. Public–private partnerships aim at delivering both infrastructure facilities and public services, and are regarded as attractive and credible solutions to the infrastructure deficit of many developed and developing States. A conceptual forecast of the legal and regulatory mapping of public–private partnerships is attempted in this think piece, and it also elaborates on the current and future legal trends within which the regulation of public–private partnerships will be developed. Furthermore, and in conjunction with the emergence of legal trends, this think piece reflects on societal needs, which need calibrating in terms of expectation, but mostly perception when faced with the modality of public–private partnerships for the delivery of public services. Finally, this think piece attempts to cast a conceptual map of the challenges for the development of the law in relation to public–private partnerships, by depicting their interface as public services instruments, as investment instruments and as growth instruments. The think piece then concludes with recommendations for law- and policy-makers in relation to the law of the future for public–private partnerships.

## 1. Background

The modern State justifies its existence through the provision of public services, a concept which encapsulates the pursuit of public interest. The delivery and regulation of public services are based on two diametrically different models, which reflect on internalisation choices or externalisation choices on the part of the State. Firstly, as far as internalisation

[*] **Christopher H. Bovis** is JD, MPhil, LLM, FRSA, H.K. Bevan Chair in Law and Professor of European Business Law, University of Hull.

choices are concerned, the notion of public services often fuses with that of State ownership of assets or infrastructure, and amalgamates the ensuing provision of services to the public. It also refers to functions which underpin essential facilities of the State (these are, defence, justice and policing), and as a result these functions are sheltered from market forces in order to ensure the integrity of their delivery. Secondly, in relation to externalisation choices of the State, public services regularly capture interests of general needs, which are delivered through market-based mechanisms where the public sector interfaces contractually or even competes with private actors. However, the externalised organisation and delivery of public services reveals that their providers interface with the State in a market place which does not correspond to the principles and dynamics of private markets, thus requiring a different type of regulation, which could be seen as an amalgam of legal, financial and policy attributes reflecting the constant changing of societal needs, expectations and requirements.[1]

## 2. The Axiom of Partnerships in Public Service Delivery

Optimal risk management is the prime advantage to the State which emerges from involving private actors through a partnership format in the delivery of public services. This axiom underlines the principle of public accountability for the modern State in a number of ways.

The private actor partner often commits its own capital resources for the funding and the delivery of public services. It is not therefore a mere contractor; it is a stakeholder which has a vested interest in the ef-

---

1 See Christopher Bovis, "The State, Competition and Public Services", in Patrick Birkinshaw and Mike Varney (eds.), *The European Union Legal Order after Lisbon*, Kluwer, 2010; Leo Flynn, "Competition Policy and Public Services in EC Law after the Maastricht and Amsterdam Treaties", in David O'Keeffe and Patrick Tworney (eds.), *Legal Issues of the Amsterdam Treaty*, Hart Publishing, 1999, pp. 196–197; Jose Luis Buendia Sierra, *Exclusive Rights and State Monopolies under EC Law*, Oxford University Press, 1999, p. 330; Aurélie Moriceau, "Services d'Intérêt Économique General et Valeurs Communes", in *Revue du Marché Commun et de l'Union Europénne*, no. 519, 2008, p. 358; Malcolm Ross, "Article 16 E.C. and Services of General Interest: From Derogation to Obligation?", in *European Law Review*, 2000, p. 22; Tony Prosser, *The Limits of Competition Law*, Oxford University Press, 2005; Cosmo Graham, "Essential Facilities and Services of General Interest", in *Diretto e Politiche dell'Unione Europea*, 2007, p. 29; Wolf Sauter, "Services of General Economic Interest and Universal Service in EU Law", in *European Law Review*, 2008, p. 172.

fective and efficient delivery of the relevant public services in order to attain its returns and recoup its investment. This attribute results in an increased certainty of outcomes, both in terms of on-time delivery (the private actor is strongly motivated to complete the project as early as possible and to control its costs, so that the payment streams can commence) and in terms of within-budget delivery (the payment schedule is fixed before construction commences, protecting the State from exposure to cost overruns). As a result, by transferring the risk of the funding required for the delivery of public services to private actors, the latter become an essential component of the State's functions, thus revealing a conceptual and strategic convergence between public and private sectors.

Private actors in public–private partnerships are often financially incentivised to offer value-for-money solutions in the delivery of public services through continuous quality improvement, innovation, management efficiency and effectiveness. As such, behavioural elements, which traditionally underpin private sector entrepreneurship, are harnessed by the State to improve the quality of public services through a transfer of operational risk to private actors.

## 3. Legal Trends in Public–Private Partnerships

### 3.1. Public–Private Partnerships as Public Service Instruments

Public–private partnerships can be viewed as public service instruments. As such, the State opts for an externalised model in the delivery of public services and heralds a departure from an "asset-based" to an "enabled-based" format in public services. Through risk transfer mechanisms, the public–private partnership is treated as an emanation of the State and reveals a different ethos in public sector management, one where the State takes on the role of an enabling and facilitating agent. However, the strategic role of private actors in financing and delivering infrastructure facilities and public services by providing input into the various phases such as finance, design, construction, operation and maintenance, reflects the need for longevity of the relations between public and private sectors. The (often) lengthy duration of public–private partnerships is justified on the basis of the affordability for repayment on the part of the public sector and on the basis of the ability of the private sector to recoup its investment profitably. Nevertheless, this could potentially result in market foreclosure. There is a pertinent need to address the competitiveness of public–private partnerships before and after the procurement process of the private actor.

A legal trend has emerged in relation to the structure and operational interface of public–private partnerships. Three operational types of public–private partnerships codify the relations between the State and private actors. All types have as a pivotal feature asset ownership and potential transfer to the public sector. The first type of such relations includes legal formats where the private actor designs, builds, owns, develops, operates and manages an asset with no obligation to transfer ownership to the public sector. Secondly, another type of public–private partnerships includes legal formats where the private actor buys or leases an existing asset from the public sector, renovates, modernises, expands it, and then operates the asset exclusively, with no obligation to transfer ownership back to the public sector. Thirdly, another legal format of public–private partnerships includes relations where the private sector designs and builds an asset, operates it, and then transfers it to the public sector when the operating contract ends, or at some other specified time. The private partner may subsequently rent or lease the asset from the public sector to deliver the related public services.

A different type of public–private partnerships has emerged through the award and granting of concessions, which are revenue-generating relations, involving an infrastructure or a service, the use of which necessitates the payment of fees borne directly by end users, and any operation or function emanating from the sale, rent or exploitation of public land or buildings. The notion of a concession is based on the assumption that no contractual remuneration is paid by the granting public entity to the concessionaire. The latter must therefore be given the right to exploit the concession economically, although this right may be accompanied by a requirement to pay some consideration to the grantor, depending on elements of risk allocation agreed between the parties.

Finally, as the private sector provides the financing for the infrastructure facilities and delivery of public services within a public–private partnership, it has emerged that a different accountancy treatment benefits the State, in that the debt financing of public–private partnerships is regarded as off-balance sheet borrowing. This means that the borrowing of the State to repay the investment of the private actor does not affect the State's public sector borrowing requirements (PSBR) and any measurements or calculations of its indebtedness. As a result of this development, the legal treatment of debt financial instruments for public–private partnerships should be standardised.

### 3.2. Public–Private Partnerships as Investment Instruments

Public–private partnerships can be viewed as investment instruments. Financing for a public–private partnership can take one of the following forms: a) a stand-alone project, where the funding raised is for only one specific project; b) a special purpose vehicle (SPV) as the borrower, where an independent legal vehicle is created to raise the funds required for the project; c) a high ratio of debt to equity through either gearing or leverage, where the newly created project company usually has the minimum equity required to issue debt for a reasonable cost; d) private lending based on project-specific cash-flow and not a corporate balance sheet, where the project company borrows funds from lenders; the lenders look to the projected future revenue stream generated by the project and the project company's assets to repay all loans; and, e) various financial guarantees, where the guarantees are provided by the private sector partners, often limited to their equity contributions. As a result, the lender receives its payment from the income generated from the project or directly from the public sector.

Secondly, public–private partnership financing can be provided via SPVs comprising consortia of banks and other financial institutions, which are set up to combine and coordinate the use of their capital and expertise as well as to share any relevant risks. Accountancy treatment of the SPV's consolidated accounts is aligned with that of the party which controls the SPV. If the private sector partner controls the SPV, its debt is recorded off-balance sheet for public sector borrowing considerations. If an SPV is controlled by the public sector, debt should be consolidated with public sector borrowing and its operations should be reflected in the fiscal accounts.

Thirdly, a public–private partnership can be financed by securitisation of claims on future project revenues. In a typical public–private partnership securitisation operation, the public sector would sell a financial asset – its claim on future project revenues – to an SPV. The SPV would then sell securities backed by this asset to private investors, and use the proceeds to pay the public sector, which in turn would use them to finance the public–private partnership. Interest and amortisation would be paid by the SPV to investors from the public sector's share of project revenue.

The cost of capital needed to finance a public–private partnership should depend on the characteristics of project related risks and not on the source of finance. However, the source of finance can influence project risk, depending on the maturity and sophistication of the risk bearing markets. On the one hand, within advanced risk bearing markets, it is irrelevant whether project risk is borne by the public sector or the private sector. On the other hand, when risk-bearing markets are less developed, project risk depends on how widely that risk is spread. This outcome might contravene the assumption that private sector borrowing generally costs more than government borrowing. However, this mainly reflects differences in default risk. The public sector's power to tax reduces the likelihood that it will default on its debt, and the private sector is therefore prepared to lend to the public sector at close to the risk-free interest rate to finance risky projects. The crucial issue is whether public–private partnerships result in efficiency gains that offset higher private sector borrowing costs.

### 3.3. Public–Private Partnerships as Growth Instruments

Public–private partnerships can be viewed as growth instruments. In the European Union, as part of the Initiative for Growth and the 2020 Growth Strategy, the European Council has approved a series of measures designed to increase investment in the infrastructure of the trans-European transport networks (TENs) and also in the areas of research, innovation and development, as well as the delivery of services of general economic interest. The UN has devised a blueprint to close the gap between the poorest countries and industrialised nations, and agreed the UN Millennium Declaration, committing its members to a new global partnership and emphasizing the potential of public–private partnerships in achieving the realisation of the United Nations Millennium Development Goals.

## 4. Trends in Regulation of Public–Private Partnerships

### 4.1. Structure Regulation of Public–Private Partnerships

The development of two distinctive legal structures/models will assist the evolution and delivery of public–private partnerships. Firstly, the contractual model, where the interface between the State and the private actors reflects on a relationship which is based solely on contractual links. Under this model and structure, it is unlikely that there would be any element of exclusive asset exploitation or end-user payments levied by the private actor. However, mechanisms of profit sharing, efficiency gain sharing as well as risk allocation between the public and private partners distinguish contractual public–private partnerships from traditional public contracts for works or services. The contractual model of public–private partnerships assumes that the private sector partner will provide the financing for completing the project and the public sector partner will pay back by way of "service or unitary charges", which reflect payments based on usage volumes or demand (that is, payments in lieu of fees or tolls for public lighting, hospitals, schools and roads with shadow tolls).

Secondly, the institutional model of public–private partnerships involves the establishment of a separate legal entity held jointly by the public partner and the private partner. The joint entity has the task of ensuring the raising of finance and the delivery of a public service or an infrastructure project for the benefit of the public. The direct interface between the public partner and the private partner in a forum with a distinctive legal personality allows the public partner, through its presence in the body of shareholders and in the decision-making bodies of the joint entity, to retain a relatively high degree of control over the development and delivery of the project. The joint entity could also allow the public partner to develop its own experience of running and improving the relevant public services, while having recourse to the support of the private partner. An institutional public–private partnership can be established either by creating an entity controlled by the public and private sector partners, or by the private sector taking control of an existing public undertaking or by the participation of a private partner in an existing publicly owned company, which has obtained public contracts or concessions.

## 4.2. Procurement Regulation of Public–Private Partnerships

Considerable emphasis has been placed on observing the public sector management principles such as transparency, accountability, competitiveness and value for money during the procurement process of public–private partnerships. When a transaction creating a mixed-capital entity is accompanied by the award of tasks through an act which can be designated as a public contract, or even a concession, it is important that there is compliance with the principles of transparency and accountability, as well as the principle of non-discrimination. The selection of a private partner called on to undertake such tasks while functioning as part of a mixed entity can therefore not be based exclusively on the quality of its capital contribution or its experience, but should also take account of the characteristics of its offer in terms of the specific services to be provided. The conditions governing the creation of the entity must be clearly laid down when issuing the call for competition for the tasks one wishes to entrust to the private partner. Also, these conditions must not discriminate against or constitute an unjustified barrier to the freedom to provide services or to freedom of establishment.

In many jurisdictions, legislation allows for mixed entities, in which the participation by the public sector involves the contracting body, to participate in a procedure for the award of a public–private partnership or a concession, even when these entities are only in the process of being incorporated. In this scenario, the entity will be definitively incorporated only after the contract has actually been awarded to it. In many jurisdictions, a practice has been developed which tends to confuse the phase of incorporating the entity and the phase of allocating the public services tasks. Thus, the purpose of the procurement procedure is to create a mixed entity to which certain tasks are entrusted.[2]

Such a solution does not appear to offer satisfactory outcomes. First, there is a risk that the effective competition will be distorted by a privileged position of the company being incorporated, and consequently of the private partner participating in that company. Secondly, the specific procedure for selecting the private partner also poses many problems. The contracting authorities encounter certain difficulties in defining the subject matter of the contract or concession in a sufficiently clear and precise manner, as they are obliged to do in this context. This in turn not only raises problems with regard to the principles of transparency and equality of treatment, but even risks prejudicing the general interest objectives, which the public authority wishes to attain.

[2] See Steven van Grasse, *De Concessie in het Raam van de Publiek-Private Samenwerking*, Die Keure, 2007. See also Alain Alexis, *Services Publics et Aides d'Etat*, RDUE, 2002, pp. 63; and Joël Arnould, *Les Contrats de Concession de Privatisation et des Services "in-house" au Regard des Règles Communautaires*, R.F.D. Adm, 2000, pp. 2.

## 4.3. Risk Treatment and its Regulation in Public–Private Partnerships

A significant regulatory trend which has emerged as a result of the strategic role of the private sector and its long-term engagement in delivering infrastructure and public services reflects on the legal treatment of risk distribution between the public and private sectors within public–private partnerships, especially the allocation and pricing of construction or project risk, which is related to design problems, building cost overruns, and project delays; financial risk, which is related to variability in interest rates, exchange rates, and other factors affecting financing costs; performance risk, which is related to the availability of an asset and the continuity and quality of the relevant service provision; and demand risk, which is related to the on-going need for the relevant public services; and residual value risk, which is related to the future market price of an asset.

Risk transfer from the public sector to the private sector has a significant influence on whether a public–private partnership is a more efficient and cost-effective alternative to public investment and publicly funded provision of services.[3] The public sector and the private sector typically adopt different approaches to pricing market risk. The public sector tends to use the social time preference rate (STPR) or some other risk-free rate to discount future cash flows when appraising projects. The private sector in a public–private partnership project will include a risk premium in the discount rate it applies to future project earnings where, under the widely used capital asset pricing model (CAPM), the expected rate of return on an asset is defined as the risk-free rate of return plus a risk premium, the latter being the product of the market risk premium and a coefficient which measures the variance between the returns on that asset and market returns.

A number of criteria have been devised to assess the degree of risk treatment in public–private partnerships, and again these criteria involve asset ownership as an essential feature. The extent of risk transfer between the parties and the quantum for such transfer can be assessed by reference to separable contractual relations in a public–private partnership, where a distinction is made between asset ownership and delivery of public service elements or non-separable contracts where asset ownership

3 See David A. Moss, *When All Else Fails: Government as the Ultimate Risk Manager*, Harvard University Press. 2002.

fuses with public service delivery.[4] For non-separable contracts, the base line for the assessment rests on the balance of demand risk and residual value risk borne by the public sector and the private operator. Demand risk, which is an operating risk and is the dominant consideration, is borne by the public sector if service payments to a private operator are independent of future need for the service. Residual value risk, which is an ownership risk, is borne by the public sector if an asset of a public–private partnership is transferred to the public sector for less than its true residual value. Residual value risk is borne by the public sector because the private operator reflects the difference between the expected residual value of the asset and the price at which the asset will be transferred to the public sector in the price it charges the public sector for services, or the revenue the public sector receives from a project. If the asset ends up being worth more or less than the amount reflected in the service payment or government revenue, any resulting gain benefits the public sector and any loss is borne by the public sector. Reference can also be made to various qualitative indicators, including government guarantees of private sector liabilities, and the extent of government influence over asset design and operation.[5]

### 4.4. Future Trends in Regulation

Future trends in regulation for public–private partnerships will reflect on the current regulatory deficit and, in particular, the conceptual limitations of anti-trust to intervene in and regulate such complex relations between public and private sectors. Such limitations have set a new paradigm, which has established that public services and the modality of public–private partnerships function in a *sui generis* market-place, where State intervention in the organisation, structure and delivery of public services reveals a type of regulation based on public law.

As a result of the importance of public–private partnerships to close the infrastructure deficit in developed and developing countries, the public law type of regulation mentioned above should be standardised.[6] Three

---

4 See Ilana Polackova-Brixi and Allen Schick (eds.), *Government at Risk: Contingent Liabilities and Fiscal Risk,* World Bank, Oxford University Press, 2002.

5 See Timothy C. Irwin, *Government Guarantees: Allocating and Valuing Risk in Privately Financed Infrastructure Projects*, World Bank Publications, 2007.

6 See International Monetary Fund, *Public-private partnerships, Department of Fiscal Affairs*, International Monetary Fund, Washington, 2004.

regulatory actors emerge with competence to accomplish such task of standardisation: firstly, the United Nations, through the specific task of achieving the Millennium Development Goals by the modality of public–private partnerships; secondly, the European Union, through its advanced legal framework,[7] which produces extra-territorial effects in third countries; and, lastly, the World Trade Organisation, which as a result of its globalised agenda in improving trade and liberalising its patterns across its member signatories, could develop standardised legal and regulatory formats for the procurement of public–private partnerships, their legal interface and corporate structure as vehicles in public service delivery and risk treatment in relations between the State and private actors.

It is worth noting that the public law type of regulation will present national and trans-national features in such a way that jurisdictional and enforcement characteristics will emerge not only within national markets but also within regional trading blocs. The national and trans-national regulation will pave the way towards international norms of coherent and standardised dimensions with a view to establishing not only standardisation of law and policy, but also uniformity of application and implementation of public–private partnerships, and an increased and enhanced legal certainty for the State, private actors and the public as end users of public services.

A new trend in societal needs which will emerge out of the route of national towards international regulation of public–private partnerships, will reflect on competing models for the delivery of public services. The State will have absolute discretion in engaging with private actors through public–private partnerships to deliver public services or advance models of public–public partnerships, which include intermediary marketisation of public services through mutual societies, social enterprise, and in-house arrangements. The competitive dynamics from the interface between public–private partnerships and public–public partnerships will present a valuable benchmark to the State for the ever-increasingly changing background, expectations, standards and needs for the delivery of public services in the twenty-first century

[7] See European Commission, Green Paper on Public-Private Partnerships and Community Law on Public Contracts and Concessions, COM(2004) 327 final.

## 5. Conclusions

The concept of public–private partnerships represents a genuine attempt to revolutionise the delivery of public services by introducing the private sector as strategic investor and financier of public services. The private sector assumes a direct responsibility in serving the public interest, as part of its contractual obligations *vis-à-vis* the public sector. The motive and the intention behind such approach focus on the benefits which would follow as a result of the private sector's involvement in the delivery of public services. Efficiency gains, qualitative improvement, innovation, value-for-money and flexibility appear to be the most important ones, whereas an overall better allocation of public capital resources sums up the advantages of engaging with the private sector in delivery of public services. Public–private partnerships as a concept of public sector management have changed the methodology of assessing delivery of public services in both qualitative and quantitative terms.

The case for the success of public–private partnerships rests on the relative efficiency of the private sector. However, this efficiency must demonstrate itself in a dynamic mode, reflecting the need for competition in the provision of the relevant services through the public–private partnership. In traditional public contracting, public procurement through tendering secured the repeated competition for a market which is inherently oligopolistic yet contestable by new entries or offerings. However, the scope for competition in the activities undertaken by public–private partnerships is more limited, because they tend to be less contestable for reasons relevant to the longevity of the engagement between public and private sectors, for reasons under which social infrastructure remains undervalued and economic infrastructure involves large sunk costs. For public–private partnerships to operate in a global competitive environment, safeguard the principles of transparency and accountability in public sector management, incentive-based regulation is paramount. Where a private sector operator can sell public services to the public, even with little scope for competition, the public sector must regulate the prices for the relevant public services. However, the challenge is to design well-functioning regulation which increases output towards the social optimum, stabilises prices in a sustainable manner, and limits monopoly profit while preserving the incentive for private sector to be more efficient and reduce costs. The Europe 2020 strategy highlights the importance of public–private partnerships for accelerating growth and boosting innovation. In addition, the Single Market Act[8] announced the adoption of a legislative initiative on concessions in 2011 in order to promote public–private partnerships and to help deliver better value for money for users of services and for contracting authorities, while improving market access for EU undertakings by ensuring transparency, equal treatment and a level playing field across the EU.

The challenges which face both the public and private sectors in public–private partnership arrangements focus on the delivery and the financing of public services respectively from a quality and efficiency perspective. They also reveal a close link with industrial policy at global and national levels, and as a result a strategic direction of certain sectors.

These challenges translated in the legal interface of the developed and developing nations pose some considerable questions in relation to the role and scope of private actors in delivering public services, the regulatory compatibility between norms of anti-trust and exclusivity of private actors in delivering public services, questions relevant to the expectations of private actors in financial, operational and strategic perspectives, questions in relation to compliance and enforcement of public–private partnership relations in the process of delivering public services, and finally, questions in relation to risk treatment arising out of such relations.

Strategically, in the author's view, the law of the future in relation to public–private partnerships will focus on regulatory standardisation. Regulatory standardisation will have recourse to both hard law and soft law. Hard law will utilise normative acts of a public law character in order to ensure a safeguard for competition, procurement and selection of private sector partners; contractual issues such as terms and conditions, guarantees, and dispute resolution; and corporate structures between public and private sectors. The role of international organisations such as the EU, the UN and the World Bank will be pivotal in shaping such instruments of hard law which will be applicable to both developed and developing nations. Their standardisation will augment legal certainty amongst public and private sectors and the society at large. On the other hand, soft law in the form of guidelines will create the appropriate consultative environment in the fields of risk management, risk assessment, financing and securitisation as well as debt treatment of public–private partnerships.

8 See Commission Communication, *The Single Market Act Twelve Levers to Boost Growth and Strengthen Confidence* of 13 April 2011.

Regulatory standardisation of public–private partnerships will emit best practice transparency and consistency in public services, ensure innovation and quality in the delivery of public service and articulate on constantly developing issues such as the competitive environment in delivering public services, as well as issues relevant to the financing, investment, control, and exit of private actors from public–private partnerships.

## 6. Sources and Further Reading

Alexis, Alain, *Services Publics et Aides d'Etat,* RDUE, 2002, pp. 63–107.

Arnould, Joël, *Les Contrats de Concession de Privatisation et des Services "in-house" au Regard des Règles Communautaires*, F.F.D. Adm, 2000, pp. 2–23.

Bovis, Christopher, "The State, Competition and Public Services", in Patrick Birkinshaw and Mike Varney (eds.), *The European Union Legal Order after Lisbon*, Kluwer, 2010.

Flynn, Leo, "Competition Policy and Public Services in EC Law after the Maastricht and Amsterdam Treaties", in David O"Keeffe and Patrick Tworney (eds.), *Legal Issues of the Amsterdam Treaty*, Hart Publishing, 1999, pp. 196–197.

Graham, Cosmo, "Essential Facilities and Services of General Interest", *Diretto e Politiche dell'Unione Europea*, 2007, p. 29.

Grasse, Steven van, *De Concessie in het Raam van de Publiek-Private Samenwerking*, Die Keure, 2007.

Irwin, Timothy C., *Government Guarantees: Allocating and Valuing Risk in Privately Financed Infrastructure Projects*, World Bank Publications, 2007.

Moriceau, Aurélie, "Services d'Intérêt Économique General et Valeurs Communes", *Revue du Marché Commun et de l'Union Européenne*, no. 519, 2008, p. 358.

Moss, David A., *When All Else Fails: Government as the Ultimate Risk Manager*, Harvard University Press, 2002.

Polackova-Brixi, Hana, and Schick, Allen (eds.), *Government at Risk: Contingent Liabilities and Fiscal Risk,* World Bank, Oxford University Press, 2002.

Prosser, Tony, *The Limits of Competition Law,* Oxford University Press, 2005.

Ross, Malcolm, "Article 16 E.C. and Services of General Interest: From Derogation to Obligation?", *European Law Review*, 2000, pp. 22–38.

Sauter, Wolf, "Services of General Economic Interest and Universal Service in EU Law", in *European Law Review*, 2008, p. 172.

Sierra, Jose Luis Buendia, *Exclusive Rights and State Monopolies under EC Law,* Oxford University Press, 1999, p. 330.

European Commission, *Green Paper on Public-Private Partnerships and Community Law on Public Contracts and Concessions*, COM (2004) 327 fin.

Commission Communication, *The Single Market Act Twelve Levers to Boost Growth and Strengthen Confidence* of 13 April 2011.

International Monetary Fund, *Public-Private Partnerships, Department of Fiscal Affairs*, 2004, Washington.

# 5.8.

# Reflections on the Legal Future of Corporate Social Responsibility

**Austin Onuoha***

In this think piece, I reflect on some of the areas in which laws could be used in the future to ensure better and more impactful corporate social responsibility (CSR). I examine the tension between the use of national legislation and the application of international law against the background of the push for soft law by the international community. Although laws act as guides for human behaviour, and the debate around CSR has been between voluntary and mandatory initiatives, I reflect that there are areas where laws could in the future be used to streamline the practice of CSR, and manage relationships between companies and communities, including individuals. Some of the areas that I reflect on include community consultation and engagement, criteria for allocation and sharing of funds for CSR initiatives, professionalisation of CSR function, monitoring and evaluation and the streamlining and strengthening of community governance structures. I conclude that the future of law should be to complement and not to compete with voluntary initiatives.

## 1. Introduction

One of the responsibilities of business identified in corporate social responsibility (CSR) theory is legal responsibility. This means that businesses have a responsibility to obey the laws of the land. However, there have been issues associated with businesses obeying the law. First, businesses are considered influential and powerful, therefore could act with impunity with minimum restraint. Corporations also have the wherewithal to navigate the legal maze in case they are found wanting. Lastly, there is the debate around who should be held responsible for corporate abuses of human rights. Is it the company or the individual managers who make the

* **Austin Onuoha** is the Founder of The Africa Centre for Corporate Responsibility (ACCR) based in Nigeria.

decisions? And because of worsening economic crises and the drive for Foreign Direct Investment (FDI), governments are proving incapable of regulating business conduct. Another issue that lends to the complexity of the issue is the nature and ownership of businesses. It is on record that many political office holders are full or part owners of businesses or they have been sponsored to political positions through donations from businesses. Because of the alleged compromise of the decision-makers, they are unable to rein in businesses when they misbehave.

Because of all of the above and more, there has been a certain level of obfuscation as to the responsibilities of businesses especially as it relates to human rights. The passing of Resolution 2005/69 on "Human rights and transnational corporations and other business enterprises" by the United Nations (UN) Commission on Human Rights was aimed at clarifying issues and standards that entangle this issue. Earlier on, the UN has developed the UN Norms. This was thrown out at the Human Rights Council because it was argued that the norms were assigning the same responsibility due to States to companies in the realisation of human rights. Because of the hostility that the norms suffered, the UN Special Representative on Human Rights and Business, Professor John Ruggie, decided to build consensus around the current mandate. It is also in an attempt to come around the legal entanglements that he decided to build consensus around the mandate. In fact, Professor Ruggie has been criticised by certain members of academia and civil society for leaning more towards consensus than principles.

The debate on CSR has revolved around whether the mechanisms and structures that deal with it should be made mandatory or voluntary. In legal terms, it is whether the initiatives should constitute "hard" or "soft" law. By "hard" law they mean elaborate legislations with accompanying sanctions, while "soft" law deals with instruments and initiatives that almost always verge on moral suasion. Most human rights NGOs opt for and support hard law because in their estimation, laws have the capacity to hold companies accountable. The business community and to some extent governments tend to lean more towards the soft law option. Interestingly, however, the soft law option has mostly been promoted by the international community, namely the UN and the European Union. The reason for this may be connected with the challenges of implementing laws at the international level, especially with the anarchy that characterises the international system

The hard law option seems to have been popular at the national levels. This may be because laws are easier to enact at the national level and such issues as extra-territoriality are not prominent. Moreover, law enforcement can prove more manageable at the national level. However, most of the companies that are targeted with legislation at the national level are multinational corporations. There is the general perception, especially in the developing world, that these companies do not respect national legislations and are more inclined to respect international laws. Paradoxically, part of the reason is the fear of litigation in their home countries.

In Nigeria, CSR has taken a beating from different commentators. This is because of the various breaches that have been experienced between companies and communities. The Niger Delta crisis is too well-known to warrant recounting. The issues that create tension between companies and communities in the Niger Delta include land, environmental pollution, oil spill compensation and clean-up, employment, contracts and recognition. Interestingly there are laws dealing with almost each one except for such issues as employment, contracts and recognition. Although subsumed in law, what is lacking has been "specificity" in these areas. For instance, how much should a company commit to community development? What are the criteria for allocation?

Already in Nigeria there has been a push to update and harmonise laws that deal with the petroleum industry, for instance. The Petroleum Industry Bill is an attempt to streamline and harmonise legislation in and around the industry. This proposed law is an executive bill which has been sitting with the national legislature for close to three years and has passed through two different legislatures. The controversies that have trailed the proposed legislation point to the challenges of law. First, some stakeholders argue that the law is not far-reaching enough. These include NGOs, human rights groups and community leaders. Others argue that it has made the petroleum industry unprofitable and therefore would not attract investors. Among these are oil industry experts, and on the process it is said that there are different versions of the proposed law in circulation.

## 2. The legal future of CSR in Nigeria

The focus of CSR law seems to have been too much on the oil industry. Although understandable, it is limited in strategic thinking. Oil for instance, may lose its importance as a strategic energy resource in the near future if the current research efforts are intensified. With the heavy investment in research, if this comes to pass, it means that nation States may have to go back to the drawing board. In my opinion, the future of CSR should focus on having laws that consider the activities of construction companies, finance and insurance, manufacturing, agricultural, chemical and allied industries. The excessive focus on the oil industry is short-sighted.

In 2009, distinguished senator Chukwumerije proposed a law to establish a CSR Commission in Nigeria. This law was amongst others aimed at compelling companies to contribute a specified percentage of their profit to a joint pool that will be used to develop host communities. The thinking was that this would reduce pressure on companies and make them focus on their business, whilst a specialised agency focuses on delivering CSR dividends on their behalf. The bill was vehemently opposed by businesses and therefore did not see the light of the day. One of the arguments put forward by the opponents of the proposed legislation was that there was already a similar law though targeted at the oil industry. This is the Niger Delta Development Commission Act 2000, which established the Niger Delta Development Commission (NDDC). It was also argued that although the oil companies contributed money to NDDC, the impact was not being felt since the NDDC has become an instrument for political patronage. Moreover, the oil companies alleged that they still experienced production disruption occasioned by perceived neglect. In other words, after contributing money to NDDC for the development of the communities, they still spent more money doing the same thing.

Recently in Nigeria, we held a series of consultations on the UN Guiding Principles on Human Rights and Business. One of the outcomes of the consultations was the push to domesticate the Guiding Principles in the form of legislation. Even after explaining that the intention of the Guiding Principles was not to make it into a hard law, the general mood was to enact it into a law. In the views of most participants, that was the only way to make it effective. This was interesting for me, because here was a group of people whose favourite past time complaint was the lack of will to enforce laws. I still could not understand the rationale and impetus for the push for a national legislation. More intriguing is the fact that the participants included people from government, business, civil society and community leaders.

My experience working in the CSR environment in the last twenty years, tells me that the issue may not be law after all. It is the process of conceptualising and initiating CSR initiatives. In my mind, the future of CSR does not lie in more laws but in more participatory processes. It also does not lie in how much corporations are committing to community development, but in how the development priorities are reached and agreed upon. Laws are mere guides to human behaviour but do not guarantee that human beings will necessarily behave better, even though law could act as a deterrent against bad behaviour.

Having said that, there is also the need to regulate and streamline expenditure, manage expectations, and ensure transparency and accountability within the CSR movement. This is where law could act as a guide. For instance, in recent research, it was found that many community members were more concerned with how oil companies arrived at the amount allocated to them for community development than the actual amount itself. In the future, laws could be made to develop criteria for the allocation of funds. Laws could also stipulate guidelines for the management of these funds. For instance, the Chevron Nigeria Global Memorandum of Understanding (GMOU) provides for a governance model for administering Chevron's contribution to community development in its areas of operation in Nigeria.

The development of this guidance by law should not be restricted to criteria for fund allocation. It could also be extended to such areas as employment, contracts and relationships with existing community governance structures. Laws could also be used to harmonise and coordinate community development efforts at the local level to achieve maximum impact. For instance, in the research that I referred to earlier, one missing piece was the lack of coordination between different development agencies at the local level. For instance, there were instances of project duplication. A law that will ensure that clusters of communities have a pool of funds for community development contributed by the various development agencies, including companies in the area, could be useful in streamlining and ensuring maximum impact.

One other area, which seems to not have received considerable attention, is when a community is fractionalised and companies find it difficult to identify leaders to engage. Over the years, companies have been accused of masterminding the fractionalisation. This is referred to as 'divide and rule'. The argument is that companies engage in activities that polarise communities with a view to distracting them from company activities. Whatever the case, in the future it might be necessary to have a law that creates community governance structures that will support development at the local level. For instance, in south-eastern Nigeria, the town development union is a strong institution but unfortunately, the lack of formalisation and institutionalisation have affected its performance especially as it relates to community development. The law will cover such issues as structure, tenure, succession, funding, discipline and election. Having a well-organised, recognisable and legitimate structure on the ground will help companies to relate better to their host, and to access and impact communities and even individuals.

Further, laws could also help in delineating the various stakeholders that a company may encounter and engage in a community. I am aware of the fact that the concept of stakeholder could be fluid and evolving, some form of legal guidance may be required to identify at least the more existing and stable ones with room for the incorporation of emerging new stakeholder groups. I make this point because the recognition of stakeholder groups in communities by companies has more often than not been left to the whims and caprices of company managers. Even though stakeholder theory suggests that more influential stakeholder groups be accorded more attention, other stakeholders no matter how less influential could also act as potential spoilers of corporate relations.

I also think that in the future, laws will prove more definitive in outlining community's role and participation in company activities, especially if we use a Phased Approach Model. For instance, when a company is coming into a community, what is the role of that community? In fact, the law of the future ought to do something about the issue of FPIC. For instance, if a community withholds its consent for a project, could that stop the project, or what is the process enunciated to get consent except through coercion? When a company has started operations what is expected of the community and when the company is leaving what is the role? Apart from outlining the roles of communities, the law will also do well to outline the roles of other stakeholders, such as government and development agencies. In the research to which I referred earlier, one recurring issue was the lack of clear allocation of roles and responsibilities in CSR initiatives.

Future laws that may deal with CSR issues may do well to institutionalise a consultation process. This is because community engagement or consultation is a much abused process. Business managers have also struggled with this issue. For instance, the law could specify the periods of consultation in which stakeholders shall be involved.

One of the most ignored issues in CSR is that of the capacity of personnel. For instance, in most oil companies, the function is managed by engineers. There is nothing wrong with this. However, what is wrong is the capacity of company personnel to "get it right". Community engagement, consultation and CSR are increasingly becoming complex and challenging. It could no longer be an all-comers affair. There is the need for a certain level of professionalism that should go into it. This professionalism calls for a certain level of certification as well. So a law that proposes the training and certification of personnel for the CSR function is long overdue. CSR is not the same as PR, it is not a personnel function and it is also not a legal affair. It calls for specialised training and the law may help in this regard. The essence of law in this regard is to specify appropriate training that will qualify personnel to carry out the function.

In 1997, Shell started a process of inspecting its community development projects. This was in response to criticisms that alleged community development projects were either non-existent or functional. The inspection team was made up of experts from the World Bank, UNDP and NGOs. In many instances, oil companies in Nigeria were accused of not executing projects, which they claimed to have executed. A neglected area, therefore, where the law could prove useful in CSR practice, would be the institutionalisation of a monitoring and evaluation mechanism for CSR initiatives.

## 3. Conclusion

Like most activities that focus on human relationship, CSR should move away from the either mentality of mandatory or voluntary initiatives. Voluntary and mandatory initiatives must complement each other. The reason why many commentators seem to favour mandatory provisions is the sanction and punishment embedded in law. This need not be so. Law ought to be aimed at correction not punishment. The future of CSR is rich and ripe for major legal intervention, this does not in any way minimise the need for voluntary measures.

# 5.9.

# Does CSR Need More (Effective) Private Regulation in the Future?

**Martijn W. Scheltema**[*]

One might expect a further increase in international private regulation in the area of CSR. However, the need for more private regulation is questionable. To date, a plethora of private regulation exists. Therefore, the effectiveness of private regulation in this area has to be assessed to distil the useful regimes. Assessing effectiveness requires an integrated approach involving legal, economic, sociological and psychological insights. Furthermore, research on hybrid systems and on the question in which cases public or private enforcement is effective, is required. As to conflict resolution and prevention, non-judicial mechanisms seem preferable. However, stakeholders experience difficulty in finding the proper ones. More research and a global facility are needed to assist stakeholders in this respect.

The future lawyer in this area has to acquire additional skills, for example on assessing effectiveness of international private regulation and its enforcement and on non-judicial dispute management and prevention mechanisms.

## 1. Introduction

In the Law of the Future Scenarios, four possibilities are discerned. One of them is the legal internet scenario in which international private regulation is predominant. International private regulation has a very broad meaning and encompasses many different private regulatory frameworks. International private regulation might be defined as a set of private norms which are established, sometimes in collaboration with others, by those who are bound by those rules, their representatives or an overarching body. The key actors in such regimes include civil society, (non-governmental organisations (NGOs)) and enterprises. Although private

[*] **Martijn W. Scheltema** is attorney at law with Pels Rijcken and Droogleever Fortuijn, The Hague, the Netherlands, and professor at Erasmus University Rotterdam, the Netherlands.

regulation has a self-binding effect in many instances, the implications thereof also affect third parties, in many cases even intentionally.

In the area of CSR, it seems probable that international private regulation will be predominant in the next decades, although legislation on some CSR issues might be promulgated in certain countries or regions, for example regarding reporting standards connected with CSR. Global understanding at the State or supranational level on the majority of CSR issues is not conceivable in the near future because ideas on what constitutes socially responsible business vary widely. For example, the obligations of countries under human rights treaties are felt in a different manner around the world, let alone the obligations to mitigate climate change and lessen the ecological footprint of business.

Therefore, CSR responsibilities are not entirely reflected in legal systems of States, a grey area exists between legal and normative standards and some responsibilities are considered to be purely social or ethical in some countries. This implicates that even if common understanding does exist to a certain extent, for example stemming from ILO conventions on child labour, forced labour and safety concerns in specific industries or treaties on industrial accidents and specific environmental issues such as oil pollution, this is not necessarily reflected in State or supranational legislation. Furthermore, differences in applicable legal norms might cause some host countries to lower their norms or to implement lower standards to be attractive for foreign investors. Besides, the enforcement of legislation, if it exists, is sometimes difficult, especially because CSR has an international reach. The responsibilities of a company in the area of CSR may go beyond its legal responsibility in a certain (host) country, although it might be held legally responsible for violations of certain CSR rules/standards in its home country. However, enforcement of these foreign judgments in the host State is rather difficult.

## 2. The Policy Implications in the Area of CSR

### 2.1. Increase in (International) Private Regulation?

To a certain extent, multinational enterprises are willing to self-regulate or adhere to international private regulation in the area of CSR, because of the responsibilities felt by these enterprises. For example, in order to create a level playing field and because it might be profitable to them, a level playing field between competitors is deemed necessary to prevent disad vantages for enterprises complying with CSR norms vis-à-vis those which do not. Besides this, some economic drivers exist for sustainable business, because economic research has revealed that it is profitable in the long run. Therefore, enterprises are more inclined to serve the public interest as reflected in CSR rules/standards, where the public interest used to be the prerogative of governments.

As multinational enterprises are more and more geared through tackling CSR-challenges and States by and large are not able or willing to regulate this area on a global level, it is not difficult to predict that international private regulation (the legal internet scenario) is (partly) going to bridge that regulatory gap.

However, international private regulation, such as the Global Compact or the OECD guidelines for multinational enterprises, is not always recognised as an effective instrument because of its rather voluntary nature. The presumption of its voluntary nature is questionable. It is contended that voluntarism with regard to CSR has long past. If a certain initiative is perceived by business as voluntary, this might be countered by NGO research and the market behaviour of citizens in the home county of a multinational enterprise, behaviour of politicians and lobby groups. The attenuation of voluntarism also is reflected by corporate governance, which entails the obligation to implement CSR policies in many countries. Hence, in the European Commission strategy on CSR of October 2011 the voluntary nature of CSR is abandoned.

The increase in private CSR initiatives implicates that private policymakers are becoming increasingly important. Indeed, many of them have taken their responsibility, with a plethora of sometimes rather ineffective international private initiatives as a consequence.

However, if effective private regulation is adopted, some States might eventually promulgate public regulation which partly reflects this private regulation. Private regulation, then, might become a standard which fills out open norms in State legislation. Hybrid systems of private regulation and public enforcement might originate. Furthermore, States might contribute to CSR in another way, for example through the UN and OECD as was done in the Global Compact and through the OECD guidelines for multinational enterprises, by funding advertisement of and research on effective private regulation in the area of CSR as well as by implementing CSR standards in their public procurement.

### 2.2. Policy Implications with Regard to Private Regulation

The policy implications of the further increase of international private regulation constitute a need for the reduction of the overwhelming amount of existing private regulation in the CSR area.

Less but more effective private regulation might be an important factor to reduce voluntarism in the area of CSR. Only effective regulation calls for effective and efficient implementation. The plethora of CSR labels causes difficulties in public procurement too. If a government or an enterprise prescribes a CSR label, applicants might contend that another label they adhere to is as good as the label prescribed. Governments or enterprises currently have no tools to assess this contention. Furthermore, international private regulation, especially when intended to create a level playing field between competitors, might cause market disruption. International private regulation should effectively meet the CSR policy requirements, while not unnecessarily disrupt markets. Effective private regulation might favour investments and might enhance trade if it is adhered to on a global level.

Governments used to be the main protector of the public interest. Private regulation must effectively equate this to be sustainable and a proper replacement for State legislation in this area. And last but not least, to date enterprises are unable to assess whether a certain initiative they adhere to is effective or whether they should implement yet another new CSR initiative. If effectiveness could be assessed, this might be a driver for enterprises to adhere to effective and efficient private regulation in the CSR area more so than they do to date and a tool for NGOs to assess whether enterprises really implement effective CSR rules.

International private regulation in the area of CSR also raises legitimacy issues. Unlike public regulation, virtually everybody might set private regulation. No instruments for control exist. If too much public regulation is enacted, democratic control mechanisms are able to reverse this: for example, by voting for other government functionaries. As far as private regulation is concerned, no or at least less democratic mechanisms for reversal of the plethora of initiatives exist. Clearly this gap has to be bridged as too much ineffective international private regulation exists in the area of CSR. Partly, this could be achieved by implementing mechanisms to enhance the legitimacy of private rule-making in the CSR area, for example by involving more stakeholders. However, as legitimate as public legislation is, private regulation is not going to be. The latter gap could be bridged partly by assessing the effectiveness of international private regulation. The more effective international private regulation is, for example in terms of economic benefits and sociological acceptance, the more reasons for its existence might be assessed. Therefore, a little less legitimacy in the traditional sense is not something to fear. In any case, legitimacy and public regulation are becoming less important on a global level, unlike for example social media, for the decision-making processes of enterprises.

The need for reversing the plethora of CSR initiatives for more uniformity in private rules/standards in this area and for assessing their effectiveness is clearly felt by many stakeholders.

### 2.3. Policy Implications with Regard to Enforcement and Dispute Resolution

Another challenge with regard to private CSR rules is the enforceability and effective conflict management and resolution. As far as the enforcement of private CSR rules is concerned, the traditional division between public and private enforcement will blur and more hybrid systems will originate. In some instances, private enforcement might be effective: for example if a private rule setting body controls market access, the threat of reputational damage exists; or NGOs, consumers or investors direct an enterprise at complying with certain rules. Certification might also play a role in this respect. In other instances public enforcement is desirable, for example if agreements are concluded or a foreign direct liability claim is honoured. Furthermore, public enforcement seems indispensable if the chance of detection of non-compliance is low. The mix of public and private enforcement seems especially feasible if open norms in public regulation might be filled out by international private regulation in the area of CSR. For example an open norm in public tort law might be filled out by international private regulation and might result in a foreign direct liability claim against (the parent enterprise of) an enterprise in its home country. If the claim is honoured, public enforcement against (the parent enterprise of) this enterprise in its home country is feasible.

Comparable public enforcement might be invoked with regard to contractual agreements and non-judicial settlements if not complied with. However, the possibility of filling out public open norms depends on the effectiveness and clarity of the international private regulation referred to. The less effective and clear these rules are, the fewer the possibilities exist to make use of them in order to fill out open norms. Only if such private norms impose clear duties on an enterprise, which effective private regulation does, it is feasible to make use of them. As international private regulation on CSR becomes clearer in this respect, the stick of, for example, foreign direct liability will be more threatening and encourage enterprises and their subsidiaries to take reasonable care. Therefore, from this point of view the effectiveness of international private regulation has to be assessed too.

As to conflict resolution in the human rights field, in the third pillar of his framework, Ruggie emphasizes the need to improve the patchwork of current non-judicial mechanisms. He and others in his research team have demonstrated that litigation is rather ineffective, for example because applicable legal norms are unclear, because of jurisdictional issues and because it might encompass parallel litigation in many jurisdictions. Litigation in many national courts has adverse effects: for example, it is slow, costly, not always predictable, and it might cause legal uncertainty. Apart from jurisdictional issues, it might entail litigation and enforcement in several countries, the difficult process of assessing applicable norms if possible at all and difficulties in gathering sufficient evidence.

It is not only in the area of human rights that litigation in national courts might be unproductive. The same may be true also in other CSR areas, for example in connection with the environment. Different environmental challenges exist in different countries, public rules differ, different stakeholders are involved in different industries and no global public supervisor exists.

Therefore enterprises have to be geared towards non-judicial dispute resolution and prevention mechanisms to resolve CSR issues, for example regarding the compliance with international private regulation in this area, instead of instigating or taking part in parallel litigation in several jurisdictions. Governments should advocate non-judicial dispute resolution and prevention mechanisms and assist in improving the current patchwork of non-judicial mechanisms in this area. Of importance in this respect is to assist enterprises, representatives of local communities, NGOs and other international bodies, like the World Bank, to find their way through the existing non-judicial mechanisms. Currently many stakeholders experience difficulty in finding the effective, legitimate, transparent and rights-compatible mechanisms. A global facility has to be established in order to provide such guidance to stakeholders because otherwise proper use of non-judicial mechanisms by stakeholders stays remote. Such a facility should provide information on available non-judicial mechanisms and a kind of "roadmap" to assist stakeholders in finding the proper mechanisms in a particular case. Furthermore, it should promote the use of such mechanisms, for example by compiling experiences of stakeholders which have made use of these mechanisms.

## 3. What We Do Know and What We Should Learn About

A lot is written on CSR cases, the binding or voluntary nature of existing public and private regulation in this area, and on conflict resolution and prevention. More and more software tools are being developed to measure the sustainability of business, notably on the environmental impact and the ecological footprint of enterprises; however, less so on labour standards, and there is little on human rights. Furthermore, enterprises are challenged to reveal their impact in the area of CSR, for example through the Global Reporting Initiative (GRI). So we do know a lot of CSR. Still, especially regarding the policy issues described hereinabove, additional research is needed.

As has been discussed before, it is necessary to assess the effectiveness of international private regulation and of dispute resolution and prevention mechanisms in this area from different perspectives. This might be achieved by finding ex ante indicators to assist private rule-makers in setting effective regulation and ex post measurement tools to assess the effectiveness of currently existing private regulation.

The ex ante indicators should stem from legal, economical, sociological and psychological insights. The legal insights mainly deal with the effectiveness of enforcement and conflict resolution. The economical insights refer to the efficiency of private regulation in terms of the increase of profit of enterprises set off against the negative external effects of their activities. The sociological insights deal with the acceptance of private regulation by those governed and affected by it. The psychological perspective is connected with the human decision-making process.

The ex post approach should mainly use the aforementioned legal, economical and sociological insights. It has to be assessed whether all these insights might be used in practice. In that respect it is important that the figures needed, especially in connection with the ex post approach, can be derived from public sources in order to enable enterprises, researchers, governments and NGO's to make use of these figures in order to assess the effectiveness of certain mechanisms. The call for transparency, advertised by, amongst others, the GRI, might support this. An integrated approach using all of the mentioned disciplines is necessary, because using them separately causes incorrect results.

However, in connection with the ex post measurement tools, the question arises whether retrieving figures, as are currently available on environmental footprint and labour standards, is feasible with regard to human rights. Additional research is needed to assess this. In this respect, the problem of sometimes unclear relationships between multinational enterprises and suppliers (in many instances not subsidiaries) and the lacking possibilities to make suppliers adhere to certain international private regulation in the CSR area have to be solved. Research is also needed as to the question of whether public regulation is more effective than private regulation in certain areas of CSR. Linked to this issue is the competition issue stemming from private regulation, especially private regulation aiming at a level playing field. This might necessitate at least some public regulation to prevent unnecessary market disruption. Beside this, it might be helpful to assess whether, and if so which, public legislation currently applied to governmental behaviour and processes might also control business behaviour and processes. As has been said, CSR rules are connected with the public interest and used to be dealt with by governments. Therefore, it would not be surprising if some of the rules with regard to governmental behaviour and processes could be of assistance to regulate business behaviour and processes. Furthermore, research is needed to assess to what extent public enforcement mechanisms are still required, and if so, which ones. Finally, it has to be assessed whether effectiveness might partly be used as a substitute for legitimacy.

As to conflict resolution we know the basic requirements of non-judicial mechanisms in the area of human rights. We are aware of the many current mechanisms and facilitators on a local level in the CSR area too. However, multinational enterprises and large international institutions like the World Bank often are unable to find them. Research has to be done in order to assist these stakeholders to navigate through the landscape and to find effective mechanisms.

## 4. The Lawyer of the Future in the Area of CSR

The lawyer of the future in the area of CSR has to acquire additional skills. To date, public regulation is mainly a fact for lawyers outside the government, and they do not participate (directly) in the rule-making process. International private regulation might change this. Lawyers outside the government might become rule-makers and could advise enterprises on which private regulatory regime to implement. Therefore they need to get acquainted with assessing the effectiveness of such regulation ex ante when advising on setting such regulation and ex post when advising on implementation of existing private regulation. Its binding force is not self-explanatory as is the case with government regulation. As private regulatory regimes in the area of CSR are mainly international or global, the classic distinction between national and supranational law and treaties becomes less prominent. They become truly international lawyers in the area of CSR. The CSR norms by and large stem from the public interest, and public law knowledge on corporate law does not suffice. One needs thorough knowledge of public law as well, not only on public substantive norms but also on public stakeholder engagement rules.

As non-judicial dispute resolution and prevention becomes more important in the area of CSR, lawyers need to acquire new skills in non-judicial conflict resolution and prevention. These skills are not (very) familiar to many of them. The classic litigation and arbitration skills are not sufficient. For example, discussions on jurisdiction, substantive norms and the enforcement of arbitral awards might become less important. Instead, a long lasting collaboration agreement between a multinational enterprise, its subsidiary or supplier, and, for example, affected local communities might prove more effective. Furthermore, lawyers do not only need knowledge on domestic court systems and international arbitration facilities, but must be able to navigate through all kinds of non-judicial international dispute resolution mechanisms in order to use them effectively and to give proper advice on them.

## 5. Conclusion

One might expect an increase in international private regulation in the area of CSR. However, the need for more private regulation is questionable. To date a plethora of private regulation exists. Therefore, the effectiveness of private regulation in this area has to be assessed to distil the useful regimes. Assessing effectiveness is far from easy and requires an integrated approach involving legal, economic, sociological and psychological insights. More research is needed in this respect.

Furthermore, more enforcement of private regulation as well as conflict resolution and prevention is tempting. As to enforcement, research is required on hybrid systems and on the question as to in which cases public or private enforcement is effective. As to conflict resolution and prevention, non-judicial mechanisms seem preferable, especially if local communities are affected. Many of such mechanisms already exist. However, stakeholders experience difficulty in finding the proper ones. More research and a global facility are needed to assist stakeholders in this respect.

The future lawyer in this area has, apart from his current skills, to acquire rule setting skills and knowledge on public legislation in general, on assessing the effectiveness of international private regulation and its enforcement, on finding proper non-judicial dispute management and prevention mechanisms as well as experience with those mechanisms.

## 6. Sources and Further Reading

Backer, Larry Cata, "Inter-Systemic Harmonisation and Its Challenges for the Legal State", in Sam Muller *et al.* (eds.), *The Law of the Future and the Future of Law*, Torkel Opsahl, Oslo, 2011, pp. 427–437.

Eccles, Robert *et al.*, "The Impact of Corporate Culture of Sustainability on Corporate Behaviour and Performance", Working Paper 12-035, 25 November 2011, available at www.hbs.edu/research/pdf/12-035.pdf, last accessed on 6 August 2012.

Eijsbouts, Jan, Corporate Responsibility, *Beyond Voluntarism*, Inaugural lecture Maastricht, Maastricht, 2011.

Eijsbouts, Jan, "International Market Regulation, Corporate Governance, CSR and Multinationals", in Sam Muller *et al.* (eds.), *The Law of the Future and the Future of Law*, Torkel Opsahl, Oslo 2011, pp. 295–303.

Enneking, Liesbeth, *Foreign Direct Liability and Beyond*, Eleven, Den Haag, 2012.

Hohnen, Paul, "Overview of Selected Initiatives and Instruments to Corporate Social Responsibility", in *Employment and Industrial Relations*, Annual Report on the OECD Guidelines for Multinational Enterprises 2008, 2009, OECD, pp. 235–260.

Kovick, David and Rees, Caroline, "International Support for Effective Dispute Resolution Between Companies and Their Stakeholders: Assessing Needs, Interests, and Models, Corporate Social Responsibility Initiative", Working Paper No. 63, John F. Kennedy School of Government, Harvard University, available at www.hks.harvard.edu/m-rcbg/CSRI/publications/workingpaper_63_rees%20kovick_june%202011.pdf, last accessed on 6 August 2012.

Lambooy, Tineke, *Corporate Social Responsibility*, Kluwer, Deventer, 2010.

Porter, Michael *et al.*, "Creating Shared Value", in *Harvard Business Review*, 2011, pp. 3–17.

Renda, Andrea, *Law and Economics in the RIA World*, Rotterdam, 2011.

Scheltema, Martijn, Effectiveness of Private Regulation: Can It Be Measured?, Inaugural lecture Rotterdam 2012 (in Dutch), Boom, Den Haag, 2012.

Scott, Colin, Cafaggi, Fabrizio and Senden, Linda (eds.), *The Challenge of Transnational Private Regulation: Conceptual and Constitutional Debates*, Wiley Blackwell, Cardiff, 2011.

Smits, Jan, "Private Law in a Postnational Society", in Sam Muller *et al.* (eds.), *The Law of the Future and the Future of Law*, Torkel Opsahl, Oslo, 2011, pp. 245–248.

Thaler, Richard and Sunstein, Cass, *Nudge*, Yale University Press, New Haven, 2008.

"Communication from the Commission on a Renewed EU Strategy 2011-14 for Corporate Social Responsibility of October 25 2011, COM (2011) 681", available at ec.europa.eu/enterprise/policies/sustainable-business/files/csr/new-csr/act_en.pdf, last accessed on 6 August 2012.

Global Compact Network Netherlands, *How to Do Business with Respect for Human Rights*, 2010.

"The UN 'Protect, Respect and Remedy' Framework of John Ruggie", available at www.business-humanrights.org/SpecialRepPortal/Home/Protect-Respect-Remedy-Framework and www.baseswiki.org, last accessed on 6 August 2012.

# 5.10.

# Collective Redress in the Cross-Border Context: Litigation, Arbitration, Settlement and Beyond

**S.I. Strong***

Globalisation has broken down numerous physical, social, economic and cultural barriers. However, one boundary that still remains involves legal barriers. Despite the creation of a single global marketplace, most types of legal injuries are compensatable only in national courts constrained by territorial boundaries. This is true even in the increasing number of cases involving large-scale injuries in the cross-border context. Rather than resolving the dispute at one time, in one forum, defendants are forced to proceed simultaneously in several different jurisdictions, with all the costs and risks associated with parallel litigation, while plaintiffs who are similarly situated in all other regards often hold different legal rights and remedies simply by virtue of their place of residence. This situation seems neither fair nor desirable. This essay considers whether any alternatives to litigation exist and whether any of these other options offer a superior means of addressing injuries of this nature.

## 1. Genesis of a Modern Legal Crisis

Globalisation has been a watchword for some time now, and it seems somewhat passé to speak of its impact on law and society. However, the creation and expansion of a global economy continues to inspire new challenges and new solutions in equal measure. This is nowhere more true than in law, which is seeing the need for and creation of a truly twenty-first century phenomenon: cross-border collective redress.

The cross-border element is easily understood: as providers of goods and services expand from a local into an international market, through either physical or virtual means, international legal injuries be-

* **S.I. Strong** is Senior Fellow at the Center for the Study of Dispute Resolution and Associate Professor of Law at the University of Missouri.

come more common. The second element – mass claims – is more subtle, but equally important: as markets open up, providers take advantage of the economies of scale and provide goods and services on a magnitude not previously possible. Thus, large-scale, international injuries are becoming increasingly common. Furthermore, the types of disputes that can arise are extremely diverse, including a wide variety of subject matter areas such as consumer law, company law, labour and employment law, anti-trust/competition law, tort law, commercial law and internet law.

Given the reality of these kinds of injuries, the question is how society – or, better said, societies – should respond. Cross-border regulation in the form of international treaties is one alternative, though the need to establish international consensus and then create a system that provides an adequate system of accountability means that the process is very slow. Furthermore, political obstacles can prove fatal at any stage of the process. Private means of redress may therefore be the best alternative, either to supplement public means of relief that are already in existence or to create some form of compensation while States are working to create other types of remedies. Several types of private action are possible.

## 2. Litigation

The most well-known type of private relief for large-scale legal harm is litigation. For years, only one nation – the United States – offered a procedural mechanism that allowed a large number of individuals to band together and assert a legal claim at a single time, in a single court. Although the class action has been severely criticised both at home and abroad, it has nevertheless inspired law-makers outside the United States to consider whether and to what extent private forms of mass relief should be allowed in their jurisdictions. At this point, over thirty civil and common law countries have adopted various forms of class and collective relief for use in domestic disputes, with other jurisdictions considering whether and to what extent to do the same. Some of these procedures resemble the US class action in certain regards, whereas other actions are entirely new.

The problem is that many of these newly developed devices have been designed primarily, if not exclusively, for use in domestic disputes. Although various States and regional bodies have attempted to find ways of establishing acceptable cross-border procedures, significant difficulties arise whenever parties reside in different jurisdictions. Some of these problems involve procedures that are acceptable in one State but objec tionable in another as a matter of fundamental or constitutional law. This issue is most commonly seen whenever US or Canadian courts attempt to create so-called "global" (meaning international) class actions. Both the United States and Canada use a form of mass relief that designates certain plaintiffs as part of the class unless they indicate otherwise by opting out. This can cause problems if some plaintiffs reside in a country that prohibits opt-out actions as a matter of public policy or constitutional law.

However, difficulties can arise even when opt-out systems are not used. For example, the European Union has recently announced its intention to create a coherent approach to cross-border collective relief based on an opt-in procedure. Although the EU has avoided certain policy issues relating to opt-out procedures, other problems arise as a result of conflicts between the parties' individual participatory rights and the primary means of establishing jurisdiction and enforcement in inter-European disputes, Council Regulation 44/2001 on jurisdiction and on recognition and enforcement of civil and commercial judgments, commonly known as the Brussels I Regulation.

These and other problems suggest that large-scale judicial actions may not be the best means of addressing cross-border collective injuries. Instead, other alternatives may be both possible and preferable.

## 3. Alternatives to Litigation

Alternative dispute resolution (ADR) is a major part of many legal systems. While ADR is most commonly used in bilateral disputes to supplement judicial means of dispute resolution, some of the mechanisms may be equally valuable in the realm of cross-border collective injuries. Two major forms of ADR, arbitration and mediation, are discussed below.

### 3.1. Arbitration Alternatives to Litigation

#### 3.1.1. Comparing Large-Scale Arbitration and Large-Acale Litigation

Arbitration is often seen as a speedy, low-cost means of resolving small-value disputes in an informal setting. As such, it is often associated with consumer or employment controversies. However, arbitration exists in many forms, and arbitration of class and collective disputes, particularly in the cross-border context, is more likely to resemble international commercial arbitration: a highly respected and often extremely formal means of resolving large, complex, high-value claims.

Class arbitration has been available in the United States since the 1980s, although the device has recently faced a variety of types of legal challenges focusing primarily on the circumstances in which class arbitration can arise. Interestingly, most of the resistance to class arbitration is the result of the unique way in which the device arose. Rather than being developed as a preferred alternative to litigation, as was the case with arbitration of bilateral disputes, class arbitration in the United States developed somewhat by mistake, at least in the eyes of corporate defendants who thought that the use of arbitration agreements in consumer, employment and similar contracts would eliminate the possibility of all forms of class relief. Since class relief provides a necessary compensatory and regulatory function in the US legal system, courts developed class arbitration as a means of giving effect to both the parties' clear desire to arbitrate and the need for a collective mechanism in certain circumstances.

As a result of this historical accident, very little research has been conducted regarding the relative benefits of class action and class arbitration. However, those analysts who have considered the matter have concluded that class arbitration may be better for the parties than class litigation for four reasons.

First, arbitration eliminates many of the problems that litigation experiences with jurisdiction over international parties, since arbitration is based on the concept of consent. Consent can arise in the context of a pre-existing contractual relationship or as the result of a post-dispute submission agreement (*compromis*). Though the latter scenario was long believed to be impossible, an international investment tribunal recently demonstrated precisely how a post-dispute arbitration agreement can be established with thousands of individual claimants.[1]

Furthermore, although there is some debate about the legitimacy and scope of certain waivers of class proceedings that can accompany pre-dispute arbitration agreements in the United States, a growing number of court cases have refused to enforce these provisions, even after the United

1 See ICSID Case *Abaclat (formerly Beccara) v. Argentine Republic*, Decision on Jurisdiction and Admissibility, Majority Opinion, 4 August 2011, No. ARB/07/5.

States Supreme Court suggested that some such waivers could withstand judicial scrutiny.[2]

Second, arbitration provides significant procedural advantages to the parties. Not only can arbitration harmonise conflicting national procedures (indeed, international commercial arbitration is well known for successfully blending common law and civil law processes), it can also provide a tailor-made mechanism specially designed for the dispute at hand. Additionally, arbitration allows parties to choose impartial and independent decision-makers who are free from national biases and who have significant expertise with the type of dispute at issue, thus taking the dispute away from juries (in the United States) or judges who may be prejudiced against foreign parties or who may not have either the technical expertise or the practical resources to deal with a large-scale, international dispute. Arbitration of mass disputes is also faster than litigation of similar disputes, since the parties do not need to wait for court dates, nor are they subject to the same kind of lengthy judicial appeals, extensive motion practice or burdensome discovery processes that mark litigation.

Third, arbitration offers parties a much easier and more predictable means of enforcing the outcome of the dispute resolution process, since the enforcement of foreign arbitral awards is governed by treaty rather than by international comity, as is the case with the enforcement of foreign judgments. Indeed, the United Nations Convention on the Recognition and Enforcement of Foreign Arbitral Awards, more commonly known as the New York Convention, is the most successful commercial treaty in the world, with 147 State Parties.

Fourth, arbitration may avoid certain conflict of laws problems relating to statutes that ostensibly provide for exclusive jurisdiction over disputes involving certain types of vulnerable parties. These statutes may prohibit foreign forum selection clauses, although some judges have been willing to uphold arbitration agreements in identical circumstances, suggesting that arbitration is the only way in which the parties can consent to resolve their disputes in a single time, in a single forum.

These four factors relate to certain tactical and legal advantages that international arbitration holds over international litigation of mass claims. However, arbitration offers another, more practical benefit, and that is

2 See Supreme Court of United States, *AT&T Mobility LLC v. Concepcion*, 1740, 131 S.Ct. 27 April 2011.

timeliness, meaning that parties can begin to resolve their disputes in this fashion immediately, without waiting for any sort of State action.

This is not to say that public officials are unable or unwilling to act. To the contrary, efforts to facilitate cross-border litigation in cases involving collective harm have already been undertaken by both the European Union and the Organisation for Economic Co-operation and Development (OECD). Relevant policy papers and practice proposals have also been compiled by organisations such as the American Bar Association (ABA), the American Law Institute (ALI), the Canadian Bar Association (CBA) and the International Bar Association (IBA). However, any form of official action is years away, and many parties simply cannot wait that long.

### 3.1.2. Developing and Facilitating Large-Scale Arbitration

Once arbitration is determined to be either a viable alternative to litigation or – as suggested here – a superior means of resolving cross-border collective claims, it then becomes necessary to find ways of developing and facilitating large-scale arbitration. Several alternatives exist.

First, the legal community can and should work to develop appropriate rules of procedure relating to international class and collective disputes, building on existing efforts reflected in the American Arbitration Association's (AAA) Supplementary Rules for Class Arbitrations, the JAMS Class Action Procedures, and the German Institution of Arbitration (Deutsche Institution für Schiedsgerichtsbarkeit or DIS) Supplementary Rules for Corporate Law Disputes. Additional insights can be gained from mass procedures adopted in arbitrations proceeding under the auspices of the International Convention on the Settlement of Investment Disputes (ICSID).[3]

However, while parties can agree to mass arbitration under existing rules on class and collective arbitration or under many of the general rule sets published by reputable arbitral institutions such as the International Chamber of Commerce (ICC), the International Centre for Dispute Resolution (ICDR) and the London Court of International Arbitration (LCIA), there are significant benefits associated with creating a model procedural framework that is not tied to a single national system, as the AAA and JAMS class arbitration rules are. For example, arbitrations that adopt a pre-existing set of cross-cultural rules appropriate for mass disputes will

[3] See *Abaclat v. Argentine Republic*, see *supra* note 1.

likely enjoy increased predictability, a higher degree of procedural fairness and lower transactional costs, since the parties will not have to create their procedures on an ad hoc basis.

Second, the international community would do well to create a roster of expert arbitrators who are qualified to serve on tribunals handling mass disputes. To some extent, reputable persons are already well known within the international arbitral community, either informally or through the rosters of the various arbitral institutions, but not everyone has the same amount of knowledge about who constitutes an expert arbitrator. Furthermore, some of these lists are only available in administered arbitrations. Therefore, a single repository of information on competent arbitrators would be welcome.

Third, the international legal community should consider whether it would be worthwhile to establish a neutral international body to help administer these types of proceedings. Although a new institution could be created, such services might also be rendered by the Permanent Court of Arbitration (PCA). Not only does the PCA have the respect of the world community, it has administrative mechanisms already in place to help parties deal with the task of coordinating a large-scale international action. There are some drawbacks to this approach, most notably with respect for the need for some form of State action to bring the dispute within the competence of the PCA. However, the PCA has experience in creating and administering a variety of mass claims processes, and thus could provide useful insights into how to devise a new form of collective redress that would resolve all or part of the claims, such as those concerning liability, in a single proceeding.

### 3.2. Mediation

While arbitration is already well established as a means of addressing collective legal injury, it is not the only alternative to litigation. Indeed, mediation has been receiving a great deal of attention in recent years as a way of resolving domestic and international disputes of all shapes and sizes, with the European Union recently passing a directive concerning the use of mediation in cross-border matters involving civil and commercial concerns.[4] This suggests a third method of resolving cross-border class and collective disputes that is based on consensus rather than adjudication.

Traditionally, mediation has been very attractive in certain types of circumstances, such as when parties wish to preserve an on-going relationship. Mediation has also been seen as a useful alternative to international commercial arbitration, which is increasingly viewed as a somewhat expensive means of obtaining relief.

At this point, mediation is a somewhat untested prospect. There is very little data on how successful mediation is in resolving international disputes, let alone large-scale international disputes. Furthermore, there are no models currently in place that might suggest how the parties to a large-scale mediation might be represented and what protocols, if any, should be put in place to protect against any procedural unfairness or collusion on the part of counsel or certain subgroups within the class or collective.

This is not to say that mediation may not be a viable means of resolving mass disputes. Indeed, the experience in the United States has been that most class actions are settled prior to trial, suggesting that many parties to large-scale legal actions prefer settlement to an adjudicated outcome. Ground-breaking innovations are always possible, as seen by the Dutch Collective Settlements Act 2005, which allows parties to an international dispute to create a class or collective for settlement purposes only.

## 4. Looking Beyond Traditional Models

Globalisation has both its positive and negative effects. While on the one hand it has opened the doors to international trade and increased opportunities for both businesses and consumers, it has also created an environment where far-flung and widespread legal injuries can arise. Fortunately, the ability to cause this type of harm is currently matched by an ability and inclination for providing legally sanctioned redress to address those wrongs.

4 See Directive 2008/52/EC of the European Parliament and of the Council of 21 May 2008 on certain aspects of mediation in civil and commercial matters [2008] OJ L 136/3.

As society considers the various means of resolving cross-border collective disputes, it will have to think beyond conventional boundaries, since the types of injuries that are now being suffered are in many ways unlike any that have come before. Public and private actors need to work together to find the best means of addressing these harms, both through litigation and through alternative dispute resolution mechanisms such as arbitration and mediation. New processes can and should also be considered. Critically, there may not be one single method of dispute resolution that works in all situations. Parties should instead be able to move freely between the different options, just as they do in bilateral disputes, so as to take advantage of the procedure that best suits their needs. In providing a number of reputable and reliable alternatives, the legal community serves both the parties and society at large.

## 5. Sources and Further Reading

Born, Gary B., *International Commercial Arbitration*, Kluwer Law International, 2009.

Born, Gary B. and Rutledge, Peter B., *International Civil Litigation in United States Courts*, Aspen Publishers, 2007.

Buckner, Carole J., "Toward a Pure Arbitral Paradigm of Classwide Arbitration: Arbitral Power and Federal Preemption", in *Denver University Law Review*, 2004, vol. 82, no. 301.

Buckner, Carole J., "Due Process in Class Arbitration", in *Florida Law Review*, 2006, vol. 58, no. 185.

Burch, Elizabeth Chamblee, "Securities Class Actions as Pragmatic Ex Post Regulation", in *Georgia Law Review*, 2009, vol. 43, no. 63.

Burch, Elizabeth Chamblee, "Litigating Groups", in *Alabama Law Review*, 2008, vol. 61, no. 1.

Gaillard, Emmanuel and Savage, John (eds.), *Fouchard, Gaillard, Goldman on International Commercial Arbitration*, Kluwer Law International, 1998.

Hensler, Deborah R., *Class Action Dilemmas: Pursuing Public Goals for Private Gain*, Rand, 2000.

Hensler, Deborah R. et al. (eds.), *The Annals of the American Academy of Political and Social Science*, 2009, vol. 622.

Monestier, Tanya J., "Personal Jurisdiction Over Non-Resident Class Members: Have We Gone Down the Wrong Road?", in *Texas International Law Journal*, 2010, vol. 45, no. 537.

Mulheron, Rachel, *The Class Action in Common Law Legal Systems: A Comparative Perspective*, Hart Publishing, 2004.

Mulheron, Rachel, "The Recognition, and Res Judicata Effect, of a United States Class Actions Judgment in England: A Rebuttal of Vivendi", in *Modern Law Review*, 2012, vol. 75, no. 180.

Nagareda, Richard A., *Mass Torts in a World of Settlement*, University of Chicago Press, 2007.

Nagareda, Richard A., "Aggregate Litigation across the Atlantic and the Future of American Exceptionalism", in *Vanderbilt Law Review*, 2009, vol. 62, no. 1.

Smit, Hans, "Class Actions and Their Waiver in Arbitration", in *American Review of International Law*, 2004, vol. 15, no. 199.

Strong, S.I., *Class, Mass and Collective Arbitration Under National and International Law*, Oxford University Press, 2013 (forthcoming).

Strong, S.I., "Mass Torts and Arbitration: Lessons From Abaclat v. Argentine Republic", in *Uncertainty and Mass Tort: Causation and Proof*, Universitat de Girona, Spain, 2012 (forthcoming).

Strong, S.I., "Cross-Border Collective Redress in the European Union: Constitutional Rights in the Face of the Brussels I Regulation", in *Arizona State Law Journal*, 2012 (forthcoming), vol. 45.

Strong, S.I., "Does Class Arbitration 'Change the Nature' of Arbitration? Stolt-Nielsen, AT&T and a Return to First Principles", in *Harvard Negotiation Law Review*, 2012, vol. 17.

Strong, S.I., "Resolving Mass Legal Disputes Through Class Arbitration: The United States and Canada Compared", in *North Carolina Journal of International Law and Commercial Regulation*, 2012, vol. 37.

Strong, S.I., "Class and Collective Relief in the Cross-Border Context: A Possible Role for the Permanent Court of Arbitration", in *The Hague Yearbook of International Law 2010*, 2011, vol. 23, no. 113.

Strong, S.I., "From Class to Collective: The De-Americanization of Class Arbitration", in *Arbitration International*, 2010, vol. 26, no. 493.

Strong, S.I., "The Sounds of Silence: Are U.S. Arbitrators Creating Internationally Enforceable Awards When Ordering Class Arbitration in Cases of Contractual Silence or Ambiguity?", in *Michigan Journal of International Law*, 2009, vol. 30, no. 1017.

Strong, S.I., "Enforcing Class Arbitration in the International Sphere: Due Process and Public Policy Concerns", in *University of Pennsylvania Journal of International Law*, 2008, vol. 30, no. 1.

Wasserman, Rhonda, "Transnational Class Actions and Interjurisdictional Preclusion", in *Notre Dame Law Review*, 2011, vol. 86, no. 313.

Weston, Maureen, "Universes Colliding: The Constitutional Implications of Arbitral Class Actions", in *William and Mary Law Review*, 2006, vol. 47, no. 1711.

Willging, Thomas E. *et al.*, "An Empirical Analysis of Rule 23 to Address the Rulemaking Challenges", in *New York University Law Review*, 1996, vol. 71, no 74.

Willging, Thomas E. and Lee, Emery G., III, "From Class Actions to Multidistrict Consolidations: Aggregate Mass-Tort Litigation After Ortiz", in *University of Kansas Law Review*, 2010, no.58, 775.

**Official Papers**

European Commission (EC), Public Consultation: Towards a Coherent European Approach to Collective Redress, SEC(173) 2011.

European Parliament, Resolution of 2 February 2012 on "Towards a Coherent European Approach to Collective Redress", P7TA, 0021, 2012.

**Working Paper and Arbitral Rules**

American Arbitration Association (AAA), Supplementary Rules for Class Arbitrations, 2003.

American Bar Association (ABA), Protocol on Court-to-Court Communications in Canada-U.S. Cross-Border Class Actions and Notice Protocol: Coordinating Notice(s) to the Class(es) in Multijurisdictional Class Proceedings, 2011.

American Law Institute (ALI), Guidelines Applicable to Court-to-Court Communications in Cross-Border Cases, 2001.

American Law Institute (ALI), Principles of the Law of Aggregate Litigation, 2010.

Canadian Bar Association (CBA), Consultation Paper: Canadian Judicial Protocol for the Management of Multijurisdictional Class Actions 6–7, 2011.

Deutsche Institution für Schiedsgerichtsbarkeit (DIS) Supplementary Rules for Corporate Law Disputes, 2009.

"Global Class Actions Exchange", available at http://globalclassactions.stanford.edu/, last accessed on 20 August 2012.

International Bar Association (IBA), Guidelines for Recognising and Enforcing Foreign Judgments for Collective Redress, 2008.

JAMS Class Action Procedures, 2009.

Organization for Economic Co-operation and Development (OECD), Recommendation on Consumer Dispute Resolution and Redress, 2007.

# CHAPTER VI

## THE PERSPECTIVE OF LAW IN ITS CONTEXT:

## LAW AS A CONCEPT WITH A PAST, A PRESENT, AND A FUTURE?

# 6.1.

# Obstructing Law's Future with Conceptions from Its Past

**Edward Rubin**[*]

The law of the future has already arrived, but it still strikes us as a disconcerting potentiality because our concept of law is tied to the legal system that modernity has displaced. This system regarded law as a set of rules governing human behaviour that were promulgated in definitive form. The law that has already arrived, and will dominate our foreseeable future, will be concerned with producing real world results, rather than specifying decision-making procedures, it will be tailored to particular situations rather than being stated in general terms, and it will be seen as a means of administrative supervision, rather than a declaration of general principles.

## 1. Introduction

Law is an instrumentality of governance. We cannot say anything about the law of a particular society until we have described its government. Any similarity among the laws of different societies is a purely empirical matter, an observed relationship that exists primarily in the mind of the observer or as a result of specific cultural contacts, and not as either a pragmatic necessity or a moral obligation. To be sure, most societies have forms of governance that can be reasonably described as law, but that is just one of the many commonalities that human societies share. It is hardly surprising that these parallel systems possess homologous structures, and that an observer can usefully describe these structures with a single term and compare their purposes and features. That does not mean, however, that any of these aspects of society, including law, has any overarching, trans-cultural reality.

The future of law in Western society thus depends on the future of its governance structures. Those structures underwent a fundamental and momentous change during the eighteenth and nineteenth centuries – the advent of the administrative State. In an earlier work, *Beyond Camelot:*

* **Edward Rubin** is Professor of Law and Political Science at Vanderbilt University.

*Rethinking Politics and Law for the Modern World*, I argue that this change can be dated to the half-century between 1775 and 1825, but the precise chronology in not important for present purposes. All that need be established is that such a change occurred sometime between the end of the Middle Ages – when our traditional ideas of law were formulated – and the contemporary era. The further point, which is necessary for any consideration of future law, is that this transformation will not be reversed.

This essay will attempt to describe the future of our legal system by focusing on this transformation of governance that occurred with the advent of modernity in the late Eighteenth century. Pre-modern Europeans would have rejected all the statements about law that appeared in the preceding paragraphs. They conceived of law as a universal principle, applicable to all societies, from which the provisions specific to each particular society could be derived. This conception of law, like all conceptions of law, was an instrumentality of the governance systems that prevailed in pre-modern Europe. In order for us – as heirs to that society and that conception – to perceive the nature of contemporary law and predict its future contours, we must understand that this pre-modern conception is not the eternal verity as it claims to be, but a specific ideology that emerged from and functioned within the systems of governance that prevailed in pre-modern Europe, which no longer exist.

## 2. The Pre-Modern Concept of Law

One well-known aspect of the medieval thought, which contributed to the concept of law as a universal principle, was natural law. Inherited from the Romans and reinterpreted as an element of Christianity, the doctrine held that general rules regarding human relations were established by God, and thus obligatory. As elaborated by St. Thomas Aquinas in his *Summa Theologica,* natural law is an application of eternal law to human relations, which is promulgated (all law must be promulgated to be effective in Aquinas' view) by God through the medium of human reason. Since humans are, in their essence, rational creatures, the eternal law is present in every human through this natural law, even if they person does not know Christ, and all people are bound by it. Natural law does not determine all aspects of the legal system – Aquinas believed most law was a purely human creation. To be valid, however, human law must be consistent with natural law and must be directed toward the common good.

Secular beliefs arising from the theory and practice of governance were equally important factors in determining the pre-modern West's concept of law. During the late Roman Empire and the Early Middle Ages, the effectiveness of central government in Western Europe steadily declined. Tenth century Western Europe consisted of a welter of small principalities presided over by semi-autonomous and perennially truculent landowners belonging to a military aristocracy. Law was viewed as essentially a local matter, a set of rights specific to each unit of governance. Thus, each large estate ruled by an earl or baron, each sub-estate ruled by a lesser nobleman, and each manor ruled by an ordinary knight, possessed its own set of laws. Enforcement of the law in this decentralised setting was intermittent and ineffective. The countryside was filled with bands of marauders, often members of the local nobility whose self-declared nobility consisted largely of their ability to buy a horse and use a sword, rather than of any solicitude for those weaker than themselves.

For various reasons, this process reversed in the eleventh and twelfth centuries, and the central governments of the royal regimes that would ultimately become modern European nation States began to reassert control. Their goal was to establish civil order, to secure the obedience of local aristocracies, end the marauders' depredations, and create stable conditions for commerce, on which their own wealth and the wealth of their inhabitants increasingly depended. Law was one of the instrumentalities by which these purposes were achieved. To do so, it had to be seen as a form of command originating with the sovereign, it had to be exclusively determined, or monopolised, by that sovereign, and it had to be uniform, or universal within the sovereign's domain.

The conception of law, as a uniform set of commands promulgated by the sovereign or under his authority, was linked to natural law and the idea that the ruler governed with God's approval, if not His direct imprimatur. A law inconsistent with these universal principles, many medieval writers held, was not a law at all, and a ruler who would promulgate such commands under the name of law was a tyrant who deserved, at least in theory, to be deposed. These closely connected conceptions of royal and natural law led to the general view that law should consist of normative statements that reflected general principles, and thus constituted a coherent body of doctrine. To rule by law meant to use such statements as a mode of governance, and the rule of law meant that the sovereign was in fact ruling in this manner. Often, it was said that in promulgating law, the sovereign was merely discovering or enacting the laws that already existed, that is, the law established by the Divine Law-maker. Everyone understood, of course, that kings issued many orders and granted many benefits that did not conform to the model of a coherent set of general rules reflecting universal principles. However, the general view was that these orders and benefits were not true to the meaning of law. Law was a system of commands issued by the sovereign that reflected general principles and fit together into a coherent whole.

## 3. The Advent of Modern Governance

The era that we call modernity results from many complex, interrelated causes, but the two most relevant to this discussion are industrialisation and urbanisation. These trends simultaneously generated an opportunity and a demand for the expansion of central government – an opportunity because people became detached from the traditional structures of local government such as the local landowner and the Church, a demand because the people thus detached were exposed to the unfamiliar miseries of urban life and the depredations of a new industrial class whose severity was not tempered by tradition. The resulting expansion did not increase the central government's control of society; that goal had already been achieved. Rather, it was an expansion of the functions that the government performed. Instead of simply keeping order and dealing with foreign affairs, government now undertook to manage the economy and provide all the social services that had previously been the responsibility of the local landowner, the village and the Church. Tocqueville describes this as the difference between governmental centralisation and administrative centralisation. As he notes:

> Under Louis XIV, France saw the greatest governmental centralisation that one could conceive of […]'*L'etat, c'est moi*' he said; and he was right […] Nevertheless, under Louis XIV there was much less administrative centrali[s]ation than in our day.

The expansion of governmental functions was related to, albeit not restricted to, the growth of democracy that occurred during the same period. Granting ordinary citizens the vote, and allowing the results of those votes to determine the identity of governmental leaders, enabled the citizens to make insistent demands upon the government. What they demanded, and to some extent received, was protection from the harshness of their employers and the rigors of the capitalist system: health insurance, disability insurance, social security, unemployment benefits and, in a later era, consumer and small investor protection. They also demanded pubic recreational facilities and environmental protection to improve their quality of life, and public education to improve the prospects for their children. Programmes of this sort were not restricted to democratic regimes. Because these programmes had the general effect of securing the loyalty of the citizens, providing more productive workers and supplying healthier and more easily trained soldiers, European autocracies were motivated to provide the same services to citizens, particularly when they were in military competition with democracies.

This massive expansion of central government responsibilities changed the character of law as a mode of governance. It was no longer sufficient to establish rules of conduct designed to confirm the authority of the central government and establish civil order. Now government needed to manage complex public institutions and benefits programs, monitor private businesses and delicately adjust the switches and levers of an enormously complex economic system. Simple statements by the legislature were inadequate; detailed regulations were now required. General statements were equally inadequate; each institution needed its own distinctive rules and regulations, each benefit its own rules of distribution, each industry its own permissions and restrictions. As a result, most rule-making functions had to be delegated to administrative agencies.

Given these new purposes and instrumentalities of governance, the commands of the sovereign could no longer be framed as general rules, universally applicable to the entire society. There was, moreover, no longer any possibility that these commands could be seen as part of a coherent totality; they were simply too numerous, too varied and too specific. Indeed, the term command itself becomes a misnomer in the modern, administrative State. Governmental purposes are often carried out by establishing institutions, distributing benefits and adjusting incentives, rather than by giving orders. To take just two examples, an act by a city council to build playgrounds throughout the city does not give commands to any citizen. Rather, it provides funds to induce a private corporation to build facilities that people can use or not use, as they so desire. Similarly, an act by the national legislature to provide medical care and income support to disabled workers does not command anyone to become disabled; it simply provides a benefit to those who suffer from this condition. To be sure, commands of the traditional sort, that is, establishing norms of behaviour, will be needed to ensure that people do not vandalise the playgrounds or falsely claim the benefits, but these are subsidiary to the primary purpose of the legislation.

None of this should have been particularly difficult for modern people to accept. After all, at the same time that the administrative State was evolving, and for possibly related reasons, secularisation was undermining the belief in natural law. In modern, democratic States, laws need not conform to any set of principles ascribed to a Supreme Being. The only test of their validity is their proper enactment by a secular legislation and, in many nations, their conformance with a secularly established constitution enforced by a secular judiciary. In other words, not only has the use of law as a pragmatic instrument of governance changed in the modern State, but the rationale that describes the purpose of and constraints upon that law have changed as well.

## 4. The Persistence of the Pre-Modern Concept of Law

Surprisingly, however, the modern world, which has had so much success in re-conceptualising other things, has failed to re-conceptualise the law. When people speak of law, they still conceive it as a set of commands issued by the sovereign that establish rules for human conduct, rules that are expected to fit into some coherent general pattern. This is essentially Hans Kelsen's definition of law; when H.L.A. Hart undertook to revise that conception, he did so by noting that law functioned as a norm as well as a command. In other words, he moved backwards toward the idea of natural law, which Kelsen had dispensed with, rather than forward into modern administrative government. His *Concept of Law* centres on the statement that "law is a means of controlling human conduct", thus excluding all the statutes appropriating funds, creating institutions, establishing benefits and adjusting incentives from that category. Hart's theory not only wrongly describes the use of law as an instrumentality of modern governance, but also preserves the empty shell of natural law, with God subtracted but the notion of overarching principles retained.

This pre-modern conception of law, perhaps because of its persistence in legal education, continues to influence governmental action, despite its conflict with the rather evident realities of modern governance. Statutes continue to be written as if they were stating general norms of behaviour; more seriously, they tend to be designed and drafted with this conception in mind. Judges continue to re-interpret statutes and regulations on the basis of this same conception. More generally, political and legal actors of all kinds express a continuing discomfort with the realities of modern administrative governance. They worry that this mode of governance is inconsistent with our norms, that it is intrinsically oppressive, that it is uncontrolled or incoherent. In other words, they worry that it violates 'the rule of law'.

## 5. Modern Governance and the Law of the Future

The law of the future will bring the long-overdue demise of this premodern concept of law. In its place will be laws that function as an instrumentality of modern administrative governance. Three aspects of this transformation are the shift from procedures to results, from generality to particularisation, and from regularity to supervision.

### 5.1. From Procedures to Results

A command tells people what they should or should not do; in other words, it gives them instructions about the way to behave. At the same time, such instructions specify a result: declaring that people should not commit murder is essentially equivalent to declaring that no murders should be committed. This may seem obvious, but the reason for the overlap is that the instruction is being given to people as separate individuals, and the instruction itself consists of a simple prohibition. Once we consider the regulatory laws characteristic of the modern State, a substantial space begins to open between these two types of instructions. Suppose, for example, the legislature enacts a law to provide benefits to disabled workers. This obviously cannot be implemented by simple prohibition, since no behaviour is being prohibited; the law is an allocation of funds, not a command. The instruction is being given to an administrative agency, a large, complex organisation, and the task to be carried out is itself complex. In other words, a large space has opened between the instruction and its implementation.

Because pre-modern law is structured in terms of command, modern law-makers, who have failed to fully re-conceptualise law in modern terms, have tended to follow the command format and instruct the agency how to go about its task. In other words, they have tended to specify procedures. Needless to say, these are not always effective; in the example, not all the workers who are eligible for the benefit will necessarily receive it as a result of the specified procedures. An alternative approach would be to legislate the result, that is, that a certain percentage of the eligible workers actually receive the benefit. It would then be the agency's task to design procedures that yielded the specified result.

There is a tendency to regard the second approach as a more extensive delegation of legislative authority to the implementing agency, but that assertion simply returns to the pre-modern concept of law and projects it into the qualitatively different modern situation. It assumes that the task of legislating necessarily consists of specifying procedures – the alternative that most closely resembles pre-modern legal commands – so that when the legislature does not do so, it is transferring 'its' power to the agency. In fact, the legislature's power consists almost entirely of its ability to instruct administrative agencies to carry out various tasks in one way or another; if it could not do so, it could only enact pre-modern, prohibitory type laws, and not any of the regulatory, institution-creation or resource-allocating laws of the modern administrative State.

The two alternative approaches are simply different ways of controlling and monitoring the implementing agency. The first approach controls the procedures that the agency uses, and suggests that the legislature will oversee the agency to determine whether it complied with those procedures. The second approach controls the results the agency achieves, and suggests that those results will be the basis on which the agency's performance is judged. The question is not, as some modern writers have suggested, which approach is more 'lawful'. Both are law, as re-defined for modern governance; the question is which approach is more effective in achieving the desired goal.

As we move into the future, we will recognise that the second approach, where the results are specified, tends to be more effective, despite being less familiar. When a programme is first established, the best mode of implementation –the best way to achieve the desired goals – is not necessarily clear. Moreover, it may change over time as circumstances change. The implementation strategy that is most effective when a program is established may not continue to be most effective once the program has matured. Discovering the most effective mode, and changing it as circumstances change, will generally not lie within the legislature's area of expertise. By specifying the goal itself, and leaving the agency to develop and adapt the implementation strategy, the legislature is more likely to achieve its desired result.

## 5.2. From Generality to Particularisation

Pre-modern Europeans regarded generality as the hallmark of law. The sovereign, typically a monarch, could engage in individualised acts of favouritism or vindictiveness, based on personal preferences, but he could also abide by the law and act through general rules that treated everyone the same, or, to be more precise, like cases alike. There was a further constraint on the content of those rules, which, if they were to be properly described as law, were expected to cohere into a consist system that reflected general principles. At present, however, Western nations are no longer ruled by single individuals with personal preferences, but by complex groups of elected officials whose authority is determined and controlled by structural rules. When a single person is in charge of government, it is relatively easy to tell when he is playing favourites and when he is acting in accordance with general rules. When an elected legislature is in charge, it will often be impossible to distinguish between its preferences and its policies.

As we move into the future, therefore, and re-conceptualise law in modern terms, we will be increasingly able to dispense with the pre-modern norm of generality and choose our mode of governance on the basis of its effectiveness in implementing our purposes. Just as that criterion will often lead to specifying results rather than procedures, it will often lead to particularised rather than general action. We have already abandoned any belief that enacted law must cohere into a unified whole. Legislators are often motivated by a general ideology of course – citizens need more protection, business suffers from over-regulation – but in implementing that ideology, they no longer argue that the idea of law itself demands internal consistency among enacted measures. If one believes that government is subject to excessive regulation, the fact that a proposed law would de-regulate one area, while related areas remain subject to regulation, would be regarded as an argument in favour of that law, not against it.

The law of the future will not only move from generality to particularity in terms of the connections among its various provisions, but also in terms of the way it relates to private parties. Because the government's relationship to business enterprises, to recipients of benefits, and to clients or inmates of public institutions is an intensive and on-going one, generalised rules are no longer sufficient or, indeed, effective. Instead, the government must design specific strategies for many of the situations it addresses. Educators generally agree, for example, that individualisation is the most effective way to teach young children – not to control them, perhaps, but certainly to obtain the results that constitute the purpose of creating public schools. The same can be said for the treatment of patients in mental hospitals. Probation and parole, without which our criminal justice system would collapse, represent efforts to individualise an area of law where uniformity and generality would seem to exercise their greatest claims.

The same is true for economic regulation. Agencies that implement such regulation will be most effective if they develop particularised strategies for each firm in concentrated industries or each recognisable group of firms (grouped according to the agency's goal) in other cases. This requires an extensive staff and massive information processing capacity, but that is precisely what the modern agency, with the assistance of the electronic revolution, now provides. Ronald Dworkin has strenuously tried to maintain the pre-modern conception of law as a coherent unity in his account of common law. His claim is only plausible because common law judges were the primary means of enforcing law in the pre-modern era; when it finally occurred to him that most modern law is statutory, his further claim that statutes should display the same unity was risibly implausible.

A current school of administrative law scholarship called New Public Governance has focused on these features of the modern regulatory process and proposed a major re-conceptualisation of the law in this area. Instead of issuing commands in an effort to control the regulated firm's practices – so-called "command and control regulation" – New Public Governance suggests that the agency should engage in a cooperative process that tailors its interventions to the specifics of the situation it confronts. Some firms will respond only to threats, but many others will comply voluntarily if given certain incentives, or if provided with expertise that would otherwise be difficult for them to acquire. This image of the regulator-as-friend may seem fatuous or insincere, but that is because command and control regulation is intrinsically adversarial. If, instead, a goal has been established, either by the legislature or the agency, then it seems entirely plausible that the agency could work cooperatively with the firm to achieve that goal. Thus, the change described above, that is, moving from specified procedures to specified results, encourages and supports the change that is being described here, that is, from generalised rules to particularised interactions.

### 5.3. From Regularity to Supervision

A particularised system of law, where State agents treat individual firms, small groups of firms, and individuals differently, in response to the specifics of their situation, naturally raises concerns about fairness. Giving a State agent authority to craft particularized treatment of a single entity, whether enterprise or individual, would seem to invite discriminatory or oppressive behaviour. Several leading critics of the modern regulatory State, notably Frederick Hayek and Theodore Lowi, have correctly identified this feature of modern governance and then used it as the basis for their condemnation. Their claim is that modern regulation violates the rule of law. This is absolutely true if one uses the medieval definition of law. According to the re-conceptualisation that is presently occurring, however, this particularised treatment not only does not violate the law, it is law – the law of the future.

When they are not simply using their arguments to express an *a priori* distaste for modernity, Hayek, Lowi and other critics seem to base their criticism on concerns about the fairness of governmental action. But generality, regularity and other features of pre-modern law that they propound are not the equivalent of fairness, as we understand that concept. Rather, they are proxies for fairness. As everyone knows, the rigid application of a rule can be as unfair as discriminatory treatment based on personal animus. In fact, it can be the same thing if the agent applying the rule is aware of the rule's effect upon the enterprise or individual in question. A uniform poll tax discriminates against the poor; a uniform literacy test for voting discriminates against those who have been denied access to education.

Pre-modern government needed to rely on this proxy for fairness since it lacked an administrative hierarchy that could deploy alternative mechanisms. Local governance, not only in the Middle Ages but often as late as the eighteenth century, was in the hands of landowners who were insulated from central government control by the idea that the area they governed was their private property. As central government developed, it relied on an analogous means of authorising officials to exercise its authority over specific subjects. In return for payment (rather than for loyalty, as in the Middle Ages), it granted them a property right in their office, which provided them an equivalent autonomy. This is not to assert that pre-modern society was non-hierarchical of course. It was extremely hierarchical, but the hierarchy was established socially, not by the government. As such, it served as a further insulation from government supervision; a low status employee of the central government would have difficulty disciplining a noble landowner or even the purchaser of an important office. Moreover, these two forms of private property insulation tended to reinforce each other; noblemen often purchased offices, and purchasing an office often conferred noble status, as in France's *noblesse de la robe*.

Modern government, as Weber observed, is characterised by officially created hierarchies, which means that each official not only receives orders and instructions from a superior, but is monitored, or supervised, by that superior. A government structured in this way does not need to rely on regularity as a proxy for fairness; rather, it can use supervision to prevent its employees from acting on the basis of personal animus, prejudice, or sheer ill will. Supervision, of course, is itself a more particularised approach that enables the supervisor to assess each subordinate's behaviour, rather than relying on general rules that can be too readily manipulated at the "street level." These administrative hierarchies are defined in exclusively governmental terms and are independent of the remaining social hierarchies. It would be virtually inconceivable for a modern US Occupational Safety and Health Administration inspector to resist disciplinary action by his superior on the ground that he came from a wealthier or more distinguished family than the supervisor.

Supervision, of course, will only achieve fairness if it is designed to implement general principles that constitute this value. That is not an exception to the nature of modern law, but an essential feature of it. Just as statutes will not be desirable unless they are designed to implement desirable policies, supervision will not be desirable unless it is designed to implement desirable values. Both policies and values are determined, in modern government, by democratic decision-making. Indeed, these are probably the only things than can be effectively determined by that process. Voters cannot possibly be knowledgeable about specific statutes, and they cannot possibly control specific governmental practices; appeals to them on the basis of such specifics tend to be anecdotal rabble rousing and scandal mongering that a fully mature democracy will hopefully avoid. Modern democratic government, where voters choose leaders rather than policies or practices, is designed to direct their choices to these more general issues. In the case of governmental fairness, the voters decide on general principles, sometimes directly and sometimes through adoption of a constitution, and then those principles are implemented through a complex, well-developed administrative hierarchy that no longer need rely on proxies for fairness like the regularity of law.

## 6. Conclusion

General principles, as just noted, are not absent from modern administrative government. They are, in fact the basic choices that the voters make, choices that constitute the essence of the modern democratic process. But these principles are not law. Law is an instrumentality of governance, a means by which the voters' basic choices are implemented in our complex, technical society. The idea that law must be procedural, generalised and regular is a product of pre-modern European ideology. It served its purpose when government's main goal was to establish control and maintain civil order, but it no longer applies when that goal has been essentially achieved, and the voter now requires government to manage economic and social systems that have grown past the ambit of tradition. The law of the future will be result-oriented, particularised and supervised. It will, in other words, be re-conceived to serve the purposes of the modern State.

# 6.2.

# Law and Policy: A Long (and Bright) Way to Go

**Mauro Zamboni***

The relations of law to politics are one of the major difficulties confronting today's legal actors, including, naturally here, legal scholars. While legal actors are educated to believe that law and politics are two distinct worlds, when faced with real issues, legal actors are forced to deal with the very responsibility of choosing a political course for an entire community. If one considers the policy of law as the transformational space of law-making, that is, the space in which the values or ideas produced inside the political arena are transformed into legal categories and concepts, the major purpose of this contribution will be to look at the way forward with respect to the relations between law and policy, and in particular on how this transformational (or policy) space can help legal actors confront the challenges presented by the (not so) future world, for example, globalisation.

## 1. Introduction

The relations of law to politics are one of the major difficulties confronting today's legal actors, including legal scholars. Though with some differences (for example as to the legal system, legal actor or legal area under investigation), one can say without much objection that, in general, legal actors are educated in the belief that law and politics are two distinct worlds. Lawyers should somehow avoid (at least explicitly) political issues as much as possible. However, when faced with real issues, legal actors not only realise that they are forced to deal with politics, but also that, occasionally, the very responsibility of choosing a political course for an entire community will fall on their shoulders.

In particular, if one considers the policy of law as the transformational space of law-making, the space in which the values or ideas produced inside the political arena are transformed into legal categories and concepts, the majority of contemporary legal actors tend to interpret this

* **Mauro Zamboni** is Professor in Legal Theory at the Stockholm Centre for Commercial Law at the Faculty of Law of Stockholm University, Sweden.

space as mirroring the general dilemma currently faced by the law. On one side, due to the high degree of politicisation of the legal phenomenon, legal actors are forced to give the transformational moment a central position in their visions of the law and its creation. For example, every lawyer or judge recognises that the right of individual private property is not a natural and neutral product of the legal system, but instead, a product of liberal political ideology. On the other side, because of the accelerating tendency towards a more specialised law, most legal actors tend to leave any further focus as to this moment at the periphery of their attention. For example, many legal actors in their everyday work operate based on the idea that the essence of the concept of property rights does not lie in any political or moral ideology, identifying it instead simply as the legal possibility to do or not to do something with their property.

Since the major purpose of this contribution is to look at the way forward with respect to the relations between law and policy, the focus here is on how this transformational (or policy) space can help legal actors confront the challenges presented by the (not so) future world, for example, globalisation. Before sketching a potential development of the future relations between law and policy, and its implications for legal actors, it is necessary to offer some clarifications as to the terminology used in this think piece. The policy of law is defined as a space that can be opened up in the law-making activity between the formation of ideas in the political world (politics of law), where political is intended in a very broad meaning (for example, the lobbying of economic actors), and the impact of the newly-made law on the surrounding non-legal environments (legal outcomes). In this space, values entrenched in political decisions (political inputs) are transformed into law, having an effect on the existing legal order (legal outputs). For example, political parties give the mandate of transforming their equality ideal between men and women (political input) into legal proposals to their legal staff or an external legal think-tank. The latter, after searching among the available legal tools, drafts a new statute realising in legal language the ideal of equality. The legal tool used by legal actors for realising equality between the sexes in the job market can be a legally compulsory system of quotas. The draft written by the lawyers of the political parties then becomes a statute that modifies both the legal duties of the employers and the legal rights to which women applying for jobs are entitled (legal outputs).

The policy of law is then a web of conversional processes and decisions located inside the legal arena. They are directed at transforming the ideas produced in the political arena (political inputs) into concepts and categories directly relevant to the legal world (legal outputs). In contemporary law-making, this space of the policy of law is mainly the domain for the work and reasoning of the actors belonging to the legal world (for example, lawyers working for the legislature or 'activist' justices). However, the borders of the policy of law as so defined, often tend to cross into the spaces in which decisions about values are taken (politics of law) and where the law becomes a socially relevant phenomenon (legal outcomes). For example, in the policy process, law-makers can prefer to incorporate in a statute a legal category of a compulsory quota system, instead of employing a taxation legal tool in the form of tax-deductions available to employers hiring women. This choice can be made because either the legal actors are aware of the political sensitivity when it comes to the ideals that should inspire taxation law, or they have witnessed successful outcomes in reality of a previous similar compulsory quota system in fighting discrimination, for example, against disabled persons.

## 2. The Policy of Law: Some Work to Be Done on the Outside

The centrality of the transformational process, defined as the policy of law, is evidently necessary in order for legal actors to better understand certain phenomena that heavily affect the legal world today and, in particular, the law-making processes. If one considers major developments affecting contemporary legal work as well as thought, for example, globalisation, the importance of such a vision of the law-making process clearly emerges not only in helping to explain larger events. This vision of the law-making process can also offer solutions to certain problems that sometimes accompany such contemporary phenomena into the legal world.

### 2.1. The Policy of Law and Globalisation

The phenomenon of globalisation from a legal perspective can be defined as the circulation of legal models (that is, legal categories and concepts) in a way that has rendered many different aspects of the different national legal systems homogeneous, in particular, with respect to such issues as human rights, capital punishment and innumerable commercial issues.

Once globalisation is defined in these terms, the fundamental contribution that a policy of law perspective can bring to the understanding of the phenomenon becomes evident, in particular by taking the legal actors' perspectives on the matter. The circulation of legal models receives a form of sanction, either *ex ante* or *ex post*, by the national or international legal actors. Legislative bodies, judges, arbitrators and lawyers become the central (although not exclusive) figures in this law-making process, allowing for the transformation of global legal categories and concepts into legal categories and concepts with a legal status in their own (international, supranational, transnational, or national) communities. One example is the increasing role played by national labour courts in the face of the declining importance of union membership as the principal route for employees to enforce their fundamental "floor of rights", as recognised at an international level.

In addition to this function of increasing the understanding of the process of globalisation, a policy of law perspective can also help to solve certain problems connected thereto. Far from being a developmental and linear phenomenon in general, globalisation also raises many issues and problems in the legal world. One is the difficulty encountered by many global legal categories and concepts in actually having a concrete effect on the daily life of the receiving community. Take, for example, Russia, where many typically capitalistic economic legal tools failed to actually implement a capitalistic mind-set in the business communities of traditionally non-capitalistic origin, attempting to take on many of the features characterising Western legal systems.

This "malfunction" of the phenomenon of globalisation can partially be explained by looking into its policy of law. First, it is necessary to distinguish, within the phenomenon of globalisation, between the globalisation of the 'policy of law' and the globalisation of the 'politics of law'. By the globalisation of the policy of law is meant that there is presently a tendency by which the same legal categories and concepts are received in many national and international legal orders. In other words, legal actors around the world tend to use the same kind of legal tools: for example, the legal category of 'limited financial liability' as a quality attached to the legal position of a shareholder. Not necessarily corresponding to this general tendency is an underpinning general globalisation of the politics of law, which is not necessarily the fact that various national and international communities similarly share the same values underlying these global legal categories and concepts.

The relatively centralised and authoritative features of contemporary law-making processes usually facilitate the adoption of a legal system of global legal categories. Few members of a drafting committee, for example, impulsively decide to embrace and impose upon an entire national community a foreign legal category, such as limited financial liability for shareholders. The introduction of new "foreign" values into a community is more difficult as the value-making process lacks authoritative force and, often, the centralised character typical for the legal phenomenon. In other words, at least in the Western legal systems, changes of the law (for example, a new legal category) can usually be expected with a (more or less) blind "acceptance" (although not necessarily endorsed) by the members of a community, while changes in the community's values are often the result of long, fragmented and complex processes.

These structural differences exist between the legal politics and the policy of law of globalisation. For example, the value underlying the adoption of a limited financial liability for shareholders in the receiving country cannot actually be the one promoting a flux of new financial resources into new economic activities, but rather the one promoting sheer financial speculation. By identifying the possibility of such gaps between the policy and the politics moments of legal globalisation, the policy of law analyst, namely, the legal professional figure with the specific task of investigating the transformational space and suggesting possible legal strategies, can play a central role. He or she can recommend that more attention be paid to the intentions of the political and social arenas (legal inputs) underlying the adoption of a law-making process suggested and/or promoted by globalising forces (for example, the World Trade Organization).

Even if one assumes that the globalisation of legal categories (policy of law) mirrors a parallel and simultaneous globalisation of the underpinning values (legal politics), the observation of the phenomenon from the standpoint of the transformational moment can help to explain and solve some of the failures of the process of globalisation. The non-legal arenas can present favourable and encouraging conditions for the acceptance of new legal categories and concepts. Political, social and economic actors can all agree on a true globalised politics of law; for instance, they can promote and sustain the necessity of transforming the idea of encouraging risk-taking in new economic activities, into the global legal category of limited financial responsibility for shareholders. In other words, the environment around the legal world is ready and sympathetic to the outcomes of a certain law-making process.

Despite these favourable conditions, globalisation processes can fail in actually implementing certain values or ideas when using global legal categories. This can happen because of the central role played by the legal world and its actors in the policy of law processes, directed at transforming certain values into legal categories. The legal world can for several reasons reject such categories by stopping the production of any policy of law output. For example, the judges of a country, educated according to a communitarian legal tradition, can consistently and generally maintain the legal irrelevancy of a new category of limited financial liability for certain economic enterprises.

Moreover, the circulation of legal models can also be stopped by conditions peculiar to the receiving legal system. When legal actors transform global legal categories into binding categories for the community, the law-making process produces some legal outputs due to the shape of the legal order. Such outputs can be rendered impotent within the non-legal arenas (no legal outcomes). For example, the receiving legal order perhaps lacks mechanisms of legal protection for those financial institutions supplying credit to newly established enterprises with limited financial liability.

It is precisely within this type of *impasse* that an articulated knowledge of the policy of law space can intervene and offer a contribution. Focusing mainly on the legal actors and their transformational role, the policy of law analyst can point out blockages in the process of introducing new legal categories into a legal order. If the globalisation of the legal system has stopped, for example, before the production of legal inputs, then the solution should start with re-educating the legal actors. Reforming teaching in law faculties, compulsory continuing legal education courses for judges, and sabbaticals abroad for legal consultants working for the legislature, are some possible ways of re-invigorating and recommencing the law-making process.

In contrast, if there are ineffective legal outputs, that is, they do not produce any outcomes outside the legal arena, then the solutions should probably be sought in more traditional directions: more attention should be given to the simultaneous reform of the surrounding legal areas and there should be longer periods of transition in which both the old and the new legal categories are accommodated.

## 3. The Policy of Law: Some Work to Be Done on the Inside

As to the policy of law and its future, the challenges for legal actors do not only concern how to confront this transformational space of the law-making with the "outside", that is, with the changing environments surrounding the law and its actors. They also face challenges as to the ways to understand and structure the 'inside' of the policy of law, that is, as to the main tools at the disposal of the legal actors with respect to the processes and decisions transforming political inputs into legal categories. In particular, the most urgent efforts should be made in the direction of answering two major questions following the recognition of the existence of a transformational moment in the law-making process: How does the policy of law work? Why should legal actors choose one legal category instead of the other?

### 3.1. How Does the Policy of Law Work?

In answering the first question, legal actors must realise that any adaptation of the policy of law to the changing external conditions will, at the same time, have to operate on its inside, by identifying the specific modalities through which the transformational processes take place. In particular, legal actors need to acquire a specific knowledge as to the mechanisms through which the political, economic, cultural or religious values become legal categories and concepts. This knowledge will have to be developed along two major converging lines of work.

First, an investigation of the modes of working of a policy process needs to take, as a central point of observation, the perspective of the legal actors, the latter playing a leading (although not exclusive) part in such processes of transformation of political inputs into legal outputs. In particular, Max Weber's distinction between a formal and a substantive legal rationality should be invoked. With it, a line can be drawn between actors working from within the legal system, whose coherence or consequentiality they are to preserve, and those social and political actors that, although active in the law-making process, strive for goals external to the internal logic of the legal system (for example the realisation of a certain political ideology or the improvement of the efficiency of an economic system).

For example, when confronted with the legal dilemma as to which legal category in taxation law can better realise the value of encouraging small enterprises, the legislative drafter (a legal actor) will choose or build the new statutory provisions according to criteria such as the 'fitting' of the new legal construction into the already existing legal regulation of the whole taxation system (formal legal rationality). In contrast, politicians or the representatives of small enterprises will propose or evaluate the new statutory provisions with criteria that are beyond (and somehow disregard) the system of taxation law as a whole. In choosing which legislative path to take, these non-legal actors are instead more focused on substantive criteria located outside the legal world, and are aiming at creating a regulation that can produce a result in the political world (for example, politicians may want to change taxation law in order to increase their support among the population) or in the economic world (for example, the representatives of small enterprises may wish to change taxation law in such a way that the small enterprises end up paying less taxes).

By drawing this line, however, legal actors will always have to keep in mind the relative nature of this distinction between legal and non-legal institutional actors (as well as their goals). Considering the vast variety of guises a legal actor can assume, it is often unclear where the latter ends and the social or political actor begins. One example of this diffuseness is in-house corporate attorneys: these are actors, educated in legal reasoning and hired as legal experts, who are in a position where, as part of their job (and under strong pressures and influences by employers), they are often required to somehow "mould", or even disregard, the basic dogmas of legal thinking in contracts law in order to fulfil some economic values (for example, the maximisation of short-term profits). Moreover, legal actors themselves (judges *in primis*), even when embracing as unique value as the maintenance of the internal logic of the legal system, are often carriers of messages of political nature: messages that are likely to surface, in particular, in the presence of hard cases. Even the most obedient judge with respect to the letter of the positive law must sometimes "go beyond the law" and rely on his or her ideological background.

There is a second major process legal actors will have to address in the near future in order to answer the question of how the policy of law works. This starts from the channels through which, in the law-making process, communications occur among the different actors. In particular, a future model explaining the policy of law should include a deep investigation of the legal language. As pointed out by movements such as post-modernism or feminist legal theory, however, in order to fully understand the point of passage from political to legal languages, it is necessary to substitute the concept of legal language with the broader concept of "legal discourse". A potential model of the policy of law needs to focus on the legal discourse since:

> [...] the concept of legal discourse is a methodology for the reading of legal texts, which places the communicative or rhetorical functions of law within their institutional and socio-linguistic contexts.[1]

Legal discourses then allow legal actors to better investigate the policy process by placing the legal phenomenon in the centre of its web of relations with the other non/legal arenas (for example, political, economic, and social). This focus on the idea of "discourse" does not absolutely mean that it is impossible to individuate the different standpoints of the different agencies participating in the discourse, that is, the "contribution" each law-making actor gives to the discourse is ignored. The use of the idea of 'discourse' simply implicates that the final product, the new legal category, has to be seen as the result of a constant and continuous interacting of different forces, different ideologies and different legal cultures.

For example, when looking at the introduction in a national law-making process of a hypothetical legal category considering the right to a marital divorce as a "human right", one should always take into consideration the fundamental fact that in the international organisation's law-making process, consideration has already been given to the (possible or factual) proposals and criticisms coming from the national States members, local communities, religious organisations and grassroots organisations. Since sometimes many of the latter do not consider "live-in partnerships" (or same-sex partnerships) equal to marriage, already in the actual creation of the right to divorce, the international organisation will most likely limit its sphere of application to "marriages" in order to prevent problems that might arise in the application of the legal category to other types of partnerships.

[1] Peter Goodrich, *Legal Discourse: Studies in Linguistics, Rhetoric and Legal Analysis*, St Martin's Press, 1987, p. 205.

### 3.2. Why Should Legal Actors Choose One Legal Category Instead of the Other?

The centrality of the legal discourse for any future model of the policy process, then, introduces the viable paths legal actors must consider in order to answer the second question: what should the motives driving legal actors in the choice (or construction) of a legal category be? Since the policy process is positioned inside the legal world, but has strong relations with the political and social dimensions of the legal phenomenon, it seems reasonable to expect that legal actors, while in this transformational space, would go beyond the mere consideration of the legal reasoning along which the law-making develops.

If the values or ideas behind a certain legal category are the starting point in understanding a policy of law process, and if a central role in such a process is played by the legal discourse, then it seems sound to expect that a normative approach to the process (that is, aiming at what ought to be done) will also sieve through the different moral, political, social, economic and cultural aspects underlying the legal reasoning. The legal actors will have to refrain from their 'purely legal' attitude and take a step into the world of moral, political, economic or cultural reasoning because, for example, the law-maker (either as a legislator, scholar or judge) must always reason and arguably rationalise his or her choices in terms of finding the correct legal category for a certain value. The law-making authority will transform a value into law, trying to be as faithful as possible to some criteria to which the authority itself (and hopefully the addressees) attributes an *a priori* validity, that is, a value-status. These criteria, as available to legal actors, can be of different natures, economic (for example, the economic efficiency of the legal order), formal legal criteria (for example, the consistency and logic of the legal order) or *stricto sensu* political criteria (for example, the idea of democracy). Regardless of the kind of criteria the law-making agencies opt for, they are all perceived and used by the legislator, judge, or scholar as axioms in their work, that is, as assumed-to-be lights guiding the work of law-makers.

Legal actors should therefore be willing to penetrate and expose the axioms underpinning the law maker's choices in favour of one or the other legal category. The illumination of such economic, formalistic or moral axioms will be necessary not only for a better understanding of the process of the policy of law. The descent into the value-roots will also be necessary when evaluating the results of the policy process, that is, both the legal inputs and its outcomes upon the community. Only by first openly recognising the political, moral, social or economic original backgrounds of the legal categories and concepts made or used in the law-making process, will legal actors be able to proceed in evaluating whether the expected effects have been realised or, to put it in famous terminology, whether the law in books has become the law in action.

## 4. Sources and Further Reading

Bell, John, *Policy Arguments in Judicial Decisions*, Clarendon Press, 1983.

Boaventura, Sousa Santos de, *Toward a New Legal Common Sense: Law, Globalisation and Emancipation*, Butterworths, 2002.

Dahl, Robert A., "Decision-Making in a Democracy: The Supreme Court as A National Policy-Maker", in *Emory Law Journal*, 2001, vol. 50, pp. 563–582.

Dworkin, Ronald, *Law's Empire*, Harvard University Press, 1997.

Goodrich, Peter, *Legal Discourse: Studies in Linguistics, Rhetoric and Legal Analysis*, St Martin's Press, 1987.

Greenawalt, Kent, "Policy, Rights and Judicial Decision", in *Georgia Law Review*, 1977, vol. 11, pp. 991–1053.

Habermas, Jürgen, *Between Facts and Norms: Contributions to a Discourse Theory of Law and Democracy*, The MIT Press, 1998.

Heineman, Robert A., William I. Bluhm, Steven A. Peterson and Edward N. Kearny, *The World of the Policy Analyst. Rationality, Values, & Politics*, 3rd ed., Chatham House Publishers, 2002.

Hill, Michael J, *The Policy Process in the Modern State*, 3rd ed. Englewood Cliffs, NJ: Prentice Hall, 1997.

Kairys, David (ed.), *The Politics of Law. A Progressive Critique*, 3rd ed., Basic Books, 1998.

Lasswell, Harold D. and McDougal, Myres S., *Jurisprudence for a Free Society. Studies in Law, Science and Policy*, New Haven Press, 1992.

Loughlin, Martin, *Sword and Scales. An Examination of the Relationship between Law and Politics*, Hart Publishing, 2000.

Lorne, Sossin, "The Sounds of Silence: Law Clerks, Policy Making and the Supreme Court of Canada", in *University of British Columbia Law Review*, 1996, vol. 30, pp. 279–308.

Summers, Robert S., "Policy on the Anvil of Law", in *Essays on the Nature of Law and Legal Reasoning*, Duncker and Humblot, 1992, pp. 191–208.

Stuart, Nagel S. and Bienvenue, Lisa A., *Social Science, Law, and Public Policy*, University Press of America, 1992.

Twining, William, *Globalisation and Legal Theory*, Butterworths, 2000.

Weber, Max, *Economy and Society*, University of California Press, 1978.

Zamboni, Mauro, *The Policy of Law: A Legal Theoretical Framework*, Hart Publishing, 2007.

# 6.3.

# Law School of the Future: Centre of Cutting-Edge Practice?

**Clark D. Cunningham**[*]

To meet the challenge of the rapidly changing future of law and to play a vital role in creating the law of the future, law schools must move beyond the delivery of static knowledge through classroom instruction and become centres of cutting-edge legal practice. The origins of modern medical education provide encouraging evidence that such a transformation is both needed and feasible. At the end of the nineteenth century, the curriculum at most North American medical schools consisted entirely of lectures, provided by part-time practitioners to supplement their income. There was no patient contact or laboratory experience. Schools varied widely in quality, as did the competence of their graduates. Then, within a matter of decades, all was changed through the widespread adoption of a powerful new model of education: the teaching hospital staffed by physician-scientists.

## 1. Introduction

The Hague Institute for the Internationalisation of Law (HiiL), working from a foundation of 49 thought-provoking essays published in 2011 as the volume, *The Law of the Future and the Future of the Law*, has developed the *Law Scenarios to 2030* as an instrument to help key decision-makers in the legal systems of the world work towards preparing for an uncertain future. These scenarios predict with some confidence a number of trends that will challenge existing legal systems over the next twenty years, including rising population; greater scarcity of food, water and fossil fuels; heightened security concerns; expanding economic globalisation; and increased access to information. However, the scenarios imagine quite different responses to such trends. For example, in terms of govern-

[*] **Clark D. Cunningham** is the W. Lee Burge Professor of Law & Ethics at the Georgia State University College of Law, Director of the National Institute for Teaching Ethics & Professionalism (USA), and Vice Chair of the Academic and Professional Development Committee, International Bar Association.

ance, one possibility is a robust global legal order with its own authoritative rules and institutions, while yet another plausible future is a retreat from global constitutionalism as legal borders thicken and State-made law dominates.

In planning for a future that we feel certain will be radically different from the present, but lacking certainty about the direction the future will take, those responsible for shaping legal education can best spend their energy altering the current institutional structure rather than fermenting by speculation new courses to be poured into the cracked and rigid vessels of today. A law school serves society in at least two ways: (1) its current staff can be a resource of knowledge and expertise for addressing immediate societal issues, and (2) its graduates will design and operate an evolving legal system over the course of their professional careers. Therefore, two questions should guide the analysis: (1) is the law school as an institution a useful resource for the current needs of the real world, and (2) are the current graduates of the law school being prepared to be effective lawyers and innovative actors in the legal system in response to changes that take place over their own professional life span?

## 2. Drawing Inspiration from Medical Education

This essay is deeply informed by the work of the Carnegie Foundation for the Advancement of Teaching, founded in 1905 by the philanthropist Andrew Carnegie. Over the past century this organisation has prompted many important changes in higher education. In the last decade a major initiative of the Foundation has been the Preparation for the Professions Program, which has overseen a series of multi-year comparative studies of the education of the clergy, engineers, lawyers, doctors, and nurses.

The Foundation's report on American law schools, "Educating Lawyers" (2007), has been widely discussed in both the profession and academia, largely because of its unfavourable comparison of the process of preparation for the American legal profession with the educational programmes of the other professions it studied, notably medicine. "Educating Physicians", the Foundation's final report, was published in 2010 and, along with *Learning to Heal* by Kenneth Ludmerer, provide the basis for much of the following information about the distinctive features of medical education that the Carnegie Foundation would have law schools emulate.[1]

## 2.1. The Twentieth Century Revolution in Medical Education

A century ago, in 1910, the Carnegie Foundation issued a blistering critique of the medical education, known as "The Flexner Report", named after its author, Abraham Flexner. Flexner found that because scientific progress had greatly increased the physician's diagnostic and remedial resources, medical education had a different function to perform. However, according to Flexner, it had taken medical schools upward of half a century to wake up to that fact. The gap between what was known and what was taught had become unacceptably wide. But how could medical schools, at the turn of the twentieth century, cope with the onslaught of new information and contend with the realisation that scientific knowledge is not fixed? Flexner advocated what he considered to be the only viable approach: to redesign medical education so that it had a procedural rather than substantive emphasis. The new objective of medical education should be to produce problem-solvers and critical thinkers who knew how to find out and evaluate information for themselves. "Though medicine can be learned, it cannot be taught", wrote Flexner. "Active participation in doing things is therefore the fundamental note of medical teaching".

The critical question was, then, what kind of institutional structure would facilitate this new educational method? Flexner proposed a new model: a four-year post-graduate programme built around faculty supervision of both patient care and laboratory investigation. The keystone of this new structure was the university-based teaching hospital, staffed by 'physician-scientists' who were competent both in the research laboratory and at the hospital bedside. Flexner asserted that no distinction should be made between research and practice, saying that "the [hospital ward] and the laboratory are [...] from the standpoints of investigation, treatment and education, inextricably intertwined". Remarkably, within twenty years, Flexner's proposed standard became the universal model for medical education both in the United States and Canada.

1 This chapter also draws from the history of the Johns Hopkins medical school provided on the school's website. An expanded version of this chapter with full attribution to sources is available at www.teachinglegalethics.org.

## 2.2. The Teaching Hospital as the Premier Provider of Health Care

Flexner pointed to the example of Johns Hopkins University in Baltimore, which had brought to America the scientific approach to medicine developed by German universities. Throughout the nineteenth century and into the twentieth, hospitals were generally reluctant to host anything more than nominal educational activities. However, Hopkins owned its own hospital and the medical school made all staff appointments. As a result the hospital at Hopkins achieved international eminence by combining patient care with path-breaking scientific research.

By 1910 the Johns Hopkins medical school was less than 20 years old, but had already demonstrated the viability of Flexner's proposal. Hopkins combined rigorous training in small classes and at patients' bedsides with an emphasis on research that was then rapidly applied to improved patient care. Teachers and students worked collaboratively on both patient care and research. The exemplar of this approach was the famous surgeon and teacher William Osler, who summed up the integration of scholarship and practice by saying: "He who studies medicine without books sails an uncharted sea, but he who studies medicine without patients does not go to sea at all".

As the Hopkins model was replicated elsewhere, a new consensus developed, held by both medical educators and hospital officials, that education and research improved the care of patients. The presence of students ensured that every detail of patient care would receive attention and served as an intellectual prod to the faculty, stimulating thorough study and discussion, and benefiting not only the immediate patient but also other patients should something new be discovered. The intellectual excitement of teaching hospitals attracted the most accomplished physicians to the staff. The most up-to-date information on the management of diseases was to be found in university hospitals, where the search for the cause, mechanisms, and cure of human afflictions was being actively pursued. Thus medical schools were continually improving medical practice through their success in discovering new knowledge and translating that knowledge into everyday medical care.

## 2.3. The Teaching Hospital as the School for Adaptable Experts

Incorporating a teaching hospital into the modern medical school not only makes the school immediately relevant to current society, the members of which turn to its hospitals and outpatient centres for the best and most innovative health care, but also produces graduates who are adaptable experts rather than mere recipients of static knowledge.

For the central experiences of medical education, the student does not sit passively gazing at the solitary teacher, but rather works actively next to her teacher and fellow health care providers, while all focus on the patient. By the end of four years of American medical school, a typical student has conducted 500 physical examinations, made 300 clinical notes on hospitalised patients, assisted in the delivery of 10 to 30 babies, and probably attended at least one death of someone for whom the student has provided care.

Actual practice becomes the primary site for producing both knowledge and skill because the compelling real-life situation provides the motivation for understanding the patient's condition from many perspectives, prompts curiosity for more knowledge, and reinforces the desire for improving patient care which is the defining characteristic of the physician's identity. As not mere didactic instructors, but rather collaborators with students in this shared enterprise, teachers are constantly calling for higher performance from themselves as well as the students, and, critically, exemplifying their own initiative and resilience in the face of disappointment and failure.

According to the authors of "Educating Physicians", becoming an expert requires not only efficiency in a core set of competencies but also the capacity to expand those competencies and the ability to innovate. Thus an educational programme fails if it produces professionals who perform routine work skilfully but fail to see new possibilities or greater complexity in their daily practice. Such skilled professionals may be experienced but are not truly experts because they do not engage in knowledge building through inquiry and improvement of the field in which they work. Experts have the ability to respond flexibly to varied situations, to modify existing practices and develop new practices to improve performance, and to cross conventional domain boundaries to explore new perspectives and develop novel solutions to persistent problems. Experts are highly aware of the limits and uncertainty of their knowledge. They recognise their interpretations as provisional rather than conclusive, their questions are open rather than closed, and they actively pursue more complete understanding rather than assuming that they already know the most important things and, thus, become indifferent to what more remains to be learned.

Medical school ideally integrates formal and experiential knowledge longitudinally over the four-year span of the curriculum, matching what the student needs to learn next with the opportunities presented by practice at the teaching hospital. The student learns how to make increasingly high-stakes decisions under close supervision that assures both effective education and safe patient care. Space is created in which the student can develop professional judgement in determining how much help she needs, and how to get it, in order to deal with a clinical problem, establishing the foundation for becoming an expert. Medical education is thus progressive, developmental, participatory and situated.

## 3. A Path Not Taken

In 1916, only a few years after the publication of the Flexner Report, the New York State Bar adopted a resolution that "every law school shall make earnest clinic work [...] a part of its curriculum for its full course". William V. Rowe, the author of that resolution, had earlier prepared a memorandum for Columbia University asserting that the "radical changes in the conditions of legal practice have now made adequate provision for clinical training and experience the most essential part of legal education" and that the "chief immediate duty [...] is to develop for law students the same comprehensive and exceptional clinical opportunities which [...] [are] open to medical students". To create such opportunities, Rowe recommended that Columbia acquire part or all of a prominent New York law practice and move it to the university campus, where it would be "a large office organization, with a very general practice, and with no restrictions upon the kind, value, or amount of business". Columbia would thus immerse its students in a practice superior even to the most prestigious private firms, a clinical experience that would be "the principal medium of instruction in all years for all subjects".

Rowe's ardour and impatience could easily be imagined as expressed today:

> We have had enough of mere debate and the time is now ripe for action [...] Why [the legal profession has] for so many years lagged behind all other professions [...] in providing systematic and experienced clinical and practical instruction

> [...] all laymen and nearly all lawyers find [...] utterly impossible to understand.

Rowe's recommendations fell on deaf ears, as did a report to the University of Chicago eighteen years later by the distinguished legal scholar and later federal judge, Jerome Frank. "Our law schools must learn from our medical schools", he wrote. "The parallel cannot be carried too far". He too proposed a legal clinic in every law school that would function as a leading law practice: "The law school clinics would not confine their activities [to legal aid] [...] They could take on important work for governmental agencies [...]". The professional work that they would do would include virtually every kind of service rendered by law offices. Such clinics, he believed, would attract exceptional lawyers, capable of becoming brilliant law teachers, who would not otherwise give up practice for what he termed "the elaborate futilities" of conventional law school teaching. The students produced by such education would be the very opposite of "mere technicians"; instead, they would have acquired "a rich and well-rounded culture in the practice of law", as well as encouragement to see that an important part of their professional future "is to press for improvements in the judicial process and for social and economic change".

## 4. The Suitability of Present Law School Structure for the Future

Although some of the Foundation's recommendations relate to distinctive features of American legal education, the central critiques of its report are relevant to legal education around the world. The Foundation begins with the premise that the "central goal of professional schools must be to form practitioners who are aware of what it takes to become competent in their chosen domain and to equip them with the reflective capacity and motivation to pursue genuine expertise". However, the Foundation found at best 'casual attention' at most law schools to teaching students how to use legal thinking in the complexity of actual law practice. The result is to prolong and reinforce the habits of thinking like students.

It is true that around the world law schools are adding elective courses involving real client representation during the academic law degree, and in many common law countries, though not the US, universities are becoming major providers of post-graduate professional training. However, such clinics and professional training programmes are, unlike the teaching hospital, not viewed by the profession or the public as the primary site where the standards of legal practice and the structure of the legal system are being constantly challenged and improved to meet the changing needs of society.[2] The teaching hospital serves the medical school both as a window and a door into the real world, making it both a vital resource for current societal needs and a dynamic site for empowering students to take responsibility for their own learning and for applying their ever-growing expertise to real-life problems. Could Rowe and Frank, writing in the early twentieth century, have been right that law schools could change their structure to create an equivalent of the teaching hospital?

## 5. The Best Law Schools of the Future

The transformation of legal education ought to be much easier than the task undertaken by medical educators a century ago, because law schools could become centres of cutting-edge legal practice without needing to make the kind of massive infrastructure investment represented by the teaching hospital. With library and information technology resources already in place, the typical law school would only need to provide additional working space and support staff to become a world-class centre of legal services if it enabled legal scholars to extend their work into practice settings and provided a site for practitioners to engage in scholarly critique and research to inform and improve their practice.

The cost of teaching in a way other than a system of solitary teachers facing large classrooms of students is almost always raised as a conclusive argument against even considering moving law schools towards the model of medical education. But medical education faced and overcame the same cynicism. In 1871, a distinguished professor of medicine at Harvard said that no successful medical school was willing to risk the large receipts produced by large classroom instruction by attempting "a more thorough education". In 1910, Flexner responded, "[p]ublic interest must be paramount and when the public interest, professional ideals and sound educational procedure concur in the recommendation of the same policy, the time is surely ripe for decisive action". By 1920 it was clear that the distinguished Harvard academic was wrong and Flexner was right.

[2] The Development of Standardized Client Assessment, available at www.teachinglegalethics.org, last accessed on 20 August 2012.

The Carnegie Foundation's study does not end with its troubling description of the limits of modern legal education; its report also asserts the conviction that "this is a propitious moment for uniting in a single educational framework formal knowledge and experience of practice".

What is needed far more than additional financial resources is a new vision of what legal education can and should be. The Future of Law Project, by moving our eyes away from the comforting certainty of the past to expand our gaze out and beyond the limiting horizon of the immediate, may do much to develop such a vision.

## 6. Sources and Further Reading

Bloch, Frank S. (ed.), *The Global Clinical Movement: Educating Lawyers for Social Justice*, Oxford, 2011.

Cooke, Molly *et al.*, *Educating Physicians*, Carnegie Foundation for the Advancement of Teaching, 2010.

Cunningham, Clark D., "Should American Law Schools Continue to Graduate Lawyers Whom Clients Consider Worthless?" in *Maryland Law Review*, 2011, vol. 70, p. 499.

Frank, Jerome, "Why Not a Clinical Lawyer-School?", in *University of Pennsylvania Law Review*, 1933, vol. 81, p. 907.

Ludmerer, Kenneth M., *Learning to Heal: The Development of American Medical Education*, Basic Books, 1985.

Maharg, Paul, *Transforming Legal Education: Learning and Teaching the Law in the Early Twenty-First Century*, Ashgate, 2007.

Rowe, William V., "Legal Clinics and Better Trained Lawyers, A Necessity", in *Illinois Law Review*, 1917, vol. 11, p. 591.

Sullivan, William M. *et al.*, *Educating Lawyers*, Carnegie Foundation for the Advancement of Teaching, 2007.

"Developing Professional Judgment: Law School Innovations in Response to the Carnegie Foundation's Critique of American Legal Education", in *The Ethics Project in Legal Education* (eds), Michael Robertson, Francesca Bartlett, Kieran Tranter and Lillian Corbin, co-authored with Charlotte Alexander, London, Routledge-Cavendish, 2010.

Global Alliance for Justice Education, available at www.gaje.org, last accessed on 20 August 2012.

International Conference on the Future of Legal Education, available at http://law.gsu.edu/FutureOfLegalEducationConference, last accessed on 20 August 2012.

International Forum on Teaching Legal Ethics & Professionalism, available at www.teachinglegalethics.org, last accessed on 20 August 2012.

The Development of Standardized Client Assessment, available at www.teachinglegalethics.org, last accessed on 20 August 2012.

The History of Johns Hopkins Medicine, available at www.hopkinsmedicine.org/about/history/, last accessed on 23 August 2012.

# 6.4.

# The Future of European Legal Education

**Miguel Poiares Maduro**[*]

Law is changing. Is European legal education addressing this change? This piece starts by highlighting a tension between law as legal practice and law as science and how that has impacted on the character of legal education. It then proceeds to review the problems with current legal education and the challenges that the changes taking place in the character of law bring to it. While doing this, the piece highlights how those challenges can become an opportunity to reform legal education.

Law is changing. Legal rules increasingly originate from different sources of political and normative authority: State, European and international legal sources. Lawyers increasingly need to operate in the context of a plurality of jurisdictions and legal sources. The market for legal services is also increasingly regionally and even globally integrated. At the same time, the social functions of law have progressively expanded and law has increasingly become a space for the resolution of social conflicts that the political process is incapable or unwilling to deal with.

Is European legal education addressing these changes? Moreover, is it ready to cope with the challenges they bring to the teaching and learning of law?

One has a reason to be sceptical, not least because these questions in themselves are surprisingly understudied. The justification for this may be found in the ambiguity surrounding the character of legal education. This ambiguity is visible in how legal scholars have dealt with legal education: on the one hand, we do not "authorise" any other social scientists to research the study of law (the presumption being that legal education cannot be understood or questioned by non-lawyers); on the other hand, we tend to focus exclusively on what law itself is and consider issues of education as unworthy of the attention of legal scholars. In other words, while we treat legal education as a subject outside the province of legal science, we do not recognise anyone else's right to address it. As a conse-

* **Miguel Poiares Maduro** is a Professor at the European University Institute.

quence, legal education is a "no man's land"; it is a subject that is practised but not often reflected upon. Apart from the usual curricular disputes, centred on the relative importance of our different legal subjects or their disciplinary borders, there is not much attention paid to how we teach the law and what ought to be the ultimate purpose of legal education.

The ambiguity of legal education reflects, in part, a larger ambiguity about the character of law as science. Is law a technical expertise or a science? Europe's doctrinal tradition of legal dogmatics has addressed this ambiguity by merging the two: law is the science of legal practice. Law becomes a science by organising and systematising the legal materials of a particular legal system. In this perspective, law is a science because it produces an organised body of knowledge that determines the practice of law in a particular legal order. It is for this reason that, in Europe, we never really faced the tensions that have dominated American law schools: the divide between the conception of law schools as professional or academic schools, or the permanent tension between legal scholarship and legal teaching. It is the existence (or assumption) of these tensions that, perhaps, explains why there is a much more developed American tradition of thinking and debating about legal education. The origin has to be traced back to the "Langdell revolution". Langdell was the first non-judge made Professor and Dean at Harvard Law School in the late nineteenth century. He considered that a good law professor had first and foremost to be a good professor, and his case-study method has forever shaped American legal education. The "Langdell revolution" has acquired such a central role in the narrative of the emergence of American law schools and their distinctiveness that it created a culture favourable to a constant questioning of the nature of legal education and of different legal methodologies: how one teaches is as important as what one teaches. However, this has not helped to resolve the tensions mentioned above. There is often a profound divide on how law is taught and thought of in the United States. The dominant conception of the law in legal scholarship is not really reflected in the way in which the law is usually taught.

To a certain extent, the US and Europe have found two opposite ways of accommodating the ambiguity of legal teaching and legal science. Americans have distinguished legal teaching from legal scholarship. The first is about the knowledge of legal materials and the teaching of the argumentative narratives made possible by them, and to be used in courts

The second is actually, predominantly, about questioning the social reality of those argumentative narratives, the underlying structures that shape them, as well as about what law ought to be. On the other hand, Europeans merged legal teaching and legal scholarship by, as mentioned, conceiving legal science as the science of legal practice. This is reflected in many other aspects of these academic communities. Notice, for example, how textbooks or treatises are considered minor (or even negatively perceived) works of scholarship in the US, while in Europe they often remain the pinnacle of a legal scholar's career.

There are problems with both approaches. Here I am concentrating on the European case and, particularly, on its impact on legal education. How can law be a science if it does not critically reflect on its own assumptions and methodological choices? It may fit the notion of science as a body of knowledge but not the scientific attitude of testing and questioning, not only of that body of knowledge but of how it is constructed. Moreover, doctrinal law is under-theorised: it mirrors reality but does not explain it. There is no science without theory (a hypothesis with both explanatory and predictive power of similarities and differences) and methodology (a reflective and critical approach to the study of the materials) and doctrinal approaches are, for the most part, a simple reproduction of the text of legal materials developed in a systematic, but largely uncritical and purely empiricist, way. Different outcomes based on the same textual legal materials are usually simply treated as inconsistencies and left unexplained. When social outcomes do not correspond to what "constitutes" the law, as doctrinally presented, the problem is treated as one of enforcement, outside the realm of the law. Law is shrunk so as to fit the dominant conception of legal science.

This has, at least, five negative consequences. First, a lot of what actually determines legal outcomes is simply left unstudied (in particular, systemic aspects that determine, aside from existent legal materials, for example, what courts do). This leads to bad legal scholarship, legal practice and law-making. Second, the nature of the relationship established between law and practice and its reflection in legal education is such that legal scholarship has become, itself, too advocacy-oriented. Third, in many instances, it has even become perfectly acceptable for legal scholarship to be a by-product of legal practice (legal opinions and legal advocacy). Fourth, legal education has become both misleading and socially perverse. It is misleading because it hides from students all the institutional variables that determine what the law is beyond the text of the existing legal materials. It is socially perverse because not only does that disconnect between what the law is and what is taught about it induces a cynical attitude in the practice of law, but it will also lead to a de-contextualised interpretation and application of the law. In other words, the disconnect will extend to the relationship between law and its social context of application. Fifth, if legal scholarship will resist embracing context, law will increasingly be dominated by other social sciences. These will put forward competing narratives of the law focusing on what legal scholarship does not explain. Though this challenge may be beneficial for law and legal scholarship, it risks, if not embraced by lawyers, simply aggravating the disconnect between law and its social context.

My argument is, however, that the current changes in the character of law offer us an opportunity to address some of these problems and rethink the nature of legal scholarship and legal education. In here, I want to focus on how they require, and may trigger, positive changes in legal education, addressing not only recent changes in the law, but also the deeper problems of legal education that I have highlighted.

The Europeanisation of legal education will be a natural consequence of the Europeanisation of the law. Such Europeanisation is measurable by the extent to which the European Union has become a primary source of law for its member States. Although this is certainly difficult to measure and there are no official statistics, most estimations indicate that the EU is responsible for at least fifty per cent of all new legislation applicable in the European States. This Europeanisation of the law is already visible at the level of litigation. Every year, there are over two hundred references from different national courts to the European Court of Justice on questions of validity and interpretation of EU law and, indirectly, on the compatibility of national law with EU rules. This number is, however, only a drop in the ocean of EU law-related litigation. Firstly, there are an even higher number of cases where EU law is pleaded directly before the two European Jurisdictions (the General Court and the European Court of Justice). Secondly, and most importantly, the (unfortunately) few existing studies measuring EU law litigation before national courts tend to establish that the cases referred to the European Court of Justice do not amount to more than five per cent of the cases in which EU law is invoked before those national courts.

Furthermore, EU law-related litigation will continue to grow, as a consequence of the expansion in the scope of application of EU law but, most importantly, of the increased familiarity with it of all relevant legal actors (lawyers, judges, et cetera). The learning process of EU law is far from being concluded and the expectation is that it will tend to permeate almost all areas of litigation. An overview of the subject-matters already addressed in recent cases brought before the European Court of Justice underscores this point. Alongside the core areas of EU law (internal market, competition and international trade), one finds subjects such as family law, contracts, sports law, tax law, consumer law, company law, environmental law, intellectual property, labour and social law, and even criminal law.

These developments must be reflected in the teaching of the law. It will not be sufficient, however, to increase the importance attached to EU law in the curricula of European law schools. A first step will be to "Europeanise" the teaching of the other legal subjects. It is no longer possible to teach contracts or consumer law, for example, without teaching EU law. However, simply to account for EU law sources would not be sufficient. In fact, EU law does not simply bring with it new rules. Such rules can only be properly interpreted and applied in the light of the particular nature of its system of law, its general principles of law and its own methods of interpretation. Legal subjects must not simply be taught in the light of a new body of rules; they must be taught in a different way, taking into account the legal culture of the EU legal order as well as the integration of national and EU legal orders.

To this, we must add the challenge arising from the increased multinational character of the cases in which lawyers are called on to assist. This creates a context in which judges and lawyers must learn to operate in a complex web of rules arising from their own legal order but also from other national legal orders and the EU legal order. This is also a natural consequence of increased economic integration and its legal implications, such as the fact that companies are being set up and operate in different States and contracts as well as other legal instruments must be drafted in light of their connection to different legal orders. As a consequence, a growing number of legal actors (in courts, just as outside courts and even in the legislative process) need to operate in a context involving different legal sources, multiple jurisdictions and diverse legal cultures. They must be comfortable "travelling" between different legal orders, so as to avoid the perils of some form of legal jet lag. This phenomenon will also increase cross-fertilisation of legal concepts and miscegenation of legal cultures. This is so for two reasons: first, the growing transnational character of economic litigation and legal services means that lawyers tend to circulate legal arguments and legal strategies among different legal orders; and, second, the circulation of legal ideas through networks of academics, lawyers and judges also entails a miscegenation of legal cultures.[1]

Though this challenge is particularly visible and important at the level of European integration, it also takes place at a global level. Increased global economic and social integration will promote some of the same phenomena at the global level, even if in a more mitigated form and without amounting to the formidable impact of the European integration.

These changes are bound to challenge not only the content of the law but also how it needs to be taught. This context of legal pluralism and legal miscegenation requires different hermeneutics and the interaction between legal cultures, which is triggered by the Europeanisation of the law, will confront each national legal culture with many of its unarticulated assumptions. Change in what you study is often the fastest way to break path-dependencies on how you study.

A second trend of relevance to the future of European legal education relates to contemporary changes in the market for legal services. The practice of law is increasingly international, and law firms reflect that. Law firms have reacted to the Europeanisation and globalisation of law by becoming European and global themselves. Top law firms have expanded into other States and have merged with law firms from those States, either acquiring them or established cross-national partnerships. An increased percentage of top law firms have lawyers from multiple nationalities, and their revenue is increasingly of foreign origin. This is favoured by, but not dependent on, the liberalisation of cross-border legal services that has taken place in Europe and is currently being promoted by the WTO at the

1 On the impact of the networks of lawyers and judges see Laurence R. Helfer and Anne-Marie Slaughter, "Toward a Theory of Effective Supranational Adjudication", in *Yale Law Journal*, 1997, vol. 107, p. 273; Anne-Marie Slaughter, "A Brave New Judicial World", in Michael Ignatieff (ed.), *American Exceptionalism and Human Rights*, Princeton University Press, Princeton NJ, 2005; Anne-Marie Slaughter, "Judicial Globalization", in *Virginia Journal of International Law*, 2000, vol. 40, p. 1103 and Mary Volcansek and John F. Stack Jr. (eds.), *Courts Crossing Borders. Blurring the Lines of Sovereignty*, Carolina Academic Press, Durham NC, 2005.

global level. A survey conducted by the magazine The European Lawyer on the European legal landscape gave an interesting, albeit tentative, perception of the recent developments in the European legal market. There are a moderate but growing number of multi-national law firms operating in a variety of European States. The tendency is for law firms to become increasingly European, following the patterns of economic and social integration. There is an even broader and already well-established tendency to create partnerships between law firms of different States at the European level. Networks continue to be the most disseminated form of internationalisation, but the so-called "organic internationalisation"[2] is increasingly gaining ground, and even leading to the emergence of truly global law firms. Another emerging tendency is for European law firms to foresee market opportunities in emerging markets (such as Russia, China or India). All law firms, even middle-sized ones, stress the increasingly international character of their work.

Another important development has been the growth of in-house lawyers[3] and, related to this, but not exclusively, the relative decrease of litigation as part of a lawyer's work. To this, one must also add the increased role of arbitration and other non-judicial forms of dispute resolution that lawyers are required to engage with. All require new legal and non-legal tools from lawyers and present them with challenges for which European legal education has hardly begun to prepare them.

Studies on the sociology and history of the legal profession have highlighted that the precise role of the legal profession is historically contingent, and that that role also impacts on the style of lawyering.4 It is inevitable that the changes in the structure and character of the market for legal services will affect the recruitment policies for lawyers and the legal

2 According to Glenn Morgan and Sigrid Quack this refers to "firms that have gradually developed their own overseas offices through a mix of methods". See Glenn Morgan and Sigrid Quack, "Institutional Legacies and Firm Dynamics: The Growth and Internationalization of UK and German Law Firms", in *Organization Studies*, 2008, vol. 26, no. 12, p. 1775. See also W, Calkoen, "The European Perspective", in Jens Drolshammer and Michael Pfeifer (eds.), *The Internationalization of Legal Practice,* 2001, Kluwer Law International, The Hague, p. 144.

3 See, for example, Abram Chayes and Antonia Chayes, "Corporate Counsel and the Elite Law Firm", in *Stamford Law Review,* 1984–1985, vol. 37, p. 277.

4 See Lawrence Friedman, "Lawyers in Cross-Cultural Perspective", in Richard L. Abel and Philip S.C. Lewis (eds.), *Lawyers in Society: Comparative Theories*, Beard Books, 1989, p. 8.

training expected of them. This is already visible. Another survey by The European Lawyer notes that there is increased competition in the recruitment process for top lawyers, with firms recruiting at an increasingly early stage and hiring external consultants to help them in the recruitment process. They also look for lawyers with international training, preferring people with diverse and multi-national training. It appears that it has become common practice for business law firms to require a foreign law degree as part of the entry requirements for young lawyers.[5] However, this is not exclusive of law firms: international legal masters are now a usual requirement to access legal jobs at international organisations and, increasingly, for in-house positions at large companies. It is also increasingly common for law firms to offer, encourage and even require their lawyers to spend some time practising or training in another State. At the moment, the tendency in Europe is for two markets to co-exist, one composed of the top-tier, large scale, elite law firms that are increasingly European (or even truly global); the other is that of small, often family based, local law firms.

Elite legal education will match the needs of the first type of law firms. I do not envisage, however, nor do I wish for, a legal education that will be simply formatted to fit the professional and specialised immediate needs of those law firms. Instead, the challenge must be met by embracing law beyond the confines to which doctrine has circumscribed it. Only the opening up of legal education will prepare students for the opening up of law. Paradoxically, the need to adapt to changes in legal practice may require a stronger theorisation of law in legal education. That is, the right theorisation of law; one that is not a mere abstraction from legal practice but genuinely engages with the institutions and processes that shape that practice beyond simply the textual legal materials. It is only by truly understanding the "mechanics" of law that students will be able to make sense of and adapt to the constant changes in the law and the different legal cultures in which they will be required to practise it. Even from a purely advocacy perspective, the move from systematising to understanding the law is much more effective for the purposes of constructing different possible legal narratives that can be successfully put forward before courts and other legally relevant actors.

5 Morgan and Quack, 2008, p. 1772, see *supra* note 2.

A third important development is the increased centrality of law in contemporary societies. This is a product of the expansion of regulation into new social domains (both as an instrument of the State where the State was not present before or to actually replace the State where it used to provide services and now simply regulates). However, it is also a product of the increased judicialisation of social and political conflicts. The current nature of the political process often entails that political pluralism is reflected in conflicting normative preferences being entrenched in strong bargaining positions that make it particularly difficult to reach a clear normative agreement in the legal rules. Such rules are bound to lead, intentionally or not, to a delegation to courts of the final decisions on those issues. This is not necessarily negative: a political community may legitimately decide to exclude certain issues from the "passions" of the political process and "delegate" them to more insulated institutions. Similarly, political communities can decide to agree on very broad principles without articulating solutions to the conflicts which will necessarily occur in the practical application of such principles. This may be so as to prevent collective action problems. We trust on the long-term advantage of committing to a judicial concretisation of such principles with its universal potential, while reducing the transaction and information costs involved in reaching particularly difficult decisions. This makes agreement possible on delicate and controversial political questions by politically deferring its practical effects to a judicial solution to be derived from a universally agreed principle.

Despite this a paradox is created. As stated, pluralism increases the centrality of law and courts, and often leads to the delegation to them of decisions of high political and social sensitivity. However, this same context tends both to increase the contestability of judicial decisions and rigidify their outcomes (because the political process is less capable of overcoming them). The only way to deal with such a paradox is by changing our understanding of the role that the law and courts play in a democratic political community. This requires an upgrading of the legal software of judges and lawyers, particularly with respect to legal reasoning. It will also bring new questions to the classrooms, questions for which doctrinal law is in no position to provide a satisfactory answer.

The fourth relevant trend allows us to relate the challenges to legal education arising from changes in the character of law to the changes taking place in the market for legal education. There is an emerging European and global market for legal education. Top American Law Schools have already for some time been developing strategies to meet the demand for global legal education.[6] They have specifically tailored their LLM programmes to fit such search for global legal education (NYU has taken this to a different level by setting up a Global Law School). That reflects itself in their faculty and course offerings but, most notably, in the composition of their student bodies which is, at the LLM level, overwhelmingly (if not exclusively) composed of foreign students. The number of international students at US law schools increased five-fold between 1980 and 2000 and the number of LLMs being offered increased from a few dozen in the early 1990s to over 100 between 2003 and 2004.7 Some American Law Schools have also, de facto, created franchises of their law degrees at foreign universities and, in some cases, are even considering opening foreign branches.

Some European law schools are also embracing the path of internationalisation. UK law schools are clearly attracting a high number of foreign students to their degrees (particularly at master level). Their faculty is also increasingly international. In the rest of Europe, one also finds a few examples of law schools that, at least on paper, appear to be embracing such internationalisation. Overall, however, the internationalisation of European law schools has been rather limited, often focusing on student exchanges in the context of the Erasmus programme. Their teaching of law continues to be largely insulated from the changes highlighted above. Their faculty, student body, courses offerings and teaching methods reflect this circumstance.

Still, things are starting to change. One first step has been the development of joint degrees. We are now also witnessing the emergence of a real European market for LLMs. More than one hundred European law schools now offer some form of LLMs open to foreign students. Only a few of these, however, are truly international in character. The international character is mostly visible in the adoption of English as the language of instruction, and in the increased offer of EU law subjects. With the exception of Germany and France, English is the dominant language.

---

6 See David S. Clarck, "Transnational Legal Practice: The Need for Global Law Schools", in *American Journal of Comparative Law,* 1998, vol. 46, p. 273.

7 David Nelken, "The Globalization of International Law", available at http://topuniversities.com/gradschool/grad_school_news/article/the_globalization_of_international_law, last accessed on 20 August 2012.

Law schools offering these programmes are attracting an increasing number of foreign students (around fifty per cent of their LLM student body). The large majority comes from other European States, but other relevant markets are Asia, the US and Latin America. Within Europe, students from former Eastern European countries are among the most mobile. European LLM programmes are thus an undisputed trend and, to a large extent, they simply answer to a market demand. In the Netherlands, one of the few European States with a large offering of law degrees aimed at international students (particularly European), the number of foreign students undertaking a master's degree in law was already over eight hundred in the academic year of 2002–2003.[8] The main example remains, however, the United Kingdom as it attracts a substantial number of foreign students to its legal programmes.[9]

However, as the European Law Faculties Association noted in a declaration entitled "For a European Space of Legal Education":

> If European legal education wants to compete with the highly successful US-American system of education for lawyers, a number of additional and more courageous steps have to be taken.

One of these steps will entail a clear division between the objectives to be achieved by legal education at the bachelor's and master's levels. The proposal of ELFA, at this stage, is to focus bachelor training on national law while the master's should offer a European and international legal education. I agree that this is a necessary development, but I would add that the pressures arising from the mobility of students and lawyers, the developments in the mutual-recognition of law degrees in Europe and the informal harmonisation of legal studies inherent in the Bologna declaration would promote such steps. In reality, the "two degree" model (bachelor's and master's) of legal education inherent in the Bologna process perfectly fits the current market demand for a two-fold legal education: national and European (or international). The expectation, in the short term, is for students to continue to do their bachelor's legal studies in their home State. However, at the master's level increased competition

8 Source: CBS, mentioned in the EURODATA Project.

9 Unfortunately, there do not seem to be easily available data specific to law schools. In total there were 100,357 foreign students attending law, social sciences and business degrees in the UK in 2002–2003. Source: EUROSTAT, mentioned in the EURODATA Project.

will emerge among European law schools. Students, particularly the best ones, will look round Europe for the best European and international legal education. It may be possible, at least in the short term, for law schools to continue to go on as usual at the level of the bachelor's degrees; however, at the master's level a European market will emerge. Formal or informal European rankings will follow, and are in fact starting to appear regarding the different master's programmes and law schools.[10] The European market for legal education at the master's level will increasingly look like the American legal education market.

The trends highlighted constitute a major challenge for European law schools and legal education. The law to be taught is different. The role played by the law is also different. Even the profile of the lawyer demanded by the market is different. Moreover, European law schools will increasingly be competing in a European market. Answering these trends requires more than simply opening up the traditional national degrees to foreign students. It requires a complete restructuring of legal education and even law schools. A European and international law degree can only be properly developed where there is a law school with a European and international culture. It will not be enough to Europeanise or globalise legal curricula. It is the teaching of law itself that must change. This presents an opportunity to rethink the legal methodologies and pedagogical approaches currently employed in European legal education. However, they must remain legal. Simply adding to the study of doctrinal law the study of other legally relevant social disciplines may do more harm than good if the right link is not established with law. The focus should always be on law and the departure point must be the existing legal sources. What is needed is for lawyers to be equipped with a new set of social, critical and analytical tools in order to really understand law and make use of its legal sources. That is the challenge.

Furthermore, a truly innovative, European and international legal education can only take place in a truly European and international context. This requires a diverse and multinational community of learning with a diverse, international faculty and student body. Only the law schools that will take these challenges seriously will succeed in the future of legal education.

[10] As a first example see the FT listing of top LLMs: available at http://rankings.ft.com/lawschools/llm-2011-listing, last accessed on 20 August 2012.

## Sources and Further Reading

Helfer, Laurence R. and Slaughter, Anne-Marie, "Toward a Theory of Effective Supranational Adjudication", in *Yale Law Journal*, 1997, vol. 107, p. 273.

Slaughter, Anne-Marie, "A Brave New Judicial World", in Michael Ignatieff (ed.), *American Exceptionalism and Human Rights*, Princeton University Press, Princeton NJ, 2005.

Slaughter, Anne-Marie, "Judicial Globalization", in *Virginia Journal of International Law*, 2000, vol. 40, p. 1103.

Volkansek, Mary and Stack, John F. Jr.(eds.), *Courts Crossing Borders: Blurring the Lines of Sovereignty*, Carolina Academic Press, Durham NC, 2005.

# CONCLUDING REMARKS

# Whither the Future of Law? Concluding Remarks

**Jan M. Smits**[*]

This concluding chapter draws a picture of the future of law that is based upon the preceding contributions and upon the views of the author. It identifies three main functions of the law – rule- and decision-making, enforcement, and dispute resolution – and asks how these functions are affected by economic globalisation and technological development. One of the main shifts identified is the one from dispute resolution to dispute avoidance: under the influence of declining national laws, and in the absence of a meaningful global law, private actors turn to alternative mechanisms such as reputational networks to order their relationships.

## 1. Introduction

In 1930, John Maynard Keynes published a short essay entitled *Economic Possibilities for our Grandchildren*. Perhaps the greatest economist of the twentieth century asked what economic life would be like around 2030. Next to surprisingly accurate predictions about future income levels, it is not too audacious to assume that Keynes will be proved wrong when it comes to his view of future working hours (he predicted a 15-hour working week in 2030) and people's mentality towards money ("the love of money as a possession – as distinguished from the love of money as a means to the enjoyments and realities of life, will be recognised for what it is, a somewhat disgusting morbidity"). The think pieces collected in this volume follow Keynes' example in reflecting upon what the world will look like in the future, but differ in two important respects. First, the contributions relate to the law, arguably to a lesser extent subject to change

[*] **Jan M. Smits** holds the Chair of European Private Law at Maastricht University and is Research Professor of Comparative Legal Studies at the University of Helsinki. He is also the Academic Director of the Maastricht European Private Law Institute (M-EPLI).

over time than the economy, and second, their horizon is not a hundred years, but only two to three decades. This makes the exercise carried out in this volume not only less speculative than Keynes' work, but also more exciting. It is likely that more than one think piece accurately describes future law.

The aim of this concluding chapter is to draw a picture of the future of law that is partly based upon the preceding contributions, and partly upon my own views of what course the law is likely to take in an age of ever-accelerating globalisation and technological progress. The goal is explicitly not to summarise all of the contributions, or to make reference to all individual authors, but rather to provide the reader with an analysis that cuts through the respective substantive legal fields addressed in this volume. This approach is justified because fields such as intellectual property law, corporate law, environmental law, trade law, competition law, cyberlaw, procedural law, human rights, health law and international law, to name the most important fields discussed in this book, all face identical problems of rule-making, of identifying the right substantive legal norms, of enforcement and of solving conflicts.

This crosscutting approach sets the agenda for this contribution. It identifies three main functions of the law – rule- and decision-making, enforcement, and dispute resolution – and asks in the three following sections not only how these functions are affected by globalisation and technological development, but also what alternatives exist. One can describe this as a functional approach. I assume that the law fulfils certain functions including the three just mentioned, and that one of the main challenges in thinking about the future is how these functions can also be satisfied, whether in a legal or non-legal way, in a globalising and technologically progressing society.

There is one methodological problem that deserves separate attention. The think pieces in this volume focus almost entirely on either finding new solutions in cases where the traditional national rules no longer function properly, as in private international law, where a jurisdictional approach is no longer in line with today's borderless reality, or on identifying a legal solution to a new problem, as in case of whether robots should have human rights obligations. In both cases, the natural tendency of lawyers is to overstress the importance of the law. However, it is likely that the problem-solving power of the law, in essence still largely of national origin, becomes less important in cases where a problem is no longer purely national. In case of a truly new problem, it also remains to be seen what the role of the law could be in solving it. Anyone writing about the law of the future should therefore take into account that the law's functions can easily change as a result of changes in society as a whole.

This may well explain why many of the contributions in this volume do not take up the grand societal challenges that the world is facing today. HiiL's *Law Scenarios to 2030* predict a rising population, greater scarcity of food, water and natural resources, including oil and gas, increasing security concerns and exposure to more, and not necessarily better, information. These trends come next to 'older' concerns about continuing rivalry among ethnic and religious groups, failed States, war, mass atrocities, nuclear proliferation, poor enforcement of human rights standards, the ineffectiveness of international law, including the adverse effects of big power politics in the United Nations, and too little attention for social justice. Added to these must be relatively new challenges such as global warming, the global financial crisis, the effects of the Arab Spring on the rights of minorities and on peace in the Middle East, and the changing balance of economic and political power in the world. The authors of the present book leave these challenges, incidentally largely influenced by a Western view of the world, almost completely aside – and probably rightly so. The law can only play a very limited role in addressing them.

## 2. Rule- and Decision-Making

If anything becomes clear from reading the contributions to this volume, it is that the Westphalian idea of States exclusively setting the norms for the people on their territory is no longer adequate. This is not only true as a description in view of the rise of international norms and of private regulation; it is also true at the normative level. As more and more problems can no longer be appropriately dealt with by national law, they need to be addressed in a different way. There are two fundamentally different ways to do this and both are represented in the present book.

The first alternative is to keep up the hope that what can no longer be done by way of national law, such as norm setting in a legitimate and effective way, could be done in a similar way at the European or global level. This leads to a belief in a global legal order and in the creation of international courts as effectively taking over the role of national judiciaries. This testifies of a continuing belief in the power of law and in official institutions being able to set rules and govern the world in much the same way as national institutions have done in the last two centuries. A prominent example of such global constitutionalism is Frank Vibert's plea for a coherent system for the judicial review of rule-making by international bodies.

The second alternative is to find functional equivalents outside of the law for the traditional national rules and institutions. This requires a different way of thinking. Instead of claiming that effective rule setting, or any other task of the State such as providing legal certainty or creating a framework for business transactions, should be provided by new international institutions, one seeks the solution in devices that can play a similar role without a need for the State or State-like organisations to intervene. This latter way of reasoning is of course informed by the reality that it is not easy at all to solve problems by way of international law-making. In some fields, such as Corporate Social Responsibility, this second alternative is already very much reality as a result of the activities of private actors. However, in areas that belong even more clearly to the public realm, it is more difficult to leave behind our old conceptions of State-made law, precisely because we feel that in public matters decision-making should take place through broad participation of the citizens or at least of national parliaments. An enlightening example is offered by Albert Lin: global warming might be addressed by geo-engineering technologies that enable us to choose a climate for the planet, but prospects of finding an acceptable answer to the question as to who should 'control the thermostat' are slim.

It would in my view be wrong to argue against the rise of the second alternative. It is the logical consequence of the changing role of law through globalisation. Globalisation requires solutions that national law cannot offer and therefore the vacuum is filled in different ways. However, this is not all. Just as important for the future of law is its potential at the national level. Here too, the role of law is due to change. Edward Rubin rightly observes that "the law of the future will bring the long-overdue demise of [the] pre-modern conception of law". Law as a set of State commands for human conduct will make place for law as an instrument of modern administrative governance, leading to a shift from democratic procedures to results, from generality to particularisation and from regularity to supervision. Rubin thus provides the theoretical framework to what others see occurring in their respective fields, including banking and corporate law, environmental law and competition law.

An interesting question is whether we can also predict anything about the future substantive course that the law will or should take. Remarkably, most contributions focus on questions of legitimacy, transparency and effectiveness of rule-making and not so much on the substance of future rules. This neutral approach can be easily explained. Any type of global law necessarily reflects diverging views of what is right. Notions of what the rule of law and fundamental rights entail already differ considerably in today's world and it is not likely that this will change in the future. In particular, if the law is to play a role in the process of economic and political development of widely diverging countries, as many contributions at least implicitly assume, it is essential to take this diversity into account. This explains why not many authors are in favour of the outright unification of laws, which presumes a view of only one 'right' substantive rule. Rather, the authors argue for recognition of diversity. As diverse views of what is right are probably best reflected by national laws, this also means that national laws remain important, shifting the question to how to coordinate these laws among each other.

## 3. Enforcement

The second traditional function of the State is that it facilitates the enforcement of the applicable law. In a Westphalian view, the State has a monopoly on both the drafting of substantive rules and the enforcement of these rules through the national courts. While the first monopoly is rapidly eroding, as we just saw, the second one still largely exists: except for some exceptional cases, of which the various international criminal courts are the most important examples, the enforcement of law is still in the hands of national institutions. This is quite logical. Today's problems may be increasingly global, but our institutions are not. Private actors and other international rule-setters thus still need to rely on the teeth of national courts to enable their addressees to claim their rights.

This age-old jurisdictional approach makes enforcement complicated and therefore expensive, a problem that is felt in particular in cross-border cases. This is true not only for data protection laws, as Lokke Moerel convincingly shows, but also in many other fields including consumer law. It leads businesses to favour private enforcement and private regulation wherever possible and prompts future customers to better assess the risk of default by the other party before even entering into the transaction (see further below, section 4). A crosscutting analysis of the think pieces confirms that litigation in the national courts is usually seen as unproductive, as Martijn Scheltema aptly describes for the field of Corporate Social Responsibility.

This finding also explains why, even in the case of new legislative instruments that allow cross-border collective redress in a national court, most parties still prefer alternatives to litigation. Arbitration and mediation are among these, but they are in the end also dependent on the State courts when it comes to the enforcement of the arbitral award or the mediation agreement. It does therefore not come as a surprise that, in a recent study, Thomas Dietz concludes that a territorially fragmented global legal order, as we have at present with separate State legal systems, is problematic in a global economy. As was already seen when rule-making was discussed, the appropriate remedy can be found in two directions. One could adapt the existing rules of private international law, for example by broadening the international jurisdiction of national courts and by enhancing mutual recognition. As this requires each individual State to change its own laws, this is not likely to happen. The alternative is that practice finds its own ways and seeks to avoid recourse to the law by assessing a party's reputation ex ante (see below, section 4).

## 4. Dispute Resolution and the Shift from *Ex Post* to *Ex Ante*

Many of the contributions could start – and some of them in fact do – with the observation that despite the globalisation of trade, of environmental concerns, of competition among companies, there is no such thing as an effective global trade law, consumer sales law, environmental law or competition law. This absence is felt in particular when it comes to dispute resolution. This is likely to lead to two shifts, the contours of which are already clearly visible today.

First, there is a shift from State courts towards forms of private justice. Private actors not only set rules, but also increasingly take care of the State function of providing access to an effective resolution of disputes. As we saw before, this includes arbitration, mediation and other forms of ADR. If we look at the provision of dispute resolution as a process of competition, in which State courts compete with other providers of problem solving devices, it seems that State courts are in decline. At the same time, State courts do take measures to remain competitive. While Western jurisdictions try to attract foreign parties to their courts, even issuing brochures, a prominent example being the English Law Society's leaflet, *England and Wales: The Jurisdiction of Choice*, Benjamin Odoki provides a nice example of how technology can help in enabling access to justice for people from distant areas. His vision of virtual courts for Uganda is worth following in many other parts of the world. It reinforces the point made by Maurits Barendrecht that we are in need of more innovative types of civil justice, also to keep State courts competitive.

The second shift is in my view even more important, at least for the area of private law. This is the shift from dispute resolution to dispute avoidance, so from *ex post* to *ex ante* dealing with potential disputes. If national law is no longer in demand and global law does not exist, private actors turn to other mechanisms to order their relationships. It is no surprise that social networks play an important role in this alternative ordering process. David Charny wrote in 1990, "One key to effective reputational controls is a system for transmitting relevant information to market participants. [...] Collective reputational enforcement should work well [...] in markets limited to small numbers, homogenous groups of individuals who are in frequent contact and thus can share relevant information. These markets are, of course, relatively rare. Conversely mass markets based on reputational bonds are feasible only with technology that conveys information cheaply to a large group of transactors [...]".

The most interesting aspect of this view is that what was still impossible in 1990 has become possible today. Due to the rise of the internet, reputational networks need no longer be based on close social contacts. Perfect strangers are often able to assess the reliability of other parties through websites that rank their previous behaviour. If one of the main functions of law is to create trust among people who do not know each other, it may well be that new technologies allow people to replace the law with new types of reputational networks. This fits in with Jim Dator's observation that order does not need law. His point that order can also exist through personal contact, and that law only becomes important in a political society sanctioned by organised force, seems to imply that a global order can exist without law as long as other methods of creating trust are in existence. In my own words, Facebook may be much more important for the future of law than any official statute or treaty.

## 5. Changing Roles of Legal Actors and the Importance of Legal Education

The functional approach adopted in this contribution sheds some light on how the role of national law, and of law in general, is likely to change in the coming twenty years. All actors involved in the legal process will have to get used to new roles. National legislatures have to accept that they are becoming just one other lawgiver and have to compete with others in setting effective rules for their citizens. Courts are likely to be increasingly called upon to fill the gaps that national legislatures cannot provide rules for. However, probably the most important change will lie in the rise of private actors, private regulation, private enforcement and above all a shift away from the law itself towards reputational networks will fundamentally change the regulatory power of law.

One group of legal actors was not yet mentioned, although their role is vital in addressing the challenges future law faces: law professors. Until now, most law professors have shown only little interest in changing the way in which they teach the law. As long as teaching focuses on learning the (doctrinal) law of national jurisdictions only, students will not grasp any of the trends identified in this collection of think pieces. There is a dire need to teach the law in a different way, not only by paying attention to rules flowing from other sources than the official ones, but also by showing alternative solutions outside of the law. Both Clark Cunningham's and Miguel Maduro's contribution show that the transformation towards such a more societally relevant curriculum is needed and possible.

One final remark is in place. While the effects of globalisation are often lamented, a majority of the contributions to this volume are optimistic about the law of the future. This may be due to the problem-solving approach of lawyers in general: no matter what the problem is, they are trained to find a solution for it. This makes it appropriate to end with a quote by economist Joseph Stiglitz. In his book *Making Globalization Work*, he quotes his wife, asking him "You have complained enough about globalisation. What would you do about it?" This is a question to which lawyers have an answer.

## 6. Sources and Further Reading

Charny, David, "Nonlegal Sanctions in Commercial Relationships", in *Harvard Law Review*, 1990, vol. 104, pp. 373–467.

Dietz, Thomas, "Contract Law, Relational Contracts and Reputational Networks in International Trade: An Empirical Investigation into Cross-Border Contracts in the Software Industry", in *Law and Social Inquiry*, 2012, vol. 37, pp. 25–57.

Keynes, John M., "Economic Possibilities for our Grandchildren", in John M. Keynes, *Essays in Persuasion*, London, Macmillan, 1935.

Muller, Sam, Stavros Zouridis, Morly Frishman, and Laura Kistemaker (eds.), *The Law of the Future and the Future of Law*, Oslo, Torkel Opsahl Academic EPublisher, 2011.

Smits, Jan M., "European Legal Education, or: How to Prepare Students for Global Citizenship?", in *The Law Teacher*, 2011, no. 45, pp. 163–180.

Smits, Jan M., *Private Law 2.0: On the Role of Private Actors in a Post-National Society*, The Hague, Eleven International Publishing, 2011.

Stiglitz, Joseph, *Making Globalization Work*, New York, Norton, 2006.

HiiL, *Law Scenarios to 2030: Signposting the Legal Space of the Future*, The Hague (HiiL), 2012.

HiiL and Maastricht University, *Maastricht Students' Perspectives on the Law of the Future*, The Hague and Maastricht (HiiL) 2012.

# LIST OF CONTRIBUTORS

**Maurits Barendrecht** is Professor of Private Law at Tilburg University and has been in this position since 1992. Prior to this, he practiced law at a major Dutch law firm from 1982 to 1997. He is currently engaged in research into dispute systems, including legal procedures, negotiation processes, ADR and informal dispute mechanisms from an interdisciplinary perspective. His research takes places within the Tilburg Institute for Interdisciplinary Studies of Civil Law and Conflict Resolution Systems (TISCO). Barendrecht has exercised leadership over several large-scale innovation projects in the realm of justice and governance, which directly address urgent justice needs. His most recent publications include Barendrecht, J.M., Gramatikov, M.A., Porter, R.B., and Verdonschot, J.H. (2012), "Towards Basic Justice Care for Everyone. Challenges and Promising Approaches", The Hague: HiiL. Barendrecht, J.M., Hoon, M.W. de, Doorn, C.J.M. van, Zeeland, C.M.C. van, Liauw-A-Joe, J., and Menting, M. (2012). Eerlijk, scherp en betrouwbaar: Een interactieve verkenning naar ijkpunten voor eerlijk zaken doen en effectieve conflictoplossing. Tilburg: TISCO. Barendrecht, J.M. (2011). (This information was adapted from the following website: http://www.tilburguniversity.edu/webwijs/show/?uid= j.m.barendrecht, last accessed on 28 August 2012.)

**Lucky Belder** is Assistant Professor, Secretary of the CIER and Co-founder of the CAAAi. As initiator and project leader in a HERA/EU-FP7-research project, her current research focuses on "Cultural heritage institutions, copyright and cultural diversity". She is a member of the Dutch UNESCO working group on Culture, Communication and Information. Her research interests include the governance of intellectual property law, the legal and normative framework of information technology and artificial intelligence, cultural rights, cultural heritage, information policies and cultural diversity. She is a Member of the Working Group Human-Robot Co-existence, Ethics and Law within RoboCom.

**Christina Biebesheimer** is Chief Counsel of the Justice Reform Practice Group in the Legal Vice-Presidency of the World Bank, which provides Bank staff and client countries with advice on how to make institutions of the justice system more effective, fair and accessible. Prior to joining the Bank, she was Principal Specialist in Modernization of the State in the Inter-American Development Bank from 1989 – 2005, and an Associate with the law firm of Milbank, Tweed, Hadley and McCloy from 1986 – 1989. Her publications include "Measuring the Impact of Criminal Justice Reform in Latin America" (in *Promoting the Rule of Law Abroad*, Thomas Carothers, editor, Carnegie Endowment for International Peace, 2006); "The Impact of Human Rights Principles on Justice Reform in the Inter-American Development Bank" (in *Human Rights and Development: Towards Mutual Reinforcement,* Alston and Robinson, editors, Oxford University Press, 2005); and *Justice Beyond Our Borders: Judicial Reforms for Latin America and the Caribbean* (Biebesheimer, Mejia, editors, Johns Hopkins University Press, 2000). Ms. Biebesheimer is a Member of the Board of Editors of the *Hague Journal on the Rule of Law*; and of the Board of Directors of Offender Aid and Restoration of Arlington County, a non-profit community organisation aimed at re-establishing former offenders as productive and responsible members of the community. Ms. Biebesheimer received her Bachelor of Arts Degree from the University of Iowa, studied at the Universidade Classica de Lisboa, and received her J.D. from Harvard Law School.

**Christopher H. Bovis** is H.K. Bevan Chair in Law and Professor of European Business Law at the University of Hull. He is Special Advisor to the UN on Public Private Partnerships and Academic Advisor to the EU Commission on the Single Market. He advises national governments and industry across the world on public sector reforms, and has been instrumental in structuring flagship public-private partnerships in the UK, EU and overseas. He is a leading authority in public procurement and public-private partnerships and specialises in anti-trust law and policy, with particular emphasis on public sector management. He has acted on behalf of governments, the defence sector and industry on numerous high profile projects. He has been Jean Monnet Chair in European and Business Law, at the Lancashire Law School, UCLAN and Visiting Professor at several academic institutions, including University of London IALS, University of Toronto, University of Montreal, Humboldt-Universität zu Berlin, the Queen's University of Belfast, University of Cambridge and University of Lisbon. In 2006 he was made Life Fellow, Royal Society of Arts and Manufacturing. He has published extensively in international legal and management journals and has produced 74 books, monographs and articles, including: *International Encyclopaedia on Public Procurement*, Edward Elgar, (2013), *EU Public Procurement Law*, Edward Elgar (2012), *Public-Private Partnerships in the EU*, Routledge (2012), and *Public Procurement: Case Law and Regulation*, Oxford University Press (2006). He is Editor-in-Chief of the *European Public Private Partnerships Law Review*. He is Contributing Editor of the *Encyclopaedia of Competition Law*, with responsibilities for transport, telecommunications and public procurement.

**Madeleine de Cock Buning** is Chair of CIER and CAAAi, Professor of Copyright, Communication and Medialaw, and Member of the board of the Supervisory Authority to the Media. She is co-leader of the Working Group Human-Robot Co-existence, Ethics and Law within the FET-Flagship Proposal Robot Companions for Citizens (RoboCom). Her research is focused on regulating the exchange of cultural information in the mass media in the field of tension between law and culture. She is specialised in the regulation of new and emerging technologies, with a view to the successful development and acceptance thereof in society.

**Roeland de Bruin** is a Junior Lecturer and Project Researcher at CIER and CAAAi. His research focuses on the intersections between law and emerging technologies, concentrating on intellectual property law. As project researcher, he takes part in the HERA/FP7-project "Cultural heritage institutions, copyright and cultural diversity", and the FET-Flagship proposal RoboCom in the working group Human-Robot Co-existence, Ethics and Law.

**Hassane Cisse** is Deputy General Counsel, Knowledge and Research and is Legal Vice President of the World Bank. Cissé, a national of Senegal, joined the World Bank in 1997 after serving for seven years as Counsel at the International Monetary Fund. He has been Deputy General Counsel, Knowledge and Research, of the Bank since 2009. In this capacity, he provides intellectual leadership on strategic legal and policy issues facing the Bank and leads its agenda on law, justice and development. He is the Editor-in-Chief of the World Bank's Law, Justice and Development Series and co-edited a book on International Financial Institutions and Global Legal Governance in 2011. Prior to his current position, Cissé served for many years as Chief Counsel for Operations Policy. He also advised on governance and anti-corruption and was appointed in 2007 to serve as a member of the Bank's newly established Sanctions Board. Cissé obtained his LL.B (High Hons.) from Dakar University, Senegal, and he also holds a LL.M degree from Harvard Law School as well as graduate law degrees from the universities of Paris I Panthéon-Sorbonne, Paris II Panthéon-Assas and a graduate degree in history from Paris I. Cissé is a Member of the World Economic Forum Global Agenda Council on the Rule of Law.

**Clark D. Cunningham** is the Director of the National Institute for Teaching Ethics and Professionalism, a consortium of legal ethics centres at six American universities. He is Vice-chair of the Academic and Professional Development Committee of the International Bar Association and a former Convenor of the Global Alliance for Justice Education. He has consulted on the development of learning outcomes for ethics and professional judgment for Australian legal education and has been admitted to membership of the world's oldest bar association, The Society of Writers to Her Majesty's Signet, in recognition of his work on teaching and assessing client relationship skills in Great Britain. He has written and consulted extensively on legal ethics, the legal profession and the reform of legal education in the US and around the world. His publications include articles and essays in the *Harvard Law Review*, *Yale Law Journal*, *University of Michigan Law Review*, *Georgetown Law Journal*, and *Cornell Law Review*; he is a Winner of the Annual Scholarly Paper Award from the Association of American Law Schools.

**Himamauli Das** is currently Assistant General Counsel for International Affairs at the U.S. Treasury Department. In that capacity, he handles a wide range of legal issues on international economic and financial matters, including those related to the international financial institutions, international banking and securities, trade and investment, sovereign debt, climate, and other matters. He has served as Attorney in the Office of the Legal Adviser at the U.S. State Department and Deputy Legal Adviser at the National Security Council. He has clerked on both the federal appeals and district courts. He received a J.D. and Masters in Public Policy at the UC Berkeley, a M.Sc. in Atmospheric and Planetary Sciences at the University of Colorado at Boulder, and an A.B. in Physics at UC Berkeley.

**Jim Dator** is Professor and Director of the Hawaii Research Center for Futures Studies, Department of Political Science, and Adjunct Professor in the College of Architecture, the Program in Public Administration, and the Center for Japanese Studies, of the University of Hawaii at Manoa; Core Lecturer, Space and Society Division, International Space University, Strasbourg, France; former President, World Futures Studies Federation; He also taught at Rikkyo University (Tokyo, for six years), the University of Maryland, Virginia Tech, the University of Toronto, and the Inter-University Consortium for Postgraduate Studies in Dubrovnik, Yugoslavia. He has worked extensively with judicial, legal, law enforcement, and corrections officers and institutions in many parts of the world and has published extensively on the futures of courts, law, police, and prisons.

**Surya Deva** is Associate Professor at the School of Law of City University of Hong Kong. He has previously taught at the Faculty of Law, University of Delhi, and at the National Law Institute University, Bhopal. Surya's primary research interests lie in Corporate Social Responsibility, Indo-Chinese Constitutional Law, International Human Rights, Globalisation, and Sustainable Development. He has published widely in these areas. His most recent publication is *Regulating Corporate Human Rights Violations: Humanizing Business* (London; New York: Routledge, 2012). Surya has also prepared two major reports on *Access to Justice: Human Rights Abuses Involving Corporations* (concerning India and China) for the International Commission of Jurists (ICJ), Geneva. He is member of a Research Team that has been awarded a competitive grant by the Norwegian Research Council on 'Sustainable Companies: How to Make Companies Contribute Effectively to Mitigate Climate Change?'. He is also the Faculty Editor of the *City University of Hong Kong Law Review*.

**Dacian Dragos** is the Jean Monnet Associate Professor of Administrative and European Law (since 2006) at the Public Administration Department, Babes Bolyai University, Cluj Napoca, Romania, and Co-director of the Center for Good Governance Studies. He is the former Vice Dean and Acting Dean of the Faculty of Political, Administrative and Communication Sciences (2008–2012); Marie Curie Fellow at Michigan State University (2005–2006); Visiting Scholar at Rockefeller College of Public Administration and Policy, SUNNY at Albany, U.S.A. (2002); Romanian Writers Association National Prize for legal research (2003); Scientific Coordinator of the Commission for drafting the Administrative Procedure Code of Romania (2006–2008) and Expert in the Commission for drafting the Administrative Code (2010–2011). He has been the Chair of the "Law and Administration" Panel of the European Group of Public Administration since 2010. His research publications include two edited books, six chapters in international books, four books in Romanian as single author, and four in collaboration, as well as over thirty papers in scientific journals.

**Claudia Dumas** is the President of Transparency International–USA, which works to strengthen integrity and combat corruption. Her focus on anti-corruption, corporate compliance and rule of law issues is informed by her more than 25 years of legal and policy work in the public, private and not-for-profit sectors. Dumas served as the first Executive Director of the World Justice Project, where she directed a global, multidisciplinary effort to strengthen the rule of law for the development of communities of opportunity and equity. She was Senior Rule of Law Advisor at the U.S. Agency for International Development from 1998 to 2005, where she negotiated and oversaw efforts to assist the countries of Eastern Europe and the former Soviet Union in implementing judicial system, commercial law and anti-corruption reforms. From 1984 to 1998, she practiced international commercial and finance law with Shearman & Sterling, IBM and Citibank, N.A. Dumas received her A.B. in Economics from Wellesley College and her J.D. from the Cornell Law School.

**Sarah Isgur Flores** is Attorney and Political Consultant, currently working as a research fellow at the Initiative on Neuroscience and the Law. She has worked on numerous State and federal campaigns and on policy issues for the Department of Justice, both houses of Congress, and the Texas legislature. Isgur Flores took her bachelor's degree at Northwestern University and completed her thesis on the Americanization of British Campaign Communication at the London School of Economics. She received her J.D. from Harvard Law School where she served as President of the Harvard Federalist Society and staffed the Harvard Journal of Law & Public Policy. She served as a law clerk to Chief Judge Edith Jones of the United States Court of Appeals for the Fifth Circuit.

**David Eagleman** is a neuroscientist, New York Times bestselling author and Guggenheim Fellow who holds joint appointments in the Departments of Neuroscience and Psychiatry at Baylor College of Medicine in Houston, Texas. His areas of research include time perception, vision, synaesthesia, and the intersection of neuroscience with the legal system. He directs the Laboratory for Perception and Action, and is the Founder and Director of Baylor College of Medicine's Initiative on Neuroscience and Law. Eagleman has written several neuroscience books, including *Incognito: The Secret Lives of the Brain*, *Wednesday is Indigo Blue: Discovering the Brain of Synesthesia*, and the upcoming *Live-Wired: How the Brain Rewrites its own Circuitry*. He has also written an internationally bestselling book of literary fiction, *Sum*, which has been translated into 27 languages and was named a Best Book of the Year by Barnes and Noble, New Scientist, and the Chicago Tribune. Eagleman has written for the Atlantic, New York Times, Discover Magazine, Slate, Wired, and New Scientist. He also appears regularly on National Public Radio and BBC to discuss both science and literature, and has been profiled in the New Yorker.

**Mary E. Footer** is Professor of International Economic Law and Head of the Business, Trade and Human Rights Unit in the Human Rights Law Centre at the University of Nottingham School of Law, and Co-director of the School's Postgraduate Research Programme. Prior to joining the University of Nottingham in 2006, she was Deputy Director at the Amsterdam Centre for International Law (ACIL) and senior lecturer at the University of Amsterdam. She has also previously held teaching posts in international law at the Erasmus University Rotterdam and University College London and was Senior Program Legal Counsel at the International Development Law Organization, Rome from 1995–1999. She has been a Fernand Braudel Senior Visiting Fellow at the EUI, Florence in 2010, and a Fellow of

Public International Law at the British Institute of International and Comparative Law, London from 1992-1994. She is a member of the Board of the European Society of International law (ESIL), a member of the Executive Council of the British Branch of the International Law Association (ILA) and a member of the ILA International Trade Law Committee. She read European History and History of Art at the University of East Anglia (BA Hons) before embarking on her law studies, with a JD in civil law from the University of the Netherlands Antilles, followed by an LLM in Public International Law from University College London and a PhD cum laude from the Erasmus University Rotterdam. Professor Footer has published widely on GATT/WTO matters, trade and investment, law and economic development, the international regulation of (agro) biotechnology, and business and human rights. She is author of *An Institutional and Normative Analysis of the World Trade Organization* (2006) and Co-editor with Julio Faundez and Joseph J. Norton of *Governance, Development and Globalization* (2000).

**Andrew R. Forbes** is a recent graduate from the School of Law at the University of Nottingham (LLB Hons, 1st Class) with a distinction in Chinese law gained at the University of Hong Kong where he spent a year studying various aspects of Chinese law and society and international law. His interests include international law; international relations, particularly between China and the rest of the world; and the relationship between trade regulation, international business and economic development. His final year dissertation focused on the "Multilateral Trading System and Preferential Trading Agreements" and he has recently worked as a research assistant on a paper about the role of credit rating agencies in providing indicators to measure transnational governance responses to the global economic crisis.

**Daveed Gartenstein-Ross** is a Senior Fellow at the Foundation for Defense of Democracies. He is currently a Ph.D. candidate in World Politics at the Catholic University of America. He earned a J.D. from the New York University School of Law, after which he worked as a law clerk in the United States Court of Appeals for the D.C. Circuit (2002–03), and as a commercial litigator. He is the author or volume editor of eleven books and monographs, including *Bin Laden's Legacy* (Wiley, 2011), and has also published widely in the popular and academic press. Mr. Gartenstein-Ross conducted field research at Joint Task Force-Guantánamo in October 2006 and July 2012.

**Ji Weidong** is Dean and Presiding Chair Professor of KoGuan Law School, Shanghai Jiao Tong University, China, since 2008. Prior to joining SJTU, he was Professor of Graduate School of Law, Kobe University, Japan, and also worked as Visiting Scholar, Stanford Law School, 1991–92; Board Member Co-opted of Research Committee on Sociology of Law, The International Sociological Association, 1994–2002; Member of Council of the Japanese Association of Sociology of Law, Japan, 1999–2011; Researcher and Member of Planning Committee, International Institute of Advanced Studies, Japan, since 2006; Fellow of the Virtual Center for Advanced Studies in Institution, the Tokyo Foundation, Japan, since 2007; Senior Research Fellow of the Department of Public Policy, China's Research Committee Economic System Reform, China, since 2008. He has studied legal culture, law and social change in Asia, focusing constitutional law, judicial reform as well as legal profession. He is the author of articles and books about legal theory and practice related to China, including: *A Hypermodern Law* (Kyoto: Minerva Press, 1999), *Legal Change in Modern China* (Tokyo: Japan Review Press, 2001), *New Views on Constitutionalism* (Beijing: Peking University Press, 2002, enlarged edition, 2005), *The Composition of Chinese Judicial System* (Tokyo: Yuhikaku Press, 2004), *Orbit of Thinking Justice* (Beijing: Law Press, 2007), *At Critical Point of Order and Chaos* (Beijing: Law Press, 2008), *Switching the Institutions* (Hangzhou: Zhejiang University Press, 2009), *et cetera.*

**Ellen Lawton** (J.D.) leads the National Center for Medical-Legal Partnership at George Washington University's Department of Health Policy and is the lead Advisor for Walmart's signature *pro bono* medical-legal partnership initiative. An expert in poverty law generally, she is a lead Editor of the textbook, *Poverty, Health & Law: Readings from Medical-Legal Partnership* (2011). A co-founder of the National Center for Medical-Legal Partnership, Lawton is internationally recognised for her leadership in developing the medical-legal partnership model, and has published an array of articles describing this work in both clinical and legal journals. Lawton received the 2011 Innovations in Legal Services Award from the National Legal Aid and Defender Association and is a member of the Blue Ribbon Commission for Public-Private Action. She is chair of the board of directors at Health Imperatives and a member of the board of directors of Community Resources for Justice. She was a 2004 Harvard Law School Wasserstein Fellow. Lawton lives in Massachusetts with her husband Jon and two sons, Louis and Charlie.

**David S. Levine** is Associate Professor of Law at Elon University School of Law, and Affiliate Scholar at the Center for Internet and Society at Stanford Law School. Professor Levine studies intellectual property law as it relates to technology and public life. His is currently focused on intellectual property law's interaction with freedom of information laws and the use of social media formats by governments. He also founded and hosts a top technology and intellectual property law radio show and podcast, *Hearsay Culture*, on KZSU-FM (Stanford University). More information can be found at www.hearsayculture.com. Facts current as of July 2012.

**Albert Lin** is Professor of Law at the University of California, Davis School of Law, where he specialises in environmental and natural resources law and also teaches evidence. His research interests include toxic torts and the relationship between technology, the environment, and law. His book manuscript exploring this relationship, tentatively titled *Prometheus Reimagined: Technology, Environment, and Law in the 21st Century*, is due to be published by the University of Michigan Press in 2013. Prior to joining the UC Davis faculty, Al was a trial attorney for the Environment and Natural Resources Division of the U.S. Department of Justice. Al received his J.D. from the University of California, Berkeley, School of Law and an M.P.P. from the Kennedy School of Government.

**Jaqueline Lipton** is the Baker Botts Professor of Law and Co-Director of the Institute for Intellectual Property and Information Law at the Houston Law Center. Prior to that, she held academic positions at Case Western Reserve University, the University of Nottingham and Monash University. Her writing and teaching is focused in the areas of commercial law, cyberlaw, and intellectual property law with a comparative and international focus. She has authored numerous law review articles in these areas, including recent publications in the *Northwestern University Law Review*, the *Iowa Law Review*, the *UC Davis Law Review*, the *Boston College Law Review*, *Harvard Journal of Law and Technology*, the *Berkeley Technology Law Journal*, the *Washington and Lee Law Review*, the *Washington University Law Review*, the *Hastings Law Journal*, the *Wake Forest Law Review*, the *Florida Law Review*, and the *Cardozo Law Review* (de novo inaugural online supplement). She is the co-author of the second and third editions of *Cyberspace Law: Cases and Materials* (Aspen, 2006 and 2010) with Professor Raymond Shih Ray Ku. She also authored *Security Over Intangible Property* (Thomson, 2000), the first text devoted solely to the issue of securitisation of intangible property, including intellectual property. More recently she completed the sole authored monograph *Internet Domain Names, Trademarks and Free Speech* for Edward Elgar (2010).

**Imelda Maher** is the Sutherland Professor of European Law at UCD School of Law. Her work focuses primarily on European law and governance with a particular interest in competition law. She was published extensively in the fields of European and international competition law. She was Director of the Centre for Competition and Consumer Policy at the Regulatory Research Network, Research School of Social Sciences, Australian National University and has held posts at the London School of Economics, University of London (Birkbeck College) and Warwick University. She was Visiting Fellow at the Institute of Advanced Legal Studies, London; Lund University, Sydney University and Notre Dame University (London Campus). She is currently Academic Director for the new Sutherland School of Law building. She was appointed a Non-Governmental Adviser by the Irish Competition Authority at The Hague meeting of the ICN in 2011. She was admitted as a Member to the Royal Irish Academy in 2011.

**Gabrielle Marceau** (PhD) is Counsellor in the Legal Affairs Division of the World Trade Organization (WTO), which she joined in September 1994 and where her main function is to advise panellists in WTO disputes, the Director-General Office and the Secretariat on WTO matters. From September 2005 to January 2010, Gabrielle Marceau was Member of the Cabinet of the WTO Director General Pascal Lamy. Marceau is also Associate Professor at the Law Faculty of the University of Geneva and Visiting Professor at the Graduate Institute of International Affairs and Development (HEID) where she teaches on WTO law and dispute settlement. Before joining the GATT/WTO, Marceau worked in private practice in Quebec, Canada, mainly in the sectors of labour law and insurance law. She has published extensively, namely in WTO related matters.

**Lokke Moerel** is Partner ICT with the international law firm De Brauw Blackstone Westbroek and chairs its global data privacy and security practice. She provides strategic advice to multinationals on their global ICT compliance. She leads the working group in which the Chief Privacy Officers of the leading Dutch multinationals developed their Binding Corporate Rules. This was done in consultation with the Dutch Data Protection Authority, which have received EU wide approval. In 2011, Moerel obtained her PhD on Binding Corporate Rules at Tilburg University. Moerel teaches global ICT law at Tilburg University, is a Member of the OECD Volunteer Expert Group evaluating the OECD Privacy Principles and Arbitrator and Mediator with WIPO and the Dutch institute for ICT disputes. She is a graduate of Leiden University and Cambridge University (British Council Foreign Office Scholarship). She is author of the first Dutch textbooks on international outsourcing and online advertising, and many international publications on data protection. Moerel is consistently ranked as a leader in ICT and data protection law in Chambers Global and Legal 500.

**Elisa Morgera** (LLM, PhD) is Lecturer in European Environmental Law and Director of the LLM Programme in Global Environment and Climate Change Law at Edinburgh University School of Law. She co-directs the inter-disciplinary Doctoral Network of the Global Environment and Society Academy of the University of Edinburgh. Morgera specialises in European, international and comparative environmental law, and researches specifically in the area of conservation and sustainable use of biodiversity, international environmental governance, corporate environmental accountability, and environmental integration in the European Union's external relations. Her publications include: *Corporate Accountability in International Environmental Law* (OUP, 2009); with Gracia Marin Duran, *Environmental Integration in the EU's External Relations: Beyond Multilateral Dimensions* (Hart, 2011); as editor, *The External Environmental Policy of the European Union: EU and Internation-*

*al Law Perspectives* (CUP, 2012); and as lead co-editor, *The 2010 Nagoya Protocol on Access and Benefit-Sharing in Perspective: Implications for International Law and Implementation Challenges* (Martinus Nijhoff, 2012).

**Richard Nash** is Counsel at the Justice Reform Practice Group in the Legal Vice-Presidency of the World Bank. Richard currently works on a range of investment projects around the world including Afghanistan (US$85 million) and Mongolia (US$5 million), as well as providing advice and cross support to client countries and Bank teams on various aspects of justice sector reform. Prior to this Richard worked as a consultant for the World Bank in Afghanistan focusing on legal and regulatory aspects of financial and private sector development in a fragile State. Before that, Richard worked as a barrister in London, with a practice focused on criminal law and in particular on financial crimes, money laundering and fraud. Richard was called to the Bar of England and Wales by the Honorable Society of Gray's Inn in 2005, he received his LLM from the University College London, his law degree from City University and undergraduate degree in History from King's College London.

**Benjamin Odoki** is Chief Justice of Uganda since January 2001. He has had a long and distinguished career in the Judiciary. He has previously served as a Justice of the Supreme Court from 1986 to 2001 and Judge of the High Court from 1978. He had earlier served in the Ministry of Justice as a Senior State Attorney and, later, as Director of Public Prosecutions. Odoki has headed many Institutions, Commissions, and Committees including the Law Development Centre, the Uganda Law Council, the Uganda Constitutional Commission, the Judicial Service Commission and the Committee to Review Legal Education Training and Accreditation in Uganda. As Chief Justice he has spearheaded the transformation of the Judiciary into a strong independent, efficient and accountable institution. He has introduced reforms, which include specialised divisions of the High Court like the Commercial Court, the International Crimes Court and the Anti-Corruption Court. He has introduced computerisation of the Courts and the use of Alternative Dispute Resolution. He has championed continuing judicial education and established the Judicial Studies Institute to conduct such training.

**Austin Onuoha** is the Founder of the African Center of Corporate Responsibility (ACCR). He is a PhD Candidate for Conflict Analysis and Resolution at the Nova Southeastern University (NSU), Florida. He is presently monitoring engagement initiative on behalf of shareholders in Chevron's in Nigeria for the Africa Centre for Corporate Responsibility (ACCR) and a member of the UN Working Group on Human Rights and Business. In the past, Austin was the executive secretary and Head of Conflict Resolution at the Human Rights Commission (now Human Rights and Conflict Resolution Centre) Abakaliki, Nigeria. In 2005, Onuoha wrote *From Conflict to Collaboration: Building Peace in Nigeria's Oil-Producing Communities and When Communities Confront Corporations: Comparing Shell's Presence in Ireland and Nigeria*. His work on "harnessing conflict energy for development" granted him the privilege of becoming an Ashoka Fellow. On top of this, he is currently a research fellow at the Netherlands Institute for Advanced Study in Humanities and Social Science (2011–2012). (This information has been adapted from the following webpage: http://emu.edu/now/peacebuilder/cjp-alumni/austin-onouha/, last accessed on 28 August 2012.)

**Luis Miguel Poiares Maduro** is Professor and Director of the Global Governance Programme at the European University Institute. He is also a Visiting Professor of Law and Gruber Global Constitutionalism Fellow at Yale Law School. Maduro received his Doctorate in Law from the European University Institute in 1996. Later, he served as Advocate General for the European Court of Justice in Luxembourg from 2003 to 2009. Maduro specialises in European Union law, international economic law, constitutional law, and comparative institutional analysis. He has been Visiting Professor at several academic institutions, including the College of Europe (Bruges), Instituto de Estudos Europeus da Universidade Católica Portuguesa, University of Chicago Law School, and the London School of Economics. In 2010 he was awarded the Gulbenkian Science Prize. He is a graduate of the European University Institute and the University of Lisbon.

**Ed Rubin** specialises in administrative law, constitutional law and legal theory. He is the author of numerous books, articles and book chapters. Rubin joined Vanderbilt Law School as Dean and the first John

Wade–Kent Syverud Professor of Law in July 2005, serving a four-year term that ended in June 2009. Previously, he was the Theodore K. Warner, Jr. Professor of Law at the University of Pennsylvania Law School from 1998 to 2005, and the Richard K. Jennings Professor of Law at the Boalt Hall School of Law at the University of California-Berkeley, where he had taught since 1982 and served as an Associate Dean. Rubin has been Chair of the Association of American Law Schools' sections on Administrative Law and Socio-economics and of its Committee on the Curriculum. After graduating from Princeton, he worked as a Curriculum Planner for the New York City Board of Education. He received his law degree from Yale University in 1979, clerked for Judge Jon O. Newman of the U.S. Court of Appeals for the Second Circuit and was an Associate in the Entertainment Law Department of Paul Weiss Rifkind Wharton & Garrison in New York. He has served as a Consultant to the People's Republic of China on administrative law, and to the Russian Federation on payments law.

**Martijn Scheltema** was Associate Professor at Leiden University from 1991 until 1997 and acquired his Ph.D. degree in the law of restitution. He became Attorney of Law with Pels Rijcken & Droogleever Fortuijn (The Hague, the Netherlands) in 1997, and became Partner in 2005. He is a Supreme Court and international litigator. He has a particular interest in international arbitration and the ensuing setting aside proceedings. His field of work also includes international dispute resolution and prevention in CSR issues. In this area, he participates in the HUGO-CSR project, which aspires to establish a global dispute management facility in the area of CSR (in The Hague). He is Professor at Rotterdam University, and also appointed Chair on Enforcement Issues in Private Law. His research focuses on the effectiveness of international private regulation, particularly in the area of CSR and standardisation.

**Colin Scott** is Dean of Law and Professor of European Union Regulation and Governance at University College Dublin. He was previously a Professor in the College of Europe, Bruges, a Reader in Law at the London School of Economics and Senior Fellow in Public Law at the Australian National University Research School of Social Sciences. His main research interests are in the field of regulatory governance. He has undertaken research projects on regulating the public sector (funded by the UK Economic and Social Research Council), communications regulation (funded by the Leverhulme Trust), reflexive governance (funded by EU sixth Framework Programme) and transnational private regulation (funded by the Hague Institute for Internationalisation of Law). He has published articles with many of the leading legal and interdisciplinary journals and is author, co-author, editor or co-editor of eleven books. He is a co-editor of *Legal Studies* and was programme chair for the ECPR Standing Group on Regulatory Governance Biennial Conference in 2010, held in Dublin.

**Jan M. Smits** holds the Chair of European Private Law at Maastricht University and is Research Pprofessor of Comparative Legal Studies at the University of Helsinki. He is also the Aacademic Ddirector of the Maastricht European Private Law Institute (M-EPLI). Jan Smits writes on European private law, legal theory, comparative law and internationalisation of law. In 2010, he was elected as a member of the Royal Netherlands Academy of Arts and Sciences (KNAW). In 2011 and 2012, he taught a course on The Law of the Future as HiiL Visiting Professor on the Internationalisation of Law. More information about his work is available via http://www.jansmits.eu.

**Sang-Hyun Song** was elected Judge of the International Criminal Court (ICC) in March 2003, for a term of three years, and re-elected in 2006 for a further full term of nine years. He was elected President of the Court in March 2009, for a term of three years, and re-elected in March 2012 for another three-year period. Judge Song has extensive practical and academic experience in the areas of court management, civil and criminal procedure, and the law of evidence. For more than thirty years, he taught as a Professor of Law at Seoul National University Law School, beginning in 1972. He has also held visiting professorships at a number of law schools, including Harvard, New York University, Melbourne and Wellington. Judge Song started his legal career as a Judge-Advocate in the Korean Army and later as a foreign attorney in a New York law firm. He has served as a member of the advisory committee to the Korean Supreme Court and the Ministry of Justice. As such, he led initiatives to reform the national litigation system and the criminal justice system, particularly the reform of the Penal Code, the Code of

Criminal Procedure, the Court Rules of Criminal Procedure, and the prison system. Judge Song has vast experience in relevant areas of international law, principally international humanitarian law and human rights law. He is co-founder of the Legal Aid Centre for Women, and of the Childhood Leukemia Foundation in Seoul, and the President of UNICEF/KOREA. Judge Song is also the respected author of several publications on relevant legal issues, and the recipient of the highest decoration of the Korean Government (MUNGUNGHWA, 2011).

**S.I. Strong** is Senior Fellow at the Center for the Study of Dispute Resolution, and Associate Professor of Law at University of Missouri. Professor S.I. Strong specialises in international dispute resolution and comparative law, with a particular emphasis on international commercial arbitration and large-scale (class and collective) suits. She has taught at the Universities of Cambridge, Oxford and Missouri and is a dual-qualified (U.S.-England) practitioner, with experience in London, New York and Chicago. Professor Strong has published numerous books and articles in Europe and the Americas, and her award-winning scholarly work has been cited as authority to the U.S. Supreme Court and in U.S. federal courts and international investment awards. Professor Strong, who holds a Ph.D. in law from the University of Cambridge, a D.Phil. from the University of Oxford, a J.D. from Duke University, an M.P.W. from the University of Southern California and a B.A. from the University of California, has acted as sole, presiding and party-appointed neutral in over a dozen arbitrations and mediations, including a number of multimillion and multiparty (three to twenty-five entities) matters.

**Rik Torfs** studied law and canon law in Leuven and Strasbourg. He has been Professor of Canon Law and Law and Religion in Leuven since 1988. He is also Dean of the Faculty of Canon Law, and guest Professor in Strasbourg and Stellenbosch. Torfs has been a Senator in Belgian Parliament since 2010 and is a Columnist for the two main Belgian newspapers, Le Soir (2008–2009) and De Standaard (since 2003). He is the Host of his own television show *Nooitgedacht* (2006–2009) and the author of 17 books and 350 scientific articles. Torfs has lectured in more than 40 countries on five continents.

**William Twining** is Quain Professor of Jurisprudence Emeritus at University College London and a regular Visiting Professor at the University of Miami Law School. Born in Uganda, he says that he had a colonial childhood, an anti-colonial adolescence, a neo-colonial start to his career in newly independent Sudan and Tanzania, and a post-colonial middle age based in several Western countries. His recent books include *Globalisation and Legal Theory* (2001), *General Jurisprudence* (2009), *Human Rights: Southern Voices* (as editor) (2010), and *Globalisation and Legal Scholarship* (2012).

**Frank Vibert** is a Visiting Fellow at LSE Department of Government having previously been a visiting fellow with LSE's Centre for the Analysis of Risk and Regulation (CARR). He is a former Senior Adviser at the World Bank and Senior Visiting Fellow at UNU/WIDER. He is the founder Director of the European Policy Forum (a London based Think Tank) and a founder member of the European Constitutional Group that published a proposal for a European constitution in 1993. He is the author of *The Rise of the Unelected* (CUP) 2007 and *Democracy and Dissent: The Challenge of International Rule-making* (Edward Elgar 2011) among other publications. He was educated at Exeter College Oxford.

**Rolf Weber** is ordinary Professor for Civil, Commercial and European Law at the University of Zurich, Switzerland, and a Visiting Professor at the University of Hong Kong. His main fields of research are Internet and Information Technology Law, International Business Law, Media Law, Competition Law and International Financial Law. Weber is Director of the European Law Institute and the Center for Information and Communication Law at the University of Zurich. Since 2008, he is Member of the Steering Committee of the Global Internet Governance Academic Network (GigaNet) and of the European Dialogue on Internet Governance (EuroDIG). In 2009, he became a Member of the High-level Panel of Advisers of the Global Alliance for Information and Communication Technologies and Development (GAID). Besides, he is engaged as an Attorney-at-law and as a Member of the editorial board of several Swiss and international legal periodicals, and serves as Expert for several international and national organisations in his widespread fields of research. Weber has intensively published in form of books and peer reviewed articles on matters of Internet Governance, of the Internet of Things, of international financial law and generally on global governance. His research focus lies on the legal problems related to his research topics, in particular the strengths and weaknesses of possible regulatory regimes. For the publication list and a more detailed CV please see: http://www.rwi.uzh.ch/lehreforschung/alphabetisch/weberr/person.html.

**Severin de Wit** was born in Düsseldorf, Germany, 1952. He has a LLM from the Vrije Universiteit Amsterdam and worked from 1978-2006 as an intellectual property attorney in several international law firms. In 2006, de Wit started an IP consultancy, Intellectual Property Expert Group (IPEG) (www.ipegconsultancy.com). He wrote several articles on intellectual property and has published many other works both in English and Dutch. Some of these works include: "Nederland als octrooiland, hebben we nog toekomst?", *Intellectuele Eigendom and Reclamerecht (IER)* (2010) and "The Case eBay Inc. vs. MercExchange LLC, It's Impact on NPEs and Patent Enforcement", *IP Cases and Their Legacy* (2010) (please see "Selected Works" at http://bit.ly/LfEIci for earlier publications). Since 2005, he writes a blog on patents, technology and innovation (www.ipeg.com). From 1994 until 2010, he was Editor of a major Netherlands IP review: *Intellectuele Eigendom and Reclamerecht (IER)*. Furthermore, de Wit is a Visiting Lecturer at Maastricht University (Advanced Master in Intellectual Property Law and Knowledge Management (LLM/MSc)). Currently he is engaged as a Key IPR Expert in a European Union funded project in Indonesia to support the Indonesian government to improve its international trade performance.

**Mauro Zamboni** is Professor in Legal Theory at the Stockholm Centre for Commercial Law at the Faculty of Law of Stockholm University, Sweden. He is also Visiting Professor at the Centre of Law and Governance in Groningen, The Netherlands, and has been Guest Scholar at Stanford University (2003–2004), Harvard Law School (2008–2009) and at The Collaborative Research Center 597 "Transformations of the State", Bremen (2009–2011). Furthermore, Zamboni has as his main topics the relations between law and politics (for example *The Policy of Law: a Theoretical Framework*, Hart Publishing, 2008) and he is currently finishing a project on transnational corporate law ("The Idea of Corporation in Transnational

Law: Setting the Legal Foundations"). He has researched and published on several topics, including Rechtsstaat, Scandinavian legal realism, legal method, and legal evolutionary theory.

# INDEX

## M



## N



## O

## P



## R



## S



## T



## U



## W

# TORKEL OPSAHL ACADEMIC EPUBLISHER

### *Advisory Board of the FICHL*

# ALSO IN THE LAW OF THE FUTURE SERIES

Sam Muller and Stavros Zouridis (editors):
*Law and Justice: A Strategy Perspective*
Torkel Opsahl Academic EPublisher
The Hague, 2012
Law of the Future Series No. 2 (2012)
ISBN 978-82-93081-82-1

www.ingramcontent.com/pod-product-compliance
Lightning Source LLC
Chambersburg PA
CBHW071337230926
51849CB00006B/510/J